D1060152

# The Cinema
# of Tsui Hark

Tsui Hark on the set of *Green Snake* (1993)

# The Cinema of Tsui Hark

*by* LISA MORTON

McFarland & Company, Inc., Publishers
*Jefferson, North Carolina, and London*

**Library of Congress Cataloguing-in-Publication Data**

Morton, Lisa, 1958–
    The cinema of Tsui Hark / by Lisa Morton.
      p.  cm.
    "Filmographies of selected collaborators": p.
    Includes bibliographical references and index.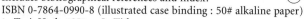
    ISBN 0-7864-0990-8 (illustrated case binding : 50# alkaline paper)
    1. Tsui, Hark, 1951–   I. Title.

  PN1998.3.T79 M57  2001
  791.43'0233'092 — dc21

                                 2001031609

British Library cataloguing data are available

Manufactured in the United States of America

*On the cover:* Tsui Hark on the set of *Knock Off* (1998)

*McFarland & Company, Inc., Publishers*
  *Box 611, Jefferson, North Carolina 28640*
   *www.mcfarlandpub.com*

# CONTENTS

# ACKNOWLEDGMENTS

Thanks first to Eric Knight, who got me started on the road to Hong Kong with two loaned videotapes. Later on, Eugene at Five Star Laser in Alhambra and the guys at Cinema Paradise in Rowland Heights (including Joey Wang—not the actress!) kept me supplied.

Thanks to Kenny and everyone at HK Movies in Hong Kong for all the help with illustrations. Stephen Jones gave me advice, encouragement and one nice big push. Tony Lane's encyclopedic knowledge of Hong Kong cinema proved both a blessing and a challenge. Ricky Lee Grove cleaned up my interviews, kept me fed, and gave me love and company during all those late viewing nights. Thanks to Brigitte Lin for an unforgettable dinner, one as entertaining as any of the films. Janet Ma and Jenny Wu at Film Workshop were very kind and helpful.

My biggest thanks must go to Nansun Shi, who gave me information, answered questions and finally lured me to Hong Kong; and, of course, to Tsui Hark himself, who endured two days of interviews with more warmth, generosity and honesty than I had any right to expect. He amply proves that a great artist can also be a great person, and I am very grateful to both those parts of him.

# AUTHOR'S NOTE

Because of the vagaries of the Hong Kong film distribution system, films often end up being available in several different versions, sometimes with completely different subtitling and character names. Likewise, Chinese names don't always translate well into English; one name will often have numerous English-language variants.

Wherever possible I have tried to use the most commonly accepted names for films, characters and actors. For example, in the *Once Upon a Time in China* series,

Rosamund Kwan's character has been referred to as both "Aunt Thirteen" and "Aunt Yee"; I've opted for the latter, not because it's the better translation, but simply because it has appeared more often than "Aunt Thirteen."

The films have been arranged in chronological order, in the hope that this will better help the reader to see the development of Tsui's themes and style.

All Tsui Hark quotes are from my interviews with Tsui unless otherwise indicated.

# INTRODUCTION

Whenever I mention the name Tsui Hark to the proprietors of the local Chinese video stores, I invariably get lectures on either Tsui's importance or reviews of one of his films. When I mention him to my *gweilo* (white) friends, I'm usually met with a resounding, "Who?"

Yet here I am, writing the first comprehensive book-length study of the cinema of Tsui Hark, and I'm another *gweilo*, and the book is in English, no less.

Chances are if you've picked this book up, you already know who Tsui Hark is; but even so, you may be weighing the book in your hands and asking, "Is there really this much to say about Tsui?" There are other Hong Kong filmmakers who are far better known than Tsui. John Woo has become practically a household name in the United States for his action films; Wong Kar-Wai has developed a worldwide arthouse following; and Jackie Chan (who, admittedly, remains unknown as a director in Hollywood) has exploded into one of the biggest superstars on the planet.

Meanwhile, Tsui Hark remains virtually unknown outside of Asia.

Why? Tsui has directed, produced, written and or acted in an amazing 64 films over the last 20 years, a quarter of which are considered classics of modern Asian cinema. Tsui is one of the most gifted film artists working in any territory, and his influence on Hong Kong cinema (and, by extension, world cinema) has been substantial.

His lack of success in Western countries, although obviously due to a complex web of factors, can probably be boiled down to three main obstructions: First, unlike much of Jackie Chan's work, Tsui's movies tend to be intensely Chinese in theme and design; second, whereas John Woo's films are almost entirely about men and male bonding, Tsui's female-driven and transgendered cinema is a tougher sell in Western culture; and third, in contrast to Wong Kar-Wai (who has directed just six features, only one of which —*Ashes of Time*, a martial arts epic — was a genre

1

film), the Hollywood marketeers simply cannot pigeonhole the prolific and versatile Tsui Hark.

I hope this book, then, will serve to introduce Tsui Hark to the casual viewer and provide the more experienced Hong Kong film enthusiast with information and food for thought. Mainly, of course, I hope this book will promote Tsui Hark's work in an entertaining way. While English-language books already exist on the other filmmakers mentioned above, it's surprising — even shocking — to me that this is the first dedicated solely to Tsui Hark's work.

Somehow I doubt it will be the last.

# 1

# Tsui Hark—
# A Brief Biography

Tsui Hark (it's pronounced "Choy Hok") was born Tsui Man-Kong in Canton on January 2, 1951, but was raised in Saigon. His father was a pharmacist and the family was large—16 children from three marriages. Tsui made his first film at 10, in which he performed a magic show. At 14 Tsui was sent to Hong Kong for his secondary education, and three years later he came to the United States to major in film (although his family wanted him to pursue a medical career). After a year at Southern Methodist University in Dallas, Texas, he transferred to the University of Austin, which he left in another two years; at school he was nicknamed "King Kong," and shortly thereafter he changed his name to "Hark," which means "overcoming." After living in both Texas and New York, Tsui returned to Hong Kong in 1976.

Within a month of his return he landed a job working in television. After he made a costume drama called *Golden Dagger Romance* (for CTV), he moved on to his first feature film, 1979's *The Butterfly Murders*. Although the film flopped financially, it firmly established the young director in the front rank of Hong Kong's "New Wave," a group of politically minded filmmakers who had trained overseas and in Hong Kong's television system. Next he went on to make the cannibal caper *We're Going to Eat You*, followed by the political thriller *Dangerous Encounter—1st Kind*. It wasn't until he directed the spy spoof *All the Wrong Clues* for the immensely successful company Cinema City that Tsui had a commercial hit.

For his next film, *Zu: Warriors from the Magic Mountain*, Tsui ventured back to the U.S. in search of special effects technicians whom he brought back to Hong Kong to train local technicians. Disappointed with studio interference during post-production of *Zu*, Tsui went on to form his own company, Film Workshop,

3

with his wife, producer Nansun Shi. Although the company was originally intended to be temporary, it went on to become one of the most successful production companies in Hong Kong. In 1986 Tsui founded Cinefex Workshop, a complete special effects company, as a subsidiary of Film Workshop. As a producer, Tsui found great success with the John Woo-directed *A Better Tomorrow*, which became one of the biggest hits in Hong Kong cinema history and also won Best Picture at the 1987 Hong Kong Film Awards. That same year Tsui directed and co-produced *Peking Opera Blues*, which is now regarded as one of the classics of modern Chinese cinema.

As an actor, Tsui's work in 1987's *Final Victory* (which was scripted by Wong Kar-Wai) brought him a nomination for Best Supporting Actor; that same year he produced the Ching Siu-Tung–directed *A Chinese Ghost Story*, which enjoyed international success. In 1991 Tsui virtually redefined the kung fu film with *Once Upon a Time in China*, which garnered him his first and only win as Best Director at the Hong Kong Film Awards (he was nominated again in 1993 for the first *Once Upon a Time* sequel). Tsui produced another box office sensation in 1992 with *Swordsman II*, which introduced audiences to Asia the Invincible, the transgendered warrior who made a superstar of actress Brigitte Lin. In 1995 Tsui received another Best Director nomination for *The Lovers*, and in 1997 Tsui finally realized his dream of bringing state-of-the-art computer imaging to Hong Kong with his animated remake of *A Chinese Ghost Story*, which combined traditional flat animation with 3D computer imagery. Tsui has since directed Jean-Claude Van Damme's last two films, *Double Team* and *Knock Off*, and recently directed a landmark commercial for a mainland China telecommunications company that told the entire history of human communications in 90 seconds.

In 1999 Tsui realized another lifelong dream with the publication of his first comic book, *Red Snow* (he is an accomplished artist as well), and began production on his latest film as a director, *Time and Tide*, released in 2000.

# 2

# Controlled Chaos and Kung Fu Queens: A Critical Overview

*"We're going to reflect the general feeling of the public, that's the thing I have in mind."*
— Tsui Hark (from Beth Accomando's interview for *Giant Robot* magazine, no. 8)

*"Tsui also suggests that by reviving older traditions you don't simply indulge in nostalgia; you link your life to a vital heritage."*
— David Bordwell (from *Planet Hong Kong: Popular Cinema and The Art of Entertainment*)

In the early 1970s the American film industry underwent a transformation: The studio system was ending, acting styles were changing, formerly taboo subjects (such as sex, violence and drugs) were being socially accepted, and the first wave of university-educated filmmakers was breaking on the shores of American-European traditional cinema. Pick three films most representa-tive of this renaissance and you might come up with Francis Ford Coppola's *The God-father*, George Lucas' *American Graffiti* and Stanley Kubrick's *A Clockwork Orange*.

In the middle years of the next decade Hong Kong cinema experienced a similar rebirth. The "chopsocky" craze of the '70s had passed, audiences were hungry for something new, and the vigorous recruiting and training by local television stations resulted in a crop of new talent anxious to break into motion pictures and revitalize a flagging industry. Choose three films to represent the new Hong Kong cinema of the '80s and you'd likely opt for *Zu: Warriors from the Magic Mountain*, *Peking Opera Blues* and *A Better Tomorrow*.

Now, what's so remarkable about those three films, aside from the way their styles and themes stand in sharp contrast to their American counterparts?

The answer is both simple and unheard-of in Western cinema: All three films were directed or produced by the same man.

Tsui Hark.

Tsui Hark is unique in world cinema, a prolific filmmaker (Tsui has directed, written, produced and/or acted in more than 60 feature films since 1979) who is also a master stylist; a political auteur and a populist; an artist with an obsessive private vision who is also commercially successful; and a filmmaker who seems to revel in deconstructing genres even while celebrating their tropes. He excels at creating chaotic situations that give the illusion of total loss of control while building careful layers of complex meaning and plot, and he will effortlessly mix opposing emotions— grief and joy, anger and love — in one scene. He may also be the world's greatest feminist director; his action films often fly in the face of convention by casting women in the leads, and even in films which star men (in aggressively masculine situations) Tsui will usually choose a female character to represent himself in the story.

## Wuxia and Sing-Song: A Brief History of Hong Kong Cinema B.T. (Before Tsui)

The Hong Kong film has a political, multilingual, complex history. China itself is a linguistically-divided region, with Mandarin being the primary dialect in the north, while the more profanity-rich Cantonese is popular in the south (all dialects can read written Chinese, though); add into the mix English (spoken by the British who occupied Hong Kong until 1997), and you'll begin to understand the proliferation of subtitles and language tracks that accompany most Hong Kong films.

In the beginning there were two principle centers of Chinese film production: Mandarin-speaking Shanghai and Cantonese-speaking Hong Kong. Cantonese movies— which featured horror films, kung fu fantasy epics and melodramas— were banned by the Chinese government in 1936 as being "morally decadent" (some things, thankfully, never change). There was, however, still a huge market for Cantonese-language films, and this became a selling point for Hong Kong film producers, insuring the survival of Cantonese cinema.

Then in 1941 the Japanese occupied Shanghai, and many Mandarin-speaking filmmakers fled to Hong Kong, where Mandarin film production found a new home. The emigres brought much of Shanghai culture with them, and such Mandarin film staples as the "sing-song girl" musical flourished (and provided considerable influence for Tsui Hark's 1984 classic *Shanghai Blues*). Cantonese cinema, meanwhile, turned more to realistic social dramas, reflecting something else the influx of exiles had brought with them: housing shortages and poverty.

In the 1960s Beijing-born director King Hu revitalized the *wuxia*, or swordplay, film with such classics as the 1965 *Come Drink with Me* and 1967's *Dragon Inn* (later remade by producer Tsui Hark as *New Dragon Inn*; Hu also worked with Tsui on 1990's *Swordsman*). Meanwhile, the introduction of local television pro-

Coming in to Hong Kong (photograph by the author).

gramming in 1967 left the Cantonese-speaking cinema in ruins. But in 1971 swordplay gave way to kung fu, and the local film was reborn as Bruce Lee burst onto the film scene, becoming the first global Asian superstar and introducing Chinese audiences to both a new style of martial arts (*jeet kune do*) and a new, intensely proud Chinese hero.

Bruce Lee was arguably the first truly postmodernist Hong Kong cinema artist. Lee took the tired conventions of the "chopsocky" genre—with its reliance on formally-executed kung fu battles and inhumanly-invulnerable combatants—and dragged them kicking and screaming into the future. Lee may have been grace-ful, but somehow his streetfighting, barechested, bloodied-lip style just looked *dirty*. He was to the kung fu film what Martin Scorsese and Francis Ford Coppola were to the American gangster film: He remade the genre forever in his own image, and after him it would never be the same again (despite the nearly one-hundred Wong Fei-hung movies that existed prior to *Once Upon a Time in China*, it does seem unlikely that Tsui's masterpiece would ever have come into existence with-out Bruce Lee).

Lee's untimely death in 1973 left the revitalized Hong Kong film industry scrambling. Anxious to maintain the excitement (and the profits) Lee had gen-erated, the Hong Kong studios looked des-perately for the next Bruce Lee. Or Bruce Li. Or Bluce Ree.

Instead they found the next Buster Keaton.

About the time Lee was still working in America on the *Green Hornet* television series, a small revolution in Chinese cul-ture was taking place: The opera schools were dying out. Traditional Peking Opera, with its dynamic acrobatics and highly-trained performers, was being replaced by television; meanwhile, new child labor laws were driving out many of the cruel masters who had run the schools. As the schools closed all over Hong Kong, a flood of acrobatic, athletic, disciplined young actors was being released into the Hong Kong film industry. Most of them gravi-tated toward that part of the film biz most like the energetic, sometimes frantic Peking Opera: stunt work.

After Lee's passing, producers plun-dered the ranks of these determined, ambitious performers. One of the most promising was a floppy-haired, slightly sleepy-eyed young man named Jackie Chan.

Fortunately for the future Hong Kong cinema, Jackie Chan wasn't interested in being merely Bruce Lee's successor. After appearing in a string of disappointing Bruce Lee ripoffs, Chan persuaded his pro-ducers to let him try what he saw in his head: a kung fu comedy, one that blended the ferocity of Bruce Lee with the comic sweetness of early American film comedi-ans such as Keaton and Chaplin.

1977–1978 saw the release of Chan's pivotal kung fu comedies *Snake in the Eagle's Shadow, Half a Loaf of Kung Fu* and *Drunken Master*. Chan's timing was, to say the least, propitious; audiences were fed up with the seemingly endless conveyor belt of Bruce Lee replicas, and what had verged dangerously on self-parody now exploded into out-and-out farce. Chan zoomed to superstardom and became the second of the great Hong Kong postmod-ern icons.

## Hong Kong and the Tube

While Bruce Lee and Jackie Chan were raising the consciousness of the chopsocky genre (and ensuring the per-manence of the Cantonese-language film), a new generation of Hong Kong filmmakers was gestating — in television studios and American film schools.

As Hong Kong television boomed in the late '60s and '70s, training programs and jobs opened up. Some future Hong Kong film notables entered the television studio internships immediately; others — like their American peers — chose film schools. Since Asian film schools were still largely nonexistent, these budding artistes came to America, the home of the world's finest film schools. Most of these temporary expatriates eventually returned home and joined the rest in the television studios.

One of these was Tsui Hark.

By contrasting the career paths of Tsui Hark and Jackie Chan, the differences between Hong Kong's New Wave and the Jackie Chan/Sammo Hung "Old Wave" become apparent: While both Tsui Hark and Jackie Chan grew up with a strong affection for American film (especially the early comedies), Tsui chose to obtain formal training. While Jackie was experiencing the school of (literally) hard knocks, Tsui was studying film history and theory, along with production. In the mid–70s, as Jackie Chan was appearing in forgettable variations on Bruce Lee themes, Tsui was directing episodic television, including a large-scale costume drama called *Golden Dagger Romance*. Then, a year after Jackie Chan freed the kung fu film from the confines of deadly earnestness, Tsui Hark put his own, bizarre spin on the genre with his feature film debut *The Butterfly Murders* (1979). Although *The Butterfly Murders* didn't achieve the success of Chan's comedies (it took Tsui's fourth feature, *All the Wrong Clues*, to do that), its combination of kung fu, mystery, horror and science fiction did mark the appearance of an authentic new voice, one with a built-in paradox: obvious admiration for tried-and-true genre conventions alongside utter disregard for same.

## Hong Kong's New Wave

Tsui Hark was at the head of a "New Wave" of Hong Kong filmmakers in the late '70s to early '80s; most critics now generally include Patrick Tam (*Final Victory*), Ann Hui (*The Story of Woo Viet*, *Summer Snow*), Allen Fong (*Homecoming*) and a short roster of others in this seminal group. While these filmmakers shared some traits with their American counterparts (an appreciation for film history, formal training), they also shared something unique to themselves: They were largely Cantonese-speaking Hong Kong natives. This was reflected in their early films, which often dealt with issues specific to life in Hong Kong (see Tsui's astonishing *Dangerous Encounter — 1st Kind*; seldom has a film been produced anywhere in the world that's such a scathing portrayal of a home town).

While the New Wave directors were producing serious dramatic films, that other Hong Kong film industry (Jackie Chan and Sammo Hung) was experimenting with genre mix-and-matching: Sammo Hung merged kung fu, horror and comedy for his 1980 *Encounters of the Spooky Kind*; and the pirate swashbuckler met slapstick comedy in Jackie Chan's *Project A*. Tsui blended New Wave social concerns with this new approach to genre splicing; *Shanghai Blues* is an ideal example, melding winsome romance, the Mandarin musical and the screwball comedy. This cross-genre approach quickly became a staple of Hong Kong cinema and still survives today (check out Wilson Yip's 1998 social-commentary-meets-the-living-dead satire *Bio-Zombie*, or Jingle Ma's science-fiction action thriller *Hot War*, produced by Jackie Chan).

The new Hong Kong filmmakers also took some of the worst elements of traditional Chinese film and turned them into assets. Hong Kong films have been traditionally shot "MOS" (literally, *mit-out sound*), meaning all sound — from the actors' dialogue to footsteps and street sounds — is added later in post-production. The chopsocky films garnered a small following in this country precisely because of their often-ludicrous dubbing and the unrealistically-hard smacking sounds of fists hitting skin (which usually sounded more like boards being struck together). But the new generation of directors seemed to recognize that they gained more than just a few extra dollars by recording without synch sound — they could also move the camera without having to worry about microphone placement. The clumsy zooms of the chopsocky films were replaced by cameras that tracked, dollied, ran and soared. The films of Tsui, Ching Siu-tung, John Woo and Sammo Hung soon became known for their wild kineticism, with camera movements and flying bodies that would be impossible to achieve in a synch sound world.

The MOS style of shooting was also at least partially responsible for another factor in the Hong Kong New Wave cinema of the early '80s: A new generation of gifted, charismatic actors was captivating audiences worldwide and bringing a fresh level of acting excellence to Hong Kong cinema. Bereft of vocal intonation to convey emotion and characters, these actors were forced to rely on facial expressions and body movements; add to that a background that consisted of actual acting work (often in the television training programs or Peking Opera schools) and not the American approach of "Method" training, and the end result was an invigorating mix

of American silent film acting techniques and the physicality of the chopsocky films. Actors such as Chow Yun-Fat, Brigitte Lin, Jackie Chan, Sally Yeh, Sam Hui and Leslie Cheung were giving rich, full-bodied (in every sense of the word) performances that broke sharply with American/European acting styles and seemed to effortlessly transcend genres: Brigitte Lin, for example, played a funny, sharp, sexy gangster moll in Jackie Chan's 1985 hit *Police Story*, then starred in Tsui's *Peking Opera Blues* as a driven, guilt-stricken revolutionary a year later. (Hong Kong actors also have considerably more opportunity to hone their craft than their American counterparts — they work almost constantly, often appearing in two or more films *simultaneously*. It's been jokingly suggested that any actor not appearing in at least four films a year is retired).

## Controlled Chaos: Tsui's Evolution

Even in Hong Kong cinema, where genres are crossed as routinely as genders, Tsui Hark's versatility is astonishing. Not only has he produced or directed films in nearly every conceivable category, he's consistently recreated, resurrected and revitalized dying or stagnant genres (or even, as with his 1997 animated version of *A Chinese Ghost Story*, created a new genre, since the film was Hong Kong's first full-length computer-animated feature). His 1983 *Zu: Warriors from the Magic Mountain* brought the American-style special effects fantasy to Chinese cinema; in 1986 he created the woman's action film with *Peking Opera Blues* and produced John Woo's reinvention of the "heroic bloodshed" gangster film, *A Better Tomorrow*. In the '90s, his *Once Upon a Time in China* revitalized the kung fu epic; and in 1995's

*The Blade* he crafted postmodern grit onto the *wuxia* picture.

Yet, despite his own consistent commercial and artistic success, Tsui's own style has undergone a distinct transformation, and his career has evolved from maverick independent to company mogul.

Tsui's first feature, 1979's *The Butterfly Murders*, was one of the first of the post Bruce Lee/New Wave films; and even if it seemed to lack the contemporary social concerns of other New Wave directors, it employed the qualities that would soon become trademarks of Hong Kong cinema: innovative photography and use of color, a melding of genres (in this case, kung fu epic, horror, science fiction and mystery), and an airborne kineticism. (The film also gave tantalizing glimpses of personal obsessions that would reoccur in Tsui's work over the next 20 years: feminine strength and the power of nature.)

Although *The Butterfly Murders* was not a commercial hit, it was well-received enough to allow Tsui to venture into even stranger territory with his next film, the cannibalistic political satire *We're Going to Eat You*. But it was Tsui's third feature, *Dangerous Encounter — 1st Kind* (aka *Don't Play with Fire*) that really established him as one of the leading filmmakers in Asia. The bleak, nihilistic, ultraviolent and finally wrenchingly tragic film was a fireball captured on silver nitrate, one of the most incendiary films ever made (and one that is almost without equal in American cinema; only George Romero's *Dawn of the Dead*— which, not coincidentally, provides most of the musical score for *Dangerous Encounter*—comes close in the sheer amount of carnage and the force of the doomsday vision onscreen). After the ferocity of this amazing trio of films, Tsui Hark seemed poised to become a sort of underground Hong Kong equivalent to, perhaps, Martin Scorsese.

Instead he made *All the Wrong Clues,* a daffy gangster comedy that became one of his biggest box office smashes and sent him rocketing into the upper echelons of mainstream Hong Kong filmmakers. *All the Wrong Clues* couldn't have been more different from the first three pictures: Where they were dark, bloody and intense, *Clues* was light, broadly comic and packed with production design that looked like a comic book come to life. Only the obvious talent of its director linked it to the other three.

Tsui had now proven himself to be a filmmaker who could work equally well in the under- or over-ground; his career could have gone either way. But in 1984 Tsui chose instead a path that confounded those expecting either direction from him: He became a company head, with the co-founding of Film Workshop. Formed with his wife Nansun Shi, Film Workshop was originally intended only as a way of allowing Tsui the filmmaker to retain some of the control he felt he'd lost on the 1983 *Zu: Warriors from the Magic Mountain.* Instead, the company became one of the hottest production units in Hong Kong, and Tsui soon found himself working as not only a director but also as one of the busiest producers around.

Tsui's influence as a producer would prove to be just as great as what he'd given the Hong Kong industry as a director. Before Film Workshop he'd brought American special optical effects to Hong Kong for *Zu*; now, as a producer, he would be largely responsible for generating the careers of such eventual Hong Kong luminaries as John Woo, Chow Yun-Fat, Jet Li, Ching Siu-Tung and Brigitte Lin, to name a few. (And Tsui's indirect influence would later be felt in the films of many of Hong Kong's "Second Wave" directors, especially Wong Kar-Wai's *Ashes of Time*, Peter Chan's *He's a Woman, She's a Man* and Andrew Lau's *The Storm Riders*.)

While Tsui the producer was building Film Workshop into a machine that churned out successful films at an incredible (by American standards, anyway) clip, Tsui the director was undergoing a metamorphosis in his personal style. With *Peking Opera Blues* and *Shanghai Blues* he seemed to have at last learned the fine arts of casting and directing actors (if the earlier films lacked in any areas, it would have been these). With 1991's classic *Once Upon a Time in China* he slowed both the frantic pace and camera work of his prior efforts down enough to concentrate more on character development; his handling of the film's epic elements also displayed a confidence born of what was now more than a decade's worth of experience. With 1993's *Green Snake* he brought his personal vision completely to the fore, creating a film that was almost the perfect antithesis of *Dangerous Encounter*: Where that film was frenetic, deliberately ugly and full of vitriol, *Green Snake* was lilting, exquisitely lovely and a tender meditation on feminine power and the nature of humanity. The new, calmer Tsui was also onscreen in 1994's *The Lovers*, 1995's *Love in the Time of Twilight*, and 1995's deliciously funny and sweet-natured *The Chinese Feast*.

Then, as if to deliberately confound critics who thought they knew what to expect from Tsui, he made 1995's *The Blade*, a film which seemed to blend the anarchic bloodshed of *Dangerous Encounter* with the lyricism of the '90s films. *The Blade*, with its emphasis on the sensuality of the human form, reflected *Green Snake*; but it was through a glass darkly, for *The Blade* is second only to *Dangerous Encounter* as the bloodiest and most vicious of Tsui's works. It served as a wakeup call that, despite his obvious mastery of the commercial feature, Tsui Hark still recognized his roots as a black-edged independent.

Rather than follow up *The Blade* with a whole new cycle of lean, mean *wuxia* films, Tsui chose not one but two very different paths in 1997: He produced Hong Kong's first computer-animated full-length feature, *A Chinese Ghost Story: The Tsui Hark Animation*, and he went to Europe to direct the Jean-Claude Van Damme vehicle *Double Team*. Although the two films couldn't have been more diametrically opposed, they both showed a new phase of Tsui's work: Tsui the technophile. Tsui Hark has always been interested in new film technologies—witness *Zu*'s optical effects—but that interest was now firmly at the front of his films. *A Chinese Ghost Story: The Tsui Hark Animation* is unique not only in Hong Kong cinema but also world cinema for its completely new way of combining traditional flat animation (foreground characters) with three-dimensional imagery (the backgrounds). And with *Double Team* Tsui turned a standard Van Damme actioner into a science fiction cyberthriller. This was even more the case in the superior follow-up *Knock Off*, in which the interior world of circuit pathways and fiberoptic networks was just as important as the exterior setting of Hong Kong.

## Kung Fu Queens: Tsui's Obsessions

If Tsui Hark's career as a trendsetting commercial filmmaker has been intriguing, then his work as a personal filmmaker has been positively mind-blowing. In his relentless pursuit of his own vision, Tsui is perhaps most comparable in American terms to David Lynch, although Tsui is plainly more interested in pleasing a mass audience than Lynch is. Tsui, of course, has also had the advantage of having been able to explore his themes in five dozen films

Zhao Wen-Zhou in *The Blade.*

as producer, director and/or writer (a figure which probably no American filmmaker, with the possible exception of Roger Corman, can match).

The one motif to appear most frequently in the Tsui Hark oeuvre is that of feminine power. From his first film (*The Butterfly Murders*) to his last as of this writing (*Knock Off*), Tsui has featured strong, smart, often funny and, most importantly, *feminine* female leads— despite the fact that these heroines are occasionally dressed as men (even men sometimes appear to yearn for femininity). Tsui has commented on how early exposure to Peking Opera— with its crossgender performances— had a profound effect on him, but his use of women is so unique that that explanation almost seems disingenuous.

While the use of women as proactive leads is hardly unheard of— Ridley Scott (*Alien, Thelma and Louise*) and James Cameron (*Aliens, Terminator 2: Judgment Day)* are probably the best of the Western filmmakers to feature female leads. Tsui Hark's use of women stands in almost complete contradiction to Cameron's and Scott's: Whereas American and European filmmakers will only allow a female action character to triumph by becoming more masculine, Tsui Hark's women triumph by remaining or becoming feminine. *Peking Opera Blues* is a good early example: Although Tsao Wan (Brigitte Lin) dresses as a man and is a forceful, resolute revolutionary, she doesn't begin to achieve her goals until she bonds with the other two female leads (note also how Tsui lets her become more feminine while not changing or lessening her character). *Green Snake* takes the theme to its logical, ultimate conclusion: White Snake (Joey Wang) completes her transformation by the act of giving birth. Of course, all of

Tsui's explorations of gender and femininity found their apotheosis in the *Swordsman* series, in which there's not only Asia (Brigitte Lin in parts II and III), the male warrior who castrates himself to achieve ultimate power, but Kiddo (Michelle Reis) in the second film, who strives to prove her femininity to her male brothers; and in *The East is Red* (part III), Snow (Joey Wang) gives up her attempt to impersonate the male Asia in order to win back Asia's love. Snow's feminine power finally becomes so great that the film's two superheroic leads—Asia and Officer Koo (Yu Rong-Guang)—attempt to annihilate each other over Snow, destroying the tragic woman in the process.

Another aspect that sets Tsui Hark's use of women apart from his Western peers is the aforementioned idea of female bonding. While John Woo was exploring male bonding (and, not coincidentally, achieving American success) in his films, Tsui was making movies in which two or more women would form such a tight-knit unit that male characters were usually left standing on the outside to look in, baffled. In *Shanghai Blues* we're presented with what could be a traditional romantic triangle—except that the film is plainly the story of the friendship between Shu-Shu (Sylvia Chang) and Stool (Sally Yeh), while the male protagonist, Tung (Kenny Bee), remains unsure (until the climax) as to which of them is his dream girl. Again, in *Green Snake* men are literally left to peep through walls and curtains at the sealed relationship between the two snake sisters. Even in a somewhat lesser film such as *Tri-Star*, Tsui seems more interested in the relationships between the prostitute Baiban (Anita Yuen) and her "sisters" than he is in Baiban's pairings with either of the male leads.

It's possible that this element of Tsui's work stems from his fascination with

inverting ideals of Western morality, because Tsui Hark may just be the most genuinely perverse filmmaker on the planet. This does not mean "perverse" as in overly sexual or fetishistic, but perverse as defined by *Webster's Dictionary*: "(2a) Obstinate in opposing what is right, reasonable, or accepted." Many critics label a filmmaker such as David Lynch perverse; but, as genuinely disturbing as Lynch's work is, most of it ultimately reaffirms traditional (American) values of love, family and gender identity. Tsui Hark, on the other hand, routinely creates action and/or fantasy films whose giddy surfaces hide true perversity: a hero who's at his best when drunk (*Swordsman II*); a heroine whose affability is unaffected by her cannibalistic tendencies (*Dragon Inn*); a villain who sacrifices himself ("Rolex" in *We're Going to Eat You*). Caucasians, or "gweilos," are often the antagonists; the handsome white stranger who would be the hero in a Sergio Leone film will be the bad guy here. Americans are almost invariably involved in illegal or unethical activities, even when the film is set in America (*The Master*). (This is obviously a key reason why Tsui Hark remains virtually unknown outside of Asia.)

If human beings need not be bound by traditional values and laws, then they also seem free of the bonds of nature and physics. In Tsui Hark's cinema, characters routinely perform exhilaratingly impossible physical feats. They walk on water or glide on top of fields, they scale cliffs in an instant, they leap, spin and soar into the sky.

This dynamic vision of human potential partly has its roots in Tsui's fondness for kineticism, but it also derives from traditional Chinese mythology. In Stephen Teo's book *Hong Kong Cinema*, he refers to Tsui as "nationalistic" due to the director's obsession with Chinese identity;

**Jet Li as Wong Fei-Hung in *Once Upon a Time in China.***

indeed, even in non-fantasy films such as *Once Upon a Time in China* or *The Chinese Feast*, mythology will make a guest appearance, usually in the form of a lion or dragon dance. The films that deal more specifically with fairy tale themes (*Zu, A Chinese Ghost Story, Green Snake*) are so steeped in Chinese traditionalism that they can seem incomprehensible to some Western viewers.

Tsui's "nationalism" also has another side to it: Despite the fact that Hong Kong cinema is usually thought of as a completely apolitical art, Tsui has made a number of films which mark him clearly as an opinionated, thoughtful and downright political filmmaker. 1981's *Dangerous Encounter* is, of course, one of the more obvious examples, with its depiction of a Hong Kong ruled by Caucasian CIA smugglers and forgotten, alienated young Asians; but the film which immediately preceded *Dangerous Encounter, We're Going to Eat You,* is a vicious satire on political systems that's thinly disguised as a black comedy/action thriller. The *Once Upon a Time in China* films are firelit by their anti-foreign-intervention sentiments; even a film as seemingly innocuous as 1992's *Wicked City* is, on second viewing, a film decrying foreign intervention (in this one the intruders are literally monsters). According to Fredric Dannen and Barry Long's *Hong Kong Babylon*, 1991's *King of Chess* (produced and co-directed by Tsui) featured a story (set partially during China's 1967 Cultural Revolution) in which "the political content... is considered daring by Hong Kong standards." Perhaps the most intriguing of Tsui's more veiled political commentaries is *The East is Red*, in which the strongly spiritual (read: strongly Chinese) Asia not only stands against Japanese and Spanish invaders, but also fights a man sometimes referred to as "Comrade" Koo over the love of the blue-eyed Snow. That both Koo and Snow lose (while Asia lives) can be interpreted as Tsui's belief that Chinese tradition is strong enough to survive the temptations of both capitalism and communism.

If Tsui seems innately in touch with Chinese culture, the same cannot be said of Chinese language. A failure of language pervades Tsui's work; the failure can be as small as two characters who mix up a pre-set password (*Peking Opera Blues, Swordsman II*), or as great as different races whose lack of communication leads to strife (*Once Upon a Time in China*). China is a land divided by its dialects, and the Hong Kong film industry has always vacillated between Mandarin and Cantonese (with some English thrown in for good measure). Tsui — who is both a master visual stylist and a canny businessman — would almost certainly have experienced difficulties caused by language (Tsui admits to one such problem in Stanley Kwan's documentary *Yang + Yin: Gender in Chinese Cinema*; when Kwan accuses Tsui of demonstrating homophobia in *The Lovers*, Tsui pleads that they simply couldn't come up with a word for "gay" that would have fit the story's period setting). Still, it may be to our benefit that Tsui and his characters occasionally struggle through some verbal dilemma — it could certainly be suggested that it has forced him to rely more on his visual skills and has created a

cinema which can be easily understood whether you speak the language (or read subtitles) or not.

As an intensely visual artist, Tsui has always been interested in new film technologies, and over the years his films themselves have begun to deal with technology. Many of Tsui's period films have featured technology that was new for the time — Tsao Wan's car in *Peking Opera Blues*, light bulbs in *Love in the Time of Twilight*, Aunt Yee's cameras in *Once Upon a Time in China I, II* and *III*, the Japanese submarine in *The East Is Red* — so it is surprising that, to date, he has made only one true science fiction film (*I Love Maria*). His most recent films definitely show him moving in the direction of high-tech imagery, what with *Double Team*'s prison island, *Knock-Off*'s fiber optic pathways, and *A Chinese Ghost Story: The Tsui Hark Animation*'s computer-generated imagery (which also featured one of the funniest examples of Tsui's interest in tech gadgetry — ghosts who flit about talking on bat-shaped cell phones). Tsui recently completed a revolutionary 90-second commercial that explored the entire history of telecommunications, and is rumored to have been in contact with American science fiction authors. It seems likely that his work in the future will continue to explore the boundaries of the evolving technologies.

While still exploding Western values, of course.

# 3

# Conversations with Tsui, Part One

Originally I had planned to interview Tsui Hark, pull out the pertinent quotes, and insert them into my overview essay. Within twenty minutes of sitting down with him, I realized this wasn't going to work.

There's no easy way to describe what Tsui Hark is like in conversation. Perhaps the closest comparison would be watching a virtuoso musician take off on a jazz riff. Or being a tachyon caught in a particle accelerator. Tsui must simply have been born with neurons that fire faster than yours or mine; the amount of thoughts, anecdotes and information that pour out of him in response to even simple questions is genuinely astonishing. I realized that it would be unfair, to both Tsui and the book's readers, to not present this interview in nearly its entirety. I've moved questions and answers pertaining to particular films to the sections on those films, and have cleaned up some grammar and

translation difficulties; otherwise, what you read is what I got.

Our interviews began on a Wednesday afternoon, in Film Workshop's offices in Kowloon Bay, Hong Kong. Kowloon Bay at first seems an unlikely spot for the combined offices of Film Workshop/Cinefex Workshop (the special effects arm); this area is a strange combination of towering, albeit rundown, government housing units and high-end shopping malls. The offices of Film Workshop sit serenely above it all, on the thirteenth floor (! — not an unlucky number in Hong Kong) of a major industrial complex.

The production offices have a feel not unlike that of their American counterparts: Assistants scurry by with faxes or hard copies, a conference area is at the hub, and one shelf unit holds nearly a dozen VCRs and/or other media players.

What's not like a Hollywood office are

**The entrance to Film Workshop (photograph by the author).**

the bookshelves. There are a lot of them, filled to bursting with *manga* (Japanese comic books, usually for adults), how-to painting books and (my personal favorite) *The Great Women Superheroes* by Trina Robbins. Inside Tsui's office proper there are even more: shelves of videotapes (I spot several episodes of both *The Prisoner* and *Monty Python's Flying Circus* among all the Chinese titles), graphic novels (a collection of Neil Gaiman's *Sandman*), art and design references (handbag and greeting card design among them), and lots of toys and figurines (Astroboy, Godzilla and American wrestling dolls included). Against the back wall is a MIDI keyboard and mixer.

Tsui has to reschedule our first meeting; it seems he was up until 7 a.m. that morning, working to finish the latest cut on his film *Time and Tide*. He merely shifts

our time to 2:30 that afternoon and shows up looking only slightly more tousled than me (I'm still suffering from jet lag).

I've heard before that he's an energetic and passionate interview subject, and today — despite the fact that he must be working on virtually no sleep — is no disappointment. He obviously puts a great deal of thought into his work and loves to talk about it.

Our interview takes two days, during which Tsui often routinely gets up to attend to business; one meeting involves pitching the proposed sequel to *Zu: Warriors from the Magic Mountain* to a major Hong Kong star. Then he returns to our talks without dropping a beat. One of the last things he said to me before I left Hong Kong was a slightly mumbled, "You know, if you ask me these same questions next week you'll probably get completely different answers."

Q: *Let's start with something basic: Did you ever have an interest in being anything besides a filmmaker?*

Actually, I wanted to be a comic artist. I think the most enjoyable thing is being a comic book artist. I'd always enjoy spending a week at home alone drawing, just laughing and giggling and listening to music. Because the thing, you see, is in making movies you have to deal with other people, which may result in a lot of unpleasant situations. This business is full of temperament; people are very emotional. They tend to say they don't like, they like, they love, they hate. These are very strong kinds of emotions. Sometimes you need to relax, take a break at home, listen to music, watch videotapes. Drawing would be something that's a way to put down something that's in your mind. Comics is also a silly kind of category; you may do a caricature of something you've seen that you hate or like, either way.

Q: *Filmmaking and comics are similar in some ways — they both tell a story visually by combining lots of small shots.*

To make a movie… you have a definite limited time, like 90 minutes, to create a viewpoint, a point of something. Even a character who has a certain kind of ambition or emotion, to carry along throughout the whole thing… You have to deal with a lot of things to do that. You have to deal with the acting of the guy, deal with the movement of the guy, dealing with the issue or angle or editing, everything, to make a point. But with drawing you can just start over and do it again. You put it down and look at it and you see the right reaction without really costing a lot of money or causing a lot of commotion because of something going wrong.

Q: *I noticed a lot of manga [Japanese graphic novels] in your offices.*

We have a big collection of manga because those things are very interesting to me. We're reading everything — we're reading manga, we're reading comic books, we're reading everything. My favorites are these outdated Chinese picture books. [He displays a stack of small, photographically-illustrated, pamphlet-style books, obviously from the '40s or '50s.]

Q: *I noticed a lot of oil painting technique books in the office as well — are you also an oil painter?*

I painted some as a kid, but I gave up that. [The oil painting books] are not for me. Those are for the photoshop guys [his CGI effects artists]. I think they need to understand some of the theory of color, the lighting, layers, perspective, sun, everything. The thing is, they complete the first level, but when they go to the second level they stop. Creating a 3-D model is like sculpting a live creature; so if you cannot sculpt a live creature, there is no way in a 3-D model you can do something we like. Low-tech to improve your high-tech technique.

Q: *You recently worked with Ma Wing Shong of* The Storm Riders *fame — was that your first comic book that was released?*

Right. Sort of, yes. I'd been thinking about drawing a lot. That book was not drawn by me, it was done by other people. I was tied to a project at the time. It happened that the artist worked for me. I always think that a comic book is two-dimensional, so it should be something you read very easily. I always think that American comic books are too graphic, too busy, too much talk, the focus is very scattered. For manga it's very simple, line drawing. Sometimes it's not very ambitious. They're very simple things that you read very fast. But American comics read very slow and are sometimes too rich (the colors). So I'd like to find a way between. I think maybe we should use a kind of

Tsui Hark's office (photograph by the author).

visual language, a simple focus. We put in some kind of like oil paintings; I think it works.

Q: *Do you consider yourself an artist as a filmmaker?*

I think if you are making money, making a living as a professional something, I believe that would be called... I don't know whether the definition of "artist" would fit into this category. I would think that "artist" means you are actually creating, using or basing on emotion of people to arouse reaction. That I would call an artist. I believe that even people who are making toys, those are artists, too. I would say the definition of "artist" is something I never really thought deeply about. I should belong to a category like that.

Q: *You said in one interview, "I always think that a female role can be very strong and very powerful." Can you talk more about that?*

The interesting thing about drama is comparison, contrast. So many people would say why; why not? So you start to create a contrast. You always play on the kind of thing people have in mind; you use that to increase the impact. For example, a female role...the majority of the stories in the movies, in Hong Kong as in everywhere, is that the females are supposed to be protected. Or even a bitchy character would cause the guy problems he'd have to solve. Or the female character would be something like — not in the main plot. So it would open up a lot of rooms, an area they haven't touched upon. Nowadays you realize that the female characters are more sensitive, in a way. More complicated than males. Males are more on the surface, where you sort of hide things. The male has a certain kind of character; everything has to be out, controlled, direct, smart, witty — witty in a way that's not obvious,

**Tsui Hark in his office (photograph by the author).**

but should be very clever. But women—they are under a kind of pressure from a lot of elements in their environment. For example, they are treated in certain ways if they have defied tradition. That is drama, that is very interesting. It's something people have taken for granted. I think that's something that's very dramatic. For example, I talked to some guy who was a producer from L.A., we talked about making a movie with a superhero, we have a lot of superheroes now, so we could create a superheroine. So he said, "Well, I'll give you an example: Kids don't like to see girly pictures." So I said, "Well, okay... How about comparing superhero to superheroine in the movie?" It's a better picture. It's very interesting to see a superheroine coming up on a screen doing something totally different from a superhero. That could have a very powerful impact. Interesting. Without seeing it right now, I have

no idea what it is about, actually. But even a character with young age or a character with a tradition which may not be very popular right now is interesting. For example, the alien in *Dragon Inn* [Dao]—he's a very interesting character. He talks in his language that no one understands, the woman doesn't understand him, and he stays on for a long time to protect the woman. That's something where I think the contrast is very warm and very dramatic.

Q: *One thing I find interesting about your female characters is that, unlike female leads in American films, your women often succeed by becoming more feminine, not less.*

In the '60s, with women's liberation and feminists, everything was finding out what should a woman be like. I would believe everything should be about yourself, you don't give in to anybody. So if a woman is built a certain way naturally, she should look that way. It's very strange for her to change her nature and become something else. Even men, a man should be what he should be. He doesn't have to be something he shouldn't be. In the '60s women were fighting all these things, how they should look, place in society... people may not do equally things that somebody younger can do. It can be a feature of the body, it's not a social thing. Mankind has so many interesting sides about themselves, man, woman — woman is very nice to look at for us men. Women are very romantic in a way... romantic is the most key word in everything. Even men, we try to be very romantic in a way. But I always think women are more romantic than men. I don't know how... if characters are going to compete, like a man and a woman, I would say that women are more romantic than men. I don't know why. It's like comparing in *Casablanca* Humphrey Bogart to Ingrid Bergman — who is more romantic? Humphrey Bogart is romantic because he is not supposed to be romantic. And when he's just a little bit romantic he's *very* romantic. That's why we sometimes take it for granted that women are supposed to be very romantic. It takes an affair of the heart to make them romantic, but then they are very romantic.

Q: *Bruce Lee is often considered to be possibly the single most influential figure on modern Hong Kong cinema — do you agree?*

Bruce Lee is one of the guys who we think of as an undying spirit. The most controversial thing about it is intellectuals don't think Bruce Lee should be the model forever of the Asian. But the reason Bruce Lee has been around for so many years is because in the '60s there was a kind of Asian student movement or civil rights thing going on. That's why Bruce Lee became such a public figure, sort of like a symbol of anti-oppression. For Hong Kong, for Asia, Bruce Lee became a legend because we saw such outstanding action from him. The audience was very excited to see something realistic, powerful and different. He was said to have a kind of real technique of fighting, and that's why he became a legend. And he died young, so everything added together... People think of him as very persistent, very strong, very uncompromising. And that becomes the kind of thing we go along with. But what is left from Bruce Lee in our movies— we don't see anything left from Bruce Lee, because we have changed. In the movie industry if you go on doing the same thing you'll be thrown out of the business. In the movies— in anything we have here in Hong Kong— we are changing very rapidly, from one point to another, to cope with the same kind of product from everywhere. For example, we see *The Matrix*, they're doing this kung fu thing, we say, "What do we have like *Matrix*? No, let's think of totally different stuff. Non-*Matrix*." And then suddenly two years later everybody's doing the same thing. It's like a video game, where you're constantly breaking open a door and you go through another door and you break the door and you're being chased by people and you have to run. This is like a non-stop type of racing. And the fun of it is suddenly you stop and look around and say, "I'm not changing anything. I'm doing the same thing again. Let's see what happens." So the thing about Bruce Lee is he sort of did the same thing. I can't really say he's had a creative influence. He's sort of a cross-culture thing. He crossed East with West. He was a guy that was very persistent, fighting something he didn't like; he was strong, he was romantic and he died young.

Q: *Didn't he bring a grittier, more realistic style of fighting to the screen?*

What he brings onto the screen is speed and power. What we see before, especially in Hollywood productions—we always think it is very silly to see John Wayne grab the guy's collar, and then he talks a lot and then swings his fist and the guy is still waiting for him to hit, and we think, "C'mon, this is a little too silly." Bruce Lee, he sort of skipped all that, he kicked ass. That's something we really like.

Q: *A lot of your contemporaries have been more interested in creating urban dramas, in which the city of Hong Kong itself is often a prominent feature, even a character, yet you've done very few films like that. Would you say you have a preference for historical rather than contemporary urban material?*

When I started in the business, not many people were doing the period material. They wanted to update stuff, they think the period films are not commercial. On TV they had a lot of that kind of thing. When you do it in movies it would take more money, the budget would be higher than usual. And people want to see something they can identify with. So I thought that would be something very interesting—a period movie or costume drama. There's still so much of the old traditional way-back stuff—Chinese, Asian... Sometimes I would look at something that's supposed to be Chinese, and that's something I've never seen before, that's supposed to belong to the culture. Like America—we go to America and we learn the language and we see things; we take it very naturally, as something not coming out of our root of origin. It's like a study. We talk about how Texans live, how Californians live, how the Anglo-Saxons coming from Europe to America live... what kind of culture developed from that history? There is so much that we don't know, so much in depth. We come back to our place—Hong Kong, China—and we realize we are supposed to know that, but I haven't seen that before! That period of time, in the '70s, I

look around and I realize the established directors, the older directors, are doing the period material. And the reason they are doing the period material is that they are not familiar with the modern stuff. So I have a real interest in going in that direction, because a lot of my colleagues are doing love story, drama, things like that. But none of them are touching the period stuff, so I say, "I want to try it." When you go into that period of time you have to find out what people are like, why people are watching it... why is it dying? Why is there no interest in that? And I found a lot of charm, a lot of magic in that area. It's like shopping, right? You pick it up, say, "This is very nice." It comes to the point where you realize it's not out-dated anymore, it can go around now. Everybody's doing it. And I felt very frustrated because they're not shooting it in the right manner. They're tearing it up and selling the pieces instead of selling the whole thing. So after a while I want to give up that area, just leave the area, don't touch it any more and do something else. But another thing about it, the reason I get into this business is I feel this is a very entertaining career to be with, because there's nothing in the world you want so much as entertainment—everything is entertaining! It's very nice to have a career like that, so I choose that career. In the '80s I start to think about why I'm making movies. Why do I like movies? You start going back, track back to when you were a kid. What was the first movie I watched, what was the best movie I saw when I was a kid? And suddenly it's a collection, there's a list of the pictures I want to see again, to compare how I feel now to what I felt before. Some of them are really impossible to get, some of them you can get. Some I felt very scared, and found it was very silly; *Seven Samurai* is one of the movies I was very scared by when I saw the trailer when I was a kid. I was really scared of this muddy picture on the screen and these people with whiskers, and they look very dirty, and they yell and they shout — we had to read the subtitles, but they're very ugly looking. But now when I saw *Samurai* again I found it was a fantastic movie, right? So there is so much difference between now and the past. I started to collect the movies I like and see them again, and feel very emotional with the characters. "Let's bring him back, let him live again"... it's like a *Frankenstein* concept. "Let's bring him to life again, let him be around with us. You can only find him in a library; let's put him on the screen again." Even *Swordsman* — that film's been done before, and it was not done well. So I said, "Let's do that again." The investor said, "Why would you do that?! That's been proven to be a failure, that didn't work!" I said, "No, no, no, the original may not work, but the character works. Let's do the character." So in my mind it's not the period or a lot of stuff, it's the character that sometimes attracts you, to bring it alive again. So I put the character into the movie I produce or direct. Sometimes it's not the script, it's the character. For example, the monkey in *Monkey King* [a classic Chinese tale] — that's a character that I would love very much to make, to create, to rejuvenate, to make live again. I don't know how — I'm going to be every excited to see that character in my studio!

Q: *Is* Monkey King *one of your dream projects?*

One of them. My fantasy I always think about is, one day I get a monkey in my studio and I say, "I want you to do this," and the monkey follows my direction. It'd be fantastic.

Q: *Maybe it can be done now with the new digital technology.*

Right. Exactly. Ten years ago the reason why I didn't really do it was that I thought it was a very interesting story and the characters need to have unlimited movement. Ten years ago I was thinking about how the character would be played by eight people, because it's going to be very strenuous. One person can only do one setup, because it's going to be impossible, wearing all this heavy, thick makeup and doing all the action and the acting. A lot of eyeball movement, a lot of facial movement... then he can do another setup? It would take him out very easily.

Q: *Have you thought about making a film with extensive use of digital technology, like George Lucas'* The Phantom Menace?

I've been following that kind of information extensively because I'm concerned about — well, how cyber can we get into now, when can it become legend? Everything is so unreal; one day we find out everything unreal is real. We won't know whether that chair is CG, or whether that chair is really a chair. And that chair looks so nice, suddenly that chair becomes a human character walking around. We get used to it some years in the future, and we become very doubtful about when something is real. We are indulging in creating something to fool our mind, fool our eyes and fool our senses, to tell you that you are not good enough to judge between real and unreal. So after a while I think that people will go in opposite directions, telling us, "I don't want this, I want *real* real. Give me something that's real, something that's breakable, something that's unchangeable, something very rigid." With *Star Wars* I think it gets to the point where the unreal characters are more lively than the real characters, it's something very bothering. Especially those actors who may not be acquainted with the kind of way of shooting on a set, they don't know how to handle a new character that's supposed to be a Jar Jar Binks or whatever. In the movie it's like you're walking through a fairy

**Figures on Tsui's office shelf.**

glass... When everything you see is created by animators, it starts to feel hollow. No weight. You want some weight. After a while you feel kind of left out. I felt left out. I saw it a second time; I liked it a little bit better a second time. You have this concept, you have this expectation, you sort of have to go through it again. It's a very simple story about Darth Vader, how he grows up, how he becomes a bad guy. Simple story. You sort of go in to see a friend. Then you walk into the theater, you see a lot of strange people, not talking to you, talking among themselves, you don't know what they're talking about, they're doing strange things, and you're left out of the movie. The second time, because you know what the movie's about, you go in with a lot of negative feeling, you pick out something you like, definitely there's something nice about it. You come out of the theater and say, "They didn't do that bad." But the first time, I was sitting there

thinking, "Okay, now Darth Vader comes out;" I was really excited. But then I realize Darth Vader is fighting ghosts, living in an empty world — there is nothing for him to relate to. And I got back home and put on the first one again. Actually it's quite similar. Only that we didn't expect that much from the first one. I always use as an example, if we're going to make *Zu* again — I am making a *Zu* sequel — and I watched *Star Wars,* and I said what is the story about? Okay, let's do a love story. Let's do *Gone with the Wind*. The background is the burning of Atlanta, but that is a love story. Very silly Southern woman, and a guy who has no morals at all. And the story has no ending. The romance doesn't have a consequence. Okay, let's do something like that — two characters fall in love with each other, yet somehow they have no way to commit to each other; they eventually split up, yet they still love each other a lot. How do they do that? Nowadays, commitment has become such a form of non-commitment. We see, very commonly, couples split up and come together and split up and come together. Never before have we seen people remarry and remarry again, with the same people. We see marry and split up and remarry and split up and remarry again — this is crazy! Three or four times. It happens. I don't know why they do that. It's like doing a series. They're doing episode one, episode two, episode three. Then, because the culture nowadays is such a series drama, everybody thinks it's so natural to do something like that. There's always a lot of taboo thing about our emotion. Nowadays people have multiple split personalities. Before, we said, "Oh, they have a split personality." Now people have multiple split personalities, and it's normal — "I have four more personalities than you, I have five more personalities than you, I have twelve personalities." The reason is because before, living and life style was very simple. You only have to deal with the environment and you handle your twenty-four thing in a very patterned, routine way. Then suddenly you have people who say this is very boring, we need to change that. So you go into something where you have choice and you have alternatives. And suddenly your character starts to split up — "I like that, but I like this one, too, when I'm in this kind of mood I like this, when I'm in this kind of mood I like that" — and that extends to more and more and more, and you start to establish different kind of tastes in yourself. Nowadays you're surrounded with products, you're surrounded with merchandise, and you are trained and educated or conditioned in a way that you start having split personalities. That's why it's difficult for a character to live in one body, let alone two characters living in two bodies — it's not two, it's like three or four, and they have arguments all the time.

Maybe one character comes back to look for this character in this body, and they live together again, then they split up again. So this is why I said let's do a movie with this kind of thinking. It's very strange... I don't know how to define emotion anymore. How to define love. It's not something as simple as a character that's a major force in your life that creates everything. Because there are several characters in your life, too. They are fighting each other sometimes. It's like a balance thing. You want to be very young — younger than what you are, at your age — and you want to give up this part, but... You wonder where it's going in the future, with hardware, software... I always have this kind of wonder; if a person sits in front of a computer monitor for 18 hours, what kind of thing will develop? Like the eyes — constantly jittery, used to colors. I'm not talking about radiation. The thing that bothers me about computer screens, television screens — everything is in a frame. You're surrounded by monitors; I don't know what kind of thing will come up when you sit there for 18 hours. Your body language is different. Like this... [demonstrates, hunching]. This generation who have this kind of life style, what kind of thing will come out of that? That'll be very interesting. What kind of visual will come out of sitting in front of a monitor for 18 hours a day? When I went to a school yesterday to understand what's going on inside, the students are all going click-click-click-click-click. They have to click on titles, and whenever they see something they don't like they have to click over and look for fingers [what a cursor becomes when it falls on a link]. They are looking for fingers all the time! That kind of life style becomes another thing now. Talk about split personality... that's another split that we have.

Q: *Are you heavily involved with the*

*writing of your scripts? Do you personally rewrite them?*

Some. A lot, as a matter of fact. Rewriting becomes a basic step. I always have this thought of meeting someone who can write a script you can just shoot, but it hasn't happened. With something you write, you have to stand back and look at it as an observer, and see what kind of things you should do with it. You have to write everything, starting from zero, you have to think about the script and you talk to the scriptwriter, and then you come back and rewrite it and rewrite it and rewrite it... You have to take the story and become one of the characters, then you're living through the story, you put in the other elements of the story. Then at the end you look at it and you say, okay, this is what I want in the movie. Usually the writing is a very basic step.

Q: *Are all of your films based on your original ideas?*

I don't know where the ideas come from. I have to say they don't come from me, because they're just flying around in the air, right? Sometimes two people have the same idea, so I say, "Okay, you gotta do it, you do it, I don't wanna do it." But usually you get the idea and then you start gathering all these people around and you talk to the investor and you say, "I have this story, are you interested?" Usually I am the person who gets these people around. Sometimes they want different concepts, and I allow that — "Okay, we'll try to put that in during development." And it's very boring to see my ideas going on forever — we need some different ideas. So in a way I'd say most ideas come from me first.

Q: *There's been a lot written during the last few years on "the death of Hong Kong cinema," but it seems to me that it's doing just fine. Where is Hong Kong cinema at right now?*

I think in the '60s the Japanese movies were very popular. Suddenly this industry died. I was asking a Japanese producer about a phenomenon like that. I said, "What happened? How could an industry so established and so popular — money-making, too — suddenly end up at the zero level?" This very strange phenomenon has happened to Taiwan, everywhere. And I was a bit worried about Hong Kong movies. But I think it's a bit different here, really. Hong Kong has the advantage of not being attached to a fixed pattern of thinking. We don't have a historical sort of a traditional linkage between what's here and what's new. I believe the filmmakers here are coming to a beginning, a point where they want to restart everything from a brand new basis. So I would say this is a new wave of Hong Kong now. You will see very interesting movies coming out, especially these next two years. Hong Kong filmmakers are very... "survival of the fittest." They believe they can get through certain difficulties in ways other people can't. They will find a way, and they will prove it. Some of them don't even have integrity. Because of "survival of the fittest," they will do anything. The intellectual will say, I will not do it because I have my integrity. But the [rest] will say, I will do it because I will survive. But this is the kind of thing where Hong Kong has an advantage, it's the worst and also the best. It's the worst because sometimes they don't have integrity, they do anything. It's the best because they are looking for a change. Now everyone is trying on a new basis. I think movies need that kind of thing — Hollywood, everywhere. We need some different charm to create another new era with the audience again, the charm, the magic. When you start to say, "Okay, we have *Star Wars*, we have CG characters walking around, we have all these things — what's gonna be next?" this is good. What's the next step? Let's do something different.

This is what is the spirit of Hong Kong, I believe.

Q: *We have seen a great deal of interesting experimentation in recent Hong Kong films. A number of them have utilized unconventional, nonlinear structures, with multiple flashbacks, to tell their stories.*

Yeah, because they are experimenting. It gets to the point where none of it is commercial, so let's do a non-commercial film. That's where they start to have new thinking. I'm very optimistic about it — this is a fun thing now. Very rich. In Hollywood you come to a studio, they say, "This is the script," and you fight for the scenes you want; and if there is some established thing you want to do in a private way, you can't do that. But here you can do anything because no one knows what is good or not good. So you play around with it. You say, "Let's do a monkey who has four legs! Let's do a vampire tiger! What is a vampire tiger?! How are we gonna do that? You haven't seen that before!" You can experiment a lot, and the audience will go along with you. They know that if you see a Hong Kong movie you know that it won't be a normal movie. It may not be an easy, understandable movie, but at least it will be something different... When you see a Hong Kong movie it's not just action now. They're not doing action now, they're doing something very different, because they were driven into a corner where they have to find a way out, and they are finding a way out now.

Q: *You've worked with certain performers over and over, to great effect. Do you have a preference for working with certain actors frequently, or do you prefer working with new talent?*

I always believe in a person as an actor or an artist or a talent. You're using him or her, they're very unpredictable and emotional; in a way they are not themselves, they are elements. So as you work with a character, with a person, you try to dig out what they like, don't like, then you try to make use of something hidden in their personality. It's sort of a very exciting experience. You work with Brigitte Lin, with Joey Wang, you sort of grow with the person, you start to know that hidden part and use that element as something very powerful. So as you work more and more with the person, you start to familiarize yourself with what she has inside. And that's sometimes good, because you think, I'm gonna use that again, let's play a bit with the character, let's put that element into that role. I love the idea of using that person to play a different role this time, how she will fit into this role. So if you have this predictable character do something significantly different, it can be very fun. So that is the fun of having a human there. Also, when you see great masters like Kurosawa, you expect to see some actors in his movies—"Ah, I haven't seen Toshiro Mifune for a long time, maybe he's in this movie..." That's sort of like a theater group for certain directors. "This guy plays a bad guy now, he plays a hero now..." Working with new people is sort of like working with new elements. You want to work with her or him because she would give you some new angle or new idea.

Q: *In your new film,* Time and Tide, *I understand you have one actor who has never acted before.*

Yeah. Not really acted in 90-minute film, only acted in 10-minutes. A couple of them. They don't think in a continuous continuity, they think in moments. So in a movie you need to get moments together; so you shoot them in a very long take to get them into understanding that it's not a moment, it should be a whole story. The character lives through this whole thing. It's a long, long, long process, and you only pick up part of it.

Q: *Do you rehearse your actors much?*

For some directors, they say, "Are you ready? Are you ready? Okay, lock it off, okay, ready—roll!" No... [quietly] "Okay, let's shoot it." Because some actors, you say, "Are you ready? Are you ready?" and they pose. It's like taking a still picture—"Ready... one... two... three... okay, now smile!" and it's bad. Every cue you become less and less yourself. That's why I say, "Okay, ready—shoot. Roll cameras—action." And then that character will move very freely. There's a guy, my friend, who's a painter, and we needed him for a movie. And he's very shy. The reason why I want him in the movie is I think he will create an impact on the tension. He's a very small guy, old, like 70 years old, very kind face—I want to make him a killer. So when people say, "He's very shy, he can't even talk straight," that's what's good about it. You would underestimate this character. So once we're set, he's doing a shot, he's doing a killing, a shooting. And he's sitting there smoking, looking very nice, and I say, "Okay, we're shooting now." But we need him to do something in the shot—"Bring up your hand and shoot." So he plays around with the gun, and I say, "Let's shoot it. Okay, you ready? You ready? You ready? Okay, let's shoot it!" And he stops smoking and starts doing very dramatic, predictable kinds of facial expression... I said, "That's not what I want. Next time you keep smoking, don't think about how we're shooting, keep playing with the gun. You don't handle a gun well—let's do some rehearsing." Then I said, "Roll the camera," and that was the shot.

Q: *So you shoot your rehearsals sometimes?*

Yeah. I shot the way he was playing with the gun. For Wu Bai [the Taiwanese pop singer who stars in *Time and Tide*], he's very nervous. He's a very well-known singer, so he's very nervous about whether he's doing well or not. He thought I was very difficult. I'd say, "Okay, let's cut it, let's do another one," and every time he'd say, "Are you giving up or just doing it the normal way?" I'd say, "I'm not telling you, I don't like telling you what I'm doing. This is not fun. You try your best, okay?" And every time we'd do it, I'd say, "Wrap it up," he'd get very curious. I'd say, "Good enough. I think that's your character. You're presenting your character, and this is recording your character. I'm not telling you whether it's good enough or not—*you* are the one telling yourself that it's not good enough. If this is your character, great. I say, let's shoot it this way. If you say, I'm not sure, let's discuss it. But this is what it should be like. You've never been on screen before, no one knows how you act. The way that you talk in the movies is a comfortable way—do it that way. You have all the freedom." And the reason why I'm doing that is because he's thinking too much. Thinking too much. Like in the script it says he gets embarrassed. He says, "How are we going to do embarrassing?" He's laboring it too much. It added up to be very funny. So I look at it on the set, and I say, "Let's do it without sound." "How can I create embarrassment?" I say, "You live in the kind of world where the world creates you, you don't create the world, okay? Pick up the gun, pick up the thing that dropped on the floor, okay? Don't do any sound." And then he did that. After that he would ask me, "Should I be myself or should I be the character?" "Your character is yourself." He said, "It's very complicated." I said, "Yes, it's very complicated. Actually, after a while it might be very funny to find out which one is you."

Q: *Do you storyboard your films?*

Sometimes. Ten years ago we storyboarded everything. And then we stopped because we found out storyboards are a restriction. If you don't storyboard, you will have room to fantasize. Storyboarding means you have to define everything, to the point where everything is fixed. The process of storyboarding is graphic design, camera angles, things like that. And usually we follow along with the storyboard as a guide. But after a while you shoot along with the storyboard very easily. So we stopped storyboarding because we say, "Let's do some key shots, and those key shots have some illustration, but the rest of them, we just shoot." But when it comes to special effects there's a problem. So we do key storyboards, yes, but we need a person on the set to tell us, "This is over the budget, it's going to be very expensive to do that. Let's do something else." We need a person to do that, but we try not to follow the storyboard, because after a while we feel very restricted. But then we sort of came back to doing storyboards again—the reason why is because we now do animatics [animated storyboards]. So we sort of see the movie before we shoot it. It's fun. When we get to live action again, we find the live action is not even as charming as the animatics. We say, "Why, why? Why is something good in graphics but not good in the real world?" This becomes a very interesting kind of experience.

Q: *Are you very involved in all phases of post-production, including sound effects, dubbing, mixing, etc.?*

Post is something like adding a texture. Like polishing. The way you treat it is very sensitive at that stage. If you treat it differently you end up with a different film. It's like a bubble, or maybe elastic— with a different kind of pressure you create a different shape. So at that moment it's like you are organically related to a piece of work. It's like giving birth to a baby. You treat the baby in a way that

it will come out right. Very sensitive, emotional stage. You may hate the movie after you edit the movie, and you go back home and you sit around with it… "Let's re-edit it. It doesn't work. Can we shoot again? Can we do something about it? Maybe we should do some good music…" At that stage it's very emotional. You will always remember the kind of thing you add to the movie, when the movie needs some kind of care or treatment—that's the moment you remember the most. When it gets to the sound effects it becomes such a routine thing that you can say, "Come on, can we do it in a very simple way, so that we can cut that step?" Mixing, too. It's usually a problem. You get very confused, because you are familiar with everything and you put it together, you are predicting everything—that's no good. If you are predicting everything, you are in no condition to watch the movie fresh. You are watching this piece you know for so long that you are looking for different stuff on the screen than the normal person. You sort of avoid doing that— you try to put yourself at a distance to observe, or you can do something very damaging.

Q: *Do you ever operate your own camera?*

In the early stages, yes. But now I think it's fun to see a great cameraman doing his work. But then I think doing the camera would be fun, too. It's like drawing—right away you think, let's do this, let's do that! That's like creating a graphic image using your camera. I would put a light behind an actor, the cameraman would say, "Why is the light behind him?" "Because it looks so good! Let's do that! Let's fool around with the lighting and forget about the continuity!"

Q: *I know you worked on a documentary just after you left film school. Have you thought about making your own feature-length documentary?*

Yes. The thing is, like *Black Mask* — if I were the director on that, I would make it like a documentary. But because I was producing, I couldn't manage to create that. I think it's more interesting to shoot a superhero in a documentary style — even more impact.

Q: *Did you watch a lot of animation as a child? What are some of your favorite animated films?*

I have a lot of favorite animation films. I like animation very much. My first animated film that I saw when I was a kid was *Bambi*. I always tell this story to explain why I have this special feeling about animated films. When *Snow White* came out, I was so excited about going to see that movie. My mother, who died several years ago, checked it out at the theater and said, "You cannot go to that movie because there is kissing in that story. Kissing is not good for kids to watch." Also, because Snow White, the princess, was wearing this low-cut dress. So my mother said, "You're not mature enough to watch this animated film!" I was quite irritated. My friends all went to see it and they'd talk about it. I couldn't see the film because my mother wouldn't allow me to see it. So then I found out later that there was a movie called *Bambi* that was all animals, and I saw it. So then I was following all these animated movies. My second animated movie was *Sleeping Beauty*. I avoided asking my mother about it, I had to go see the movie by myself. So from that point on I started to realize that animation had its own charms. I caught up with the rest of the stuff later on, and eventually saw *Snow White*. Actually, I would say *Snow White* is my favorite movie; even now you can see how much detail is in the movie. And I don't know whether there's enough craft out there to create *Snow White* again, because you see the birds, animals… There's one scene where Snow White walks across a frame, and you see exactly there's a little detail of every animal following Snow White. Now, with the budgets, I don't think they'll ever do anything like that again. Also, Snow White is not the kind of design we see now. She's like Shirley Temple. Now we have all these big eyes. So I would believe that *Snow White* is my most favorite movie.

Of course, then, later on, we saw other kinds of movies, like *Laputa* [by Japanese animator Hayao Miyazaki]. I like Miyazaki a lot.

Actually, I did a lot of drawing when I was a kid because of a special kind of response to animated films. I think my first movie concept was when I drew on a large piece of glass with ink, then got a flashlight and projected it on the wall, telling a story with music, everything. I found out some of my colleagues did that, too.

Q: *I've heard that your first film was about a magic show?*

At school there were several people doing a performance for the end of the semester, so I thought we should try something different. So I said, "Let's do some magic." So I went to learn some magic. Later, whenever we could grab a camera, we shot us. I was the actor, doing the magic show, performing.

We were a very small size, our hands were so small there were some tricks we couldn't do. The trick of pulling a card out of the air — I couldn't do it. That was real fun. Three of us, we're performing everywhere — parties, annual balls, factories, everywhere.

Q: *I noticed some figures from the Japanese comic* Lupin III *on your shelves. [*Lupin III *was also animated by Hayao*

Miyazaki, especially in the feature film *The Castle of Cagliostro.*]

I think Lupin III is a very interesting character. I've been working with some people from L.A., trying to put the movie through. We've been hanging around on how Lupin III should look. We'll do it live action.

*Note:* Additional comments by Tsui may be found in the following chapter under individual films.

# 4

# THE MAJOR FILMS

## *The Butterfly Murders*

Director, 1979. Cantonese: *Dip Bin*. Mandarin: *Die Bian*. Literally: *Butterfly Transformation*. Screenwriter: Lam Chi Ming. Cinematography: Faan Gam Juk. Action Design: Wong Shu Tong. Editing: Wong Chi Hung. Music Score: Joseph Koo. CAST: Lau Siu-Ming ("Fong Sai Yuk"), Wong Shu Tong ("Tien Fung"), Michelle Chan Kei-Kei ("Green Shadow"), Eddy Ko Hung ("Kwok"). Opening Date: July 20, 1979.

SYNOPSIS: In China's distant past, scholar Fong Sai Yuk wanders a desolate landscape of drought, bandits and clan wars. After he is summoned to the mysterious Shum Castle, he encounters Tien Fung, the powerful leader of the Tien Clan and the Ten Flags; and the Green Shadow, a slightly inexperienced but enthusiastic young female superheroine. The Master of Shum Castle has asked for the help of this unusual group because of bizarre deaths which have recently occurred at the Castle, apparently caused by killer butterflies. The mystery deepens after Master Shum is killed by the butterflies, and his widow reveals that he's left a will instructing her to call the Thunders—three mighty warriors—to the Castle. When two of the Thunders—Li, who fights with small handheld weapons, and Kwok, an expert in explosives—show up, they declare immediate war on the Tien Clan, and soon the Castle is awash in blood. But both groups soon find themselves fighting a third antagonist, the invincible "Armoured Man," who accidentally murders Madam Shum before revealing himself to be Master Shum. Shum tells Fong Sai Yuk and Green Shadow that he faked his death, and called the Thunders and the Tien Clan together so they would fight and destroy each other. Shum has been amassing a highly-advanced arsenal of explosive devices, and he used his wife's ability to control butterflies to kill the Castle's spies. But Shum's plans are interrupted when

33

Tien Fung and Kwok both turn against him; Tien finally removes Shum's helmet and kills him, but then Tien and Green Shadow are annihilated by the vengeful Kwok's last explosive, which brings the Castle crashing down. Only Fong Sai Yuk survives, wandering the same corpse-strewn desert he walked at the beginning.

REVIEW: To call *The Butterfly Murders*, Tsui Hark's debut feature film audacious is roughly like saying *Citizen Kane* wasn't a half-bad first film. Which is not to say *The Butterfly Murders* equals Orson Welles' astonishing achievement — its structure occasionally clanks as loudly as its "Armoured Man" — but what it lacks in focus it more than makes up for in energy and genre-jumping. It practically burns with the excitement of a gifted young filmmaker who loves movies and wants to pay homage to an art form he simultaneously challenges on several levels.

It's possible that if Tsui Hark had never made another film, *The Butterfly Murders* would have a place in the history of Hong Kong cinema as little more than a brilliantly-mounted curiosity; but, given Tsui Hark's eventual importance in the Hong Kong film industry, the film will forever have an identity as "Tsui Hark's first film." And, indeed, it's hard to imagine a first film that more perfectly exemplifies a filmmaker's style and obsessions: Here, right out of the gate, are Tsui's strong female action lead, his emphasis on Chinese tradition, the love/hate relationship with nature, interest in technology (anachronistic as it is here), and his fast cutting, freeze frames and layered images. It also displays problems that would plague some of Tsui's later films: uneven casting, cutting that is occasionally *too* fast, and a story that nearly disintegrates as it approaches its unwieldy climax.

*The Butterfly Murders* must have felt like a sure bet to its investors. The period kung fu film craze of the '70s hadn't completely died out, Cantonese-language films had made a comeback, and they had the hot young director of television's successful costume drama *Golden Dagger Romance*. Unfortunately for the investors (but fortunately for us!), what they got was a genuinely unique combination of horror, kung fu, mystery and science fiction. Not only did *The Butterfly Murders* mix and match genres with astonishing ease, but it also asked audiences who were used to non-stop action in their films to follow a torturously complex plot. It's almost as if Tsui intended his first film to do more than introduce his talents — he wanted to challenge his audience to think about film in an entirely new way (in the article "Artist Provocateur — on Tsui Hark's Artistic Character" in *Hong Kong New Wave: Twenty Years After*, mainland film scholar Lee Yi-Chong says that *The Butterfly Murders* "subverted the traditional Chinese martial arts genre").

After a brief setup of historical events given by Fong Sai Yuk in voiceover, the film launches into its first real scene, set in a printing shop. A man enters, claiming to have an unpublished eight-page manuscript by Fong Sai Yuk describing butterfly murders, and suggesting that there's a great deal of money to be made. The printer informs the man that the document is fake — he knows Fong's handwriting, and this isn't it. Later the printer is found dead, his throat cut, his blood the color of ink on the stone floor.

The sequence immediately sets up *The Butterfly Murders'* interest in Chinese tradition. The men drink tea (and even comment on it) while they discuss the manuscript; in the next room the workers sing folk songs as they arrange printing plates. Everywhere, printed sheets of Chinese characters flutter, the ink still drying. Throughout the rest of the film Chinese tradition will reappear as dragons, embroidered silk, ancestral feasts, birds and, of course, butterflies.

If *The Butterfly Murders* is completely Chinese in design, it is paradoxically largely Western in style (a few shots lifted from Kurosawa notwithstanding). Tsui must certainly have been influenced by the new wave of American and European horror films of the '70s; sequences such as the early one in which two desperate, sweating peasants attempt some nocturnal grave-robbing could easily be straight out of a Mario Bava or Joe Dante film. The flesh of the men gleams in the warm amber tones of their lantern, and the cutting moves back and forth between the anxious diggers and the butterflies perched in a nearby tree. It's to Tsui's credit that, when the butterflies finally attack, it seems quite plausible that the small, fragile insects can actually kill these large, powerful men.

Where Tsui's approach to horror differs from that of his Western counterparts (especially the Americans) is in making his horror *beautiful*. Even after we've seen the insects massed together to commit brutal, gory murder, Tsui shows us the butterflies flitting about in a lovely, pastoral setting or celebrated in the art of an exquisite embroidery. When Tien Fung crushes one that's lit on his hand, we actually find his action repugnant, even though a few scenes later we sympathize with him when he finds his trusted scout "Big Eyes" dead, apparently another victim of the butterflies. Of course, eventually the butterflies will be revealed as mere pawns of a manipulating human being; in Tsui's films, nature may be cruel, but there's only one species we should really fear — and it walks on two legs.

Although *The Butterfly Murders* was made at the end of the '70s Hong Kong kung fu film cycle, it seems blissfully free of the stylistic excesses found in those pictures. Tsui's camera is seldom locked down; it runs through tall grass, pushes through dark caverns or spins to follow a punch. The zooms that had become cliché in the earlier films are almost avoided here; the few times they are used are appropriate, providing emphasis on some startled reaction or revelation. Tsui also utilizes natural lighting throughout, and since most of the film is set at night or beneath Shum Castle, it's largely dark, with high contrast light and shadow on faces. The choice of subdued lighting imbues the film with a sense of mystery and dread; it's jolting — and apt — when Fong Sai Yuk ends the film by walking out into a brightly-lit (albeit corpse-strewn) desert, both bringing the film full-circle and signaling that the mystery has been solved.

The rapid editing that is one of Tsui's trademarks is plainly visible here in his first film. *The Butterfly Murders* may have the lighting of a moody, somber, Western-style horror picture, but the cutting is completely Tsui Hark. No scene is lingered on, no shot held down too long; new information is presented constantly, a dynamic which almost works against the story — it's difficult to be frightened when you're just trying to keep up. Likewise, in some fight scenes action is sometimes lost because of the cutting; on the other hand, the editing also never loses the screen direction and the flow of the fights. And since the actual fight choreography seems less adept than in Tsui's later films, the editing also creates movement and excitement.

If Tsui Hark the young filmmaker already knew how to use his camera and had his own editing style, he seemed less certain with his actors. Tsui has always empathized most strongly with the outsiders in his stories (they are usually his protagonists), so it's no surprise that the two most interesting characters are the ones who live outside of any clan, Fong Sai Yuk and the Green Shadow. Green Shadow, in particular, is delightful, bringing a grinning vitality to scenes that could otherwise be too somber. She's the perfect foil for the stoic hero Tien Fung, who, in fact, is reduced to almost a background character by her in many scenes; it's unfortunate that actress Michelle Chan Kei-Kei seemed to disappear after this film. Master Shum, by way of contrast, comes across as a Peking Opera stage actor who hasn't quite learned film acting yet; he occasionally strikes theatrical poses that Tsui's fast editing fortunately doesn't let become comic. The best villain on display is the literally explosive Kwok, and actor Eddy Ko Hung (the one member of the cast who would go on to become a popular Hong Kong character actor, and who would star in Tsui Hark's next film *We're Going to Eat You*) plays him with malignant glee.

Despite its relatively minor flaws, *The Butterfly Murders* is so brimming with enthusiasm and ideas that one can only imagine how disappointed Tsui Hark must have been with its poor box office performance. Little could the youthful filmmaker have suspected that it would eventually become one of the most widely-watched and written-about Hong Kong films of 1979; unlike many of its contemporaries, *The Butterfly Murders* has actually improved with age.

ABOUT THE MOVIE: *The Butterfly Murders* played one week, taking in $1,152,756.20. It placed number 69 in the year's box office (the number one film of the year was Jackie Chan's kung fu comedy *Fearless Hyena*), wedged in with low-budget films the likes of *The Magnificent Ruffians* and *Sexy Night Report*; even the poorly-made American import *Phantasm*

fared better. The film's box office take was particularly disappointing considering its large ($3 million) budget, possibly the largest budget for any of the debut films by the Hong Kong New Wave directors (who included Patrick Tam, Ann Hui and Allen Fong).

Composer Joseph Koo also scored *A Better Tomorrow, A Better Tomorrow II, Happy Ghost III* and *Terracotta Warrior* for Tsui; Koo recently collaborated with favorite Tsui composer James Wong on a series of sold-out music concerts in Hong Kong.

Actor Eddy Ko Hung would star in Tsui's next film, *We're Going to Eat You*, as the villainous Chief. Actor Wong Shu Tong ("Tien Fung") also choreographed the film's action choreography and wire rigging.

*The Butterfly Murders* is still generally well-regarded within critical circles, and was a major feature in the Hong Kong International Film Festival's retrospective *Hong Kong New Wave: Twenty Years After*.

TSUI HARK ON *THE BUTTERFLY MURDERS:* Actually I wanted to do a modern piece [for my first film], but the producer said, "I want you to do an action movie, a period action movie." At that period of time I was not really into that kind of film. I was thinking about doing a modern drama. But when I thought about it, I said, "Why not? Let's try that." So that's why I did *The Butterfly Murders.* But *The Butterfly Murders* is very strange, I'm kind of creating my world of period drama... before I thought, there's so much that's been done in that genre, that's why I said I'd like to do something different. And I tried to create my own kind of... it's not quite science fiction. Kind of my own category.

[On the experience of directing his first film]: That was a nightmare for me.

I think I was so inexperienced, and making movies was different from making a TV feature; and so I was sort of like an inexperienced director on a set trying to handle very complicated material. And I had a problem with the line producer; I did get very temperamental at that moment. After that I realized that I was so inexperienced that I was doing everything wrong. After a while I thought about, if I were the producer, how would I handle this director? When I was a producer, I referred back to my first experience. I'd think, maybe he's not aware of it, maybe I should tell him that angle's not good, instead of handling everything very nicely. At the end you have a bad film. So that movie sort of gave me a very, very good experience in seeing myself. I was doing something I think I was not ready to do. But no one was ready. I don't think anyone on that set was ready, even the actors. The first time my friend came to the set he said, "Why don't you use optical effects?" I said, "I never thought about it." In our Hong Kong productions we never thought of optical effects. We did everything real. When I went home I started looking at books, I started looking at movies and things in an optical way, and realized actually it's not a new thing in Hong Kong movies, and it's not a new thing in my experience. I've done things like that before, even in school — why don't we do that in real movies? Because there's a lot of things where they create some kind of traditional way to do something among the people in the crew... every day was a disaster. Some days we'd be in the air, everybody hanging on wires, and it's too dark, we don't have enough lights, and there's no crane, so we put a scaffold there with the cameraman on top of the scaffold. And the ground is very soft, so after a while the scaffold starts to fall down. I have this problem with heights. When I was five I'd

stand up on top of a ladder or even a staircase and I'd be attracted by the bottom of the staircase and just fall towards the bottom. It's kind of ... psychology. So after a while I would stand on top of the scaffold and I would remind the people around me that I have this problem, so if anything happens, grab me! So I was on the scaffolding several times, and every time I was on the scaffolding I would feel like it was sort of slanted at one angle. It's not very flat, something's wrong with it, it's standing on an angle. Every time, these other people would say, "It's not true." Every day it's getting more and more slanted. And then it's falling — with the cameraman, the assistant director and me. I don't know how to stop it and it's happening! The cameraman grabbed the camera and luckily it stopped on a wall. A few days later I said, "I am not going up there. You go up there — that's good enough."

[In the interview with Ting Wai Ho conducted for *Eastern Heroes* Magazine Special Edition #5, Tsui noted another problem encountered on the set of *The Butterfly Murders*]: You can never really get the butterflies to fly in the air when you want them to fly in the air, they simply hide away under the ceiling, under a rock, under the trees, they never come out...eventually we found a way to handle the butterflies and that's to use human urine and that really attracted the butterflies a lot, they just go crazy over the urine...close to the end of the production we sort of enjoyed making fun of the butterflies by just peeing everywhere.

[On a DVD release]: I don't know. The processing is not very good. That's why it looks very grainy, a lot of scratches, and the sound quality is very bad. Sometimes I look at my old movies, and it's worse than what we had in the black-and-white period. The colors sometimes fade to really strange colors.

## We're Going to Eat You

Director, 1981. Cantonese: *Dei Yuk Mo Moon*. Mandarin: *Diyu wu men*. Literally: *Hell No Door*. Also Known As: *Hell Has No Gates*; *Kung Fu Cannibals*; *No Door to Hell*; *We Are Going to Eat You*; *We're Going to Eat You!* CAST: Norman Chu Shiu-Keung ("Agent 999"), Eddy Ko Hung ("The Chief"). Opening Date: April 2, 1980.

SYNOPSIS: Agent 999 of the "Central Surveillance Agency" is pursuing a mysterious thief called "Rolex." The hunt leads him to a small, isolated village whose inhabitants routinely capture and eat any and all passersby. Although the village's Chief of Security originated this institutionalized cannibalism, the villagers are on the verge of rebelling because the Chief is taking more and more of the "meat" for his security officers and leaving less for the villagers. Agent 999 is in peril until he's rescued by Rolex himself, who's been posing as the Chief's Aide in the hopes of redeeming his criminal career with an act of justice. After narrowly escaping masked cannibal butchers, a deformed priest and a cross-dressing giant, Agent 999 finally rescues himself and his new love, Eileen, and they escape the evil village.

REVIEW: After the densely-plotted *The Butterfly Murders* left audiences cold, Tsui Hark's second directorial effort, *We're Going to Eat You*, seemed, on the surface, to be a much simpler, straight-arrow action film... while indulging in at least three different genres and hiding a wicked satirical heart. As with *The Butterfly Murders*, the influence of Euro-American horror films and Spaghetti Westerns is apparent, but once again the film somehow manages to avoid stereotypes and plays as a unique and original work. Although the fight scenes still seem slightly stagey and static compared to Tsui's later work (i.e., *Peking Opera Blues* or *Once Upon a Time in China*), the pace has his trademark speed, the visuals his kineticism, and the story his layering.

*We're Going to Eat You* works as horror film, kung fu actioner and slapstick comedy. Tsui sets the tone early on with the scene in which our young hero, the arrogant and slightly dense Agent 999, first confronts the cannibal butchers near the mysterious village. 999 has been ensnared by the butchers' traps in the forest, by both hands and feet, and now hangs horizontally six feet above the ground. He somehow manages to twist his body around to avoid his attackers' blows, and even uses their own knife blades to sever his bonds; his opponents eventually split their own heads accidentally (never has a film featured so many images of accidental impalement). The scene is simultaneously exciting, as 999 fights for his life; funny, as both 999 and the cannibals take pratfalls and engage in silent-movie-style slapstick; and horrific, as the human-skin-masked cannibals wield a variety of blades in no uncertain terms. It would be a remarkable feat for any director to juggle all three of these genres in one film, but for a director making only his second feature to hold all three tones together in a single scene is nothing less than amazing.

*We're Going to Eat You* may be most noticeable in Tsui's oeuvre as his most overtly anti-Communist film. The Chief's inequitable distribution of the "meat" to his starving masses, his military uniform, the armbands some of the villagers strap on when running to the latest distribution call, all state Tsui's intent clearly. Even the village's funeral parlor — the "People's Funeral Parlor" — is in on the gag. If some of Tsui's later films have been interpreted to show his unease about the 1997 handover of Hong Kong to China, then *We're*

*Going to Eat You* could be thought of as conveying a director absolutely horrified at the prospect.

But *We're Going to Eat You* isn't any easier on religion, intellectuals or love than it is on Communism — anything's an open target for Tsui's satire. The village's priest, a deformed little man who's also the peasants' cowering representative in dealing with the vicious Chief, thinks nothing of interrupting a funeral service when the prospect of fresh meat arises; at one point Agent 999 encounters the village's black-garbed scholar and finds that his book is now the paper wrapping for a human steak. When Agent 999 falls for the Chief's lovely girlfriend, Eileen, he is willing to sacrifice himself to help her escape the village — and yet in the film's climax, when Eileen offers him her heart it's not a paper Valentine. One of the film's oft-stated jokes is that the entire world is full of cannibals, so perhaps it's the world at large that Tsui's poking fun at.

Tsui's influences in the film are plentiful and witty. Agent 999 brings to mind Sergio Leone/Clint Eastwood's *The Man with No Name*, as he lights his handrolled cigarettes while squinting up from beneath his wide-brimmed hat. Nods to the American horror films of the mid-to-late '70s — especially *The Texas Chainsaw Massacre* — are here, and when the final escape from the village involves exploding firecrackers blackening the faces of surprised villagers, we can only blame the cartoons of Tex Avery or Chuck Jones. Tsui even includes a reference to classical Western theater — when Rolex finally breaks into the Chief's quarters to take him on, he finds the sobbing leader engrossed in a copy of *King Oedipus*.

*We're Going to Eat You* also contains a number of elements which Tsui himself would recycle in his later films. The deformed villagers would reappear a dozen years later in the prologue of *Green Snake*; a razor magically pops out of a captive's mouth to cut the net that holds him, a trick that would reappear in the Tsui-produced *Black Mask*; and, perhaps most fascinating of all in light of Tsui's later work, *We're Going to Eat You* contains his first cross-gendered individual, the giant/ess who so lusts after Agent 999 that s/he sobs hysterically at the prospect of his murder. This may not be Asia the Invincible of the *Swordsman* films, but s/he's still a more interesting character than any of those in the American films Tsui riffs on.

But to note *We're Going to Eat You*'s various influences is partly unfair to a film which remains so determinedly original and exciting throughout. And don't let Tsui's anti-Communist ideas confuse the issue — any film which has a scene of a starving villager complaining that he can't even "get a pubic hair" is obviously aimed first and foremost at pure entertainment.

ABOUT THE MOVIE: *We're Going to Eat You* took in $1,054,986.50, placing it at 113 in the year's Hong Kong box office (the same year Tsui Hark's *Dangerous Encounter — 1st Kind* placed at number 33), taking in even less money than Tsui's first film, *The Butterfly Murders*.

Much of the soundtrack of *We're Going to Eat You* is from Dario Argento's classic 1976 horror film *Suspiria*.

The name of the cannibal island is Tai Kar Heung, meaning "Big Village." However, "Heung" is also part of Hong Kong's original name (meaning "fragrant"), and is also a slang word for "dead."

In *Hong Kong New Wave: Twenty Years After*, Ng Ho says of *We're Going to Eat You*: "Tsui smudges the line between Jean Vigo and Luis Buñuel." In the same volume, in an article entitled "Artist Provocateur — On Tsui Hark's Artistic Character," mainland film scholar Lee Yi-Chong suggests that *We're Going to Eat You* is Tsui's most neglected picture, adding: "The film causes us to be aware that where a society is closed, without rule of law and democracy, and authority is exerted instead by a patriarchy, its value system exploits the worst excesses of human behavior (such as fear, greed, selfishness, etc.) to engender fanaticism and mob rule."

TSUI HARK ON *WE'RE GOING TO EAT YOU*: I don't know, maybe it was my student movement experience [explaining the film's parody of communism]. I sort of, like, put that in. Usually student movements are a lot of political things, kind of like arguing about direction, programs, what kind of plan will we lay down to create something. Maybe all student movements are leftist. It's sort of like the people are very naïve, following a leader who has a problem with integrity, putting out a mixed statement of something he may not be able to follow; yet he's pushing that kind of discipline on the group. It's sort of a sarcastic way of looking at all kinds of isms and political philosophy followers. In the '60s and '70s a lot of people were talking about ideology. So I sort of took a sarcastic look at that. And the funny thing is, I feel a little bit embarrassed because the producer asked me to do a kung fu action movie and I shot a political satire, something very weird. I think they were a little bit disappointed by seeing me doing something they weren't expecting. And I was a little bit confused, too. I was thinking we were actually shooting a martial arts action movie, but it ended up as a political satire.

It was fun to shoot on the set, because you could ask the actor to do something based on someone you know. It's really fun to see someone you know on the set. It's sort of like a game, too, I think, to ask somebody to do what you think another person would do.

[On the film's use of existing music]: The reason is, during that period of time we didn't have the budget for music. Like in *The Butterfly Murders*, part of the score is canned music. Until we got to *All the Wrong Clues*, which is when we said, "Okay, let's not use the canned music any more, because we're talking big budget." We had to convince the producer of different ways to handle things. We'd say, "We should use original music." They'd say, "Not necessary. You have all the great composers in the world doing great music, we don't have any great composers, why don't we use their music?" It took time to convince them. Now everyone is doing the music. But you look back and say, "Some of that canned music is really good!"

## Dangerous Encounter— 1st Kind

Director/Writer/Cameo, 1980. Cantonese: *Dai Yat Lui Ying Ngai Him.* Mandarin: *Di4 Yi1 Lei4 Xing2 Wei2 Xian3.* Literally: *First Kind of Danger.* AKA: *Dangerous Encounters of the First Kind; Playing with Fire; Don't Play with Fire.* Co-Writer: Roy Szeto Cheuk Hon. Cinematography: David Chung. Action Design: Ching Siu-Tung. CAST: Lo Lieh ("Pearl's Brother"), Lin Chen-Chi ("Pearl"). Opening Date: December 4, 1980.

SYNOPSIS: Hong Kong police are investigating a circle of American smugglers who have 800 million Japanese yen they're passing from courier to courier; the case takes an unexpected turn when their main witness is brutally stabbed to death at his athletic club. Meanwhile, three young boys — Paul, who is rich, and the poor Ah Lun and Ah Gow — go joyriding in a car they can barely drive. They hit and kill a pedestrian, then try to flee, but they have been seen by a young girl, Pearl. When they have a second chance encounter, Pearl threatens to expose them unless they help her; the boys may be criminals, but they soon realize Pearl is genuinely disturbed — after she covers Paul's car with animal intestines. She tries to lead them in a scheme to rob a busload of Japanese tourists, but the boys fail and she retaliates by tracking them down the next day and trying to set them on fire. Her attempted arson is interrupted by the arrival of one of the American couriers; Pearl is blocking the road, and when he attempts to use violence to remove her the boys begin to stone him. Pearl takes advantage of the mayhem to steal the courier's briefcase; after a chase down an urban hillside, Pearl escapes and discovers the fortune in Japanese yen money orders. After an attempt to pass one of the notes at a bank is unsuccessful, Pearl goes to local Triad leader Uncle Hak. Uncle Hak sets her up with a local moneychanger, and after he's certain that the notes are worth something, Hak and his gang attack Pearl and the boys, demanding all of the notes. Pearl makes it home, while the three boys head for the hills, where they hide out in a cemetery. But the American smugglers have also located Pearl, and Pearl's brother, a policeman, comes home just in time to see Pearl thrown out the upper-story window of their apartment onto the spiked fence below. The Americans don't find the yen, but the cops do — hidden in the cage of Pearl's white mice. At the cemetery the three desperate boys engage in a suicide pact, but only Ah Gow goes through with it, downing a cup of poison; as he convulses and foams, Paul runs to a nearby store to get milk for him. The store clerk is a police informant; he

recognizes Paul and calls Pearl's brother, Ah Dan. Ah Dan arrives at the cemetery, trailed by the American gang, and a shootout ensues. Ironically, the only survivor is Ah Gow, presumably still dying from the poison he's ingested and driven mad — he laughs hysterically and fires an automatic weapon into the necropolis around him, interspersed with black-and-white images of the Hong Kong Colonial riots of 1967.

REVIEW: The word Tsui Hark uses most often in discussing why he made *Dangerous Encounter — 1st Kind* is "anger." While most critics assume this to mean Tsui was angry at the existing political/socioeconomic situation in Hong Kong, *Dangerous Encounter* doesn't really play like a political thriller; it's not really interested in making you think, and if it expresses any kind of philosophy, it's existentialism. More likely, Tsui's anger was directed at his audience; he had already made two films which certainly he felt were good, and yet they had been almost completely shunned by ticket-buyers. His third feature film feels less like a political commentary and more like venom spat in the face of commercial film. It's a film completely devoid of anything beautiful or sympathetic; watching it is like being dropped into the middle of hell and told there's no way out. Ironically, of course, it performed well at the box office. No wonder Tsui made a comedy (*All the Wrong Clues*) next.

Bluntly put, *Dangerous Encounter* is probably the most nihilistic film ever made. It opens with images of oppression and brutality: barbed wire, a storm, mice running aimlessly in a wheel in their cramped cage, a needle driven through the head of one of the innocent creatures. For the following 90 minutes Tsui makes no attempt to relieve the ugliness; he's not trying to make ugliness into anything else, he

Original poster for *Dangerous Encounter—1st Kind.*

just wants to show it for what it is. There's only the barest attempt really to cleave to a plot; there is no traditional resolution to the story, and there are really no heroes to root for. The three young boys, who would normally be the protagonists, are guilty of a hit-and-run, and they later eye the grave of a young boy with either callous disregard or, at best, mild curiosity.

The character driving *Dangerous Encounter* is Pearl, a completely unlikable psychopath. If *Dangerous Encounter* succeeds in making us understand how she is a product of this rotting and rotten environment, it does nothing to make us like her. She's completely reprehensible. She's sadistic, greedy and manipulative — and these are her *best* qualities. To her considerable credit, young actress Lin Chen-Chi plays by Tsui's rules, and although attractive, Pearl is never for an instant cute or coy; Lin's steely, dispassionate gaze makes for some of the film's most memorable images.

Then why does *Dangerous Encounter* work? There's no denying that it *does* work — it's among the most compelling 90-plus minutes of film in all of cinema. The easy explanation is the "car accident" theory — that you hate it even while you can't take your eyes off it. But car accidents don't last for an hour-and-a-half; even the most ardent rubbernecker would move on sooner than that. No, something else is at work in this remarkable film.

When Tsui talks about his reasons for making films, he often discusses the idea of presenting an audience with something entirely new, something they've never seen before. Certainly *Dangerous Encounter* falls into this category; it is a completely unique film, in either Hong Kong or American cinema. Black filmmakers in America have explored the plight of the inner city many times, but always with a sympathetic hero, one you usually root for to escape his or her environs; the only film which comes close to *Dangerous Encounter* in terms of sheer, numbing, anarchic violence is George Romero's *Dawn of the Dead* (which, interestingly enough, provides much of *Dangerous Encounter*'s stolen score), but even that film is considerably leavened by black humor.

*Dangerous Encounter* may be without a shred of humor, but it is propelled by action; in fact, apart from its nihilism it's a spanking good action film. It marks the first time Tsui and soon-to-be-long-time collaborator Ching Siu-Tung worked together, and although some of the fights still look slightly primitive compared to their later work, they have a raw, visceral energy missing from the more carefully-choreographed films. When Pearl escapes from the blond American courier, there's no question that the actress is desperate to keep her footing on the slippery grass; later, the same courier meets his end in a car, in a fight so fast it seems paradoxically ultra-real, without any showy camera moves or martial arts stances. In fact, only once in *Dangerous Encounter* is there anything like a hint of directorial technique: That's a freeze-frame on the three boys when they aim an obscene gesture at the blonde American smuggler. The three boys are already half-naked, having stripped after Pearl threw gasoline on them, and so the gesture literally has a naked power behind it. Curiously, the American himself is not visible in the shot, which is almost played into the camera, leaving it open to debate as to whether Tsui is issuing his "up yours" to Western culture or his Hong Kong audience.

Another of *Dangerous Encounter*'s strengths is the way that it provokes emotions, emotions most films would never dream of trying to inflame: fear, disgust, hatred and — of course — anger. One of the film's most potent themes is anger towards society's treatment of marginalized groups: women, the poor, the young, even gays (part of the police investigation involves a gay bar, which Tsui neither sensationalizes nor trivializes). His choice of a young girl for his lead psychotic flies in the face of all Western film convention, but he well justifies the choice by surrounding Pearl with examples of violence toward women: Street toughs expose themselves to her, an old man tries to rape her, even her brother ties her up. Once again, it doesn't make us like Pearl or even sympathize with her, but we do feel Tsui's anger toward the forces that have molded her. Combined with its heart-pumping action, it's a roller coaster ride through regions most of us have forgotten existed (or tried to). Tsui is asking (or demanding) that we experience feelings most of us shy away from — but because he's made the asking so exciting, we give in. By the time the film ends you may feel a little queasy — but also strangely exhilarated.

If *Dangerous Encounter* is Tsui Hark's darkest film (it's *anybody's* darkest film), it's also one of his most atypical in terms of direction. The individual shots have a stark, gritty quality (despite the use of odd, sometimes exaggerated angles); they're cut together for maximum impact, shots slamming up against each other like colliding cars. He often holds on closeups, inviting us into his ravaged characters, letting us experience their rage or frustration. Only in the action sequences is there a glimpse of the usual Tsui Hark style, as the camera moves furiously to follow action, tracking with running characters or pushing up over a rim to reveal something hidden.

*Dangerous Encounter* also seems strangely ahead of its time in the way Tsui surrounds his characters with mass media: There are a large number of scenes in which radios or televisions blare in the background. In one quick sequence an audience in a theater is watching a war film when a bomb goes off in a theater, to which one character's blithe response is, "Not *another* bombing… " Newscasts rattle on about abortion or crime; Pearl watches insanely violent cartoons on television. Tsui is plainly suggesting a link between the characters' violent tendencies and mass media, and more than a decade before the topic became a hot one in both the U.S. and Hong Kong. And although *Dangerous Encounter* is certainly a wildly-violent film itself, it stands apart from the mass media it accuses by virtue of the very negative emotions it arouses. Unlike films such as Andrew Lau's *Young and Dangerous* series (which Tsui's wife Nansun Shi refers to as "Triad recruitment films"), no one is likely to commit an act of violence after viewing *Dangerous Encounter*. If anything, they're far likelier to feel what Alex the Droog feels after his reprogramming in Stanley Kubrick's *A Clockwork Orange*: intense, even physical revulsion.

ABOUT THE MOVIE: *Dangerous Encounter — 1st Kind* performed surprisingly well at the box office (possibly to Tsui's chagrin), coming in at number 33 for the year and grossing $2,248,034.50 (far better than either of Tsui's first two films).

Roy Szeto Cheuk Hon also worked on *Shanghai Blues*, *Zu*, and *Once Upon a Time in China and America*; David Chung also shot *The Lovers*, *Once Upon a Time in China* (along with a host of other cinematographers) and *Web of Deception* (which he also directed); he directed *I Love Maria*.

Tsui appears briefly as the men's room attendant in the athletic club who discovers the murdered "Augustus" near the film's beginning. Tsui Hark frequent collaborator John Sham plays one of the cops investigating the smugglers.

The film uses music from George Romero's *Dawn of the Dead* (score by the

Italian rock group Goblin) and Jean Michel Jarre's classic '70s album *Oxygene,* among others.

*Dangerous Encounter* was banned by the Colonial censors upon its initial release in Hong Kong, but was an immense critical success for Tsui, assuring his status at the top of the New Wave heap. In the article "Hong Kong New Wave: Modernization Amid Global/Local Counter Cultures" from *Hong Kong New Wave: Twenty Years After,* critic Law Kar says of *Dangerous Encounter:* "It was Tsui's extreme metaphor for the local people under the cultural and economic domination of foreigners." In the article "The Confessions of a Film Archivist" (ibid), Ng Ho notes, "Man as trapped animals— this is the popular theme of the New Wave and the one enduring image in their narratives." In the book *On Hong Kong Genre Films* (by Law Kar, Ng Ho and Cheuk Pak-tong), Law Kar also said: "It is one of those very rare films in the history of Hong Kong cinema that brims with accusation and subversion, and whose use of violence has a special significance."

Influential Hong Kong film critic Shu Kei called it simply Tsui Hark's masterpiece (in *Hong Kong New Wave: Twenty Years After*).

TSUI ON *DANGEROUS ENCOUNTER—1ST KIND*: At that period of time people were expecting I wouldn't do anything that is commercial at all. I didn't do anything that had success at the box office at all. I've always had this kind of very strange way of telling a story. Strange because it's not very generic, it doesn't really belong to any genre at all, sort of a very marginal combination of everything. So maybe I can do a commercial movie for the next one — there's always hope. So they asked me to do a modern drama. I said, "I don't want to do any period things any more. Kind of boring. I'd like to try a modern drama." So I did *Don't Play with Fire* [aka *Dangerous Encounter*]. And I was so angry, angry with myself, angry with everybody in the industry, so that's why I was being very… beast-like. Sort of like… I devolved every character to a very animal, basic instinct, very primitive state of mind. Survival is the attitude. And suddenly I realized, with all the characters in the movie there was only one woman there. The actress, she worked at Shaw Studios, she played in several movies there. She was not very popular, but I realized something about her: She had very strange eyes. She looked at things like a cat, like a predator, looking for food. That's why I started creating around this character. The film is very strange that way.

The fun was to play around with the graveyard, to create an environment in a graveyard and put the characters into that situation. That is something fun. Eventually they couldn't get out of that — I enjoy that a lot! We were around that graveyard for days.

Sometimes you see the character at the end of their journey, and there's the part where they receive the sentence from the story where they should die or shouldn't die. For some characters at some point in shooting I would judge that they should die.

## All the Wrong Clues

Director, 1981. Cantonese: *Gwai Ma Ji Doh Sing.* Mandarin: *Gui Ma Zhi Duo Xing.* Literally: *Zany Wiseguy.* AKA: *All the Wrong Clues…for the Right Solution; Wrong Clues…Right Solution.* Producers: Carl Mak (Mak Ka), Dean Shek Tin. CAST: Teddy Robin Kwan ("Chief Inspector Robin"), Carl Mak [Mak Ka] ("Ah Capone"), George Lam Chi-Cheung

("Yoho"), Eric Tsang Chi-Wai ("Killer"). Opening Date: July 23, 1981.

SYNOPSIS: When gang leader Ah Capone is released from prison, Police Chief Inspector Robin is forced to call on the help of private detective Yoho, Robin's one-time rival and the only man who ever put Capone behind bars. When Capone's not trying to wreak revenge on Yoho, he's trying to bilk an old man out of a fortune in bonds, a scheme that Yoho and Robin must thwart, despite Capone's gangsters, molls and gags.

REVIEW: In the Tsui Hark timeline, *All the Wrong Clues* (his fourth feature) was the point at which Tsui went commercial (or sold out, depending on your personal preference). After experimenting with genres and political overtones in *The Butterfly Murders*, *We're Going to Eat You* and *Dangerous Encounter—1st Kind*, Tsui took on a purely escapist comedy with *All the Wrong Clues*, a film gleefully lacking avant garde elements or even a whiff of social commentary. In some respects, *All the Wrong Clues* is the gangster spoof Mel Brooks never made; in the hands of Tsui, however, it becomes the spoof Mel Brooks couldn't possibly ever make.

Because, despite its broad humor and ridiculous characterizations, *All the Wrong Clues* has style to burn and the quirkiness of the other features. *All the Wrong Clues* is one-part gangster spoof and one-part living comic book. Background sets are rendered in bright, primary colors, with little or no decoration to mar perfect lines; characters frequently break the fourth wall, almost seeming to pop out of the frame like superheroes breaking the confines of comic book panels. Some scenes are even shot with figures completely in silhouette, swaths of black moving against the colorful backdrops.

But Tsui's got the gangster jokes down, too, and *All the Wrong Clues* amply demonstrates his familiarity with (and obvious affection for) film history. His gangsters could have stepped out of any James Cagney film, and the femme fatales (there are quite a few in the film) pose with a sly knowingness that James M. Cain would have recognized immediately.

Tsui's visual wit occasionally wanders into territory uncharted by any gangster film. A party of New Years revelers don bizarre masks and fight around a jaded pianist; a villain tries to escape but finds himself on an endless series of Kafkaesque stairwells going nowhere. While these sidetracks are often amusing, the film as a whole meanders, sometimes confusing in its proliferation of molls and elaborate scams.

*All the Wrong Clues* also betrays the same problematic casting that cursed Tsui's films until *Shanghai Blues*. His heroic police inspector (Teddy Robin Kwan) is tiny and shaggy-haired; his hardboiled detective (George Lam Chi-Cheung) is more of a sunny-side-up kind of egg; and the women are all completely interchangeable. Fortunately, there's Carl Mak to save the day, giving a sneering, snarling and utterly hilarious performance as Ah Capone.

Despite the film's drawbacks and frequent left turns into near-surrealism, *All the Wrong Clues* is a delightful, whimsical comedy that is light years more visually sophisticated than the American spoof films which probably partly inspired it.

ABOUT THE MOVIE: *All the Wrong Clues* was Tsui Hark's first real box office success; it came in at the number four spot on the year's box office list, with a gross of $7,479,976.00. It also inspired a sequel, *All the Wrong Spies* (directed by Teddy Robin, and featuring Tsui in front of the camera as Japanese spy "Hiroshima Tora").

Tsui won the Taiwan Golden Horse Award for Best Director for *All the Wrong Clues*, his first major award (the film also won Best Cinematography and Art Direction).

The indifferent pianist in the New Years fight scene is played by John Sham, who would later co-star with Tsui in *I Love Maria* and *Yes, Madam*.

At the time *All the Wrong Clues* was made, the production company Cinema City was probably the biggest company in Hong Kong. The company had become immensely successful on the basis of its comedies (especially the *Aces Go Places* series), and would be a force in the Hong Kong film business throughout the '80s. Founded originally by Carl Mak, Dean Shek Tin and Raymond Wong in 1979 (as the Fun Dao [Task] Film Company; they changed the name to Cinema City a year later), by the early '80s the company was run by a group occasionally referred to as the "Gang of Seven": Carl Mak, Dean Shek, Raymond Wong, Tsui Hark, Nansun Shi, Eric Tsang and Teddy Robin. Part of Cinema City's success lay in their philosophy of giving work to new directors, who included Eric Tsang, Ringo Lam, Ronny Yu and Clifton Ko. Unfortunately, their comedies finally fell out of fashion by the end of the '80s, and the company fell apart. It was recently reformed, but Tsui wryly noted that they hadn't asked him to re-join yet.

*All the Wrong Clues* engendered some curious responses among Hong Kong critics. Although most praised it, a few regarded it as the end of the New Wave, and used the film's comedic tone and financial success to accuse Tsui of having "sold out." In his 1997 article "A Magical Witch's Brew: *A Chinese Ghost Story*," Sam Ho offers a new reading of *All the Wrong Clues*, suggesting that, in the film, "history was rewritten to pump up the Hong Kong people's role in the colony's early days."

TSUI ON *ALL THE WRONG CLUES*: Cinema City was looking for directors with the potential for making good movies. And they talked to me because I'd been around the industry as a director who had potential for creating a fantastic movie somewhere in the future. [They thought,] "Not yet ready, but still has this potential, has a very fluid way of telling a story. Material is something he needs to study, to use commercial elements." They started to pull in a list of directors who are going to make a movie for them. So when they got to me, I said, "Let's do a silly movie. All the movies I've done before were very serious and very depressing. Let's do a very silly movie, absent-minded and mindless. Let me relax and enjoy the movie." So that's why we did *All the Wrong Clues*. Nothing very serious; very *un*-serious movie!

[The film's comic book approach] sort of worked against all the logic. You get a friend like Teddy Robin to play the cop, right? When I talked to Teddy Robin, I told him the story, the whole thing, and he thought he was the private detective. I said, "No, you're the cop." He said, "Isn't there supposed to be a standard of recruitment for a cop? Height, weight? That sort of thing?" I said, "I don't know how we could have you as a cop, but you are a cop, okay?" And Lam — he said, "Who's the cop?" I said, "Teddy Robin's the cop." He said, "Whoa! We'll look weird." I said, "No, you look very normal, you'll be a very fashionable figure on the set. Only thing is, everything you do is wrong. Everything you do is dumb."

## *Zu: Warriors from the Magic Mountain*

Director/Cameo, 1983. Cantonese: *Suk Saan San Suk Saan Gim Hap*. Mandarin: *Shu Shan Xin Shu Shan Jian Xia*. Literally:

Original poster for *Zu: Warriors from the Magic Mountain.*

*Suk Mountain: New Suk Mountain Sword Heroes.* AKA: *Warriors from the Magic Mountain; Zu: Time Warriors.* Producer: Leonard Ho Koon-Cheung. Action Directors: Corey Yuen Kwai, Yuen Biao, Fung Hak-On, Mang Hoi. Screenwriter: Roy Szeto Cheuk Hon. Cast: Yuen Baio ("Ti-Ming Chi"), Sammo Hung ("Long Brows"/ "Red Soldier"), Adam Cheng ("Ting-Yin"), Brigitte Lin ("The Countess"), Moon Lee ("Chi-Wu Shang"), Damian Lau ("Hsiao-Lu"), Mang Hoi ("Yi-Chen"), Judy Ong ("Lady Li I-Chi"), Norman Chu ("Heaven's Blade"). Opening Date: February 5, 1983.

Synopsis: In China's 5th century, warring troops fight to possess Mount Zu, a strategic point located in the western region; but Zu is more than a military nexus, it's also a center of mystical forces. When Ti-Ming Chi, a young scout working for the West Zu army, is attacked by his own comrades, he flees and soon finds himself in the company of an enemy soldier from the East Zu army. Although they begin as antagonists, they soon find they have more in common, and protect each other during a fierce forest battle. The battle literally pushes them to the brink, and Ti-Ming falls into a mysterious ravine. A storm breaks out, and the young scout seeks refuge in a cavern full of ruins—a haunted cavern, as he discovers when he is attacked by demonic creatures. He is saved by the virtuous Ting-Yin, and pursues his whiteclad hero, begging to become his student. He is disenchanted, though, when they meet a rival monk, Hsiao-Lu, and his assistant Yi-Chen; an argument breaks out, which ends only when Hsiao-Lu tells them he and Yi-Chen have been following the Evil Disciples for three years, and now is the time to confront them. Poor Ti-Ming soon finds himself following the other three into the Evil Temple, where a supernatural battle breaks out, one which the

four humans barely survive, defeated. No sooner have they fled the Evil Temple than they encounter the Blood Demon, an ultimate evil being who badly injures Hsiao-Lu. The rest are saved only by the appearance of Long Brows, an aged magician who tells them he can hold the Blood Demon off for only 49 days, and unless they can find the Purple and Green Swords on Heaven's Blade Peak, the Blood Demon will be invincible. Their first step is to take the stricken monk to the Fort, a commune of women warriors led by the Countess, a healer. She successfully heals the monk and finds herself drawn to Ting-Yin; even though their relationship begins with a playful battle, it ends with an embrace. But when Ting-Yin himself is possessed by the Blood Demon, the Countess is too weak to save him. It's up to the two young students, Ti-Ming and Yi-Chen, to make it to Heaven's Blade Peak, accompanied by the young female Fort commander Chi-Wu Shang. At Heaven's Blade Peak the trio encounters Heaven's Blade, an aged guardian who protects the world from the fiery doorway leading to the Evil Territory. The trio finds Lady Li I-Chi, who gives the Purple and Green Swords to Ti-Ming and Yi-Chen, with the admonition that they can only destroy the Blood Demon if the swords are united. Suddenly the possessed Ting-Yin appears and attempts to keep the two young heroes apart until time runs out; but the Countess appears and sacrifices herself to destroy Ting-Yin, allowing the swords to unite. The Blood Demon is defeated, and the young heroes return to their troops to try and bring peace to their war-torn land.

Review: In film criticism circles, *Zu: Warriors from the Magic Mountain* is typically discussed as the film that introduced American optical effects to Hong Kong cinema. Certainly this alone would earn

*Zu* a place in global film history; but *Zu* is far more than merely a showcase for special effects. Not only is it one of Tsui Hark's most exciting and extravagant films, it's also (atypically for a fantasy film) packed with ideas that challenge social, religious and political norms.

*Zu* is sometimes referred to as the Chinese *Star Wars*, but where George Lucas' space fantasy reaffirms existing values (the wisdom of age, the role of female as "damsel-in-distress," sharply-defined good and evil), *Zu* is a far more complex social document. Near the beginning of the film we meet Ting-Yin, the swordsman whose prowess and confidence would lead us to believe he will be the hero; yet, after losing time while arguing with his peers, he finally becomes the embodiment of the Blood Demon, an ultimate evil. The generals who lead poor soldiers like Ti-Ming Chi into battle are cruel, egotistical warlords who hold no regard for those who serve under them. The story's various quests — to heal the monk, to find the Two Swords — all lead to women, who become integral figures in the action. The only characters who can work together are the young, impoverished (i.e., working class) Ti-Ming Chi and Yi-Chen. Even traditional Chinese concepts are challenged: In *Zu*, fate is something that can be taken and changed, not something to be serenely accepted. The film's ending clearly states that the future lies with this next generation — if they can learn to live peacefully, which *Zu*'s ending seems to put in doubt.

What's fascinating about *Zu*'s social challenges is the way they bubble just beneath the surface of a frenetically-paced fantasy masterpiece. *Zu* features many of the tropes of classic Western *Lord of the Rings*–style fantasy: quests, wizards, warriors, princesses, forests, caves, temples, encounters with evil creatures, magical doorways, enchanted all-powerful weapons.

Yet, set within the Chinese design and played out with the unexpected twists and turns provided by Tsui's social challenges, the movie plays like something entirely new. Even when we're watching swordfights with what look suspiciously like *Star Wars* lightsabers, any thought of similarity is banished by the milieu. After all, nobody in *Star Wars* could fly.

*Zu* is the first Tsui Hark film to suggest that the ability to fly can be achieved by intense training. Even in *The Butterfly Murders* — the first film to feature extensive wire-rigging — characters were propelled through the sky by ropes and wires. In *Zu* (as in the later *Swordsman* films), flying is as natural to most of the main characters as walking. In an American fantasy we'd get a five-minute explanation about how they do it; in a Tsui Hark film we're simply launched into it. In Tsui Hark's world the ability to fly seems to be a freedom that need not be explained or discussed — it's there to be enjoyed, a celebration of human power and discipline.

There's another force that propels *Zu*, though, and that's Tsui's unique and justly-famous editing style, which reached its peak (pun intended) in this film. During action sequences few shots seem longer than a dozen frames; the number of different setups (angles) is often astonishing. In his later films Tsui created more movement with the camera, but here in *Zu* his camera is often static, presumably limited by the vast amount of effects. And effects there are, in nearly every frame of *Zu*; while the optical effects vary from mediocre to excellent, the physical effects are even more plentiful and uniformly superb. One memorable scene features more than a dozen performers flinging themselves upward to escape the possessed Ting-Yin (one can only imagine the complications involving the wire-rigging there!). In another sequence — one of the film's most astonishing — Ting-Yin and the Countess begin their romance with a playful fight conducted in mid-air, while they fly seated atop giant stone animals; the sequence has the thrill of the world's greatest unbuilt amusement park ride. In a typical bit of Tsui Hark visual wit, the sequence ends with a lovely close-up of the pair as sparks literally fly around them.

*Zu* sparkles throughout with humor, which Tsui directs in such a way that it feels natural, never intruding on the suspense or action. There's the above-mentioned visual wit, often displayed in the performance of Yuen Baio, one of Hong Kong's best physical comic actors (see Yuen's performance in *Once Upon a Time in China* as another example of his fine talent). Yuen is delightful, whether jostling to free himself from Long Brows' sticky gray hairs or leaping after a mischievous fish (who literally laughs at his frustration!). The forest battle near the film's beginning is a stunning example of comic martial arts, with Yuen and the equally-talented Sammo Hung almost acting out what feels like a Marx Brothers skit as they trick soldiers into attacking each other, only to have their tricks turn against them. Despite *Zu*'s emphasis on optical effects, such sequences remind us that actors alone can still provide the most special of all effects.

*Zu* also brims with wonderful, wry verbal humor. Take, for example, the scene in which the possessed Ting-Yin, with sickly silvery pallor and sunken eyes, turns to his student and asks, "How does my face look?" Ti-Ming struggles for a second to rein in his obvious disgust, then tries to sound reassuring as he responds, "Not *too* bad..." In another of the film's funniest lines, after Ti-Ming and Yi-Chen mistake the Countess for the Blood Demon and start a furious fight, Ting-Yin reprimands them, "Don't call every woman you see a witch!"

Technically, *Zu* is just as wondrous as its direction and script. Kwan Shing Yau's score is the first great one from a Tsui Hark film, with its epic themes and complex orchestrations. The sets are both huge and exquisitely-detailed; the Fort, for example, consists mainly of a huge central space filled with stone sculptures and columns, but close-ups reveal lovely bas-relief murals adorning the walls. Even the fabulously creepy cavern near the film's beginning has artbook-worthy wall paintings. Setting off the sets to maximum effect is the perfect lighting, which Tsui often allows to go dark to create mood and unease (as he did with *The Butterfly Murders*).

Costuming also deserves a special mention in *Zu*. Tsui undoubtedly recognized from the start that *Zu*'s script and furious pacing would not allow much time to set up characters, and he lets the costuming do much of that for him (very successfully). The warring troops in the beginning are easily distinguished by their vivid red, blue, orange, yellow and green uniforms (which spark a marvelous comedy line when one of our young heroes, caught in the middle of the opposing forces, blurts out, "What a colorful battle!"). The Countess is clothed in long streamers that suggest her supernatural radiance. At the end of the film the two young heroes are clothed by Lady Li I-Chi in their new roles as world saviors; they even look down at themselves in awe at the impressive — yet simple, as befits working class heroes — new garb.

*Zu* also boasts one of Tsui's biggest and best casts. Aside from Yuen Baio, there's Sammo Hung in a duel role as both Long Brows and the red soldier who befriends Ti-Ming in the film's beginning; Hung brings both sage wisdom and humor to Long Brows, and matches Ti-Ming's

**Brigitte Lin as "The Countess" in *Zu: Warriors from the Magic Mountain.***

agility as the red soldier. Adam Cheng is genuinely eerie as the possessed Ting-Yin and conveys the swordsman's plight with sympathy and grace. Judy Ong is also a stand-out as Lady Li I-Chi; she brings a deep benevolence and joy to what is nearly a cameo role.

Of particular note among the actors is, of course, Brigitte Lin as the Countess. This is the first time Tsui directed Brigitte, and although her performance in *Zu* differs sharply from her later gender-bending work with Tsui (in *Peking Opera Blues*, *Dragon Inn* and the *Swordsman* films), her work here has much of the same dignity and intensity she would bring to the other roles. In her battles with Ting-Yin she seems easily his equal, and yet she never loses her femininity. Although she's decked out here in traditional woman's clothing, it's not hard to see why Tsui would eventually remold her into a sort of gender avenger.

ABOUT THE MOVIE: Although *Zu* was a critical hit for Tsui, it was not an immediate financial success, not even performing as well as *Dangerous Encounter — 1st Kind*. It placed number 119 on the year's box office list, with a disappointing gross of $1,587,851.00 (it had an astonishing budget of $30 million). However, it went on to become a financial success over time, drawing well in other Asian territories (especially Taiwan).

It was recognized by the Hong Kong Film Awards, receiving nominations for Best Picture, Best Actress (Brigitte Lin), Best Art Direction (Cheung Suk Ping), Best Action Choreography (Yuen Kwai) and Best Film Editing (Shek Chi Kwong).

*Zu* actually had an American release under the title *Zu: Time Warriors*. For this release a wraparound story was added in which a contemporary Yuen Baio suffers a head injury in an accident, and while in the hospital he apparently "dreams" the rest of the film. One major additional scene was added to the period footage, in which the ongoing war situation is explained in depth by a man Yuen encounters in the forest. Needless to say, the wraparound felt completely superfluous and probably left American audiences far more baffled than the film would have in its original cut.

Tsui has a cameo appearance at the very end of the film as the blue-clad soldier fighting Sammo Hung.

Brigitte Lin tells an amusing anecdote about being left hanging above the floor in her wire rigging one day while the entire crew adjourned for lunch!

Tsui On *Zu: Warriors from the Magic Mountain*: All the sets were built from scratch. Now it'll be better when we make a sequel. The first time we had 30 people sitting in a room, everybody has to have their own *Zu* world, so I have to draw a lot — draw, draw, draw, draw, draw! None of them really look like what you want. Actually, we were creating from what we'd see in the environment. We'd see some corridor that'd look very interesting, and we'd say, "That should be in the movie." We'd see some character, "He should be in the movie." We'd see an empty studio and look around — "This should be in the movie." Like Brigitte Lin's temple — it looked like our office, our lobby. In our lobby area there were these two big props that we put on the set. We translated our experience into the movie. In the end we put everything into the movie and it looked kind of fun. I think the difference between designing and seeing things in real life — designing is doing everything on a flat piece of paper. And when it comes to a 3-D thing, maybe you have a problem with a grandscale look, or maybe you have a problem with how these things relate to the drama. Usually, with *Zu*, in the preparation period

the artists would do all this designing, and it had nothing to do with the characters. You'd ask, "Where do we put the character?"

And at that period of time when we were trying to put together the sets, we had a problem because we had a group of students who were coming from school to work on our big effects. They stayed away for six months and came back with one or two shots. And I had found out one day — very shocking — they forgot to put the filter on the optical printer, so the film coming out wasn't the right color. And there was something about how they lost some of the test pieces by giving them the wrong catalog number, so they couldn't find them any more ... all these problems. That's one part of the production where I felt so frustrated. I was a cameraman for that, and also I'm a photographer, so that's why I'd say, "Let's try that, let's use some darkroom techniques in the movie." We also had some people out from L.A., who had done *Star Wars*, and they gave us a lot of information and knowledge about the way we handled some of the shots.

So the most important thing is, how should the film look? How should the characters look? They shouldn't look boring. They need to look very interesting. They should look very fresh, they should look different from other movies. The story background should look unusual, fairy tale, fairyland. When Brigitte Lin was standing in a room we dressed her for a week. We'd put one piece of fabric on her, take another piece out — she was standing there for a week! We felt very sorry for her, because we couldn't find a costume for her. One time there was a piece of fabric that we put on her and we realized that piece of fabric looked great on her. And we put it back again, and it was only a piece of something, not a costume, so we had to take it off!

# Shanghai Blues

Director/Cameo, 1984. Cantonese: *Soeng Hoi Zi Je*. Mandarin: *Shang Hai Zhi Ye*. Literally: *Shanghai Nights*. Screenwriters: Chan Koon-Chung, Raymond To Kwok-Wai, Roy Szeto Cheuk-Hon. Production Designer: Hing Yee Ah Yeung. Editing: Chew Siu Sum. Film Score: James Wong. CAST: Sylvia Chang ("Shu-Shu"), Kenny Bee ("Tung/Do-Re-Mi"), Sally Yeh ("Stool"), Loletta Lee Lai-Chun ("Shu-Shu's assistant"). Opening Date: October 11, 1984.

SYNOPSIS: It's World War II, and Shanghai is under attack by the Japanese. While the wealthy foreigners bask in the knowledge that their quarter of the city is protected, natives Tung and Shu-Shu are caught in the stampede of frightened victims. Tung pulls the panicked girl to safety beneath a bridge, and a romance begins, even though Tung is on his way to the war. They vow to return to the bridge after the war has been won, to seek each other once again. Ten years later, Tung is an impoverished musician and Shu-Shu a struggling nightclub performer, both still hoping to find the other some day. When Tung moves to Shu-Shu's rooftop, he begins a new romance with Shu-Shu's naïve roommate (whom he nicknames "Stool"), unaware that the girl of his dreams is right under his feet. It isn't until Shu-Shu accepts a club client's proposal of marriage that Tung discovers her identity and must pursue her, even if it means abandoning his attraction to "Stool."

REVIEW: For all of those who have walked out of recent Hollywood films grumbling, "They just don't make 'em like they used to…," here's a film that proves they do—provided, of course, "they" refers to Hong Kong, not Hollywood. *Shanghai Blues* is probably the best American Depression-era romantic comedy never made in America.

Although Tsui Hark intended *Shanghai Blues* to be the first film in a "Blues" trilogy, the film bears more resemblance to an American '30s comedy, such as *It Happened One Night*, than to Tsui's own *Peking Opera Blues* (part two of the trilogy—he never made part three). In fact, *Shanghai Blues* is so continually laugh-out-loud funny that its title is somewhat deceptive (but then again, *Peking Opera Blues'* lightning-fast action renders it virtually blues-free as well).

Like the best American Depression-era films, *Shanghai Blues* is firmly entrenched in a milieu of "haves" vs. "have-nots," with our sympathies obviously in line with the latter. In *Shanghai Blues* (as in its American predecessors), poor chorus girls dance in glitzy jazz clubs and vie for dates with wealthy gangsters. Tsui even includes some of the old films' archetypal characters: The golddigger whose own heart is gold, the naïve country girl, the young man torn between responsibility and romance.

But where Tsui veers sharply away from those old films is in giving *Shanghai Blues* a genuinely hard edge. Beneath its pratfalls and embraces is a world seething with vice and greed. In one scene an old man's head is smashed into a glass window by the roiling crowd lined up behind him; and Shanghai's mean streets are overrun with pickpockets, gangsters, whores, drunken sailors and unscrupulous merchants.

Where another director might condemn all this, Tsui revels in it, finding great joy and humor, and giving *Shanghai Blues* its own distinctive sense of life. Merchants may be overcharging so much that poverty-stricken ex-soldiers must sell blood just to survive, but this means that acquiring a handful of vegetables is a cause

Original poster for *Shanghai Blues* (featuring, left to right, Sally Yeh, Sylvia Chang and Kenny Bee).

for celebration. There's a rich dramatic moment in which the opportunistic Shu-Shu hurls herself from a rich man's car to make her way back to Tung, and in the process breaks a leg — which, of course, provides for numerous jokes involving the ensuing plaster cast. All of this chaos and hysteria keeps *Shanghai Blues* from ever becoming melodramatic or maudlin, although it remains just as moving in the end as its American kin.

*Shanghai Blues* is also one of the finest examples of Tsui Hark's ability to create a sense of controlled chaos. To thoroughly synopsize the film would take as long as the film itself, because nearly every sequence provides some new twist to the plot. And yet the plot never threatens to spin out of control, nor do individual scenes, which are occasionally astonishingly manic (a standout being the scene in which Shu-Shu attempts to perform a seductive tango before a sold-out audience and becomes aware halfway through the number that her dress has a large hole burned in the rear). Jackie Chan (the director, that is) loves the setup in which too many people, all occupying the same house or room, try to hide from each other; yet he's never pulled it off as well as Tsui does here, when Tung, Shu-Shu, Stool, the pickpocket and Tung's army friend all frantically maneuver in the tight confines of Tung's tiny rooftop apartment. For one thing, Chan has a tendency to let his farcical scenes run long, but there's probably no single sequence in all of *Shanghai Blues* that occupies more than five minutes of screen time.

Visually, *Shanghai Blues* is a splendid example of Tsui's love of vivid primary colors. The main title sets the tone, with red, green and blue light scintillating across lapping waves. The opening attack on Shanghai is lit in hard crimson, with deep shadows; it's lovely, but it also makes

it believable that the lovers can't recognize each other later. Tung, who makes his barebones living as a clown-for-hire with his uncle, is always dressed or made up in reds and blues, while Shu-Shu's nightclub is awash in a rich yellow glow (Tsui also filters his lens here to flare out the many lights in the club, giving the scenes a romantic, fairy-tale quality).

If *Peking Opera Blues* feels distinctly Chinese, *Shanghai Blues* is in line with *All the Wrong Clues* in seeming thoroughly Western. Even though *Shanghai Blues* is a direct descendent of the earlier Mandarin-language "sing-song" girl Chinese musicals, its tale of post-war poverty could easily have been set in Europe (especially the Italian Neo-Realist cinema); with the exception of Shu-Shu, the characters don't dress in traditional costumes. One of the first shots in the film almost states its Western themes clearly, as Tung is framed by French, British and American flags; later, Tung almost seems to mock Peking Opera as he and Stool perform a parody dressed (respectively) in minstrel blackface and pajamas. Even the nightclub musical numbers involve tangos (as does most of the film's score) or Big Band jazz. And although the film flirts briefly with the notion of evil gweilos (the French laugh at the local economic crisis), it never becomes a major theme.

What does, though, is female bonding, which is probably *Shanghai Blues'* closest link to its sibling *Peking Opera Blues*. Although the film opens with the wartime meeting between Tung and Shu-Shu, the bulk of the film is about the relationship between Shu-Shu and Stool. Indeed, both the Shu-Shu/Stool friendship and the Shu-Shu/Tung romance are played in similar ways: Both "meet cute" (Tung pushes Shu-Shu under the bridge, and later Stool pushes her into the river); both follow the formula of boy-meets-girl, boy-loses-girl, boy-wins-girl-back; both are even scored with the same lush, romantic theme. If Shu-Shu and Stool are the pair that must ultimately split for the Shu-Shu/Tung couple to survive, it's also because the women have become so bonded that they've switched identities at the end: Shu-Shu is now the plainly-dressed girl on the train, while the elegantly-attired Stool is assisted by the same young girl who used to help Shu-Shu at the nightclub.

Which is not to say that *Shanghai Blues* is not also drenchingly romantic. Stool falls in love with Tung before they've even met, as she nearly swoons listening to his violin playing beneath neon and moonlight. Later, during a power outage, Tung and Shu-Shu try to save her dying goldfish while Tung carries a goldfish-shaped lantern; Shu-Shu is obsessed with her burning hope, which has clearly just passed to Tung. Attraction flowers between them, an attraction whose denouement occurs on a crowded train, as Tung desperately pushes his way through to Shu-Shu. It's a scene nearly as old as the movies themselves, but Tsui plays it with a comic touch (the other passengers' heads swivel in perfect unison from Tung to Shu-Shu and back) that seems to reinvent it.

*Shanghai Blues* is the turning point in Tsui's ability to work with actors. For the first time one of his films received acting nominations at the Hong Kong Film Awards (for Sylvia Chang and Loletta Lee), and deservedly so. Maybe it's because *Shanghai Blues* is the film wherein Tsui seemed to also learn how to create real, vital, sympathetic characters; or perhaps it's the caliber of the performers themselves. Whatever the reason, the performances are one of the chief delights of *Shanghai Blues.* Sylvia Chang demonstrated a minor comic genius in Tsui's *Aces Go Places 3,* but here she creates a fully-rounded human being, not just a cartoon

caricature. Shu-Shu may be the classic hooker-with-a-heart-of-gold, but in Chang's hands she seems more like a tired workaholic who still desperately clings to a cherished dream. Sally Yeh displays a rubbery-faced comedic talent that will surprise those who know her best from *The Killer;* and Loletta Lee steals several scenes as Shu-Shu's dim and perpetually-panicking young protégé. As the male lead stuck in the middle of all this, Kenny Bee performs with enough youthful energy to power a dozen typical Hollywood-actor performances.

*Shanghai Blues'* influence on the Hong Kong film industry is still being felt a decade-and-a-half later. The subplot involving Stool entering a contest and winning the top prize because of her "ordinariness" seems to have been copied wholesale for Peter Chan's delightful 1994 comedy *He's a Woman, She's a Man;* and Tsui's style of often ending scenes with a freeze-frame seems to have later become a trademark of John Woo.

Would that *Shanghai Blues* had been a major influence on American cinema as well; Hollywood could use a major injection of its humor, charm and lovely imagery.

ABOUT THE MOVIE: *Shanghai Blues* was moderately successful, placing number 18 on the year's box office list and taking in $11,625,564 (a more impressive figure given that the film's budget was under $4 million!). It received eight nominations at the year's Hong Kong Film Awards— for Best Picture, Best Director, Best Actress (Sylvia Chang), Best Supporting Actress (Loletta Lee Lai-Jan), Best Art Direction (Hing Yee Ah Yeung), Best Film Editing (Chew Siu Sum), Best Original Film Score (James Wong) and Best Original Film Song. It was also named one of the ten best Chinese films at the Hong Kong Film Fes-

English-language poster for *Shanghai Blues,* featuring Sylvia Chang.

tival in 1985 and appeared at over 20 other international film festivals.

Most critics (including Sek Kei, in the *Ming Pao Evening News,* 1/4/85) regarded *Shanghai Blues* as one of the best films of 1984 and saw in it a poignant take on Hong Kong's past and future. Roger Garcia said, "Tsui Hark uses the past as a vantage point from which to view the future," and Li Cheuk-To said that Tsui "came up with the most mature and touching of the 'political' films" (both quoted in *Hong Kong New Wave: Twenty Years After)*. At least one major critic was not so kind: In *Film Biweekly,* No. 153 (1/3/85), Shu Kei gave the film a negative review because of its "fence-sitting tactics" in regards to its politics.

Tsui has referred to *Shanghai Blues* as his personal favorite among his films, mainly because it was the first film to be produced by his company, Film Workshop.

Look for Tsui in a cameo as the passerby whom Stool accidentally douses with a tub of water.

Tsui on *Shanghai Blues*: The idea for the film came from a story I heard from my friend who was this actress. She was doing a performance on stage and she was playing a very poor character, and she's wearing a diamond ring — a big diamond ring. She's very poor, in rags and everything, and she suddenly realized there's this diamond ring on her finger, glittering! And she felt really terrible. I felt that she was really funny, a fun person, and the character started formulating in my mind. The person that started formulating was Sylvia Chang. Then I needed a person for a duo, so that's why I created Sally Yeh. I never thought of that as being in the '40s; I thought it was supposed to be now. So I was travelling in Nepal and I started thinking about it. I was trying to conceptualize the story of a woman surviving the world

of performing, being hypocritical and self-pitying, but still a very charming and touching character. And I started thinking about it, and I realized … actually, that was a period where everybody was thinking about 1997. And I hate to say, let's tell the story in 1997. So I thought, let's do everything backwards, in 1941 or '38, something like that. To go back to a period with that same kind of mood of fear, to compare to what we have now. I think it was not appropriate to date something several years in the future, when it won't be true, it won't happen that way. Like a movie like *2001*; now it's 2000 and we're still sitting on earth, worrying about the ozone. And that is why I changed everything back to the '40s.

And it's so nice to see them playing the two characters and using the sets — there were only three sets, because the budget was a limited amount. So we made use of the sets all the time — that's one of the conditions you have, doing a movie. After I made the movie, people would say it was very similar to some of the pictures they'd seen from the '50s. Maybe because of the limited sets. We definitely needed a set of a home, a set of the exteriors, and the staircases. It's very similar to movies from earlier stages; the only difference is our movie's in color! But anyway, I believe the similarity of this movie to other movies is because of the style itself. When I went to Japan, they said, "This is a Japanese film — it's *Under the Bridge!*" "Really? What's the story about?" "Well, after several years of war time, the guy comes back to look for the girl." I said, "Exactly like that?" "Exactly like that!" It's difficult to avoid something like that. It looks similar to a lot of other movies.

[On the music]: When you really listen to the song, it's about Hong Kong, as a matter of fact. It's about how people can share the moment together.

That's the movie I feel so emotional about because it's the first of Film Workshop. Because I had problems with Cinema City. They cannot read our thoughts on movies any more, so there's no way we can collaborate any more. At Cinema City you have a certain type of production, and if you want to suggest another type of production you have a problem, because everything was successful — like a golden brand. So anything that would cost or damage that golden brand thing — it's like a sentence of death. So that's why I said, "Maybe we should prove it outside." So that's why we have the Workshop and *Shanghai Blues*.

In an interview with Stephen Short from Time@CNN.com (5/3/2000), Tsui named Sylvia Chang as a major influence in his use of women in film: "It was during the shooting of *Shanghai Blues* in 1984. In that movie you've got women playing male roles, and Sylvia encouraged me to explore what female psyches could bring to a male persona. She kept telling me that females were richer subjects, more complex than guys and at first I questioned that. By stretching the dimensions of the gender of the characters in that movie, I realized she was right. Her thinking enhanced the whole movie and much of my thinking."

## A Better Tomorrow

Producer/Actor, 1986. Cantonese: *Jing Hung Bun Sik*. Mandarin: *Ying Xiong Ben Se*. Literally: *Heroic Character*. AKA: *The Color of a Hero*; *Gangland Boss*; *True Colors of a Hero*. Director: John Woo. Screenwriters: John Woo, Chan Hing-Ka, Chan Shuk Dut. Cinematography: Wong Wing Hang. Art Direction: Lui Chi Leung. Action Design: Blacky Ko, Stephen Tung.

Editing: Ma Kam. Music Score: Joseph Koo. CAST: Ti Lung ("Ho"), Chow Yun-Fat ("Mark"), Leslie Cheung ("Kit"), Waise Lee ("Shing"), Emily Chu ("Jackie"), John Woo ("Inspector"), Kenneth Tsang ("Ken"), Tsui Hark ("Music Judge"). Opening Date: August 2, 1986.

SYNOPSIS: Ho and the carefree, suave Mark are two moderately successful members of a Hong Kong Triad gang who specialize in counterfeiting and assassination. Although Ho has always kept his criminal activities secret from his idealistic young police officer brother Kit, the truth comes out when Ho and Mark are set up and Ho is captured by police. After three years in prison, Ho comes out determined to go straight, only to find that his brother has rejected him, Mark is a broken cripple parking cars for a living, and Ho's former Triad protégé, Shing, has taken over and is determined to get Ho involved again. As the pressures on Ho increase from every side, he reluctantly agrees to aid Mark in a desperate plan to steal and ransom a printing plate used in the Triad's counterfeiting process. After a bloody shoot-out on the Hong Kong docks, the brothers Kit and Ho finally resolve the situation and find a measure of respect for one another at last.

REVIEW: *A Better Tomorrow* may have been the crowning jewel in Tsui Hark's Hong Kong Triple Crown (with *Zu: Warriors from the Magic Mountain* and *Peking Opera Blues*), but there's no question that this is a John Woo film. Unlike the films directed by Tsui's frequent collaborator Ching Siu-Tung (i.e., *Swordsman II* or *A Chinese Ghost Story*), *A Better Tomorrow* reflects virtually none of Tsui Hark's characteristic themes or style. The story is about two men trying to retain some shred of dignity while betrayed by other men;

the only woman in the film (Jackie, Kit's girlfriend) serves no other purpose than peacekeeper, and she even fails at that. *A Better Tomorrow* tells a clear, linear story, with none of Tsui's usual frenzied plotting; it's a tragedy with action elements, not a dramatic-comedy-fantasy-action-tragedy. It's probably the closest thing to a Hollywood film Tsui has ever been involved with, and, ironically, it became his biggest hit.

In some ways *A Better Tomorrow* is to Hong Kong cinema what *The Godfather* was to American film: a deconstruction of the gangster mythos. Both films show mobs as essentially business organizations, with mobsters as businessmen (in *A Better Tomorrow* the accoutrements of the successful executive—the tailored suits, the briefcases, the chauffered limos—are obviously important to Mark and Ho in the beginning of the film); both films feature a central character who desperately wants to "go straight" but can't find a way out. Both films are also about family: In *A Better Tomorrow* Ho is torn between his real family—his brother Kit, who won't accept him—and his Triad family, Mark, who would (and does) willingly sacrifice himself for his friend.

Where *The Godfather* and *A Better Tomorrow* differ most is in the style of storytelling; *A Better Tomorrow* still wants to abide by some of the rules of the gangster picture even while annihilating them. The amount of abuse that Ho is willing to take in order to "save face" causes the story to veer dangerously close to melodrama; that it manages to avoid crossing that line is due primarily to one element: the performance of Chow Yun-Fat as Mark.

It's often said that *A Better Tomorrow* made Chow Yun-Fat, but the reality is that Chow Yun-Fat made *A Better Tomorrow*. Prior to *A Better Tomorrow*, Chow Yun-Fat had been in some excellent films, including Ann Hui's *The Story of Woo Viet*, but he was primarily known as a minor comic actor. With *A Better Tomorrow*, Chow became more than a superstar—he became an icon. His performance is so deeply impassioned that actors as dependable as Ti Lung and Leslie Cheung nearly cease to exist in scenes with him. Mark's transformation from dapper, jokey ladies' man to broken, desperate amputee is the engine driving *A Better Tomorrow*; it's the kind of heartwrenching, fiery performance most actors can only dream of giving. It's a pity that much of Chow's later work required him to play stoic, lantern-jawed hitmen, because, when allowed a full range of emotions to lay before a camera, Chow proves himself to be one of the finest film actors in the world.

If Chow's later work was a minor letdown, Woo's work only got better. His direction in *A Better Tomorrow* lacks many of the visual flourishes that would later become his trademarks—the freeze-frames, the intricate cross-cutting—and in fact, *A Better Tomorrow* feels like the work of a director just coming out of the '70s "chopsocky" style (which is basically what Woo made prior to this film). Woo still uses zooms (compare to Tsui's moving camera in *Peking Opera Blues*), and the lighting is flat. The film's one brief attempt at humor—when Jackie knocks over the music stand during her cello audition—is forced, and the scene where a mobster tries to attack Ho and Kit's father in a dark apartment plays like a parody of a '70s slasher film. It isn't until the blood-drenched final gunfight on the docks (which Woo later recycled in his finest film, *Bullet in the Head*) that *A Better Tomorrow* really comes alive visually; it's almost as if Woo was slightly behind his audience in realizing that "heroic bloodshed" (as this style of film was later known) was his real calling.

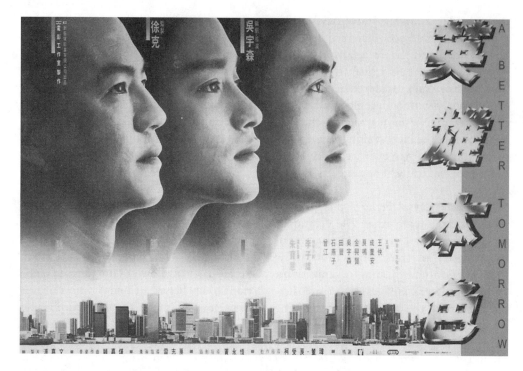

**Original poster for *A Better Tomorrow* (featuring, left to right, Ti Lung, Leslie Cheung and Chow Yun-Fat).**

*A Better Tomorrow* must have been a bittersweet success for Tsui Hark; as producer, he took home a Best Picture Award at the Hong Kong Film Awards, while the film he directed that same year —*Peking Opera Blues*— was not mentioned for either Best Picture or Best Director. In Fredric Dannen's excellent book *Hong Kong Babylon*, a poll of critics placed *Peking Opera Blues* at number 4, one notch above *A Better Tomorrow*, so perhaps, in this case, the test of time is on Tsui Hark's side.

ABOUT THE MOVIE: *A Better Tomorrow* is the most successful film Tsui Hark has so far been associated with. It was the number one film of 1986, with a take of $34,651,324. At the 1987 Hong Kong Film Awards, *A Better Tomorrow* won for Best Picture (Tsui Hark and John Woo) and Best Actor (Chow Yun-Fat), and was nominated for Best Actor (Ti Lung), Best Art Direction (Lui Chi Leung Lui), Best Cinematography (Wong Wing-Hang), Best Director (John Woo), Best Film Editing (Ma Kam), Best New Performer (Waise Lee), Best Original Film Score (Joseph Koo), Best Screenplay (John Woo) and Best Supporting Actor (Waise Lee).

*A Better Tomorrow* and its two sequels virtually began Hong Kong's "heroic bloodshed" genre and inspired a host of imitators, the most obviously-titled being Wong Jing's *Return to a Better Tomorrow*, which, despite a solid cast (Lau Ching Wan, Ekin Cheng and Michael Fitzgerald Wong are the three leads), essentially plays as John Woo Lite.

*A Better Tomorrow* is loosely based on the 1967 Hong Kong film *The Story of a Discharged Prisoner*, directed by Lung Kong.

TSUI ON *A BETTER TOMORROW*: It's a revision of a movie already made by director Lung Kong, and Lung Kong is one of my favorite directors from the '60s. So I came back to Hong Kong from the States, and when I was thinking about movies I always remembered that as a movie that attracted me. So when I got back to Cinema City, where it was all comedies, I said, "Let's do something that's not a comedy. Let's do something like a drama. Let's do *A Better Tomorrow*." They got very uncomfortable: "How can you make a non-comedy movie? Everybody wants to be happy! Why do you have to do a serious drama? No one's going to go in and watch the movie!" Then I was in Taiwan — at that period of time I was still friendly with John Woo. So I talked with John Woo about *A Better Tomorrow*. I said, "I want to make the movie, but they don't believe in it. They think it's too serious, no one wants to see an unhappy movie." So when I came back from Taiwan — I was acting for John Woo [in *Run Tiger Run*] — I came back from Taiwan to Hong Kong again and we started doing something different. At that period of time I was writing stories like *A Chinese Ghost Story*; I started to think that maybe we should divert from comedy movies to find out the possibility of movies. So John Woo came back to Hong Kong, he was looking for a project. I said, "Let's do *A Better Tomorrow*. I'll try to convince people to do *A Better Tomorrow*." I thought that maybe doing something different would help the industry. So that film was done in that kind of atmosphere. It was made at the same time we were doing *A Chinese Ghost Story*.

[Did the film's success surprise him?] Well... yes and no. Yes, because we always think that we're going to be back at zero! No, because when this kind of thing comes to you, suddenly you feel like you can do anything in the world. James Cameron, after the success of *Titanic*, said he could do anything in the world. That kind of feeling was distressing to me, because I felt like I wasn't ready for it. It's fun to be like a carefree person, but you start to carry the weight of responsibility, obligation. Especially because of the success of that thing, it started creating politics around it. That's something very bad, and I don't like it. I'm not a character that would live in a world of politics. I'm very bad at it. So we started to see some very weird phenomena in the office, and I didn't like it.

Anyway, so *A Better Tomorrow* became a big hit, and then *A Chinese Ghost Story*, so we passed the period where people were feeling very skeptical about our chance of commercial success. They always had a problem thinking this director never knows what sells, or what won't sell, and he's using our money to prove a point. You want to go into a different place. Of course we knew the reason *A Better Tomorrow* was such a success was because the drama was really still a very powerful element for the people. Some of the people feel very strong about friendship, romance, care... before that, everything was so—insincere. I always say that Hong Kong culture is a salesman culture — they are selling something and they don't know what they're selling, they just keep selling because that's the way they make their living. But they never put time into learning something they already have in their daily life — a little bit of care, a little bit of love, a little bit of romance, a little bit of friendship, a little bit more to yourself than what you are — and it's a nice movie. It has great feeling. When you have great feeling you have a great movie.

[On the casting of Chow Yun-Fat]: When we were thinking about that role, we were all thinking about Chow Yun-Fat. Chow Yun-Fat had done nothing good before. Chow Yun-Fat was always great on camera, but the movies were not good. So he tried comedy, he tried action, tried romantic love story—didn't work. So we cast Chow Yun-Fat, and everyone was against it. *Everybody* was against it. "Come on, we don't want to watch the movie with him." We said, "Chow Yun-Fat is a great actor, and Ti Lung is a great actor. We put these great actors together, do some drama. Let's do something serious instead of comedy." So Chow Yun-Fat said he didn't have the window for the movie. So we said, "Let's wait; let's wait for Chow Yun-Fat." Everybody was laughing at us. And Ti Lung also gave us a problem. He was playing in another movie called *The Legend of Wisely* at the same time, and the director [Teddy Robin] wanted him to have long hair. In our movie, when he's in jail, he definitely needed to cut his hair. So I went to see the director and asked if his ponytail could be a fake ponytail, so he can cut his hair so we can make our movie? So the director turned around and said, "No, no! You are not respecting me at all! Now you want to take the character and—!" [Tsui moans] He was jumping around. So now we didn't have Ti Lung, either. So all we had was Leslie—"Let's do something with Leslie!" But then after a while Ti Lung said he wanted to make the movie, so he would try to help us out by cutting the hair so it won't look long or short. Then we went after Chow Yun-Fat and said to him, "Give us a schedule and we'll start making the movie." Funnily, Chow Yun-Fat's character only lasted for 10 days or 15 days. It ended up that we needed more schedule. We ran over budget, so I said, "We don't have Chow Yun-Fat any more. Can we convince Chow Yun-Fat to be in the movie a few more days?" Chow Yun-Fat looked at the movie, and he felt so good about it that he said, "Okay, I'll give you five free days. Free of charge." Everything was on an unstable basis, sort of like walking on

a boat—everything is moving, shaking, unbalanced.

In an interview with Stephen Short from Time@CNN.com (5/3/2000), Tsui talked about how he wanted to cast *A Better Tomorrow*: "I remember clearly wanting Michelle Yeoh playing the Chow Yun-Fat role. Rather than examine the relationship between a group of men, I wanted the relationship to be between women. From very early on, I wanted to do movies without any guys."

## Peking Opera Blues

Director/Producer, 1986. Cantonese: *Do Ma Daan*. Mandarin: *Dao Ma Dan*. Literally: *Knife, Horse, Dawn*. Action Director: Ching Siu-Tung. Screenwriter: Raymond To Kwok-Wai. CAST: Brigitte Lin Ching-Hsia ("Tsao Wan"), Cherie Chung Cho-Hung ("Sheung Hung"), Sally Yeh ("Pat Neil"), Mark Cheng Ho-Nam ("Pak Hoi"), Wu Ma ("Mr. Wong"), Kenneth Tsang Kong ("General Tsao"), Paul Chun Pui ("Fa"). Opening Date: September 6, 1986.

SYNOPSIS: In 1913 three women become unlikely allies during a period of civil unrest: Tsao Wan, a General's daughter who must reluctantly betray her beloved father by stealing a document he is carrying that would expose the current political regime; Sheung Hung, a greedy young musician who will happily take the revolutionaries' money without supporting their cause; and Pat Neil, daughter of the local theater owner who only wants to act in Peking Opera but is denied her dream because of her gender (no women allowed in the theater). Along with Pak Hoi, a handsome guerilla fighter, and Tung Man, a former soldier who now sides with the democrats, the women must avoid lecherous soldiers and corrupt government

Original poster for *Peking Opera Blues* (featuring, left to right, Sally Yeh, Brigitte Lin and Cherie Chung).

agents to protect the stolen document, even at the cost of their loved ones or life-long dreams.

REVIEW: *Peking Opera Blues* is often considered to be Tsui Hark's best film, and, indeed, in many respects it is the perfect, archetypal Tsui work: The leads are strong, complex women; the main setting — Peking Opera — is uniquely Chinese; the story is often comical, but with strong political overtones; the colors are rich and variegated, the camera movements fluid, the editing fast; and (most importantly of all, of course) Brigitte Lin appears in Edwardian male drag throughout the film.

That said, *Peking Opera Blues* is a difficult film to describe, because it's a film that seems to float free of the entire history of cinema, with few obvious influences; it's a film that created its own genre (the period-comedy-women's-actioner?). Its wild, multi-layered comedy scenes bear some resemblance to the American Marx Brothers comedies of the '30s (especially in the mix of verbal and physical humor — the "Peking Duck" password gag even sounds like the classic "why a duck" Marx Brothers bit), but we've never seen a Marx Brothers film that featured deeply-felt grief or rage, let alone showed scenes of graphic torture. The period setting may have been partly inspired by Jackie Chan's seminal 1983 *Project A*; but then again, *Peking Opera Blues* looks more like *Project A — Part II*, which (coincidentally?) came out in 1987, a year after *Peking* was released. Tsui may have seen Chu Ping's daffy 1984 *Golden Queen Commando* (an action film with seven female leads, two of whom were played by Brigitte Lin and Sally Yeh), but it's doubtful that he (or anyone else) thought seriously about that film past the moment it ended. The likeliest predecessors to *Peking* are Tsui's own *Shanghai Blues* and his first film, *The Butterfly Murders*, which also featured a spectacular nighttime rooftop chase.

One test of any great work of art is that it creates its own unique world, and *Peking Opera Blues* is so successful on that count that it's surprising to realize this film actually ends after only 104 minutes. It's a perfectly-realized domain of candlelit interiors and claustrophobic nighttime streets, of mansions and theaters, bloated rich and toothless poor, leeching officials and virtuous freedom fighters. In Tsui's *Peking* world, we all at some point must choose between authority (Tsao Wan's and Pat Neil's respective fathers, even Sheung Hung's lust for gold) and freedom. In contrast to the later *Once Upon a Time in China*, *Peking Opera Blues* seems relatively free of nostalgia, of yearning for the past — its protagonists are firmly dedicated to the future. Also, unlike the Wong Fei-Hung films, the characters in *Peking Opera Blues* are more concerned with the forces of evil from within, not without; Tsao Wan in particular is enamored of Western ways, and her Western geography lesson even awakens a sense of adventure within the materialistic Sheung Hung.

What *Peking Opera Blues* does share in common with *Once Upon a Time in China* is a notion of romance as something that's sweetly sensual but chaste. Pat Neil is obviously smitten with the handsome Pak Hoi, but their relationship can go no farther than the moment in which she awakens to realize she's fallen asleep on his chest, and immediately closes her eyes again, seemingly hoping to prolong her rapture. Pak Hoi, however, is drawn to Tsao Wan, but, similarly, the relationship is limited to comforting embraces. It's telling that the most sensual scene in the film is one involving only the three

women, when they get drunk together and don Tsao Wan's Western-style lingerie. Tsui seems to be suggesting that women can only find joy when in the company of other women, a strangely feminist idea that he reworks often throughout his career (*The East Is Red*, *Dragon Inn*, *Green Snake*).

While it's tempting, then, to call *Peking Opera Blues* a feminist film, such a label belies its brilliance as both a comedy and an action thriller. The carefully controlled chaotic situations that Tsui began working with in *Shanghai Blues* are integrated here into an essentially dramatic story, and one of the most astonishing things about *Peking Opera Blues* is that its occasionally extreme tone shifts work so well. Take, for example, the scene in which the corrupt "Ticketing Officer," Mr. Liu, propositions the actor Fa in the theater. After Fa's comical shock (he passes out and bumps down a flight of stairs), Liu tries to torture Fa into compliance, using a device to crush Fa's fingers. The scene is graphic and excruciating, and — impossibly — flows naturally out of the pratfall that's preceded it. Tsui wants to give his audience a roller coaster ride, and *Peking Opera Blues* manages to involve, at some point, nearly every possible human emotion. We feel grief when watching Tsao Wan cry quietly over her impending betrayal of her father, but at nearly the same time we're laughing at the onstage antics of Sheung Hung and Pat Neil, impersonating members of the theater repertory; we feel horror at the gruesome torture of Tsao Wan after she's captured by the Ticketing Officer's men, yet only a few scenes later we're cheering on the action as the women help Pak Hoi and Tung Man effect their prison escape.

Such opposing reactions would probably have been impossible to elicit had Tsui not set up his characters so well and cast them so adroitly. Sheung Hung is the first one we meet, as she plays for the Stalin-like General Tun, surrounded by his 28 wives and blithely plotting to make Sheung Hung wife number 29 while his unpaid men riot outside. Sheung Hung is greedy, lusting after the gold adorning the General and his wives, but we laugh with her as she outmaneuvers both the General and the riot in pursuit of a stolen box of jewelry. Tsao Wan is introduced as Sheung Hung is captured in the streets outside; when Tsao Wan sees the frightened woman surrounded by soldiers, she leaves her father to take over frisking Sheung Hung, whom she releases with a polite nod and smile. Last is Pat Neil, who is trying to sneak on stage with the other actors in the Peking Opera when her father catches her, forcing her to wash her face and throwing her out to cook. Within the first few minutes of the film Tsui and screenwriter To Kwok-Wai have set up three very independent characters whom we have already come to care about and like, which also means (in Tsui's typically audacious thinking) that we will accept them in any emotional context.

Not only do the emotional transitions work, but the scenes they surround are virtually textbook examples of comedy, action and suspense. *Peking Opera Blues* is probably most famous for its astonishing climax, which occurs after the protagonists, in a desperate attempt to escape the government forces closing in on them, all masquerade as actors in the onstage drama and escape through the roof of the theater. Here Tsui calls on the services of action genius Ching Siu-Tung, who will later direct both *A Chinese Ghost Story* and *Swordsman II* (among others), and *Peking*'s rooftop chase is an absolute masterpiece of Hong Kong action cinema. Bodies hurtle through the nighttime sky, thanks to Ching's wire-rigging (still fairly understated here, as compared to such later films

as *Swordsman II*); Tsui's use of slow-motion compresses and captures the action so effortlessly that we forget it's not normal time. It's exhilarating and breathless, with the sheer cinematic "ballet of violence" often associated with John Woo's later work. Tsui also knows that all great action sequences must be driven by a character, and this one is about Tsao Wan's quest to avenge her father's death; at one point when escape still seems possible, she chooses instead to turn and face the pursuing Mr. Liu. Her friends, of course, stand with her, and together they overcome and literally ride off into the sunset (*Peking*'s final scene shows the five friends on horseback, parting ways but promising to reunite at some point). *Peking*'s ending also brings the film full circle as it tells us that the document our heroes risked their lives to capture did indeed expose the evil President Yuen's conspiracy, but that he was swiftly back in power. Meanwhile, the same bold laughter that played over the opening titles scores the ending, but with fresh irony.

If *Peking Opera Blues* has any flaws, it would probably be in Tsui's occasionally "Keystone Kop"–like depiction of the government soldiers, who stumble into each other and leer broadly (a little too broadly) over displays of wealth. And the choice of music is sometimes incongruous; Tsui dispenses with the otherwise excellent score during at least one action scene in favor of American synthpop. Tsui's musical choices throughout his career have been known to promote more head scratching than resonance.

But *Peking*'s look is so dazzling that it more than compensates for the audio lapses. In 1986 John Woo, in *A Better Tomorrow*, still seemed slightly stuck in the '70s "chopsocky" mode of directing, with zooms in place of actual camera movement; but Tsui's camerawork of the same period is always assured. In *Peking Opera Blues* it's hard to spot anything that looks like a traditional master shot; most scenes are covered from several very different angles. And while Tsui has always had a painter's eye for color, he outdoes himself in *Peking Opera Blues*, taking full advantage of the colorful costumes of the actors, blending and contrasting them with the sedate grays and blacks of Tsao Wan and the military men. Most of the interiors are lit by fire, imbuing shots with a rich amber glow; as with *Shanghai Blues* and *All the Wrong Clues*, Tsui eschews the Hollywood style of comedy (flat lighting, emphasis on the performer) to present a world as richly visual as it is funny.

Although they'd worked together in *Zu: Warriors from the Magic Mountain*, *Peking Opera Blues* is the beginning of Tsui Hark's long exploration of gender identity via Brigitte Lin. Lin's Tsao Wan should be *Peking*'s dashing young male hero, with her meticulously tailored suits and youthful romantic ideals; and yet Tsui also does nothing to hide her obviously feminine beauty. She's not in disguise, no glasses or fake hairpieces, she doesn't even wear a hat; Tsao Wan herself assures her female friends that she's one of them, and only dresses that way because it tends to confuse men and made it easier to receive her Western medical training. Tsao Wan's manner of dress probably has less to do with the story of *Peking Opera Blues* than it does with a filmmaker who simply wanted to explode the usual notions of female/male; this may be the single most defining theme in the oeuvre of Tsui Hark, beginning with his very first film (the young female superhero in *The Butterfly Murders*) and continuing right on up to his most recent directorial effort (*Knock Off*, in which *uber*-hunk Jean Claude Van Damme has the stuffing beaten out of him by several different women).

*Peking Opera Blues* is also an exploration of different kinds of femininity: In addition to the crossdressing Tsao Wan, there's the completely feminine, flirtatious, giggly Sheung Hung (the comic heart of the film, thanks to Cherie Chung's delightful performance); the practical down-to-earth Pat Neil, who would rather simply knock a man out than follow the guerillas' rules and secretly drug him (this is Sally Yeh, the only holdover from *Shanghai Blues*, in another dynamic and impassioned performance — no wonder she's one of Tsui's favorite actresses); and even the actor Fa (Paul Chun, subtle and sympathetic), whose onstage portrayal of graceful womanhood so inflames the villainous Mr. Liu that Fa's actual gender seems unimportant. In fact, *Peking Opera Blues* takes one of the most nonchalant stances on homosexuality of any Hong Kong (or American, for that matter) film: The actors seem to be largely gay, as does Mr. Liu, but (with the possible exception of the theatrical troupe playfully teasing Pat Neil) there's no overt mention made of this. In the world of *Peking Opera Blues*, sex is far less important than family obligation and political responsibility.

*Peking Opera Blues*' ending — our five heroes on horseback in a rural setting, completely separate from the rest of the film's urban locale — seems slightly strange until you consider that it was meant to set up a third "Blues" film. Tsui originally intended *Shanghai Blues* and *Peking Opera Blues* to be the first and second parts of a trilogy, but unfortunately he never got around to part three. Perhaps he feared (and possibly rightly so) that the magnificent, daring *Peking Opera Blues* was simply untoppable.

ABOUT THE MOVIE: *Peking Opera Blues* took in $17,559.357, making it number 7 on the list of top-grossing Hong Kong

**Tsao Wan (Brigitte Lin) confronts the government officials over the death of her father in *Peking Opera Blues.***

films that year. It fared equally well at the 1987 Hong Kong Film Awards, where it was nominated for Best Action Choreography (Ching Siu-Tung), Best Actress (Sally Yeh), Best Art Direction (Ho Kim-Sing, Leung Chi-Hing and Vincent Wai ), Best Cinematography (Poon Hang-Sang), Best Film Editing (David Wu) and Best Supporting Actor (Paul Chun); strangely, Tsui was not nominated for Director.

Watch the end credits of *Peking Opera Blues* carefully, and you'll see a scene that was cut from the finished film of Pat Neil performing some very impressive kung fu fighting.

The film's literal title, *Knife, Horse, Dawn,* refers to the name of a type of Peking opera character. The final opera (which leads into the rooftop chase) is the classic *Eight Immortals Cross the Sea.*

TSUI ON *PEKING OPERA BLUES:* The reason I used those three characters was—

there are several reasons. One reason is that any one of them could get married and retire very easily. For that moment they are very fantastic and silly characters in the movie; probably later they would never have that chance again. Another point is at that period of time, before *A Better Tomorrow,* all of the stars in the movies are like Carl Mak, Sammo Hung, Bruce Lee — they have this kind of characteristic face. And those pretty faces, those women, were all hidden behind them. So I said, "Why don't we just make a movie with no guys, just women? And doing all male customs." I had a big problem with how do I make this believable? There's something about women in the Chinese viewpoint — when I start to go into that, I start to see women in early, early, early Chinese history. And to make a comedy of it is kind of like an unholy thought, because that period in history, those political situations, shouldn't be made fun of.

When I said a comedy, people didn't really like it at all. But I feel the only way to solve a problem is with a light heart. It's '97 syndrome stuff. The three women represent the Chinese mentality — what we have now they also had in that period. One is an adventurer, one is an artist, one is a businesswoman. Cherie Chung said, "Why do you have to make me so money crazy in the movie? Is that the way you think of me?" I said, "You are the simplest mind among the three. So — yes. Seriously — yes." I think Cherie has the simplest mind; Brigitte and Sally sometimes don't know what they're thinking.

Also, I have this thing for Peking Opera. I always thought Peking Opera was good material for a comedy, so I made use of that.

[Where did the English title come from?] The titles are created by Nansun. In *Shanghai Blues* it was because of the music. And then when it gets to *Peking Opera Blues* it's sort of like a continuation of *Shanghai Blues*. I was thinking about maybe just *Peking Opera*, but *Peking Opera Blues* was more interesting. So we added Blues to Peking Opera. Actually, there are no blues in Peking Opera at all!

## A Chinese Ghost Story

Producer, 1986. Cantonese: *Sin Nui Yau Wan*. Mandarin: *Qian Nu: You Hun*. Literally: *Sien: Female Ghost*. AKA: *Fair Maiden, Tender Spirit*. Director: Ching Siu-Tung. Screenwriter: Yuen Kai Chi. Music: Romeo Diaz, James Wong. Action Directors: Ching Siu-Tung, Kwok Chui, Lau Chi-Ho, Tsui Chung-Sun, Wu Chi-Lung. CAST: Leslie Cheung Kwok-Wing ("Ning"), Joey Wang Cho-Yin ("Hsiao-ting"), Wu Ma ("Swordsman Yen"). Opening Date: July 18, 1987.

SYNOPSIS: In China's past, Ning is an impoverished debt collector sent to a distant town where anarchy and violence hold sway. Unable to perform his tasks because his account has been ruined in a storm, Ning asks for a place to spend the night and is sent to the haunted Orchid Temple, three miles outside of town. After being chased by fierce wolves, he arrives at the Temple only to find himself caught in a battle between two mighty rival swordsmen. He manages to break up the fight but finds himself warned away from the Temple by Swordsman Yen; with no other place to go, he reluctantly stays. Outside the Temple the other swordsman, Hsia-Hou, is seduced by a beautiful woman, Nien Hsiao-Ting; however, Hsiao-Ting — who is actually a ghost — abruptly abandons Hsia-Hou to a malevolent creature that sucks him dry, reducing him to a withered corpse. Swordsman Yen finds the corpse and uses a magic spike and scroll to lay it to rest; he is unaware that poor Ning, in Orchid Temple, is about to fall prey to a band of similar desiccated zombie creatures. Ning leaves the pavilion when he hears music, and he follows the sound to a waterside pavilion, where he meets Hsiao-Ting. She tries to seduce him, but when he saves her twice (once from a snake and then from Swordsman Yen) she discontinues the fateful seduction and flees. Ning returns to the Temple — and the waiting zombies; but Ning's own clumsiness saves him, and the creatures are reduced to puddles of slime by the morning sun. The next day Ning returns to the village as a minor hero for having survived the night in the haunted temple; he tries to buy a painting he'd seen the day before, showing a lovely girl washing her hair, but the painting is now gone. He finds it again that night when he follows the sound of music to a waterside pavilion and discovers that Hsiao-Ting has taken the painting.

**British poster for *A Chinese Ghost Story*.**

When her matron appears, Hsiao-Ting hides Ning in a tub of water, and he narrowly escapes detection; while in hiding he overhears that Hsiao-Ting is betrothed to the hateful Lord Black and will be married in three days time. Smitten with her, and believing Swordsman Yen to be an escaped murderer, he tries to save her, and she realizes she has fallen for the young debt collector. They make love, and Hsiao-Ting eventually tells Ning the only way to free her spirit and give her a chance to reincarnate is to collect her ashes and take them to a clean place of burial. Then Hsiao-Ting vanishes, in an effort to save him from the clutches of the Matron, who is in actuality a 1,000-year-old tree demon. When Ning tries to turn Yen in, he finds out the swordsman is, in fact, not a criminal but a skilled Taoist exorcist. Together they take on the Matron, who transforms into an immense tongue. Yen defends them with the Sutra, a magic book, and

the Blessing Sword, an enchanted weapon. They escape and Ning begs Yen to help him retrieve and move Hsiao-Ting's ashes; the swordsman reluctantly agrees, and they dig up Hsiao-Ting's grave. They take the ashes to an inn, which they realize is haunted when they find a pot of severed heads in the kitchen. The evil spirits kidnap Hsiao-Ting and take her to hell for her marriage to Lord Black. Yen and Ning follow, and they soon find themselves battling the very hordes of hell. With Hsiao-Ting's help they finally defeat Lord Black and return to earth, where Ning and Hsiao-Ting must bid farewell to each other before her urn is reburied and she is freed to reincarnate.

REVIEW: *A Chinese Ghost Story* may be Tsui Hark's biggest global success to date (the film was released theatrically throughout Asia and Europe), and it's not hard to see why: Although it contains just enough Chinese design and content to seem

**Joey Wang as Hsiao-Ting in *A Chinese Ghost Story*.**

exotic, its story of undying love and Good vs. Evil is told in the style of an American horror film on speed. An astonishingly rich mixture of horror, humor, romance, action and special effects, *A Chinese Ghost Story* is among Tsui Hark's most crowd-pleasing pictures.

*A Chinese Ghost Story*'s plot is one part Chinese fable, two parts *Evil Dead*, and the rest pure Tsui Hark. It uses elements from several stories in Pu-Sing Ling's classic 17th century collection *Strange Stories from a Chinese Studio*, sort of the Chinese equivalent to *Grimms' Fairy Tales*. Typically in these short pieces a young scholar finds a beautiful, imperiled woman who is either a spirit or an animal in human form; the scholar saves the woman and wins her through an act of courage, kindness or skill. (Contrast this with the typical European hero, who is either a brawny woodcutter or knight who chops his way to victory.) There are even eccentric Taoist monks involved in a few of these fables. Nowhere, however, will you find immense flying tongues or androgynous harem-keeping tree demons; the former is shot in a style reminiscent of Sam

Raimi's *Evil Dead* films, while the latter is another entertaining example of Tsui Hark's obsession with the meaning of gender.

*A Chinese Ghost Story* has an uncanny ability to blend humor and horror. Its closest American counterpart is obviously Raimi's crazed-zombie series, but Raimi seems to be trying to create live-action cartoons; the broad performance of his leading man, Bruce Campbell, plays more like a parody than a counterbalance to the horror. *A Chinese Ghost Story*, on the other hand, builds its horror steadily, never letting the concurrent running humor detract from the growing dread; because the humor arises naturally, it never overwhelms the chills. *A Chinese Ghost Story* has the good-natured feel of the old-fashioned carnival spookhouse, while Raimi seems more intent on crafting a merry-go-round.

Where *A Chinese Ghost Story* is way ahead of its American counterparts is in its use of romance and sensuality. In Western horror cinema, only vampire films have displayed any real eroticism, and certainly *A Chinese Ghost Story* could be thought of as a vampire film: Its heroine can't withstand sunlight, cowers before religious objects and seduces men to their doom. But where eroticism in vampire films typically arises from a connection between blood and sex, the lyrical eroticism of *A Chinese Ghost Story* has more to do with genuine romance. While Hsiao-Ting's seduction of swordsman Hsia-Hou in the beginning of the film is certainly rife with sexual elements, it's the scenes of Ning protectively cradling Hsiao-Ting or simply falling against her that carry the strongest charge. Possibly the film's finest moment is when Hsiao-Ting pushes Ning's head underwater to hide him from her sisters, giving him a long kiss while small violet blossoms float around them; it's one of the loveliest kisses in all of modern cinema. In *The Butterfly Murders* Tsui suggested that horror could still be beautiful; here he suggests it can be beautiful and can elicit love.

*A Chinese Ghost Story* isn't content just to capture the heart and gut — it goes for the head as well, with a poignant theme about the dangers (and joys) of retreating from the real world into fantasy. The Taoist swordsman Yen initially turns down Ning's entreaty for help in moving Hsiao-Ting's ashes by telling him that he can't stand the idea of returning to the "mundane" world, that he's more comfortable with ghosts. Indeed, by setting up the outside world as a cruel, greedy place run by oppressive cops and brutal shopkeepers, we can understand Yen's point of view. But Yen has removed himself from the good parts of the outside world as well — he plainly envies the love between Ning and Hsiao-Ting. Tsui and Ching have created a great fantasy film that is simultaneously a warning against the dangers of fantasy; they ultimately suggest that, like Ning, we must learn to revere and love our fantasies without living for them.

While much of *A Chinese Ghost Story*'s pacing and genre-crossing is certainly due to its director and producer, a considerable amount of credit must also go to its stars, especially Leslie Cheung. Cheung — known to Western audiences mainly for his work in the dramas of mainland China director Chen Kaige — is one of Hong Kong cinema's most versatile and likable actors. Cheung's range has always been astonishing — he seems to move effortlessly between comedy and tragedy, drama and action film, romantic leading man to gay lover, naïve to world-weary; his work always seems so effortless that it's easy to overlook the art that goes into it.

In *A Chinese Ghost Story* he is required to hold long stretches of the film entirely on his own — witness his night in the Orchid Temple near the film's beginning — and that he manages to do so without his performance seeming the least bit narcissistic is a tremendous credit to him. His Ning is idealistic without being naïve, clumsy without being foolish, romantic without being maudlin, and frightened without being weak; it's easy to see why Hsiao-Ting would fall for him.

And vice versa, with Joey Wang's performance as Hsiao-Ting being one of the loveliest in any Hong Kong film. Her use of stylized, almost Peking Opera–ish gestures works tremendously well, giving Hsiao-Ting the feel of an elegant, classic character. She handles the physical requirements of the role well (meaning she looks poised in Ching's wire rigs!) and conveys Hsiao-Ting's regret perfectly; it's no wonder she became Tsui's ideal tragic heroine in such later films as *Green Snake* and *The East Is Red*.

And then there's Wu Ma, who may have the best character of his career in swordsman Yen. Wu turns Yen into a melancholy wildman, a brilliant but morose exorcist who would rather dance drunk alone in the forest than deal with another human being. In any other film Wu would be the aged sage, the Father Merrin or Don Corleone character, doling out wisdom and valor; here he seems to alternate between being arrogant and pathetic. It isn't until the end that he becomes a true hero, sacrificing his own desire for solitude to help Ning and Hsiao-Ting; in Wu's splendid, fierce performance he is a warrior reborn.

Wu's rebirth is aided considerably by the film's gorgeous special effects. Indeed, *A Chinese Ghost Story* may boast the best effects of any Tsui Hark film. The optical effects, which include lovely matte shots of the town, making it seem like it's filled with towering pagodas, and a magical gateway to hell, are impressive, but it's the physical effects that really dazzle. Whether it's the Matron's endlessly-long tongue or Yen chasing Hsiao-Ting in mid-air through the treetops, the physical effects are flawless. Ching's direction shows them off to perfect advantage; he favors low angles, canted angles and travelling shots, all of which help to establish the film's pace and off-kilter approach.

Only in one sequence does *A Chinese Ghost Story* falter — that's a scene in which Ning rushes into an official court, believing swordsman Yen to be a wanted killer. The scene is fairly long and seems completely divorced from the rest of the film, bereft of any supernatural or romantic elements whatsoever. In fact, it seems so pointless that it's hard to understand why it was left in the film.

But before long *A Chinese Ghost Story* is back on track, literally taking us to hell for its climax. At this point Tsui and Ching dispense with the humor to focus on the action and the chills, and the confrontation with Lord Black is a hugely satisfying mix of effects, action, heroism and love. Despite the brief, bittersweet epilogue — Hsiao-Ting and Ning must be parted so she can be reincarnated — the film still concludes with a sense of excitement and leaves audiences wanting more — which they got via two sequels and an animated version.

**ABOUT THE MOVIE:** *A Chinese Ghost Story* performed well financially, placing number 15 on the year's box office list and taking in $18,831,638. It also performed well at the year's Hong Kong Film Awards, where it received nominations for Best Picture, Best Director (Ching Siu-Tung), Best Actress (Joey Wang), Best Supporting Actor (Wu Ma), Best Cinematography (Poon Hang-Sang, Lee Ka Ko, Lau Moon Tong, Wong Wing Hang), Best Action Choreography (Ching Siu Tong, Kwok Chui, Lau Chi-Ho, Tsui Chung-Sun, Wu Chi Lung) and Best Film Editing (SNS Group); it won for Best Art Direction (Yee Chung-Man), Best Original Film Score (Romeo Diaz and James Wong) and Best Original Film Song (it was actually nominated three times in this category). This makes *A Chinese Ghost Story* the most nominated film in Tsui Hark's career (it beats out *A Better Tomorrow* by one); it is second only to *Once Upon a Time in China* as the film which won the most awards. It also picked up four awards at 1987's Taiwanese Golden Horse Awards and five awards at the First Hong Kong Directors Guild Awards.

*A Chinese Ghost Story* also gained international recognition, winning the special Jury Prize at the Avoriaz festival in France, and the Best Film Award at the Opporto Festival in Portugal that same year.

Tsui had been interested in making *A Chinese Ghost Story* as early as 1978, when he suggested it for television production at TVB, but the producers there felt it was not suitable for television. In "A Magical Witch's Brew: *A Chinese Ghost Story*" (from *Fifty Years of Electric Shadows*) Sam Ho suggests that Tsui at least partly modeled the film on *The Enchanting Shadow* (1960).

*A Chinese Ghost Story* has withstood the test of time well. In Sam Ho's above-mentioned article (from 1997) he suggests that *A Chinese Ghost Story* is the link between the popular kung fu comic horror films of the '80s (*Encounters of the Spooky Kind, Mr. Vampire*) and the later epic fantasy films (*The Bride with White Hair, The East Is Red*). Ho said the film "is the crystallization of the industry's technical maturity, rich genre traditions, an intimate rapport between filmmakers and its audiences and, finally, the visionary zeal of an artist... it is no doubt the sign of a system that had come of age."

Tsui on *A Chinese Ghost Story:* Ching Siu-Tung wanted to do something with me. I said, "Let's do *A Chinese Ghost Story.*" He said, "What's it about?" "It's a love story." "Love story? I just did a love story, it didn't work." "It's not romantic enough — let's do a *romantic* love story. A ghost story." "Come on, a ghost story... everybody's looking for horror in a ghost story, they're not looking for romance in a ghost story." "Ah — let's do a romantic non-horror ghost story." Then one day one of the guys at the higher level talked to me and said, "We have a great story for *Chinese Ghost Story.*" I said, "Actually *Chinese Ghost Story* is adapted from a book." "No, no, this story is about a cop woman who blah blah blah..." I said, "I tell you, this is a period piece, there won't be a cop or anything like that." He said, "Period piece?! How can you do a period piece now? A period piece will never sell." I said, "Well, think about it. Maybe it's fun to watch a period piece."

So we started making the movie, and no one knew what it was going to look like, even Ching Siu-Tung, because he had just done another one. It was not a very successful movie, he was scared of a love story. So right from the beginning he said, "Ah, great — let's do a horror movie."

[On the adaptation]: We changed so much to fit our drama. We found out later that the story is pretty much against our interpretation. We changed so much that it didn't end up looking like the story.

[On the score]: James Wong had actually been around for a long time. He was writing songs for singers — pop songs, TV theme songs. The first movie he did the music for was *Shanghai Blues.* He just did the song and a bit of the music. The movie

that he actually worked on as the first one would be *A Chinese Ghost Story.* I think at that period of time he didn't even know how long it took to make a piece of music for the movie, and how much music to put into the movie. We argue a lot. Sometimes it's things like there should music there, or music there. It's a very strange kind of relationship. But on *A Chinese Ghost Story* it was really fun for him, and for me, too.

[On directing any of the films in this series]: Actually, I was thinking of doing all of them!

## *Once Upon a Time in China*

Director/Producer/Writer, 1991. Cantonese: *Wong Fei Hung.* Mandarin: *Huang Fei Hong.* Co-Writers: Yuen Kai Chi, Leung Yiu Ming, Dang Bik Yin. Cinematography: David Chung, Bill Wong, Chan Tung-Chuen, Arthur Wong, Angy Lam, Tung-Chuen, Wilson Chan. Art Direction: Yee Chung-Man. Action Design: Yuen Cheung-Yan, Yuen Shun Yee, Lau Ka-Wing, Bruce Law. Editing: Mak Chi Sin. Music Score: James Wong. Cast: Jet Li ("Wong Fei-Hung"), Rosamund Kwan ("Aunt Yee"), Yuen Biao ("Fu"), Jacky Cheung ("Bucktooth Sol"), Kent Cheng ("Porky Lang"), Yan Yee Kwan ("Iron Robe Yim"), Wu Ma ("Uncle"). Opening Date: August 15, 1991.

Synopsis: Wong Fei-Hung is a nineteenth-century martial artist and physician who is asked by a departing commander to organize his men into a local militia in order to protect the native Chinese from foreign invaders. Assisted by the virtuous and adoring Aunt Yee, the faithful Lee, the Western-educated "Bucktooth" Sol and the feisty "Porky," Wong fights off

**Poster for *Once Upon a Time in China*.**

rival kung fu master "Iron Robe" Yim while protecting the town from an extorting local gang and vicious American slave traders. Wong must also decide between his firm belief in Chinese traditions and the need to understand Western progress.

REVIEW: *Once Upon a Time in China* is usually considered one of the two best films Tsui Hark has directed (the other being *Peking Opera Blues*), and the film which virtually re-created the dying kung fu genre. Although Jackie Chan had already done that once in the late '70s and early '80s by taking the genre in a comic direction (one of his biggest hits, *Drunken Master*, also centered on real-life folk hero Wong Fei-Hung), it took Tsui Hark to remake it as a legitimate, serious art form. In the process he created one of the greatest films to ever celebrate Chinese nationalism (a theme Jackie would later borrow for his *Drunken Master II*).

*Once Upon a Time in China* is a stunning achievement on any level. Aside from the beautifully paced and emotionally rich script, Tsui assembled one of the finest casts ever to grace a Hong Kong film; and his quest for visual perfection led him through six different cinematographers (it's to Tsui's credit that the film has a completely unified look). Add to that a lovely romance and some of the most spectacular kung fu ever caught on film, and you end up with that rarest of hybrids: the art film that's also massively entertaining.

Tsui sets up his main theme even before the opening credits, when Wong takes over a dragon dance after the original dancers are accidentally shot at by French sailors. Wong is more concerned with completing the dance than wreaking vengeance; what's most important to him is that the dragon not be allowed to fall because of *gweilo* intervention. After Wong completes the dance and agrees to train the

departing commander's men into a local militia, main titles roll over an exquisite montage of Wong leading the troops through their moves on a beach at sunrise. The final shot of the credit sequence is an audacious—and wholly successful—attempt to establish a new icon for China: Wong Fei-Hung, robes blowing in the wind, standing proudly before a fiery sky.

Now that Tsui has introduced the hero who will protect China from foreign intervention, he next brings on the character who will cause Wong to question and finally alter his position: Aunt Yee, who has been travelling for some time and has acquired certain Western ways. She dresses like a proper Victorian woman, carries a box camera and has American friends; her Westernization is so effective, in fact, that she's at first mistaken by one lead character for a *gweilo*. Yee tries to tell Wong that China must change, that it must open itself to some Western advances—or be crushed. And although Wong initially dismisses her arguments, he will finally succumb to her logic.

It's also worth noting that Tsui depicts Yee and Wong's budding romance as shadow play; in one exquisite sequence, Yee, who is hopelessly smitten by Wong, tenderly strokes his shadow while he remains oblivious. Thus Tsui makes the metaphorical nature of his two lead characters paradoxically bright: The "shadow play" of ideas, of old vs. new, tradition vs. progress (Wong himself finally puts the conflict into the form of "kung fu vs. bullets").

Tsui also swiftly lines up his delightful cast of supporting characters. At Wong's clinic (he is, after all, a healer) we meet Wong's disciples: "Bucktooth" Sol (Jacky Cheung, almost unrecognizable in fake teeth and glasses), who has trained in Western medical techniques and splutters helplessly when trying to speak his native tongue — although he has no problem with English; Fu (the always-energetic Yuen Biao), the country boy who can't decide between kung fu and Peking Opera; "Porky" Lang (Kent Cheng), the butcher who doesn't see the point of knowing kung fu if you can't get into a good fight from time to time; and Lee, the usually practical assistant who, like Lang, also wants to see some combat.

Two other supporting characters worth mentioning embody another theme that will appear in virtually all of the *Once Upon a Time in China* movies: the Chinese who betrays his own people by selling out to the *gweilos*. In this first film it's both the gangster who extorts protection money and sells slaves to the Americans, and Master "Iron Robe" Yim, the penniless kung fu master who takes money from the foreigners to destroy Wong. Yim is first seen in a particularly beautiful visual metaphor: After he performs a feat of strength for money, he carefully retrieves each coin from the rain-sodden street but ignores a lovely flower. Later, Yim's repentance will come when he must again pick up dropped coins, but this time in front of a gang of mocking gangsters. Yim, of course, must finally pay the ultimate price for not following the Chinese way.

No sooner has Tsui set up his major themes and characters than he launches straight into the action: While Wong, Sol and Lee lunch with the Americans and the French in a posh *gweilo* restaurant, Fu runs afoul of the local gangsters and seeks Lang's help. Within seconds a fight breaks out which covers seemingly every inch of the city, from shore to crowded alley, and gives Tsui a chance to show off Yuen Biao at his acrobatic best, as he flips, leaps and swings over his opponents. Finally, the combatants crash through the windows of the very restaurant where Wong is dining,

and although Wong eventually quells the fight, the *gweilos* (and the steadfast but misguided local police) blame the fight on Wong. Dispirited, Wong and his men are confined to Wong's clinic; for the first time Wong questions his own resistance to Western ways. Wong is even more disillusioned when he catches the gangsters in their extortion routine but can't find anyone to testify against them. After the gangsters are unable to kill Wong themselves (although they do manage to destroy most of his clinic), they make a fiendish deal with the American corporation: They'll supply women for the Americans' Chinese slave-laborers if the Americans will dispose of Wong. In one of the film's blackest jokes, the Americans set up an assassination attempt in a theater (remember, this is the nineteenth century, presumably not long after Lincoln's death in a theater); although the attempt fails, Wong and Yee witness the deaths of many Chinese, shot by the Americans who panic at the prospect of a riot. Tsui lingers on the scene, his camera capturing both the horror itself and the horrified reactions of Yee and Wong. Although the slow-motion massacre brings to mind both Sam Peckinpah and Akira Kurosawa, the scene is still powerful and uniquely Tsui.

After Yee is captured by the gangsters and her virtue threatened, Wong finally puts his principles of pacifism aside and launches into a full-scale attack. Although it's easy to see this as yet another variation of the age-old "hero rescues the damsel in the nick of time" trope, Tsui gives it his own spin by having the captive women wreak their own vengeance on their captor: They push him into a furnace. And then it remains to Wong Fei-Hung to find a way to balance kung fu and bullets: Wong finally defeats the ultimate American villain (curiously named "Jackson") by using his bare fingers to snap a bullet into the

**Jet Li and Rosamund Kwan as Wong Fei-Hung and Aunt Yee in *Once Upon a Time in China*.**

man's head. Although the scene veers perilously close to fantasy—such an act is really not possible, is it?—the metaphor is obvious and made even more plain by the last shot: Wong, in full Western suit, poses with Yee for a photo. Wong Fei-Hung has learned at last to step into the future—and is bringing China with him.

*Once Upon a Time in China* also contains one of the most justifiably famous fight scenes in all of Hong Kong cinema, as Wong finally battles it out with Yim in a dockside warehouse. The fight is conducted mainly atop ladders, which the two men use at various points as stilts, levers and weapons. It's almost less a true fight scene and more an extended sequence of pure cinematic kineticism, movement for its own glorious sake (in *Planet Hong Kong: Popular Cinema and the Art of Entertainment*, David Bordwell notes that this fight alone consists of nearly 300 different shots). Even the whipping motion of the

combatants' long hair becomes crucial, especially when Wong realizes that Yim's hides a treacherous blade. It's a stunning display of directorial virtuosity and certainly one of the best action sequences in Tsui Hark's oeuvre.

*Once Upon a Time in China* made Jet Li into a Hong Kong superstar, and it's easy to see why: If Sean Connery was THE James Bond, then Jet Li is equally THE Wong Fei-Hung. Li's innate mix of stoicism and intensity, toughness and tenderness brings what could easily have been a comic-book superhero to witty and wonderful life. And, of course, there's Li's astonishing physical grace and agility; Jackie Chan's Wong Fei-Hung might be more acrobatic, but it's hard to imagine anyone else pulling off Li's two-footed kicks, sideways rolls and fearsome punches with his precision. And then there's that chemistry with Rosamund Kwan's Aunt Yee; is there another couple in all of cinema that radiates so much heat with so little obvious fire? Even though Kwan is far more feminine than the Tsui Hark women of other films, she still has more feistiness and Machiavellian guile than a dozen heroines in *gweilo* films (when she gets angry at Wong she dresses like a true Chinese — Chinese man, that is — just to spite him).

It's undoubtedly partly due to this superb cast that *Once Upon a Time in China* seems to have marked a turning point in Tsui's visual style. The lightning-fast, occasionally choppy cutting of earlier films now gives way to a more assured pace, as if Tsui were confident about letting his actors create movement within the frame instead of constantly moving the frame itself. The new style — which became even more marked in such later films as *Green Snake* and *The Lovers*–works in Tsui's favor, allowing him the time to explore more diverse and complex emotions.

*Once Upon a Time in China* also marks a welcome new direction in Tsui's use of music. Scored by James Wong, it's the first time Tsui seems to have been confident enough in the original score to not rely on any "temp tracks" or music not belonging to the score (i.e., the American action film synthpop that breaks into *Peking Opera Blues'* score at one point). This soundtrack is one rich with traditional instrumentation and themes, and boasting a bold male chorus (in almost comical opposition to the strictly female vocals the same composer would later use in his scintillating *Green Snake* score).

Although *Once Upon a Time in China* remains unknown to most Western audiences (undoubtedly due to its less-than-favorable depiction of Westerners as largely villainous slave traders and assassins), it's a magnificent epic that deserves its own place in cinematic history — regardless of who the good guys and bad guys are.

ABOUT THE MOVIE: *Once Upon a Time in China* was a smash hit, coming in at number 8 on the year's box office list (one mark above James Cameron's *Terminator 2: Judgment Day*), with a gross of $29,672,278.

At the 1992 Hong Kong Film Awards, *Once Upon a Time in China* won Best Action Choreography (Yuen Cheung-Yan, Yuen Shun-Yee and Lau Ka-Wing), Best Director (Tsui Hark), Best Film Editing (Mak Chi Sin, who was also nominated for *A Chinese Ghost Story III*) and Best Original Film Score (James Wong, likewise nominated for *A Chinese Ghost Story III*). It was nominated for Best Art Direction (Yee Chung-Man, who won for *Saviour of the Soul*), Best Cinematography (David Chung Chi-Man, Bill Wong, Arthur Wong, Angy Lam, Chan Tung-Chuen and Wilson Chan), Best Picture and Best Supporting Actor (Jacky Cheung).

There's really only one way to see *Once Upon a Time in China* (unless you're lucky enough to catch it on a big screen), and that's on the Media Asia DVD. Astonishingly enough, this is both the only official release which is subtitled and also the only release which contains the complete film; at 128 minutes, it's considerably cut on both VHS and laserdisc (the VCD is probably a safe bet, though). In fact — as unbelievable as this sounds — on tape and laserdisc the entire ladder fight sequence between Yim and Wong is gone. Don't be tempted by that bootleg VHS at the convention or the cheap rental copy — aside from the bad quality, you'll miss one of the great fights in modern cinema. The DVD also includes trailers, a section about the film and a superb booklet on Wong Fei-Hung written by *Hong Kong Action Cinema* author Bey Logan. Both the transfer and the subtitling are excellent.

TSUI ON *ONCE UPON A TIME IN CHINA*: I always have this problem of getting

**Wong Fei-Hung (Jet Li) leads the Lion Dance in *Once Upon a Time in China.***

attached to the background of a story. For the flow of the story or the flow of the drama there's a stop sign there. Every time I look at [*Once Upon a Time in China*], it doesn't really come from one point or the other; it sort of stops dead, hangs around. I was too much into the visual stuff, so it just sort of hangs around, it doesn't really flow. It's only my pattern, my style of storytelling that I want to change — it always took me three reels, four reels, to establish something like that. There's some more about the characters I'd like to create. I could get into a more interesting style of the characters.

[Does Aunt Yee represent Tsui's viewpoint?] I think everybody in the movie is part of me. The thing about Wong Fei-Hung is he's always this kind of male family leader. So when I put a woman character into the story, I set her up so she doesn't belong to the family. And it's fun to see someone who doesn't belong to the family giving advice, giving some sort of suggestion to whatever happens to them.

I was kind of hesitant to have Rosamund become the victim of a kidnap in the end of the story, but that was the natural direction that the story moved, because if it's not so, then I think the romance between the guy and Rosamund doesn't really come about in the end.

I think it's fun to pull back the perspective and see what the characters really are. The woman doesn't belong to that era; she comes in telling them they are outdated, they don't know what's going on in the future. It's a bit sad in a way, but it's also fun to have to tell them that a gun is more powerful than crane style or tiger style. I always wanted a character coming in to tell him he was outdated, but because it's a woman I think it's even more interesting. It could be a guy, you know!

[Why was *Once Upon a Time in China* cut so badly for its laserdisc release?] I don't know. I was very frustrated because originally it was a 120-minute film, and they wanted me to cut it to a 90-minute film. So I was very frustrated at the beginning, and I told them I would try to cut it as much as possible, so I cut it to a 90-minute film. And later I found out that they sold it to laserdisc, and they made it into a 120-minute film. And the music and everything was kind of weird. In another case they tried to make it into a Dolby system and all that sound went totally different. So I was a bit frustrated. I said, "If you want to do that, let me do it!"

In an interview with Ange Hwang for *Asian Cinema*, Vol. 10, No. 1, Fall 1998, Tsui explained the choice of setting for *Once Upon a Time in China*: "One of the biggest obstacles I had was that I studied in Hong Kong. For the last 20 years we studied under the colonial education system. Because of Taiwan and mainland China, we, as students, were discouraged from knowing too much about modern history. Maybe it's because of the colonial way of governing which involves controlling the upcoming generation's thinking… I decided that if I had the chance, I would link Wong Fei-Hung with every incident in the modern history of China. That's why when it was time to decide the English title for the film, I thought, why don't we call it *Once Upon a Time in China* just to imply that actually *Once Upon a Time in China* can be now, can be the future."

## Once Upon a Time in China II

Producer/Director/Writer, 1991. Cantonese: *Wong Fei Hung Ji Yi: Naam Yi Dong Ji Keung*. Mandarin: *Huang Fei Hong Zhi Er: Nan Er Dang Zi Qiang*. Literally: *Wong Fei Hong 2: Man Should Be Self Sufficient*.

Action Director: Yuen Wo-Ping. CAST: Jet Li Lian-Jie ("Wong Fei-Hung"), Max Mok Siu-Chung ("Foon"), Rosamund Kwan Chi-Lam ("Aunt Yee"), Donnie Yen Ji-Dan ("Lan"), David Chiang [Keung Dai-Wai] ("Luke"), Xiong Xin-Xin [Hung Yan-Yan] ("Priest Kung"), Paul Fonoroff ("British Consul"), Yan Yee Kwan ("Governor"). Opening Date: April 16, 1992.

SYNOPSIS: The film opens in 1895 in Canton, with the White Lotus cult, who believe the ancient Chinese gods have granted them powers that have made them invulnerable: They can't be cut by blades, they can swallow burning embers without being scorched, and their leader, Priest Kung, is impervious to bullets. They are dedicated to eradicating China's foreign invaders, and are even shown burning a Dalmatian dog as part of their ritual, believing it to be diseased. Cut to Wong Fei-Hung, who is heading for a doctor's convention in Canton with Aunt Yee and his new assistant, Foon. Wong's attitude is now markedly different from the beginning of the first film; he's genuinely interested in trying the Western food, even if he finds it uncomfortable to eat aboard the moving train. The trio arrives in Canton to find the city in chaos; China has just lost Taiwan to Japan, and the country is ruled by dissension. Aunt Yee's Western-style clothing instantly marks her as a target for the White Lotus members; when she makes the mistake of trying to photograph a White Lotus ritual, she and Foon are nearly torn apart by the angry crowd. Wong Fei-Hung appears at the last moment, fighting off the vicious White Lotus members and rescuing Foon and Aunt Yee. The next day Wong addresses a gathering of Western doctors on the uses of acupuncture. His demonstration is met with bewilderment until a man steps up to translate for him: The man is Dr. Sun Yat

Sen, the actual historical figure who, in 1911, led the overthrow of the Qing Dynasty and the founding of the Provisional Republican Government. Although Wong doesn't know it yet, he and Dr. Sun will cross paths again, forming a friendship that will change history. Wong's newly-translated demonstration is finally rewarded by applause — and cut short by the White Lotus' flaming arrows. Wong, Sun and Foon barely escape the massacre, which signals the beginning of major civil unrest in Canton: While a blind old man plays a traditional ballad on the erhu (a two-stringed Chinese violin), riots erupt, rebels attempt to destroy the Telegraph Office and the British flag is burned. Wong, worried about Aunt Yee, tries to teach her some kung fu, but she only learns one move ("Grappling Hand") before losing herself in romantic fantasies about Wong. Meanwhile, Canton's police, headed by the righteous Lan, are worried that they don't have enough men to keep the peace; but when they request reinforcements they find out the Governor is more worried about tracking down Sun Yat Sen and his assistant Luke, believing them to be revolutionaries. Wong, Foon and Aunt Yee try to leave Canton the next morning but are delayed by the discovery of a troop of abandoned children whose school has been destroyed by White Lotus. Wong goes to Lan, begging for assistance, but Lan's hands are tied, so Aunt Yee and Foon finally take the hapless young students to the British Consulate for protection. White Lotus wants to take the Consulate, and Lan cuts off their lines of communication, in the belief that they're harboring Sun Yat Sen (they are). Finally, White Lotus attacks the consul, and Lan takes advantage of the situation to kill the British Consulate himself; unfortunately, the act has been witnessed by Wong Fei-Hung. Wong finally decides to take the battle to

**Wong Fei-Hung (Jet Li) takes on the White Lotus Society in *Once Upon a Time in China II*.**

the White Lotus sect itself; he and Luke enter their temple, where Wong fights off the members and laughs at their idols. Priest Kung emerges to fight Wong and is finally killed when he is flung against the upturned hand of the cult's idol. Wong and Luke try to escape Canton now — they have a name book which must reach Sun Yat Sen at the docks by seven — but they're caught by Lan and his men. Luke is killed, barely managing to burn the name book in time and begging Wong to get an important piece of cloth to Sun; Wong takes on Lan in a battle that goes from a huge storage house to a narrow outside alley. Finally, Wong finishes Lan, and he and Foon head for the docks, where they arrive just in time to see the boat with Aunt Yee and Sun Yat Sen pushing off. Aunt Yee uses "Grappling Hand" to protect Sun from a soldier, and Wong hurls him the piece of cloth, which turns out to be a flag. Foon and Wong Fei-hung promise to meet Aunt Yee at the other end of her journey.

REVIEW: One of the biggest rules in Hong Kong cinema is that a successful film will beget sequels; often the sequels are rushed into production with little thought given to their scripts. They tend to be either essentially remakes of the first film (*Aces Go Places 2*), or expand on the more extreme elements of the first film, under the "bigger is better" theory (*A Better Tomorrow II, A Chinese Ghost Story II*).

Well, happily, *Once Upon a Time in China II* is that rarest of creatures, a sequel that neither recreates the first film nor expands on the wrong qualities. It manages the nearly-impossible feat of continuing the first film's themes and historical setting within the context of a completely new story; and, in an even more impressive accomplishment, it almost completely reverses its hero's moral stance from the first film. It is, to be blunt, an absolutely brilliant sequel to a brilliant first film.

It begins by introducing us to the fearsome White Lotus sect, in a prologue that is exciting and just a little eerie, with a hint of the supernatural. This prologue ends as a young girl within the sect smiles directly into the camera while it pulls up and away from her. The shot is an audacious one, breaking the filmic fourth wall in a drama; yet it works perfectly to establish a sense of dread where the White Lotus sect is concerned. After all, they now seem to be coming for *us*.

After a brief comedic scene aboard the train (which sets up the humorous interplay between Aunt Yee, Foon and Wong), the action resumes when Wong and White Lotus meet for the first time. The scene is almost free of wire-rigging, allowing Jet Li to fully display his astonishing skills. It's from this sequence that one of the most famous martial arts photos of all time is derived — a low-angle shot of Wong standing ready, dressed in gleaming white.

Shortly thereafter Tsui inserts a montage showing the chaos all around Canton. The sequence is most interesting in revealing more about Hong Kong in 1997 than Canton in 1895: A British flag is burned while an old man plays a traditional ballad. Although the sequence is exhilarating, it also betrays anxiety towards the then-coming 1997 handover (an anxiety which was fortunately nullified in the peace that actually followed).

As the White Lotus sect rampages through town, Wong finds himself fighting on the side of the foreigners, first to protect a group of students from a foreign-language school, then to defend the British Consulate. In the first film Wong was so deadset against foreign intervention that he at first refused to even be measured for a Western suit; now he's fighting on their side — in the same film that offers a compelling image of a British flag in flames. Likewise, there's no "Jackson" (the *gweilo* bully from the first film) in *Once Upon a Time in China II*; instead, the foreigners are all victims who try to operate within the Chinese culture with understanding. Wong — who has seen immense prejudice and hatred perpetrated against Aunt Yee just because of her clothing — now accepts that ideologies are the true evils, not those oppressed by said ideologies. By extension, Tsui is telling us that while the 1997 handover would spell the end of British colonialism and the return to Chinese nationalism, it would be disastrous to use it to attack individuals simply because of their color or citizenship. *Once Upon a Time in China II* may well be one of the most compassionate action films ever made.

And what an action film it is. If *Once Upon a Time in China* recreated the martial arts film, then Part Two nearly re-recreates it. The action choreography by Yuen Wo-Ping makes excellent use of the abilities of its two leads, Jet Li and Donnie Yen; their workout battle is an outstanding early example, as Wong Fei-Hung visits Lan merely to ask for assistance and ends up dueling with the policeman in a battle that becomes too intense to be simple training. Tsui's direction is particularly outstanding here; his camera follows the combatants as they move right, then left. He never loses the screen direction and follows every move with crystal clarity, occasionally pausing long enough for a close-up of Lan. Yen's performance is superb in two regards: his physicality and his intensity. Those close-ups reveal that he takes his contest with Wong a little too seriously; we understand that these men — who are both on the side of justice — must eventually fight to the death, and we understand it for no other reason than Donnie Yen's face in the first confrontation with Wong.

If *Once Upon a Time in China II* is missing anything from Part I, it would be the stunning supporting cast; Wong felt like part of a family in the first film, surrounded as he was by Porky, Sol and the rest. But *Once Upon a Time in China II* also has better villains than Part I; aside from Lan (who can barely be called a villain), there's Priest Kung, the arrogant, fierce head of the White Lotus sect. Xiong Xin-Xin endows Kung with such awesome ferocity that a motion picture frame can barely contain him. His fight with Wong in the temple is one of the film's high points, and is the only sequence that makes considerable use of wire-rigging, as Wong and Kung battle atop a teetering collection of tables. The wire-rigging lends the scene a slight fantasy feel, which is shattered when Wong rips Kung's top aside to reveal the source of his ability to withstand bullets: A metal plate. In a macabre moment of visual irony, Kung dies when pierced by a finger of the sect's idol, while his followers nearly convulse with fear and confusion. Once again, ideology is the evil—even though Kung is evil himself, without the ideology of the White Lotus cult he would be nothing but a lone bully.

As good as the villains are, the heroes are every bit as fine. Jet Li gets the opportunity to add some new layers of moral understanding to Wong, especially in the scene in which he takes on Kung and the White Lotus sect—he becomes frightening himself as he mocks their belief in their gods, bursting into nearly-demonic laughter. He and Rosamund Kwan also shine in the film's most touching moment, when Wong calls Aunt Yee by her name (Sin-Qun) for the first time. Max Mok is a delightful addition as Foon, the comic relief for Wong's intensity; he may not be as acrobatic as Yuen Biao was in the earlier film, but he has his own endearing style, especially when mooning over Aunt Yee.

Rosamund Kwan isn't quite as involved in Part II as she was in Part I, but it is worth noting that she gets in the film's final blow (when she uses Grappling Hand against the soldier who is about to arrest Sun Yat Sen). Only in the cinema of Tsui Hark would a martial arts epic conclude with its heroine—rather than its hero—delivering the coup de grace.

**ABOUT THE MOVIE:** *Once Upon a Time in China II* may not have performed quite as well as Part One at the box office, but it placed a respectable number 12 in the year, with a gross of $30,399,676. It was also well recognized at the year's Hong Kong Film Awards, where it actually received more nominations than its ancestor (nine, as compared to the first film's eight). Nominations were awarded for Best Picture, Best Director (Tsui Hark), Best Supporting Actor (Donnie Yen), Best New Performer (Xiong Xin-Xin), Best Cinematography (Arthur Wong), Best Art Direction (Ma Poon-Chiu), Best Film Editing (Mak Chi Sin, who was also nominated this year for Tsui's *Swordsman II*) and Best Original Film Score (Richard Yuen, Johnny Njo); it won for Best Action Choreography (Yuen Wo-Ping). It's worth noting that Tsui ruled the 1992 Hong Kong Film Awards, with an astounding 21 total nominations (the other Tsui Hark produced/directed films to be nominated that year were *Swordsman II*, *Dragon Inn* and *King of Chess*).

**TSUI ON *ONCE UPON A TIME IN CHINA II*:** The camera is nice because it has so many things attached to the meaning of it—modernism, technology, science and also something to register how they are living. And it's good for the acceptance part of it — eventually they accept that. I think it's good to register that acceptance thing as the camera.

## *Swordsman II*

Producer/Writer, 1992. Cantonese: *Siu Ngo Kong Woo II Dung Fong Bat Baai.* Mandarin: *Xiao Ao Jiang Hu II Dong Fang Bu Bai.* Literally: *Laughing and Proud Warrior: Invincible Asia.* Director: Ching Siu-Tung. Co-Writers: Chan Tin Suen, Dang Bik-Yin. Cinematography: Lau Moon Tong. Action Design: Ching Siu-Tung, Yuen Bun, Ma Yuk Shing, Cheung Yiu Sing. Editing: Mak Chi Sin. Music Score: Yuen Cheuk Faan. CAST: Brigitte Lin Ching Hsia ("Asia the Invincible"), Jet Li ("Ling"), Rosamund Kwan ("Ying"), Michelle Reis ("Kiddo"), Waise Lee ("Hattori"), Lau Shun, Fennie Yuen ("Blue Phoenix"), Yan Yee Kwan ("Master Wu"). Opening Date: June 26, 1992.

SYNOPSIS: During the Ming Dynasty, Ling, his young female friend Kiddo and their clan "brothers" are a group of martial artists who are on their way home to retire in peace and seclusion. On the way home they stop at an inn to see Ling's beloved, Ying, and discover that Ying's clan, the Sun Moon Sect, has split into warring factions. Ying's father, Master Wu, has been captured and imprisoned by Asia the Invincible, a super-warrior who has castrated himself to achieve ultimate kung fu power. Ling finds himself attracted to Asia, who has transformed into a beautiful woman; but it isn't until the ultimate battle between Wu's forces and Asia's Japanese allies that Ling realizes the mysterious Asia is his nemesis. In the final fight

Ling must choose between saving Asia or protecting Ying and Kiddo.

REVIEW: One man is torn to pieces, a eunuch's head is severed, a battleship is destroyed, two men race while running three feet above the ground, a man risks his life to protect his wine gourd and a horse is split perfectly in half — all in the first seven minutes. If that doesn't convince you that *Swordsman II* is one of the most giddily demented films ever made, the next 100 minutes certainly will. This is gonzo filmmaking, with a complexity of vision and a surety of skill that are continually jaw-dropping.

After helping to craft the screenplay, Tsui chose to hand the directorial reins over to his frequent collaborator Ching Siu-Tung, but there's never any doubt that this is a Tsui Hark film. *Swordsman II* continues and expands Tsui's preoccupation with gender identity in ways that no other filmmaker on earth would even dream of. In fact, it's safe to say that *Swordsman II* is one of the most non-traditional martial arts films ever made (which is particularly unusual considering that the first film was a fairly staid entry in the genre). First, there's the narrative structure: Although there is a plot (Ling and his brothers must choose between helping to defeat the evil Asia or pursuing their retirement), the film is really more interested in turning plot clichés upside-down. If *Peking Opera Blues* was an emotional roller coaster, then *Swordsman II* is a moral Tilt-a-Whirl: The hero is an unrepentant, likable "alcoholic womanizer" (as one friend refers to Ling); the villain is standing up for an oppressed clan; men become women (Asia), and women become like men (Kiddo, whose own brothers refer to her as "a strange yin-yang beast"); the ancient master (Wu) is a homicidal maniac; and the object of Ling's affection carries a whip and threatens to

Ling (Jet Li) goes after Asia the Invincible in *Swordsman II*.

cut out the tongue of her faithful servant. Even the meaning of insects is inverted in *Swordsman II* (Ling is delighted by a fearsome black scorpion, which he says will produce a wine that leaves one drunk for three days).

*Swordsman II* threatens at every turn to simply fly off into the stratosphere, but it remains thankfully tethered by the sheer, awesome craftsmanship on display and the genuine, impassioned emotions of its players. Ching Siu-Tung may not quite match Tsui's color sense or his lovely, diffuse lighting, but what he brings instead to *Swordsman II* is a distinct sense of horror, with sharp, blue night tones and shadowy dungeons. He's also the world's greatest wire-rig wizard, and he uses that talent in *Swordsman II* to create a fantastic world where people, swords and sewing needles (Asia's eventual weapon of choice) routinely escape the bonds of gravity. The physical effects are genuinely amazing: In

one memorable scene Master Wu fights seven or eight opponents in a forest clearing, all leaping and twirling thirty feet into the air over his head. Even a scene as simple as Ling's joy over a new wine gourd becomes magical in Ching's camera, as Ling laughs and spins sideways in delight. The net effect of all this frenzied motion is a dizzying idea that human beings are capable of anything, whether it's flying or changing sex at will.

It may be Ching's camera, but what he's capturing are Tsui's obsessions. Asia the Invincible represents Tsui's notions of female power taken to their ultimate endpoint: While Asia's power increases after his self-mutilation (which has taken place before the film starts), it's not until Asia puts on female clothing and make-up and feels sexual attraction to Ling that his/her power reaches its zenith. At that point Asia can destroy with only a nod or a gesture, yet is undone by her hesitation in killing Ling. Here's one of *Swordsman II*'s most subversive moral suggestions: That women are ultimately more powerful than men — until they allow the power to be taken.

But *Swordsman II*, like *Peking Opera Blues*, spins out ideas far past the easy feminist reading. Like the *Once Upon a Time in China* films, one of its themes is the futility of spoken language. The heroes are surrounded by Asia's Japanese-speaking allies; they try in vain to mimic the language and just wind up fighting instead. Even among themselves the spoken word can be a trap, as when Kiddo and Ling agree to use a password, then nearly run each other through when the password becomes confused. It's worth remembering that Hong Kong is a territory in which three different dialects/languages (Mandarin, Cantonese and English) are spoken, and this has doubtless been a major influence on the development of the Hong Kong action film in general. Not everyone can understand a Cantonese word, but we can all relate to a punch or a pratfall. Tsui Hark may just be the first filmmaker to concretize Hong Kong's language dilemma. Actions most definitely speak louder than words in his films.

The mixed-up world of *Swordsman II* also serves to evoke powerful emotional responses. There's no doubt that it is first and foremost an action film, with enough adrenaline pumping through it to fuel a dozen more ordinary films, but *Swordsman II* works equally well as a horror film. The best horror films, after all, strive to unseat us from our comfortable reality, to disturb and unsettle; and, as such, *Swordsman II* is filled with some genuinely horrific moments. A human body is torn apart by a nod, a woman discovers her lover has transformed into a crossgendered demon, a madman is hung by giant hooks through his back.... Few American horror films can equal *Swordsman II*'s visual terrors (or even the amount of blood it sheds).

*Swordsman II* — normally one would say "paradoxically," but this is a Tsui Hark film — also has moments of transcendent joy and deep sadness. There's that aforementioned sight of Ling whirling into the air over the gift of "perfect wine"; by the end of the film, Ling will be whirling in the air while he watches Asia, whom he's still strongly attracted to, plummet to her death. What makes *Swordsman II* a great film (instead of merely an interesting curiosity) is that the emotions are as intense as the action (and the warped morality).

Tsui Hark and Jet Li made three films together in 1991–1992 — *Swordsman II* and *Once Upon a Time in China* Parts I and II (Li in particular deserves some kind of endurance award!) — and Li was launched into Hong Kong superstardom. His performance as Ling is as frenzied as his Wong Fei-Hung is dignified; he has an easygoing charm in *Swordsman II* that has seldom been seen in his work since. He's even cast opposite his *Once Upon a Time in China* co-star, Rosamund Kwan, who plays Ying with a venom (almost literally — her clan uses snakes as secret weapons) that would melt her demure Auntie Yee. The film's second oddest performance is Yan Yee Kwan's Master Wu (another carryover from the cast of *Once Upon a Time in China*), who has apparently been driven mad by Asia's torture and winds up a vengeance-obsessed psychotic; he laughs, bellows and glares his way through the film, often at the same time.

But performance-wise, *Swordsman II*, of course, belongs to Brigitte Lin. Hong Kong acting styles are often reminiscent of American silent-film acting, and nowhere is this more apparent than in Lin's Asia the Invincible (particularly since she doesn't speak in most of her scenes with Ling, her voice being the last masculine thing about her). Her gaze is so forceful that she's absolutely believable as a powerful warrior; yet, as with her Tsao Wan in *Peking Opera Blues*, there's no attempt made — or needed — to hide her striking beauty. It's ridiculous, certainly, that anyone would look at Lin and believe her to be a man, but her sheer authority and power so dominate any scene she's in that we simply forget we shouldn't be buying this.

*Swordsman II* also features a throbbing, dread-inducing score by Yuen Cheuk Faan, and Lau Moon Tong's shaded, dense, cinematography makes it a technical triumph as well.

ABOUT THE MOVIE: *Swordsman II* was a huge hit for Tsui, his second most successful film ever (behind *A Better Tomorrow)*; it grossed $34,462,861 and was number eight for 1992 (the top five films that year all starred comedian Stephen Chow).

At the 1992 Hong Kong Film Awards *Swordsman II* won for Best Costume and Make Up Design (William Cheung and Yu Ka On), and was nominated for Best Action Choreography (Ching Siu-Tung, Yuen Bun, Ma Yuk Shing, Cheung Yiu Sing), Best Actress (Brigitte Lin), Best Art Direction (James Leung, Chung Yee-Fung), Best Film Editing (Mak Chi Sin), Best Original Film Score (Yuen Cheuk Faan) and Best Original Film Song (James Wong, for the song "Jek Gei Gam Woo Siu," or "Only Remember Today Lake Smile").

Although several of the main characters from the first *Swordsman* film returned for the sequel (Ling, Kiddo, Ying), there's only one holdover from the cast — Fennie Yuen as Blue Phoenix.

TSUI ON *SWORDSMAN II*: I got the idea [for Brigitte Lin as Asia] during *Zu*. I have this picture of her in this red costume, and

I looked at her and I thought, this is a character I want for another movie. So that had been around for several years — eight years. So I always said I wanted to shoot *Swordsman*, and so more people said, "Why *Swordsman*? That is an impossible story to work on, it's so long and has so many characters and that writer has never worked on screen, only on television, because he tells such long stories." I said, "This one is interesting, it's got all the interesting characters in it." For episode one — *Swordsman I* — I was writing all the characters on a big white board and we were discussing how we were going to cut this story into pieces and tell the story in a very interesting way. And it got to the point where suddenly we don't have Brigitte Lin at all — Brigitte Lin is not in the story of the first episode. And it's not my wish to cut out the character, but somehow I cannot leave the character in — she's so powerful. The role is too powerful to be just part of the story — she has to be the focus of the whole story. That's why I have to cut her out; otherwise she's going to destroy the structure of the first episode. And it would destroy her character, for sure. That's why I left her for the second episode.

When we were shooting *Swordsman II* the writer asked me out to dinner. And he seriously said to me, "Brigitte Lin is not the right casting for this role." He didn't expect the role to be cast with a pretty woman; he thought it should be a male impersonating a woman. I thought Brigitte Lin could be a very, very interesting cast for the role. I suspect that's why the writer didn't want to do any more work for me; that was the end of my collaboration with him! And Brigitte wanted to read the novel; I said, "No, don't read the novel. It's only ten pages." She said, "Ten pages? I thought it was a very big book!" "No, the whole novel's circling around that character, but the character only runs ten pages."

**Brigitte Lin as Asia the Invincible in *Swordsman II*.**

But even though it's only ten pages, right from the beginning of the novel people are already talking about this character. When I read the novel I was expecting so much about this character, and it ended up with only ten pages. I was a bit disappointed. Then, when I started thinking about the movie, it was about the character by itself. So I said, "Brigitte, don't read the novel. Just read the script."

The thing about writing is you don't know how it should look. We had a couple of people working on the look of that character. It's kind of a mixture of Japanese things and Chinese culture. In *Once Upon a Time in China* I really wanted the art director to go to England to get all the costumes, because I think it's right to be authentic. As much as the budget would allow, I would insist on that. So we created this image of Brigitte Lin, and during production I went up to her and said, "I have to tell you something. I was sort of hesi-tant to tell you this before production, but — your voice will be dubbed by a male voice." She looked at me very calmly, I couldn't tell if she was shocked or not shocked. Anyway, she went along with it... it became very popular. Of course, she'd been popular for years and years in China and Taiwan.

It was a convenient thing that we had just finished *Once Upon a Time in China* and we were preparing for *Swordsman II*, and so many of the people were standing around, so we'd just get them for a role.

The night we wrapped, Brigitte invited me to dinner. She was going to leave the next morning. So we went out to dinner, and I sat there, and the majority of the film was cut, and in the middle of the dinner I said, "What time does your plane leave Hong Kong?" She said, "Two." "Can you come in the morning so we can do some re-shooting?" She said, "WHAT?! I was supposed to finish the movie already!"

## New Dragon Inn

Producer/Writer, 1992. Cantonese: *San Lung Moon Haak Jaan*. Mandarin: *Xin Long Men Ke Zhan*. AKA: *Dragon Inn*. Director: Raymond Lee. Co-Writers: Cheung Taan, Hiu Wing. Cinematography: Lau Moon Tong, Arthur Wong. Art Direction: William Cheung Suk Ping, Chiu Gok San. Action Design: Ching Siu-Tung, Yuen Bun. Editing: Poon Hung. Music Score: Chan Fei Lit. Associate Producer: Ching Siu-Tung. CAST: Maggie Cheung ("Jade King"), Brigitte Lin Ching-Hsia ("Yau Mo-Yin"), Tony Leung Ka-Fai ("Chow"), DonnieYen ("Tsao Siu Yan"), Xiong Xin-Xin ("Eunuch"), Lau Shun ("Eunuch"), Lawrence Ng ("Eunuch"), Yan Yee Kwan ("Ho Fu"), Elvis Tsui Kam-Kong ("Frontier Commander"). Opening Date: August 27, 1992.

SYNOPSIS: During the Ming Dynasty a group of eunuchs, led by the evil Tsao Siu Yan, have seized power. After killing the Minister of Defense, Yang Yu-Hin, they plot to take the army by using Yang's children to lure his partner Chow out of hiding. With the eunuchs' highly-trained Black Arrow Troops in close pursuit, the children are sent into the desert, where they're rescued by Chow's lover, Yau Mo-Yin. Yau Mo-Yin flees to the isolated Dragon Inn to await her rendezvous with Chow. The Inn is a wild frontier watering hole run by Jade King, a feisty, proud businesswoman who routinely kills her guests to provide the filling for her spicy meat buns. When Yau Mo-Yin appears, Jade smells profit and tries to spy on Mo-Yin, an attempt which leads to a playful battle between the two women — one which ends with Yau Mo-Yin wearing Jade's clothes while Jade winds up naked on the inn's roof. Just then Chow arrives, and Jade is immediately attracted to the handsome stranger, even though he and Mo-Yin are

obviously involved. Things really heat up, though, when the eunuchs arrive, disguised as travelers. A fierce storm traps everyone in the inn, and a dangerous game of cat-and-mouse follows. The game is interrupted temporarily by the arrival of Jade's friend, the Customs Officer, who becomes a pawn between Chow's group and the eunuchs. Chow contrives a way of escape, but to implement it he must marry Jade, much to the dismay of Mo-Yin; the attempt is successful, and Chow, Mo-Yin and Yang's two children escape into the desert, just as the Black Arrow Troops arrive. Jade's men are slaughtered, and she kills two of the eunuchs herself in retaliation; then she and her barbarian chef Dao join Mo-Yin and Chow. Their escape is cut short when they reveal themselves to Tsao Siu Yan, and the film's final battle is a four-way swordfight between Tsao, Chow, Mo-Yin and Jade. Mo-Yin is killed, and Chow and Jade are badly wounded, but they're saved by the surprise appearance of Dao, who uses his barbarian butcher skills to carve Tsao into a gruesome part-skeleton. In the end Jade burns the Dragon Inn down and takes off after Chow, accompanied by the devoted Dao.

REVIEW: First, imagine an "Eastern Western" — an Asian film that relies on many of the motifs of the traditional American Western; now add the epic, operatic style of 1960s Hong Kong icon King Hu; and then give the whole thing a distinctly Tsui Hark spin (meaning several major gender switches), and you might wind up with something like the magnificent — and magnificently strange — *New Dragon Inn*.

Like the earlier *Swordsman*, this one began life as an homage to one of Tsui's major influences, King Hu (it's a remake of King's 1967 *Dragon Inn*); and, also like *Swordsman*, what emerged on the other

Chow (Tony Leung Ka-Fai), Mo-Yin (Brigitte Lin) and Jade (Maggie Cheung) face the eunuchs at the end of *New Dragon Inn*.

end looked more like Tsui than King. Unlike *Swordsman, New Dragon Inn* is a fully realized, superb work of filmmaking.

Right from the start, *New Dragon Inn* has a distinctly different look from nearly every other film in the Tsui Hark library. Shot on location in the deserts of mainland China, it possesses a stark, barren beauty, not unlike the great western landscapes of John Ford. When the plot moves to the actual inn (where at least two-thirds of the movie takes place), the exquisite, complex set would barely be out of place in any frontier American town — built completely from wood, there are tables, chairs, counters, an upper level for the guest rooms, and a spitfire barmaid.

Where *New Dragon Inn* is plainly an Eastern, not a Western, is, of course, in its use of swords and martial arts over guns and fisticuffs. And where it's a Tsui Hark

film is in the fact that the best fighters in the film are its female leads, Mo-Yin and Jade King. Even its male protagonist, the cool Chow, seems more like a strategist than a fighter, leaving the more physical work to the women. Of course, *New Dragon Inn* is also shot in a way that plainly emphasizes the women (both of whom we meet well before Chow). Although there is a romantic triangle between the three leads, the real attraction seems to exist between the women; in the film's most famous scene, Jade is stripped naked by Mo-Yin during a fight, while the two exchange compliments about each others' figures. It's an astonishing scene, one as charged with eroticism as action. Later, Mo-Yin's flute — the symbol of romance throughout the film — is passed between the women, not between one of them and Chow. In one of the film's final

Chow (Tony Leung Ka-Fai) tries to evade Jade's (Maggie Cheung) seduction in *New Dragon Inn*.

shots (after Mo-Yin's death), the flute lies forgotten in the desert as the wind blows through it, causing wavering, lonely tones; the flute tells us this was a doomed romance, since the women couldn't love both Chow and each other at the same time.

If the male protagonist, Chow, seems slightly impotent compared to the two female leads, it could also be that he's surrounded by castrated men — the villainous eunuchs. If much of *New Dragon Inn*'s plot seems politically charged, it probably has less to do with the historical intrigues than with the suggestion that men can only achieve power by becoming more like women. In this it is thematically similar to the last two *Swordsmen* films, although in a more implicit, playful way (although, in all fairness to King Hu, his films — including the original *Dragon Inn* — also often featured women warriors as protagonists).

It also shares some of *Swordsman II*'s cast, notably Brigitte Lin, Lau Shun and Yan Yee Kwan. Where some of Tsui's films (i.e., *The Raid*, *The Magic Crane*) have nearly collapsed under the weight of a large cast, *New Dragon Inn* handles its own panoply of characters superbly. For one thing, there's a definite emphasis on Mo-Yin, Jade and Chow; the rest are obviously supporting characters or villains. And since the bulk of *New Dragon Inn*'s action is confined to the inn itself, the large number of characters keeps the proceedings from becoming dull; there's always another fight to cut to. Also, the actors — most of whom had worked together on other projects — have excellent chemistry together, especially Maggie Cheung and Brigitte Lin (for another film in which they play best friends, see Yim Ho's touching *Red Dust*). It's also a pleasure to see the actors assembled to play the eunuchs: Lawrence Ng (*The Magic Crane*), Xiong Xin-Xin and

Lau Shun (these two from *Once Upon a Time in China III, IV* and *V*), and Donnie Yen are like a Who's Who of Tsui's bad guys. Yen in particular shines here as the effete, pasty-faced Tsao; the structure of the film plays wittily on its audience recognizing Yen as a famed martial artist, and saves his fight for the last. That climactic battle is one of the greatest in the martial arts cinema, with Tsao simultaneously battling Mo-Yin, Jade and Chow amidst the desert sand and swirling winds. The camera tracks furiously with the four combatants as they leap, parry and thrust at astonishing speeds; the grand finale, as the barbarian Dao appears from beneath the sand to deftly butcher Tsao in seconds, is as gruesome and blackly-funny a scene as any in Hong Kong cinema. It's another scene that sets *New Dragon Inn* firmly apart from its Western kin; certainly no John Wayne or even Clint Eastwood film would ever end that way.

*New Dragon Inn* also boasts a stunning musical score by Chan Fei Lit. The original King Hu film was scored with Peking Opera music (in fact, in the program book for the *22nd Annual Hong Kong International Film Festival*, Stephen Teo says that the original *Dragon Inn* was "the induction to King Hu's application of Beijing Opera to his cinematic narrative style"), and that motif is carried on here; the score is both richly Chinese and tremendously exciting, with strong percussion that propels the action at top speed. At times it also has strange echoes of both Ennio Morricone's spaghetti western scores and American western music, with banjo-like instruments and flutes taking the lead. It's probably the finest non-James Wong-composed score in all of Tsui Hark's films.

ABOUT THE MOVIE: *New Dragon Inn* performed well at the box office, placing

at number 16 for the year, with a gross of $21,505,027. It also did well at the Hong Kong Film Awards, where it was nominated for Best Actress (Maggie Cheung, who won the award for *Centre Stage*, against Brigitte Lin for *Swordsman II* and *Handsome Siblings*), Best Cinematography (Lau Moon Tong and Arthur Wong), Best Action Choreography (Ching Siu-Tung and Yuen Bun, who were also nominated for *Swordsman II*; Yuen Wo-Ping won for *Once Upon a Time in China II*) and Best Film Editing (Poon Hung).

*New Dragon Inn* is one of the best films to illustrate how Tsui works with the same collaborators from film to film. Director Raymond Lee worked as associate producer on *The Magic Crane, Iron Monkey, Wicked City,* and *Once Upon a Time in China II*, and as associate producer and director on *The East Is Red*. Cheung Taan also wrote *Once Upon a Time in China II* and *III*. Lau Moon Tong also shot *Once Upon a Time in China V, The Magic Crane, The East Is Red, Swordsman II, The Raid, A Chinese Ghost Story* and *A Chinese Ghost Story III*. Arthur Wong shot *Tri-Star, Iron Monkey, Twin Dragons, Once Upon a Time in China I, II* and *III*, and *A Chinese Ghost Story II*. William Cheung did art direction/costume on *The Blade, Love in the Time of Twilight, The Chinese Feast,* costumes on *The Lovers* and *Swordsman II,* and art direction on *A Chinese Ghost Story II* and *It Takes Two*; he also worked on nearly all of Wong Kar-Wai's films. Chiu Gok San worked on *Once Upon a Time in China II* and *V* (costume on both). Ching Siu-Tung has worked on *The East Is Red, Swordsman II, The Raid, Terracotta Warrior, A Chinese Ghost Story I, II* and *III* (all director/action design); *Swordsman, The Killer, A Better Tomorrow II, Peking Opera Blues, Happy Ghost III,* and *Dangerous Encounter — 1st Kind* (action design). Yuen Bun also did action design on *The Blade,*

**Action designer Ching Siu-Tung at work: Tsao Siu Yan (Donnie Yen) tries to fight off Mo-Yin (Brigitte Lin) and Jade (Maggie Cheung) in *New Dragon Inn*.**

*The Chinese Feast, Once Upon a Time in China V, Swordsman II* and *A Chinese Ghost Story III,* and directed *Once Upon a Time in China IV.* Tony Leung Ka-Fai did *King of Chess* (for which he received a Best Actor nomination), *The Banquet, The Raid, A Better Tomorrow III* and *Gunmen* with Tsui. Donnie Yen was also in *Iron Monkey* and *Once Upon a Time in China II.* Yan Yee Kwan, one of Tsui's favorite heavies (playing a mercenary working for the good guys in *New Dragon Inn*) also appeared in *The East Is Red, Iron Monkey, Swordsman II,* and most memorably as "Iron Robe" in *Once Upon a Time in China.* Maggie Cheung played the title role in the Tsui-directed *Green Snake* and also appeared with frequent co-star Jackie Chan in *The Twin Dragons.* Brigitte Lin, of course, is probably the one performer

most associated with Tsui Hark, having been seen in *All the Wrong Spies, Zu: Warriors from the Magic Mountain, Peking Opera Blues,* and as the amazing Asia the Invincible in *Swordsmen II* and *The East Is Red.*

Brigitte tells an amusing anecdote about the difficult making of *New Dragon Inn:* One day on location in the desert the cast awoke to such intense cold they were certain they wouldn't be able to work that day. They got together and approached Brigitte, who they knew was closest to Tsui, begging her to plead with Tsui to suspend the day's work. Brigitte called Tsui and explained the situation, but Tsui's legendary response was, "No! We will shoot today even if it is raining knives and swords!" (The joke turned out to be on Tsui when the day's footage was unusable because the actors were so obviously suffering the effects of the extreme cold.) *New Dragon Inn* was also a dangerous film for the performers—Brigitte was hit in the eye during one fight scene and suffered numerous lesser bruises.

TSUI ON *NEW DRAGON INN*: The movie was about 80, 85 minutes [but was extended on its laserdisc release]. I think they can sell it at a higher price if it is two laserdiscs, so they extended it. That's one of the most frustrating things that happens, and it happens all the time here. That's why we fight so much to protect our work. I'd always ask people to watch *Dragon Inn*—like Maggie, right? She'd never seen that movie, so I said, "You gotta buy the laserdisc." So I bought the laserdisc, and she saw the movie, and she said she didn't like the movie. I said, "Why?" She said, "I don't know—there's something weird about it." So later I watched the movie on laserdisc, and I found out they put some more scenes in there. There's a lot of horse-riding, and that's not supposed to be in that long. It's like cover shots—they're using all the cover shots, they're using all the masters to put everything in, to extend the laser. Some of those scenes I'd cut out because they hindered the flow of the movie. But they were all there! And the music was different. And the dialogue—they redubbed it. That's why we always sign contracts telling them all the laserdisc versions need to be approved by us, the characters cannot appear in other movies... otherwise you see the characters from your movie end up in some other movie, doing something else, and that's very bad. That's why we always try to stop that, by telling them not to do it. And they don't understand! You tell them not to do it, that legally they cannot do it, and they get very mad.

# The East Is Red
# (Swordsman III)

Producer/Writer, 1993. Cantonese: *Dung Fong Bat Baai 2: Fung Wan Joi Hei.* Mandarin: *Dong1 Fang1 Bu2 Bai4 2: Feng1 Yun2 Zai4 Qi3.* Literally: *Invincible Asia 2: Turbulence Again Rises.* AKA: *The East Is Red.* Directors: Ching Siu-Tung, Raymond Lee Wai-Man. Co-Writers: Szeto Wai-Cheuk, Cheung Taan. Cinematography: Lau Moon Tong. Art Direction: Ma Poon-Chiu. Action Design: Ma Yuk Shing, Dion Lam. Editing: Chun Yue, Geung Chuen Dak. Music Score: Woo Wai Laap. CAST: Brigitte Lin Ching-Hsia ("Asia the Invincible"), Joey Wang Cho-Yin ("Snow"), Yu Rong-Guang ("Koo"), Jean Wong Ching-Ying ("Dai"), Lau Shun ("Warden of the Black Cliffs"), Eddy Ko Hung ("Ching"). Opening Date: January 21, 1993.

SYNOPSIS: Four months have passed since Asia the Invincible disappeared over the edge of the Black Cliffs. Naval Officer Koo has come to this haunted place with a contingent of Spaniards who are supposed to retrieve the goods lost with the Dutch ship Asia destroyed. Koo encounters a mysterious warden who leads him to Asia's grave; then the Spaniards reveal their real purpose: They've come in search of the mysterious Sacred Scroll, which grants its user supernatural powers. Koo tries to stop them from defiling the grave and is shot; he's rescued when the warden destroys the Spaniards, then reveals herself to be Asia. Koo tells Asia that, since she vanished, dozens of impostors have risen, all claiming to be Asia; Asia will let Koo live if he takes her to the impostors. One of the fakes is Asia's former concubine Snow, who now leads the Sun Moon Sect in Asia's name; Snow tries to buy arms from a Japanese warship, but the Japanese commander betrays her and attacks instead. She beats off the attack with her own impressive kung fu, and later that night discovers one of her own concubines to be a ninja in disguise. After killing the spy, Snow mourns the loss of her lover Asia, unaware that even now Asia is carving a bloody path through the countryside, slaying fake Asias, warlords and innocents alike. The path eventually leads to Snow, and the two women fight, although Snow surrenders and allows herself to be wounded. Koo, attracted to Snow, tries to save her, but Snow finally leaves Koo to return to Asia. When Snow finds Asia again, Asia has captured both the Japanese and Spanish warships, with the intention of creating her own naval power; but her plans are thwarted by the arrival of Koo. Koo and Asia fight over Snow, destroying the ships and killing Snow. Finally, Koo blows up with the last ship, and Asia sails away, grieving over Snow's corpse.

REVIEW: *The East Is Red* is one of the most difficult films in Tsui Hark's career — difficult to describe, to penetrate and (for some) to like. It's a sequel to *Swordsman II* that has virtually nothing to do with the previous films (despite a lengthy prologue recapping events from the other movies). It has no real hero, no real plot and no clearly expressed goals for the characters to achieve.

All that said, it's also one of the most audacious works of genius in the history of the fantasy film.

Tsui Hark's personal goal, expressed both in his films and his interviews, is to challenge his audience. This is the filmmaker who has given us the nihilistic *Dangerous Encounter — 1st Kind*, the female-driven action pieces *Peking Opera Blues* and *New Dragon Inn*, and the utterly distinctive animated feature *A Chinese Ghost Story: The Tsui Hark Animation*; yet none

of these challenges in the ways that *The East Is Red* does. Even the bleak *Dangerous Encounter* has characters who we pity and feel for; but *The East Is Red* is almost gleeful in its utter disregard for traditional storytelling techniques. Its predecessor, *Swordsman II*, was a frantic exercise in brilliant weirdness that at least had a likable leading man and an obvious goal (to stop Asia the Invincible); but *The East Is Red* is more of a fantasia, an exploration into notions of gender, love, identity, ambition, corruption and power.

In the hands of any other filmmaker, Asia would be the villain and Koo the handsome, upright hero; but not only is Koo a morally (and mentally) ambiguous character, by the end he and Asia are indistinguishable in their shared madness. In one of the first scenes, after the warden of the Black Cliffs has told Koo s/he's actually Asia the Invincible, Koo begs her to shed her disguise so he can have a look. She asks if he's willing to die for one glimpse, and he willingly agrees. In some way this makes Koo a shadowy reflection of Tsui Hark himself: Koo is so obsessed with a figure of Chinese legend (what Asia has become in the four months since her "death") that he would sacrifice himself for it. Tsui has always been the most traditionally Chinese of Hong Kong directors, but in *The East Is Red* he seems to question that interest, finding in it both salvation and doom.

The film then moves to the first sequence with Snow, Asia's one-time love. Snow, now masquerading as Asia to hold the Sun Moon Sect together, is attacked by the Japanese warship led by Mo Yan Lu Chong, a powerful figure in frightening black Japanese armor. When Snow's vessel unleashes its cannons, the Japanese warship escapes by turning into a submarine; in the world of *The East Is Red* nothing — not even a boat — is what it seems.

That night Snow selects the lovely

**Brigitte Lin as Asia the Invincible in *The East Is Red.***

young Dai from her courtesans, and what follows is both the film's most erotic scene and its most bizarre. As Snow and Dai share liquid opium, which they pass from tongue to tongue, Snow recalls a similar scene from her past with Asia; the two love scenes (which involve three women) are intercut with a languorous rhythm until the abrupt moment when Snow discovers Dai is actually a man. The scene is a veritable Chinese box of identities: Snow, a woman masquerading as another woman who used to be a man, seduces a woman who really is a man, while thinking of the woman who used to be a man. Significantly, this scene is followed by one in which Asia gruesomely slays an entire clan led by an impostor Asia; Asia is being driven mad by her loss of identity, stolen from her by impostors. And Koo's identity is completely consumed by Asia's; at the film's conclusion the demented Koo screams her name over and over until he's destroyed in an explosion.

All three lead characters (and nearly all of the supporting characters as well, such as the Japanese commander and Dai) have given away their sense of self and pay with either their lives or their sanity. Combined with a rich vein of Chinese tradition in the film, the ultimate message of *The East Is Red* may be one for Hong Kong itself: It can't rush to give away its own history, or it will become a city of the mad. When *The East Is Red* was made, the handover was four years away, so surely its coming was an immense influence on all of Tsui Hark's films at the time.

If Asia has given away her identity, she's gained immense power, and *The East Is Red* is surely one of the most outrageous examinations of feminine power ever committed to film. In *Swordsman II* it was enough to simply have the one character who had castrated himself for his ambitions and finally achieved full power upon his complete conversion to womanhood; but in *The East Is Red* an entire nation is pretending to be feminine to achieve power. (One almost expects to hear the code phrase shouted by the army at the end of 1983's *All the Wrong Spies*: "I am woman!") Even when Asia gives in to a whim to experience life as a commoner and masquerades as a prostitute, the scene is curiously skewed towards the women: Taken prisoner with the other whores, Asia manipulates two groups of men until one is destroyed. It's also interesting that the only moment of genuine friendship in *The East Is Red* occurs between Asia and the prostitutes' madam; once again, Tsui assigns the finer attributes to the working class.

*The East Is Red* also features one of the most frightening assessments of love ever seared into film. Before Snow and Asia meet, we've seen Snow's memories of their affair, so we know it was intimate and genuine. Yet when Asia discovers that Snow has been posing as her, her fury is unleashed on Snow, who offers no resistance. Only Koo saves Snow from Asia's wrath; Asia's love is no match for her rage. And Snow pledges her love to Asia by offering her life; when she's left alive but badly injured, she seems to treasure her pain as if it were a love offering. It makes sense that the psychologically-damaged Koo would fall in love with the physically-injured Snow; his obsession with Asia naturally (if tragically) transfers itself to Asia's lover. Koo, unlike Asia, at least has some sense in the first half of the film that he's becoming unhinged; when he blurts out his desire for Snow at one point, he looks shocked while Snow just smiles bitterly. But it doesn't stop him from pursuing his love interest, even though she makes her disinterest in him clear; he will pursue her to his (and her) end. In *The East Is Red* love is ultimately a sickness that leads to death.

But then, of course, it could be argued that *everything* in *The East Is Red* leads to death, for it may be the bloodiest film with the highest death count in Tsui Hark's filmography. The film might as well have been called *This Film Is Red*, for red is the overriding color throughout; most characters are clothed in red, ships are painted red, and gallons of blood adorn the fights. The constant use of red throughout not only makes the film seen exceptionally gory, it also makes it feel paradoxically vibrant and passionate; certainly, passions run high to the point of insanity in *The East Is Red*, a point driven home by the rich crimson color palette.

Red is the color of both passion and violence, and, indeed, *The East Is Red* is exceptional in both areas. If it is a rich and complex psychological fable, it's also a rip-roaring good action film, with extremes of grief and love, rage and horror. Ching Siu-Tung brings his characteristic verve to the action sequences, which include such memorable images as Asia atop the back of a flying swordfish, Koo's cheeks being pierced by a flying needle, and Snow puppeteering two Ninjas she's just slain. The film is awash not just in blood but in tears; it is deeply tragic, with each of the three characters isolated from the others by their own fate: Koo knows he's in the grip of increasing dementia, Snow is literally dying for Asia, and Asia is so lost in rage that one of the film's biggest shocks is when she finally mourns for Snow at the film's conclusion.

After *Swordsman II*, Brigitte Lin became the most famous androgyne in Hong Kong, playing a male figure in such films as *Ashes of Time*, *Deadful Melody*,

**Gender confusion: Jean Wong as Dai and Joey Wang as Snow in *The East Is Red*.**

Tsui's own *New Dragon Inn* and more; but in *The East Is Red* Lin doesn't simply play a crossgendered wo/man, she also embodies Asia's rage, confusion and passion. Lin must certainly be one of the most fearless performers in the world; her performance as Asia in *The East Is Red* never feels dishonest or overtly glamorous. Her poise is so natural that she never seems to be posing, even when she stops abruptly; she certainly knows exactly when the camera is lingering on her, but she's willing to be ugly as well as beautiful in those moments. After she finishes slaughtering the highlander clan, for example, her sheer exultation actually causes her to stagger. She makes Asia a terrifying figure — without resorting to special make-up or optical effects.

But just as good is Joey Wang as Snow. Wang has occasionally been thought of as "just a pretty face," but in such films as *The East Is Red* and Tsui's *Green Snake* (where she holds her own with another formidable acting challenge, Maggie Cheung) she proved herself to be a major talent, apart from her beauty. A lesser actress could easily have imbued Snow with maudlin sentiment, but Wang is nearly as fearless as Lin in choosing to create a character who is not easy to empathize with. Her Snow takes sick, sad pleasure in taunting the lovestruck Koo; the scene in a military camp when she seduces an amorous captain just to make Koo jealous is genuinely cruel. She does a fine job of imitating Lin's Asia as well (although she's even less believable as a man than Lin is).

As the male leg of this warped triangle, Yu Rong-Guang is superb. In *Iron Monkey* his size and masculinity worked well for his portrait of a hero, and here those same qualities work to trick the audience into initially believing that Koo will be a hero — and then Yu's acting skill takes over, as Koo descends faster and farther.

The film also features an excellent supporting cast, including Tsui regulars Lau Shun (Wong Fei-Hung's father in the *Once Upon a Time in China* series), Jean Wong (Aunt May from *Once Upon a Time in China IV* and *V*) and Eddy Ko Hung (*We're Going to Eat You*). There was also a cast of the usual Tsui suspects on the other side of the camera, including cinematographer Lau Moon Tong (*Swordsman II*, *New Dragon Inn*, *A Chinese Ghost Story III* and others) and composer Woo Wai Laap (*Shanghai Grand*, *Love in the Time of Twilight*, etc.). Woo's score deserves special mention — it's a rare synth score that feels grand, not repetitive and throbbing, as is so often the case. It fully captures both the emotional and visceral aspects of this lush, intricate film.

**ABOUT THE FILM:** *The East Is Red* was moderately successful in Hong Kong, placing at number 38 on the year's box office list, earning $11,248,506.

It received one nomination from the Hong Kong Film Awards, for Best Make Up and Costume Design (William Cheung, Chiu Gok San; Cheung was also nominated for *Green Snake*).

**TSUI ON *THE EAST IS RED*:** I thought *Swordsman II* was the end of that character [Asia the Invincible]. And then it became a big hit, and people were asking for a sequel. That's something that wasn't my best doing, because I thought that character had died already. And now it ends up they want her to live again.

That movie was chaos, because we ran out of people, we ran out of actors. Brigitte Lin was shooting two movies at the same time, the director was shooting three movies at the same time, the cameraman, *everybody* was working on several projects. So I think that was a film that sounded the toll announcing the future death of Hong Kong movies. The doomsday toll.

I was very involved with the script. It was with that one that I was announcing the death of costumed swordplay movies. Everybody was imitating the character. I think Brigitte did almost ten movies playing the same role.

[On Joey Wang's contact lenses]: Both of them are wearing contact lenses. The way they look with the contact lenses, I think they have a little bit more substance in their character.

## *Green Snake*

Director/Producer/Writer, 1993. Cantonese: *Ceng Ji*. Mandarin: *Qing1 She2*. Also known as: *Blue Snake*, *White Snake*. Co-Writer: Lillian Lee Bik Dut. Based on the classic "Bai She Zhuan" ("White Snake Story"). Cinematography: Giu Chiu Lam. Art Direction: Bill Lui. Editing: A Chik. Costume Design: Ng Po-Ling, William Cheung. Music: James Wong, Mark Lui Chung Dak. CAST: Maggie Cheung ("Green"), Joey Wang ("White"), Zhao Wen-Zhou ("Fa-Hai"), Tien Feng ("Hsui-Xien"). Opening Date: November 4, 1993.

**SYNOPSIS:** Fa-Hai is an arrogant monk who holds himself equally above both humans and animals, and lives in denial of his own desires. One day he encounters an old man in the forest, and, upon realizing the man is actually a spider in disguise, he captures him and forces him back into his spider form, taking his magic beads. Later on, Fa-Hai repents his act and passes the magic beads on to a pair of kindly snakes, who transform into two beautiful human women. White has been training for 1,000 years and takes humanity very seriously; Green, on the other hand, has only trained for 500 years and wants experience without responsibility.

The women set up house in a small town and manage to thwart the efforts of an evil Taoist monk who wants their life essence. White moves in with a naïve young scholar, Hsui-Xien, and Green attempts to seduce Fa-Hai; her partial success leads the self-righteous Fa-Hai to seek vengeance against the women, a path which ends in wholesale slaughter and ultimate tragedy.

REVIEW: I first discovered the joys of Hong Kong cinema sometime around 1993, when a friend gave me two mediocre-quality videotapes of movies by a then-unknown director named John Woo. My friend assured me they would knock my socks into the next state, and he was right. Despite the muddy-looking copies, *The Killer* and *Bullet in the Head* intrigued me, and I had to have more. I had to have them on a big screen.

I was in luck, because at this time there was a nearby theater that actually ran a different HK double feature every few weeks. The local paper gave a rave review to the latest, so off I trundled, expectations high.

The first film I saw that night was Clarence Fok's 1992 *Naked Killer*. It was not an auspicious beginning—I found the film to be sordid, inane and visually cheap. The audience loved it, though.

The second feature was the one that had received the intriguing rave, and it was late by the time it started. My fellow cineastes were still amped up from *Naked Killer*, and you could feel their energy wane as this second film (whoever was insane enough to pair *Naked Killer* and *Green Snake*?!) wore on. They roared at the occasional shoddy effects. They drifted out.

I didn't care, because I was utterly transported. This film was (is) like nothing I'd ever seen. Its sensuality bore some resemblance to the works of British directors Nicolas Roeg and Peter Greenaway,

but it had a sort of (to coin a phrase) epic playfulness that would have been unimaginable in an English film. It took me to another realm, one where torn-up love poems became cherry blossoms, where a cup of tea hurled heavenward invoked a rainstorm, and snakes transformed themselves into lovely women. It was positively heady in its beauty.

To this day, *Green Snake* remains my favorite Tsui Hark film. Maybe it's because it was my first encounter with Tsui Hark as director, or my first HK mythological fantasy, or the film that most represents Tsui Hark's thematic obsessions... whatever the reason, the film has been a minor obsession of my own ever since, and has led me to seek out whatever I could find by this remarkable filmmaker.

That said, we can move on now to talk about why *Green Snake* is technically not a particularly good film... and why that doesn't matter.

No other Tsui Hark film so divides his admirers (and detractors) as *Green Snake*: Half think it's one of his masterpieces, while the rest consider it one of his biggest disasters. My own opinion—objectively it's a severely mixed film, subjectively it's brilliant—is a microcosm of the greater debate. The roots of this dichotomy lie in the film itself, which changes viewpoints so often and abruptly that *Two-Headed Snake* might have been a more appropriate title. Although the film begins and ends with the story of the conflicted priest Fa-Hai, who commits acts of callous violence in his arrogant self-righteousness, the middle of the film (and by far the better part) concentrates almost solely on the story of two snakes who strive to become fully human. When the film focuses on the snake women, it's erotic, funny and sweet-natured; when Fa-Hai is the center, it becomes a morality play, with sins committed repaid in tragedy. It's like trying to

Original poster for *Green Snake* (featuring Joey Wang and Maggie Cheung).

cut *Gone with the Wind* and *The Wizard of Oz* together. Just because they were made in the same year (1939) by the same director (Victor Fleming) doesn't mean you'll end up with anything but a schizophrenic nightmare. That *Green Snake* works as well as it does is surprising. (A hint: Try watching *Green Snake* sometime without the beginning and end. Start it at exactly 11:30 in, and end it when White reveals that she's pregnant. You'll come away with a very different sense of the film.)

When *Green Snake* does work... well, some of its best sequences involve virtually no dialogue, and indeed words don't begin to do it justice here. "Sensuous" and "erotic" may be two of the most misused words in the vocabulary of the American critic, applied as they often are to scenes that would be more properly termed "gratuitous nudity," but Tsui Hark understands that "sensuous" best refers to all the senses, while "erotic" is a mood, not a motion.

In *Green Snake*, not just sense but also sight, sound, taste and smell are used to tempt and arouse. What you'll be most likely to carry away from a viewing *of Green Snake* is not story or dialogue, but images and sounds: Green shadows floating across moonlit canvas walls, Ravi Shankar's sitar twining throughout a shimmering orgiastic dance tune, a half-eaten fish sliding to a floor in slow-motion, forgotten during a seduction. When Hsui-Xien deeply inhales the intoxicating scent of a lotus blossom, or bites into a fresh seedy grape, as if tasting it for the first time, we realize that what Tsui has really made in *Green Snake* is a film that celebrates all of the rich sensuality of everyday life.

*Green Snake* is also a film that wants to explore life itself, life as a constant transformation. Even after the two snakes transform they continue to study, in order to progress and evolve. Hsui-Xien is awakened by White's attention, transformed from a stern, joyless teacher into a man who literally screams his love for the world as he's carried to his doom by the vengeful Fa-Hai. The film's biggest montage involves the change of the seasons, summer to winter to spring.

It's perfect, then, that Tsui's main visual motif in *Green Snake* is water, the constantly-changing essence of life. The film opens with water as serenity: Fa-Hai witnesses a celebration of deformed, brutal villagers, and to escape his disgust he imagines water and transports himself to a peaceful sea grotto. A few scenes later water becomes birth and sex, as Fa-Hai witnesses a woman delivering a child in a rain-drenched forest and finds his thoughts returning again and again to the image of the woman's dripping thighs. In the next sequence water becomes transformation itself, as the two snakes assume human form during a rainstorm in a city of canals. Water is seduction: White first flirts with Hsui-Xien in a boat, and Green later seduces Fa-Hai in a lake. Water is power: White controls the elements, using rain to wash away the sulfur an evil Taoist priest tries to use against her. Water eventually becomes violence and death, first when the two snakes and Fa-Hai join together to stop a flood from destroying the city, and in the final battle, when the sea itself becomes the ultimate weapon of horrible destruction. Images of water begin and end the film, and are glimpsed in virtually every frame.

*Green Snake*'s use of the water motif is clearly tied to its themes of feminine power and bonding. Water is part of birth, and the ability to conceive a child is what finally marks White as fully human (just as the ability to shed tears is what completes Green's transformation). But water is also associated with snakes (Green in particular seems to be a type of water snake), and Tsui's characteristic humor and love of chaos play out in the numerous scenes in which the half-reptilian Green tries to hide in water while White tries desperately to redirect Hsui-Xien's attention.

Like the triangle in *Shanghai Blues*, Tsui seems less concerned with the romantic entanglements in *Green Snake* than he is with the relationship between the

**Maggie Cheung as Green in *Green Snake*.**

women. Tsui has always been interested in exploring female bonding, but here the ties between the two women are so strong that they are literally psychic — the two share each others' feelings. They laugh together and revel in their power over men (particularly in a delightful early scene where their serpentine walk causes boatmen to collide and fall into the water); they make mistakes and argue, but also willingly sacrifice themselves for each other. In the end, Green will even sacrifice Hsui-Xien, whom she has mildly lusted after, to White, who has finally come to refer to Green as "sister."

While it could be argued that the inclusion of the Fa-Hai story line was necessary to provide both the male counterpart to the two women (Hsui-Xien is really too weak a character to serve this purpose) and the moral contradiction, his scenes instead feel simply crushing after the whimsical, beautiful interludes with Green

and White. After the stunning, extended sequence when the snake women enter the town on a stormy night, Green joining in a drug-and-music-induced party while White is drawn to the sound of students chanting, the film cuts to Fa-Hai being tortured by pale-skinned, tail-sporting demons of lust (whom he violently dismembers). The rhythm and tone so carefully built during the introduction of Green and White are shattered. Again, at the end of the film, the bittersweet revelation of White's pregnancy and Green's refusal to part from White are suddenly annihilated by an extended fight with Fa-Hai. Tsui may have demonstrated a mastery of emotional tone shifts in other films, but in *Green Snake* it simply devalues the film.

The above-mentioned "moral contradiction" is paradoxically contradictory unto itself. Any other filmmaker would include Fa-Hai to show the dangers of indulging too much in pleasure, and the story's final tragic outcome seems to support this viewpoint. But Tsui Hark is an artist who loves to test and invert accepted codes of morality (see *Swordsman II* or even *Tri-Star*), and so Fa-Hai finally serves to validate the snakes' upside-down morality. For the snake women, sex is both useful and fun: useful because it teaches them about humanity, and fun — well, in contrast to most American love scenes, White and Hsui-Xien actually laugh, giggle and tease during their lovemaking. Where the monk would be the upstanding hero in a Western fantasy, here he's a vindictive poor loser who is so intent on fighting his own lust that it doesn't matter what he annihilates in the process. The exorcist is not a tower of virtue, but is instead a blind, greedy old man who, like a vampire, wants to suck the snakes' life essences. Animals are kinder than humans, serpents are protectors of the homeless, and serenity is a betrayal of life — these are all examples of *Green Snake*'s unique moral universe.

Much has been made of *Green Snake*'s notoriously poor special effects, and while they are wildly inconsistent throughout the film, it isn't until the final battle between the women and Fa-Hai that they become conspicuous. Although the giant snake head that White rides during the battle is undoubtedly the same one that scared Hsui-Xien to death earlier, it stands out in the finale only because Tsui shoots it in bright, harsh daylight and invests it with no emotional response. Or compare the fight that occurs between the two women in the house: It technically isn't any better than the denouement, but because it is consistent in photographic style and lighting with the rest of the film, it works, where the ending does not.

Maybe the real point of all this is that Tsui's biggest mistake lay not in a few bad effects but in making a film that was two-parts intimate, small-scale, gentle fantasy and one-part cast-of-thousands epic swordplay. With Joey Wang and Maggie Cheung as White and Green (respectively), Tsui had two of the finest, most photogenic actresses in Hong Kong; and when he creates a simple, tight two-shot filled with those faces, the effect is magical indeed, focusing the film perfectly. As White, Joey Wang is sweetly seductive, regal and, lastly, heartwrenchingly tragic; although her performance in Tsui and Ching Siu-Tung's original *A Chinese Ghost Story* had already set her up as a supernatural tragic heroine, her performance here has an earthy, smart quality lacking in the more spectral roles. And Maggie Cheung aptly demonstrates why she's possibly the finest actress in the world today: Granted, Green doesn't offer the kind of challenges that the role of Ruan Ling-Yu in Stanley Kwan's stunning *Centre Stage* does, but Cheung makes Green vibrantly funny, curious, confused, jealous and very alive. The free-spirited, youthful Green is the emotional heart of the film, and Cheung's risky performance (she can make Green seem even slightly menacing without ever losing the audience's sympathy) is one of the best in any Tsui Hark film. Together the two actresses have a comfortable, deep rapport, and Tsui's often ingenious and witty blocking (i.e., the scene when Green and White jockey for Hsui-Xien's attention while bathing) clearly accentuates both their closeness and competitiveness.

It's perhaps inevitable that any male actor would suffer by comparison, but even so, Tien Feng seems miscast as Hsui-Xien. He's neither so charismatic that we understand why the women would vie for him, nor is his transformation from prude to lover as clearly defined as it could be; it's a role that Leslie Cheung, with his easy ability to move from priest to playboy, could have been divine in. Zhao Wen-

Zhou fares better as Fa-Hai — he has a genuinely interesting chemistry with Maggie Cheung, and handles the role's physicality superbly — but even he can't overcome the leaden character of Fa-Hai.

Effects aside, *Green Snake* is a technical achievement of the highest order. Even the Fa-Hai scenes are noteworthy for the exquisite lighting and design, especially the opening in the animalistic village: Fa-Hai stands serenely above a mob of vicious grotesques who stage peacock fights and carve monstrous idols. Tsui and cinematographer Giu Chiu Lam shoot the scene in reds and browns, giving the opening a hellish contrast to the cool blue and green pastels of the snake women sequences. Much of the film's lighting is deliberately artificial, with gradated filters and moving bands of color, but Tsui uses the very artificiality as a transitional device, linking two disparate locations with the same intense colors. The end is a puzzlement — why Tsui chose to shoot the final battle in harsh, unfiltered, revealing daylight instead of cool, shadowy night — but the vivid red of Fa-Hai's surplice filling the sky is nonetheless memorable. Bill Lui's art direction is exquisitely, intensely Chinese, with graceful draperies, lotus blossoms, arching bridges and large, sparsely-furnished rooms; *Green Snake* often looks more like a traditional painting than a modern movie. Equally impressive is the costume design, with the snake women clad in glimmering greens and pinks that suggest both shiny snakeskin and femininity; the costuming and the performances do more to suggest the women's reptilian nature than the occasional make-up touches, which consist of little more than fangs and scleral contact lenses.

*Green Snake*'s score deserves special attention. Nearly every second of *Green Snake* is accompanied by music, and this may be the finest score to ever grace a Hong Kong film. James Wong (who had already provided Tsui with the excellent scores to *Peking Opera Blues* and *Once Upon a Time in China*) and Mark Lui Chung Dak deliver a musical score that combines traditional Chinese instrumentation, Indian themes and current Cantopop. Where Wong's *Once Upon a Time in China* score featured bold male choruses, there's nary a male voice to be heard in *Green Snake*'s score, which makes use of female vocals (including Joey Wang's) in at least half of its cues. The songs in HK films are sometimes excruciatingly banal or inappropriate, added on for no other reason than formula, but the songs in *Green Snake* are so perfectly integrated it's impossible to think of the film without them.

*Green Snake* may have been a notorious financial bomb in its native Hong Kong, but it's also gained a small cult following in the West. Perhaps Chinese audiences were disappointed when *Green Snake* didn't meet their expectations for a period fantasy (it has neither the frantic pace of *A Chinese Ghost Story* nor the lunatic action of *Swordsman II*), whereas some Western viewers came to the film with fewer preconceptions and were more willing to embrace a film which (in direct opposition to most American films) celebrated sensuality and feminine power. In any case, if *Peking Opera Blues*, *A Better Tomorrow* and *Once Upon a Time in China* are the main jewels in Tsui Hark's crown, then *Green Snake* is the cracked emerald: imperfect, uneven, but with depths of meaning and beauty that make even its flaws seem precious.

ABOUT THE MOVIE: At 1993's Hong Kong box office, *Green Snake* ranked number 51, with a gross of $9,497,865.

At the 1994 Hong Kong Film Awards

*Green Snake* was nominated for Art Direction (Bill Lui), Costume and Make-Up Design (William Cheung and Ng Po-ling), and Original Film Score (James Wong and Mark Lui Chung Dak).

*Green Snake* actually differs slightly depending on what format you're watching it on, most significantly in the main title: In the "Gold Edition" laserdisc, for example, the film's title appears on a still shot of the snakes' garden, but in other releases it's over a moving shot of the water which flows throughout the main credit sequence.

*Green Snake* is based on the traditional Chinese legend "The Tale of the White Snake." According to *Women in Chinese Folklore* (published by Women of China, 1983), it's one of "The Four Great Tales of China," along with "The Cowherd and the Weaving Maid," "Seeking Her Husband at the Great Wall," and "The Story of a Tragic Love" (the latter was the basis for Tsui's film *The Lovers*). "The Tale of the White Snake" first appeared at the end of the Tang Dynasty (618 A.D.–907 A.D.) and has evolved ever since. In one version, Fa-Hai was the hero who imprisoned the White Lady in the Leifeng Pagoda (an actual structure that stood until 1929). In the most generally-accepted form of the story, White is the central figure, while Green is merely her maid. Fa-Hai is even more vile (he deliberately unleashes a plague on the populace, hoping the victims will turn to his temple for help), and after White gives birth he captures her in his magic alms bowl and imprisons her under the Leifeng Pagoda. Green retreats to the mountains and practices her swordplay for several years, after which she returns to best Fa-Hai, who finally transforms into a crab in a last effort to escape. The story ends happily, a distinct change from Tsui's tragic end.

The story has been adapted to film numerous times most recently in the 2000 film *Phantom of Snake*, which brought the snake women into contemporary Hong Kong. It has also been the basis of a number of novels, including the one by Lillian Lee which served as the basis for *Green Snake*; and American fantasist E. Hoffmann Price adapted it for his 1979 book *The Devil Wives of Li Fong*.

TSUI ON *GREEN SNAKE:* [The monk and the women] should be in the same story, but I put too much emphasis on the monk, maybe. It comes from a traditional fairy tale. The monk comes in very late, at the end of the story, when he starts to pull the male scholar away from these two women. And I didn't want to exploit the gay thing about the monk; I think it's too easy to do that. I think the monk is a very frustrated personality. That's why I chose a young guy with a very pretty face, so he's an ideal person. He thinks he's too perfect, and at the end he runs into the same problems as all human beings. He's kind of a statement I give to people who think they are better than other people. And the most difficult thing for religious people is to fight temptation. It's very strange, when everybody is enjoying temptation, for religious people to fight temptation, so he's a very frustrated guy. And I think human nature is fun to analyze again; how frustrating and contradictory they are! They want to be disciplined, but they hate boredom; they want happiness, but they hate temptation. I also have the monk in there to make a statement on how, if you make a mistake, you can redeem it by doing something good. What happens if you do something good and then you do something bad? Is that also the same pattern? So if you do something bad, then you do something good — that's a good sign. But if you do something bad again, do you have to do something good again? This is silly logic.

**Temptation: Green (Maggie Cheung) attempts to seduce the virtuous monk (Zhao Wen-Zhou) in *Green Snake*.**

In *Green Snake* one woman says, "I've been expecting human beings to be such smart creatures, but I've found they haven't any answers." The monk is a reflection of people who have this ideology, who are stuck in any position or level in our world, like government or officers. The character would be like all types of leaders in the spiritual world. In the book the emphasis is on White Snake, but we shifted it to Green Snake, then shifted it again to the monk, because I think the monk is a very interesting character to play with. If he was in real life, things would come very easily to him, but he wouldn't want to grab them. This is human nature.

[On the film's music]: Music is very attractive. The most different music I have in the movie is the Indian dance. The lyrics come from the Buddhist scriptures. "Mofuloku" is the god of snakes, said to be the symbol of lust. I really love that piece of music. I talked to James and said it should be a happier tone; and James said it should be romantic.

[On reusing certain pieces of music in the film]: Probably it was my mood at that period of time. Because I felt very involved in the movie, the color and the women. I think these two women in the movie were having big problems in real life with relationships, with their boyfriends.

[On the film's use of color]: We were shooting with five, six filters in front of the camera. The cameraman was worried about the sharpness of the image, but it turned out to be quite interesting. This is the movie where we used the most filters. It was crazy.

## The Lovers

Director/Producer/Writer, 1994. Cantonese: *Leung Juk.* Mandarin: *Liang Zhu.* Literally: *Leung & Chuk.* Co-Writer: Hui Sa-Long. Cinematography: David Chung. Art Direction: William Cheung, Cheong Kwok Wing. Editing: Mak Chi Sin. Music Score: James Wong, Woo Wai-Laap, Mark Lui Chung-Pak and Wong Ying-Wah. Costumes: William Cheung. CAST: Charlie Yeung Choi-Nei ("Chuk Ying-Toi"), Nicky Wu [Ng Kei-Lung] ("Leung Shan-Pak"), Carrie Ng Ka-Lai ("Ying-Toi's Mother"), Elvis Tsui Kam-Kong ("Ying-Toi's Father"), Lau Shun ("Cheung Kwai"). Opening Date: August 13, 1994.

SYNOPSIS: Chuk Ying-Toi's ambitious parents decide they must marry her to a high official to gain power at the court; unfortunately, Ying-Toi is too tomboyish and uneducated to lure a husband. Even though colleges are limited to male students, Ying-Toi's mother arranges to have her accepted at the same one where she studied, disguised as a boy. Accompanied by her devoted servant Cheung Kwai, the disguised Ying-Toi is placed in the school, where she is befriended by impoverished but hard-working Leung Shan-Pak. Shan-Pak and Ying-Toi grow closer and begin to question their feelings for each other. Shan-Pak reaches graduation and takes the government examination, earning a post as a low official; meanwhile, Ying-Toi's parents have arranged a marriage and send for her. She gets a message to Shan-Pak, and they have a last rendezvous, where Ying-Toi reveals her gender and they con-summate their relationship. Shan-Pak promises to marry her promptly; but when he meets her parents, he is dismissed and beaten to the point of death. His dying request is to be buried by the side of the road where Ying-Toi will pass by on her wedding procession. Her parents try to arrange a different route, but storms and landslides force the wedding party to pass by Shan-Pak's tomb. Ying-Toi tears off her wedding gown and races to the tomb; supernatural winds keep Cheung Kwai and the others from reaching her. The ground gives way beneath her and she's instantly buried alive. A monk friend of Shan-Pak's finds a drawing of butterflies Ying-Toi did in happier times, and when he tears the paper butterflies out they become two real butterflies and flutter off together.

REVIEW: When I was on my way to Hong Kong to interview Tsui Hark, I sat on the plane next to a delightful young man who was bound for home after a year abroad as a foreign exchange student. We struck up a conversation, and when he found out the subject of my visit, he was absolutely thrilled. He told me that *The Lovers* was his favorite movie, that when he was a teenager he and his friends had seen it over and over and played the songs from the film to death.

Is *The Lovers,* then, Tsui Hark's attempt to crash the teen-movie market? If it is, it's a damn good one — not only was *The Lovers* a hit for Tsui, it's also one of his most beautiful films and a poignant meditation on love.

*The Lovers* is based on a traditional tale and has been filmed several times before, but Tsui manages to make the story very much his own. His *Lovers* is set in a world run by women, where the men waste their days vainly grooming themselves; in this world nature is vitally important, a force that nourishes, kills and resurrects.

Original poster for *The Lovers* (featuring Nicky Wu and Charlie Yeung).

Tsui's interest in exploring gender is obvious and well-discussed, but his thematic fascination with nature itself is just as apparent in *The Lovers*. He's always had a love-hate relationship with natural forces; in his first film, *The Butterfly Murders*, nature was a great power and a mortal danger (even while it was appealing in outward appearance). Likewise, *A Chinese Ghost Story* presented a tree demon; *The East Is Red* and *The Magic Crane* both feature antagonists who fight with water; and in *Green Snake* weather, water and sulfur can all kill. But in *Green Snake* nature — as represented by the snake women and the spider monk — can also be more compassionate than humanity.

*The Lovers* — like *Green Snake* — surrounds its characters with nature partly to create a complete fairy tale world, but also to comment on how man's fate is interconnected with nature. The *Lovers* opens with Ying-Toi's love of butterflies — she keeps some in a jar and draws more on a sheet of paper she uses as a lamp shade. Her wealthy home skillfully incorporates nature, with lovely fountains, ponds and gardens; but later on, Shan-Pak's monk friend comments on the horror of imprisoning ornamental fish in man-made ponds. The school that Shan-Pak and Ying-Toi attend is located in the midst of a lovely glade, surrounded by trees and lawns; the setting adds to their growing love an innocent, unspoiled quality. During the rendezvous when they finally acknowledge their physical attraction, nature works for them by granting them a rainstorm and a sheltering cavern; when the storm stops they return to Ying-Toi's waiting attendants covered in mud. While the implication would be obvious in a Western film — they've been dirtied by their experience — in *The Lovers* it seems more as if they've also consummated their relationship with nature. And at the film's

conclusion nature literally becomes their fate, as storms force Ying-Toi to Shan-Pak's tomb and finally to her own death. Nature has granted them the unity their human parents tried to deny them — but nature has also taken Ying-Toi's life.

*The Lovers* also continues Tsui Hark's obsession with the meanings of male and female. Ying-Toi can apparently only succeed if she is disguised as a boy; and yet the all-male college she's sent to is run by a woman. Ying-Toi's own family is clearly run by her mother, a cunning and cruel manipulator who plots while Ying-Toi's father spends endless hours making himself up. Tsui spends virtually no time trying to convince *anyone* that Ying-Toi is male; her disguise consists of nothing more than binding her breasts and slightly lowering her voice. In fact, Tsui seems to be suggesting that Ying-Toi would be better off simply acknowledging her femininity and taking her place alongside her mother and headmistress.

*The Lovers* also takes an amusing but ultimately compassionate look at homosexuality. In his documentary *Yang + Yin: Gender in Chinese Cinema*, filmmaker Stanley Kwan virtually ignores Tsui's treatment of women and concentrates instead on the use of the word "real" in *The Lovers* to describe the love between Shan-Pak and Ying-Toi. Kwan believes Tsui is disparaging homosexuality with this particular phraseology, but in fact the word fits in with *The Lovers'* fairy tale approach to its story — Shan-pak is correct in saying that he and Ying-Toi can't have a "real" love (Tsui defends the word by saying that there was no popularly-accepted alternative for the film's time period). Kwan also ignores the film's contingent of gay students at the college, led by Mong-Chun, a student who develops a crush first on Shan-Pak, then on Ying-Toi. When Ying-Toi needs help getting a message to Shan-Pak, it's Mong-

Chun who comes to her rescue, sacrificing his own feelings and risking his standing at the college.

When Shan-Pak first feels affection for Ying-Toi, rather than deny the sensation he begins to question his own (and Ying-Toi's) orientation. Peter Chan's 1994 *He's a Woman, She's a Man* would carry this theme farther, with its hero finally openly embracing the object of his affection irregardless of gender; if Tsui chooses instead to have Ying-Toi reveal her sex before they embrace, it's largely because he's addressing the subject of love — not homosexuality — in a different way. In *The Lovers* friendship is what finally leads to romantic love; before they finally kiss we've seen Shan-Pak and Ying-Toi study together, eat together, play together, support each other through tough trials — in short, they've developed a deep, mutual respect and friendship before they acknowledge any physical attraction. *The Lovers* may look like a fairy tale, but just under its summer-afternoon surface lurks a surprisingly sophisticated notion of romance.

*The Lovers* has a fine cast, particularly its two very appealing young leads (Charlie Yeung and pop singer Nicky Wu), but it's the behind-the-camera elements that make the film a triumph. David Chung's cinematography makes use of much of the same lighting and filtering that served *Green Snake* well, and *The Lovers* has a similar soft pastel look. Tsui wisely downplays his use of exaggerated angles and rapid cutting, favoring instead a simple, moderately-paced style for the film. But best of all is the score, led by Tsui's great composer James Wong. The score incorporates an orchestra, traditional instruments and minor use of synthesizer, all supporting an exquisite main theme that soars, bobs along happily during the comic sequences and wrings tears at the conclu-

sion. It stands alone as a magnificent achievement from this gifted composer.

If *The Lovers* suffers in any regard, it would be the abrupt tone shifts incorporated into the script. The film's first two-thirds is sweet-natured, simple and comic in tone (Shan-Pak and Ying-Toi become friends partly because they make faces at each other); in its last third it becomes cruel and tragic, as first Shan-Pak and then Ying-Toi die. And its final denouement is supernatural and mystical, as the lovers are reborn as Ying-Toi's beloved butterflies. Tsui has gone on record at length defending the change from humorous to serious, but this shift is less problematic than the one from natural to supernatural. Prior to the film's ending there has been virtually no mention of mystical forces (excepting the film's fairy-tale setting), so it comes as a strange surprise when reality gives way at the end. It also makes the ending — when Ying-Toi's butterfly drawings take on life — seem forced; some set-up earlier on would have paved the way for a smoother transition to the ending's spiritual happenings.

Still, that's a minor complaint for a film that is, for the most part, an utterly gorgeous examination of love, humanity and nature.

ABOUT THE FILM: *The Lovers* came in at number 16 on the year's box office list, with total earnings of $18,643,478.

At the year's Hong Kong Film Awards it received five nominations: for Best Director (Tsui Hark), Best Supporting Actress (Carrie Ng Ka-Lai), Best Art Direction (William Chang, who won for *Ashes of Time*, and Cheong Kwok Wing), Best Costume and Make-Up Design (William Cheung, who also won for *Ashes of Time* here), and Best Original Film Score (James Wong, Woo Wai Laap, Mark Lui Chung-Tak and Wong Ying-Wah).

As with *Green Snake, The Lovers* is based on an ancient legend known as one of "The Four Great Tales of China" (the other two are "The Cowherd and the Weaving Maid" and "Seeking Her Husband at the Great Wall"). "The Story of a Tragic Love" was first conceived in the Northern and Southern Dynasties (420 A.D.–581 A.D.), and developed into its present form in the early Tang Dynasty. In the afterward to *Women in Chinese Folklore*, Wu Chao indicated that the story "stands for freedom of choice in marriage," a privilege not often enjoyed in early China. Although most of the story is remarkably similar to Tsui's film, in the original the lovers changed into birds at the end; Tsui also added the character of the monk.

"The Story of a Tragic Love" has been filmed numerous times before, most famously in Li Hanxiang's immensely successful *The Love Eterne* (1963), on which King Hu served as "Associate Director."

TSUI ON *THE LOVERS*: For *The Lovers* I was doing it in a very short time. It was a very short schedule. I only had a month to do that movie, including preparation — that's a crazy schedule. Probably most of our sets were existing sets.

A lot of people cried in the theater; I didn't expect that. I thought it was supposed to be romantic, not a sad movie. One funny thing was when I showed the rough cut (it didn't have sound) to the actors... I showed it to the two young kids. And they saw the movie and they cried like hell. And I said, "What's wrong with the movie?" This was in a hotel room, they were watching a tape, they were watching the middle of the movie and they started crying. And after they finished the movie, they went into the toilet to clean up, and I said, "What's wrong with the movie? It's not supposed to be so sad!" And then in the theater everybody starts to cry in the middle, because they know the story already. It's a well known story, like *Romeo and Juliet*, so they expect the ending. It's like at the end of *Romeo and Juliet*, he dies, and then Juliet, too. And the way I treated it was a very harmless beginning, and everything's harmless, and even when it comes to very major things it's still harmless. And that's something that would create some kind of very strange mood for the audience, because he dies. They feel like I'm luring them into something unexpected. I make them feel easy, relaxed, but they know at the end it's going to be a big massacre, bloodshed, things like that. If you know the story, it has different feelings. They hate each other, they don't like each other, but they start to be friends. If you know the story, these things are not important; what's important is when you encounter the parents. And that's the most tragic thing about it. And that changed a lot from the story, because the story was not like that. It was sort of like a story about people in different subclasses. That was a very practical phenomenon in our real lives, our social situation. I changed that because the kid knows that — he's not blind, he's a smart kid. Still, he tries to break through that barrier. In the original story there's no way — the guy spits blood right on the house of the girl. It's kind of silly — you've been friends with a guy for a period of time, and it ends up that it's a girl. How could he get so frustrated at not being able to marry a girl? When he found that's a girl, he spit blood right on the house! That's a bit impossible for me to imagine. What kind of thing would frustrate you to the point where you really spit blood and die? I think something is symbolic about this — what he can never change is the social system. He has been sentenced already, condemned to a death sentence. And you can't change anything and you die. That's very symbolic in that he cannot fight something that's been around for years, that's stood for so long. And his character dies because of that. So for that we needed to add several scenes. Actually, the young guy dies because all of his obligations, all his morals, come down on him. He spits blood because there's no way this character can exist in this world.

With the girl I said, "How are you going to be 16 years, have no contact with other people your age, staying in a male school, and with people not knowing you are female? Can you imagine that? I cannot. So you should be isolated." In the original story she is not isolated, but I feel that is difficult to comprehend. So she should be isolated, somebody should know she is a young girl and is protecting her. Otherwise there is no way — when she takes a shower, when she has her period — there is no way she can avoid being noticed by the males. There's this awareness of the different sex at that age, especially when you have to take up so much of the obligation to love someone. This is very interesting. It's not something impossible that you may not be interested in at all, you may just be curious. I think love may be too easy a word to say. When you are at this age and you have this first experience with a guy, it's kind of easy to say "love," but I think it's more curiosity than anything. Because youth can be a reason for emotional ups and downs. I say, "When you die, how are people going to look at you? I don't want people to take it as a suggestion for solving a problem by killing yourself, that's very bad thinking." Actually, in the story she jumps into the grave, the two of them become butterflies and fly out of the grave. I said, "You can jump, but what does that mean? You're tired of talking, so you make this statement and you are together, right? And spiritually — the butterflies should be your spirits, it's

not just the butterflies coming out." So I changed that a bit. I had a difficult time doing that. I wanted her to be very strong on the set.

And I added the make-up there, because it's symbolic. It means something. It's actually true that these people did make-up, in festivals or happy occasions. Even the males did make-up. And the funny thing is, they put on make-up, and it was not thick enough. I said, "Let's make it *real* thick, like a clown." The make up people were trying really hard. Even for the girl I wanted her to look very clownly, so when the rain comes down and washes it off, she looks better. A girl like that, she looks kind of pale after the make-up's off; I think that's good, too — let's make her pale.

The butterfly thing, I was thinking a lot about how are we going to treat the butterflies? Then I put in the monk. But do you realize that is not a monk — that is just a person who shaved his head, and he's not actually a monk. That's an intellectual character who is also a social outcast; there is no way he can get into their social world with his thinking. So is the school principal — she's also a social outcast. She cannot help, she cannot do anything, she is not part of the power structure, the hierarchy of the society. They intellectually understand the situation, and they understand that's all they can do — nothing else.

## *The Chinese Feast*

Director/Producer/Writer, 1995. Cantonese: *Gam Yuk Moon Tong*. Mandarin: *Jin Yu Man Tang*. Literally: *Gold Jade Full Hall*. Co-Producers: Raymond Wong Bak-Ming, Li Ning. Co-Writers: Ng Man-Fai, Che Chung Taai. Cinematography: Peter Pau. Art Direction: William Cheung Suk Ping, Man Lim Chung.

Sun (Leslie Cheung) and Au Ka Wai (Anita Yuen) watch an amazing meal in *The Chinese Feast*.

Action Design: Yuen Bun. Editing: Mak Chi Sin. Music Score: Lowell Lo. Costumes: William Cheung Suk Ping, Man Lim Chung. CAST: Leslie Cheung Kwok-Wing ("Sun"), Anita Yuen Wing-Yee ("Au Ka Wai"), Kenny Bee [Chung Chun-To] ("Liu Kit"), Law Kar-Ying ("Master Au"), Zhao Wen-Zhou [Chiu Man-Cheuk] ("Lung Kwun Bo"), Xiong Xin-Xin [Hung Yan-Yan] ("Wong Wing"), Lau Shun ("Kawasaki"). Opening Date: January 28, 1995.

SYNOPSIS: A major cooking competition is taking place in a Beijing hotel. The last two contestants are Master Liu Kit and Master Lung Kwun Bo. The two men are tied; as the competition proceeds, these master chefs prepare rice, exotic sculptures and finally fish, all with tremendous joy and skill. Just before the final round Kit receives a call from the hospital, telling him that his girlfriend Bing is having a miscarriage. He tries to go back to the competition but realizes he can't continue. His hesitation has cost him: When he arrives at the hospital his girlfriend has lost their baby and left behind only a note for him, telling him their affair is over because cooking is obviously more important to him. He leaves the hospital, crushed. Cut to: Five years later, another cooking contest — but this one is to recruit chefs for hotels in Canada. Sun wants to emigrate to follow his girlfriend, but he can't cook; he tries to cheat but makes a fool of himself and is thrown out. Sun is a successful triad loan shark who desperately wants to leave the business; when Lung Kwun Bo happens to overhear him, he offers him an introduction to the owner of Qing Han Restaurant, Master Au. Au hires him to work in the kitchen, but Sun seems completely incompetent until the day a triad meeting takes place at Qing Han and Sun quickly quashes the situation. Sun also gets involved with Au's punkish daughter Ka Wai, who wants to be a singer; when he sees her mauling an old standard at a karaoke bar, he's smitten. Ka Wai and Sun are both there the day the restaurant is visited by Wong Wing, an arrogant master chef who challenges Master Au to a cooking duel: They will invite gourmet judges and see who can best prepare the Qing Han Feast, a legendary three-day affair involving 108 dishes. The stakes: Wong Wing's 50 million against the Qing Han Restaurant; Wong Wing wants to take over all of Hong Kong's restaurants, and is starting with this one because it's the oldest in the district. When Master Au suffers a heart attack after Wong Wing's visit, Sun and Ka Wai realize it's up to them to prepare Qing Han Feast in Master Au's stead, so they go in search of Kit, the only other chef in China qualified to prepare the meal. They find him a shattered, half-dead drunk in Guangzhou; they use his girlfriend Bing to lure him back to Hong Kong, where Bo begins reawakening Kit to his cooking talents. Finally the first day of the contest arrives, and Kit succeeds in tying with Wong Wing; but on the following days the devious Wong cheats, sabotaging Kit's equipment. When the piece de resistance involves monkey brain, Wong Wing tries to have Kit arrested, alleging he's committed an illegal act in killing a monkey; but Kit reveals he substituted tofu for monkey brain, and the judges are so impressed they award him the championship. In the end Bing and Kit are reunited, Sun and Ka Wai are together, and Master Au has recovered; they all join together at Qing Han Restaurant to prepare a celebration.

REVIEW: *The Chinese Feast* is easily Tsui Hark's most delectable comedy since 1984's *Shanghai Blues*. Not only is it consistently amusing and often fall-down funny, it's also a wry political commentary that offers possibly the most hopeful vision of post-handover Hong Kong in Tsui's entire library.

*The Chinese Feast* is also a visual homage to food. It opens with a long, high shot that tracks over a seemingly endless array of gorgeous, multi-colored dishes, while a simple, very Chinese main theme plays. After the credits it proceeds directly to the first of the film's three cooking competitions, as Bo and Kit face off. Tsui endows all of the cooking scenes in *The Chinese Feast* with the panache and agility of the martial arts duels in the *Once Upon a Time in China* series. Bo and Kit (and later, the vile Wong Wing) spin bowls, whirl knives, carve at lightning speed and flip flaming meats high into the air with astonishing precision. But what sets this apart from the typical martial arts scene is that Bo and Kit have an obvious admiration for each other; they smile and nod as they watch each other prepare the exotic dishes. It's as if food is so precious to them that they will take any opportunity to learn better ways to prepare it, even if it means expressing an interest in one's rival.

Food is obviously the central metaphor in *The Chinese Feast*, and Tsui uses it to represent everything from love to greed to apathy. Food is what drives Kit and his girlfriend Bing apart (while she's giving birth, yet — Kit has chosen food over life at this point), but food is what brings them back together; in the film's most touching scene, Bing fixes dinner for Kit, and as they share the food their faces reflect fondness for both the tastes and each other. Food represents Kit's apathy — when he's a used-up drunk he crunches through Sun and Ka Wai's horrible concoction of spices, bottle tops and clothespins without batting an eye. Food becomes Wong Wing's arrogance when he uses technological devices to prepare bear claw in the Qing Han competition. But mainly food represents community; throughout *A Chinese Feast* food is the focal point of large gatherings. The only time anyone eats alone in *The Chinese Feast* is when the drunken Kit goes to a street vendor for his evening meal; Kit's lonely, tasteless meal marks him as a pathetic figure. Food is virtually the glue holding society together in *The Chinese Feast.*

In 1991's *The Banquet* food finally united rich and poor; in *The Chinese Feast* food finally unites more than economic classes. Kit is a mainland chef located in Guangzhou (formerly Canton). To win the Qing Han competition, Hong Kong chef Master Au must unite with mainland China chef Kit; their competition is Wong Wing, director of "the Super Group," an enigmatic but obviously very capitalistic company. Wong Wing drives a gleaming red Mercedes Benz, dresses flamboyantly and plots to take over all the restaurants in Hong Kong; he's the worst of 1990s money-grubbing. When he and his assistants dress in traditional Chinese robes for the final contest, it seems less as if they are venerating tradition and more as if they're making a mockery of it, with their high-tech freezing units and injection devices. The Qing Han feast, of course, is important because it represents Chinese tradition; in the past it was used to unite the Qing and Han clans. The final message of *The Chinese Feast* seems to be that Hong Kong and mainland China must revitalize themselves to come together in the best interests of China.

Curiously enough, *The Chinese Feast* also seems to disparage parts of the same past it celebrates. Neither of the contestants at the end of the Qing Han competition are willing to prepare monkey brain; Wong Wing wants to set his opponents up, so he uses goat brain; while Kit and Bo simply can't bring themselves to kill a sweet-faced, intelligent-looking monkey. Tsui plays a slightly cruel trick on the audience, leading them to believe that not only have Kit and Bo killed the monkey, they're even serving its brain raw while it shrieks in terror; when he reveals that the brain is tofu and the screams are a recording, we're likelier to feel dismayed than relieved, especially considering the competition judges have happily eaten what they believed to be fresh monkey brain. In 1988's *I Love Maria* the two heroes adopt a dog rather than eat it, even when they're starving; here Tsui goes for a heartwrenching close-up of the caged monkey. It almost seems as if Tsui simply couldn't reconcile his own affection for animals with his interest in Chinese tradition.

But, politics aside, *The Chinese Feast* is a sidesplitting comedy that deftly mixes physical humor with sweetly funny characters. Anita Yuen may be Hong Kong's funniest woman, and here she outdoes herself as the magenta-haired, bopping Ka Wai. She's a rubber ball of energy, bouncing her way through scenes with a delightful insouciance. The film's most hysterical scene comes when Master Au tells Sun to kill a gigantic fish; the fish slithers from Sun's grasp right into the restaurant, where it's pursued by Sun, Ka-Wai and the rest of the staff. The scene is a veritable comic masterpiece, with some slightly odd shots (one of which places Sun's struggle with the fish in the background) lifting the sequence to ever funnier heights.

It's also delicious to see two of Tsui's leading martial arts experts (Zhao Wen-Zhou and Xiong Xin-Xin) in essentially non-martial arts roles (note the use of the word "essentially"—those cooking scenes call for some deft moves). Zhao exudes warmth and camaraderie as Master Bo; after seeing him as the stoic Wong Fei-

**Lung Kwun Bo (Zhao Wen-Zhou) and Sun (Leslie Cheung) light up *The Chinese Feast*.**

Hung and *The Blade*'s On, who'd have guessed he has the most endearing smile this side of Julia Roberts? And Xiong Xin-Xin makes Wong Wing just the slightest bit fey, a perfectionist who is as concerned about his nails as his meals.

Is it just coincidence that the name "Wong Wing" is one English letter off from Wong Jing, Hong Kong's premiere B-filmmaker who recently opened a "Super Group"–like agency in Hong Kong? On top of everything else, *The Chinese Feast* has a field day throwing out in-jokes referencing Hong Kong's film industry. At one point Bo is trying to restore Kit's sense of hearing via acupuncture, and instead Kit begins picking up radio signals. He mentions a pop song, and Ka-Wai and Sun ask him who's singing. "Leon Lai," he responds, "not Leslie Cheung." Ka-Wai and Sun both express their displeasure in no uncertain terms.

*The Chinese Feast* was presented as a Lunar New Year release, and so it falls into the subgenre of New Year's "Gung Hey Fa Choy" movies, which traditionally end with the entire cast turning directly to the camera and toasting the audience. In *The Chinese Feast* the gesture feels genuine; it's a perfect finale to an honestly presented feel-good movie.

**ABOUT THE FILM:** *The Chinese Feast* is the most successful film yet directed solely by Tsui Hark; only *A Better Tomorrow*, *Swordsman II* and *The Twin Dragons* grossed more. The film was the sixth most successful movie of 1995, with a gross of $31,117,576. Strangely, it was completely ignored by the Hong Kong Film Awards.

Look for Tsui in the closing shot, as he raises his glass to toast the audience.

The song that Anita Yuen mangles in the karaoke club (and which is echoed in the film's musical score) is "Habanera" from Bizet's *Carmen*. This was traditionally performed with castanets, which explains the stylized stance Yuen has at the beginning of the karaoke number.

Tsui on *The Chinese Feast*: The script had been around for quite some time. Eventually someone wanted to do something, so I pulled that from the shelf and said, "Let's do this one." It's been around for a long time. (In the interview conducted by Ting Wai Ho for *Eastern Heroes* Special Edition #5, Tsui explains the reason for the long wait to make *The Chinese Feast*: "Actually, after I made *Once Upon a Time in China* I already planned to do *The Feast*, but then the star of the film, Yuen Biao, I never expected that after I told him the story, he'd make another film called *Shogun and Little Kitchen* and I was quite shocked. I stopped making the production and waited till the film came out…I tried to plan again and found out that Ang Lee is making *Eat, Drink, Man, Woman*, so I stopped again.")

[Was it a fun film to make?] Definitely yes. The script had been around since *Once Upon a Time in China* — even earlier than that. The script was on the shelf for a long time, and I started to be skeptical about the idea. I thought that would be a very fun film to watch, lots of food, lots of funny things going on with the food.

I still have the sequel script around; I think it's fun, too. The location of the sequel is Japan; they start doing Japanese food! So what happens is, it's a restaurant run by the daughter of the boss. And the daughter's cooking is very bad. And the restaurant is always packed! This traveler comes to the restaurant, orders a bowl of noodles or rice, and it's very bad, but the restaurant is packed, and she says, "Why?" Then the daughter comes out, and she's very pretty. So the traveler — who is also a woman — tells her that the food is very

bad: "No one here would tell you the truth, but I will tell you the truth — the food doesn't taste good at all." So she walks out, and the daughter runs after her, saying, "How bad is the food?" "The food's really bad. Test it." So they put it outside, people eat it, and the food is thrown away. So she has been living in an unreal world. And she asks the traveler to be with her, so she knows the truth. Eventually she was to imitate a cook, and she has to learn how to cook, and she has to be a cook. The sequel's on the shelf, too; I don't know when we're going to put it out or do it.

It's fun making a movie about food. We had four or five different chefs on the set cooking all the time.

In a 1991 interview with Law Wai-Ming and Lo Man-Hing, "Laughter in the Deep Blue Sea — Tsui Hark on His Recent Developments" (from *City Entertainment*, 1991), Tsui talked about his ideal comedy film; even though the interview predates the release of *The Chinese Feast* by four years, it perfectly sums up his approach: "It was not productive to tell stories with the psychology of 1997… it was more important to overcome Hong Kong people's sense of being marginalized…."

## The Blade

Director/Writer/Associate Producer, 1995. Cantonese: *Diy.* Mandarin: *Dao.* Co-Writers: Hui Nyn, Siu Man Sing. Cinematography: Gam Sing. Art Direction: William Cheung Suk Ping, Bill Lui, Yau Wai Ming. Action Design: Mang Hoi, Yuen Bun, Stephen Tung. Editing: Gam Ma. Music Score: Woo Wai Laap, Wong Ying-Wah. Cast: Zhao Wen-Zhou ("On"), Xiong Xin-Xin ("Lung"), Austin Wai ("Ling's father"), Moses Chan ("Iron Head"), Michael Tse Tin Wah ("Bandit Leader"), Jason Chu

On (Zhao Wen-Zhou) takes on his father's killer at the climax of *The Blade.*

Wing-Tong ("Bandit"). Opening Date: December 21, 1995.

SYNOPSIS: Ling is a young girl who has been raised in the sword factory run by her father; she is infatuated with two of the laborers, Iron Head and On, and dreams that they will one day fight over her. When On overhears Ling's grandmother talking about how his father was horribly murdered by a tattooed man "who could fly" named Lung, he takes his father's broken saber and goes in search of the killer. Ling follows after him and is captured by bandits; when On hears her cries, he tries to help her. In the fight with the bandits On loses his right arm and falls over a cliff, disappearing. He's found by Black Head, a young orphan girl who lives in the wilderness on a small farm; she nurses him back to health, but their world is shattered when bandits torch the farm and torture On. In the ruins of the farmhouse Black Head finds half a kung fu practice book, and On uses it to train himself. Meanwhile, Ling is languishing, griefstricken over the loss of On, until Iron Head takes her out to search for On. Their quest leads them to a town where Iron Head falls for a prostitute, whom he steals from one of the bandits. The bandits also take a beating from On, who puts his new kung fu skills to use when they attack the farm again. When the townspeople try to proclaim On a hero, he and Black Head leave the farm. In the town they run into Ling and Iron Head. Just as the bandits try to re-capture Iron Head's prostitute; during the fight On accidentally kills the prostitute. When the bandits' leader finds out, he hires Lung, the tattooed killer, to go after Iron Head, who has returned to the sword factory. The bandits and Lung attack the factory, and On finally has the chance to go head to head with his father's killer. After a lengthy swordfight, On defeats Lung, then leaves

with Black Head. Iron Head also leaves, and Ling is left to grow old in the deserted factory alone.

REVIEW: *The Blade* is Tsui Hark's homage to the "wuxia" (swordplay) films he grew up with. Based on Chang Cheh's 1967 classic *The One-Armed Swordsman,* Tsui has taken the traditional martial arts epic and transformed it into a turbocharged, dark, raw classic for the '90s.

Perhaps no other film in Tsui's career so emphatically delineates the differences in style between new Hong Kong cinema and old as *The Blade.* Chang Cheh's earlier film is an archetypal '60s kung fu film, with its stately pace, stylized sets and short fights; long passages of dialogue and philosophy discussions are photographed with simple two-shots and a static camera. To modern audiences the film may seem stilted and slow; despite the similar story, it's virtually the antithesis of Tsui Hark's hyperkinetic, primitive remake.

But what distinguishes *The Blade* as a Tsui Hark film — and not just any other contemporary, post–'70s martial arts epic — is its reliance on a feminine point of view. Even though *The Blade* revolves around On, who will become the one-armed swordsman, the story is told by Ling, the daughter of On's boss and his secret admirer. In both the 1967 film and this 1995 edition, the boss's daughter is a sheltered, lovely and lonely young girl who secretly yearns for the gifted young student swordsman; in Tsui's updating, Ling actually becomes a more proactive character, leaving the safe confines of her home to go in search of On. What she finds instead is a world so awash in brutality and lust that she flees back to her enclosed birthplace, spending the rest of her life there. She is plainly so appalled by the violence she sees that she prefers the life of a hermit; she paradoxically serves then to both condemn the film's extreme violence and to condemn those who choose to deny its existence, for she ends up leading a solitary life punctuated only by occasional (platonic) visits from On and Iron Head.

The Blade does in fact mirror Tsui Hark's own fascination/disgust with violence. Its fight scenes are brilliantly choreographed and are undeniably exhilarating; yet The Blade is also set in a world where violence is so constant that characters seem isolated, helpless and perpetually victimized. Just as in his earlier Dangerous Encounter — 1st Kind, Tsui is not afraid to acknowledge this contradiction in himself; and, again, just as with that ultraviolent film, there is no easy resolution or happy ending.

Just as terrifying as violence is sex. Ling fantasizes about On and Iron Head fighting over her, yet when finally confronted with an actual sexual act (Iron Head and the prostitute), she is utterly terrified. The Blade features shot after shot of half-naked, gleaming bodies (including, in the opening, Ling's), yet sex is one more violent act (Iron Head leaves the prostitute tied during their encounter) to be feared.

The best that can be hoped for in The Blade's world is friendship, which is a redemptive force that saves On and educates Ling. The film's two most interesting relationships are its friendships: On's with the feral orphan Black Head, and Ling's with the cynical prostitute. On and Black Head bond by saving each other; Ling and the prostitute have nothing more than mutual femininity to draw them together. Tsui also uses the friendship between Ling and the whore to emphasize the tragedy of the latter's death; just when we had begun to care about her as someone who could offer the naïve Ling support, strength and advice, she's accidentally slain by On — who had once desired her.

If the swords are phallic symbols (desire is certainly dangerous in The Blade), they're also the film's most potent political statement. In the original One-Armed Swordsman the plot revolved around the typical kung fu-film nexus of the martial arts school; but Tsui has wisely avoided that cliché-laden trap and substituted instead a sword factory. In the beginning of the story the swords are beautiful to Ling; they reflect light in a way she loves. None of the laborers are adept swordsmen, and when they approach the master with their desire to avenge the death of a monk, the master literally beats the idea out of them. He worries about his company's reputation should it become known that those who make the swords can also use them; in the end the bandits break into the company compound and take the swords. They are finally defeated by the laborers, but the company has suffered such a heavy loss that the implication is that the factory closes as a result. By taking no responsibility for the weapons they produce — and which have empowered an entire generation of bandits to lay waste to the land — the manufacturers pay the ultimate price, falling victim to their own sabers. Certainly Tsui intended the message of The Blade to be a contemporary one, and it's just as appropriate to the atomic present as the sharp-edged past.

Tsui's image of China's past is like no other; certainly nothing could be farther from the opulent costume dramas of the '60s. This past features bandits who paint their faces in death-white make-up, heavily-tattooed men who don exotic headdresses, and bandits who use steel-jawed traps. If parts of The Blade seem slightly anachronistic (the traps, for instance, seem to come from a later period), it all fits in Tsui's vision of a world ruled by ancient passions. Costume design, sets, make-up and the stunning, percussive musical

The male form: On (Zhao Wen-Zhou) forges *The Blade.*

score all reflect the rough, frontier-like ambiance. The gasp-inspiring fights rely less on wire work and more on the extraordinary abilities of their performers; the final showdown between Zhao Wen-Zhou's On and Xiong Xin-Xin's Lung is certainly one of filmdom's great fights, with blood, sweat, whirling blades and the fast-as-lightning combatants. And Tsui has dispensed with his usual exaggerated camera angles and movements in favor of documentary-like zooms (which is almost a witty commentary on the martial arts films of the '60s and '70s, when zooms were often overused to the point of self-parody) and jerky handheld shots, which make this world feel ultra real. It's almost a shock when *The Blade* ends and you realize it was a work of fiction.

In the end *The Blade* may be as much a tribute to Tsui's idol Akira Kurosawa as to any of the Chinese filmmakers. It has

the dirty, down-in-the-mud, almost existential quality of *The Seven Samurai* or *Yojimbo,* but it also has a completely distinctive look that belongs to Tsui Hark alone. He may have been influenced by Kurosawa and Chang Cheh, but it seems likely that future filmmakers will be just as influenced by Tsui Hark and his remarkable accomplishments in *The Blade.*

ABOUT THE FILM: *The Blade* was perhaps just too dark for Hong Kong audiences, as it performed somewhat dismally at the box office. It placed at number 97 for 1995 (it played into 1996 but didn't place on the charts), for a total gross of $3,308,775.

It was recognized at the Hong Kong Film Awards with nominations for Best Action Choreography (Yuen Bun, Mang Hoi and Stephen Tung), and Best Costume and Make-up Design (William Cheung).

TSUI ON *THE BLADE:* At that period of time I wanted to switch to something totally different. Actually, I am closer to *Blade* than anything I've done before. I'm actually a documentary cameraman, so I would go for a vérité look more than some types of shots. I think I'm still going in that direction

There was one time I asked the cinematographer, "Let's shoot the scene with no clear idea of lighting. Let's do different lighting in every setup." He said, "No, I cannot do that." "Why not?" "I'm trained in a way that I do everything in continuity." "Okay, let's put up the light and let's shake the light!" He was going crazy. I said, "Let's use a spotlight. Spotlight everything — a spotlight following the guy." He said, "Can we do that? Can we do a spotlight?" "Yeah, why not? Let's do a spotlight!"

In a May 3, 2000 interview with Stephen Short from Time@CNN.com, Tsui responded to a comment about the incessant violence in *The Blade:* "It didn't start out that way, it just grew. I just thought to myself that war is brutal and violent and there's no point pretending otherwise. If you're a person who grows up in a world full of fighting, then that world would be full of tormented people with tormented thinking — a life with no guarantee of safety, a life that's perpetually fragile."

## *A Chinese Ghost Story: The Tsui Hark Animation*

Producer/Writer/Actor, 1997. Cantonese: *Siu Sin.* Mandarin: *Xiaoqian.* Character design: Frankie Chung. Character animation director: Tetsuya Endo. Music: Ricky Ho. Executive producers: Nansun Shi, Tsuneo Leo Sato, Charles Heung, Meileen Choo. Directed by: Andrew Chen. Voice Cast (Cantonese/ Mandarin): Jan Lam/ Nicky Wu Chi-Lung ("Ning"); Vivian Lai/Linda Wong ("Lan"); Tsui Hark ("Solid Gold"); Eric Kot/ Tommy Su Yu-Pang ("Ten Miles"); Raymond Wong/ Sammo Hung ("White Cloud"); James Wong/Lee Li-Chun ("Red Beard"); Anita Yuen/Sylvia Chang ("Shine"); Charlie Yeung/Liu Jo-Ying ("Butterfly"); Kelly Chan/Yon Fan ("Madame Trunk"); Jordan Chan/Lo Ta-Yu ("Mountain Evil"); Ronald Cheng ("Fu"). Opening Date: July 31, 1997.

SYNOPSIS: Ning is a poor travelling tax debt collector who roams the countryside with his loyal dog, Solid Gold, hoping desperately to make enough money to impress the girlfriend, Lan, who rejected him some time ago. When he enters a village whose inhabitants are only too happy to load him down with gold, he's overjoyed — until he realizes he's entered a city of the dead populated entirely by ghosts and monsters. He falls in love with Shine, a beautiful ghost, who at first merely wants to suck his soul out for her evil mistress; however, eventually Shine is won over by his trust, and together they plot to catch the Reincarnation Train so they can be reborn as human lovers.

REVIEW: Tsui Hark is a talented artist and great aficionado of comic art; his live-action style has always included cartoon-like elements (vivid colors, frenetic action and a love of chaos), and so it was perhaps inevitable (to say nothing of desirable) that he would eventually turn to the field of animation. And yet what he's rendered in his retelling of his own live-action classic *A Chinese Ghost Story* is so far from any existing form of animation that it nearly deserves to be considered a new subgenre.

To begin with, the look of this ani-

**Nicky Wu voices Ning in *A Chinese Ghost Story: The Tsui Hark Animation*.**

mated *Ghost Story* is unique, combining 3-D computer generated imagery (CGI) with Japanese anime-style flat animation for the characters. While this technique is not one-hundred percent successful, its net effect is to create a visual style never seen before (unless one counts the non-Hark live-action epic *The Storm Riders*, which similarly employed CGI backgrounds with live actors matted in). At worst, seeing a two-dimensional drawn character walk through a fully-rendered background is merely disorienting; at best, it renders a magical, mythical world where anything can — and will — happen.

Because Tsui understands that one of the advantages of animation is that you can do anything, *A Chinese Ghost Story: The Tsui Hark Animation* positively exults in its wild visual leaps and bounds. Consider that while Disney employed its considerable resources to recreate a world that actually once existed in *Mulan*, Tsui is creating instead a world that cannot possibly exist anywhere — outside of the world of

animation. Tsui has expanded his original *Ghost Story* to fit this exciting new world. Our young hero no longer encounters his ghostly love in an isolated pavilion; he's now in a massive, colorful ghost city, populated by hundreds of bizarre spectres and monstrosities. His tree demon now has a trunk that rises hundreds of feet into the sky; montages impossibly layer images of ghosts, butterflies, toys and flowers; reincarnation is no longer enabled by simply moving ashes, it now involves a golden Reincarnation Train chugging across the night sky, with a full cargo of anticipatory spirits.

Despite a number of design elements borrowed directly from *A Chinese Ghost Story III* (notably the long-lobed elderly monk "White Cloud"), in many respects this animated extravaganza is as much of a reworking of *Zu: Warriors from the Magic Mountain* as any of the *Chinese Ghost Story* films. Within a few moments of the film's opening, the naïve young hero (who even looks more like *Zu*'s Yuen Biao than *Ghost*

*Story*'s Leslie Cheung) goes from encountering a temple full of eerie spirits to being caught between two warring factions of monks. Yet the story retains both the original *Ghost Story*'s unnerving images (Ning's brief visit to a restaurant serving human body parts is a standout) and its lush romance; the original film's sensuality is toned down slightly here, replaced with love songs and montages.

Speaking of love songs, *A Chinese Ghost Story: The Tsui Hark Animation* also benefits from a spectacularly lovely score (by Ricky Ho). Even the songs (which are principally by the fabulous James Wong, whose vocal performance on Red Beard's number is spectacular) are witty, particularly when the mile-high red-eyed demon king Evil Mountain sings a song about his love for himself. The score itself employs traditional themes and instrumentations in a '90s synth/orchestral setting that is genuinely majestic and moving throughout.

If the film lacks in any area, it is the occasional bad dubbing—voices often don't come close to matching animated mouth movements. But when the eye is so often taken to Tsui's and director Andrew Chen's exquisite palettes and designs, this becomes a very insignificant flaw indeed.

*A Chinese Ghost Story: The Tsui Hark Animation* represents more than just a significant advance in the art of Hong Kong animation; it's also a challenging venture from an artist who keeps moving forward, pushing his vision in bold new directions. This is one cartoon that should reawaken the sense of wonder in even the most jaded adult.

ABOUT THE MOVIE: *A Chinese Ghost Story: The Tsui Hark Animation* performed only adequately at the box office; its gross of $8,158,200 placed it at number 47 for the year (amusingly, this placed it one point above *The English Patient*).

At the 1997 Golden Horse Film Festival *A Chinese Ghost Story: The Tsui Hark Animation* won Best Animated Feature.

In 1999 Viz Films released an English-dubbed version of *A Chinese Ghost Story: The Tsui Hark Animation*; unfortunately, they apparently couldn't afford to completely dub the songs into English, so in most cases one verse is sung and the rest of the song finishes as an instrumental.

*A Chinese Ghost Story: The Tsui Hark Animation* had an exceptionally large budget by Hong Kong standards ($7 million American dollars) and spent nine months in production (not counting pre- or post-production). Tsui hoped it would spark an interest in animation again in Asia, and his wish may be coming true: Mainland China recently released the animated film *Lotus Lantern*, which featured the voice work of some of Hong Kong's hottest young stars, including Nicholas Tse (who stars in Tsui's *Time and Tide*).

*A Chinese Ghost Story: The Tsui Hark Animation* was also a critical success, and several Hong Kong reviewers saw it as an allegory for the 1997 handover. In a review on the *Hong Kong Film Critics Society* web page, Long Tin said: "Retreating from the Door of Reincarnation is indeed obvious (Hong Kong Chinese giving up on immigration and resuming their rightful identities), and [Tsui Hark's] intent can also be seen in the frolicking Hades (isn't Hong Kong's prosperity also transient?), the Black Mountain Monster (Big Shot from the north) who demands worship (the ghost of Mao?), and the people who would rather walk with ghosts." Author Stephen Teo lauded the film as "one of Tsui Hark's pioneering efforts to bring new technology and production methods into the Hong Kong film industry" (*Hong Kong Panorama '97—'98*).

**Tsui Hark as Solid Gold, the dog, in *A Chinese Ghost Story: The Tsui Hark Animation.***

Tsui on *A Chinese Ghost Story: The Tsui Hark Animation*: I think I'm very good at animation. I think I can be a much better animated filmmaker than live action. But when I did the film I found that it wasn't the thinking that would make a difference — the organizing takes the most energy. Most of the time we were fighting the people who were working on the project. Somehow, because it's an animated film, you have to fight your way to the point where people believe in what you say. Most people we used were experienced animation artists; they had their own style, they had their own way of telling a story. So I think that film took me a lot of effort in arguing with people who thought it should look like something else. Even in the end it's still like a fifty-fifty result — of what was originally in the design. Especially some of the scenes; because of the money, the budget, we had to sacrifice some parts. Like we could not have too long a fight sequence, because we didn't have the money for the 3-D, and the film is too long

so I have to cut it short, things like that. And some of the characters— I think there was not enough policing of the quality. The cue sheets were not enough to make sure of the look of the character. For the second animated film, I think it will be much better. And I always think that I am a better filmmaker on animation than live action.

There were no cels— only paper and pencil, and inking. It took us some time to get a system together to synchronize the pencil drawing with the 3-D animated backgrounds. We had a schedule to meet. We had a problem with the animators, because they didn't work with our designs. They were traditional-type animators, they didn't know how to work with a wireframe 3-D model, they didn't know how to deal with these backgrounds. Also, we had a problem of working with people on the 3-D, because there were not enough artists in our industry to do that. And we trained people, so they were not at the same level in terms of quality.

[Was there anything you'd wanted to

do in the live action films that you couldn't afford, so it went into the animated script instead?] I was thinking from a totally different perspective. Live action is designed for mature people, not kids. So we combined the element of kids and their parents— or maybe their brothers— to create a totally cute version of the film. It took us some time to decide what it should look like. In the beginning, it should be very original, very pastoral. Originally the characters looked older, but after a while I started to think maybe we should bring the age of the characters down to younger, to make it funny. It's kind of silly to see these kids talking about marriage, love, that sort of thing. I think it's more fun that way, than to see a teenager who is 17, 18 years old running around doing that. I think that's too Disney. So we just brought the age down to make it more silly. People were criticizing it — they were expecting romantic, pretty faces, pretty design, and they looked too young to do that sort of thing. But was my intention to do that, so they looked sort of cute. Silly, too. They all look 12, 13 years old.

[On the dog]: I was thinking that maybe the dog should talk. I think that's again too Disney. I put a lot of effort into designing that dog, but because we didn't have enough money, we lost part of the dog's animation. The dog has a lot, lot, lot of character. (In an interview with Patrick Macias for *Animerica* magazine, Vol. 7, No. 10, Tsui had this to say about doing the voice of the dog: "Well, I had been asking my friends, performers and stars, to do voices for the film, but I didn't know who to ask to do the voice of a dog. I didn't know if it was rude…eventually the schedule was getting tight and I really only wanted to demonstrate how the voice should be done, but I ended up doing the whole film.")

In a conversation with Stephen Teo in *Hong Kong Panorama '97–'98*, Tsui

describes *A Chinese Ghost Story: The Tsui Hark Animation* as "a deliberate attempt to make a cross between Japanese *anime* and American Disney."

## Knock Off

Director, 1998. Producer: Nansun Shi. Script: Stephen E. De Souza. Second Unit Director: Sammo Hung. Editor: Mak Chi Sin. Music: Russell Mael and Ron Mael. CAST: Jean-Claude Van Damme ("Marcus Ray"), Rob Schneider ("Tommy Hendricks"), Lela Rochon ("Karen Leigh"), Michael Wong ("Lt. Han"), Paul Sorvino ("Harry Johannson"), Carman Lee ("Ling Ho"), Glen Chin ("Skinny Wang"), Jeff Wolfe ("Skar"), Michael Ian Lambert ("Russian Mafia"). Opening Date (U.S.): September 6, 1998.

SYNOPSIS: When con man and "knock off king" Marcus Ray lands a cushy executive position with V-Six Jeans, he and his partner Tommy Hendricks think they've got it made — until their jeans become part of a terrorist plot to export deadly nano-bombs (button-sized explosives) to the U.S. Then, during the pageantry surrounding the 1997 Hong Kong handover, they must reluctantly team up with Hong Kong Police and the C.I.A. to find out who's behind the plot and stop it from happening before it's too late.

REVIEW: Where Tsui Hark's first outing with Jean-Claude Van Damme, *Double Team*, placed the Muscles From Brussels in the safe role of super-heroic secret agent, *Knock Off* takes the opposite approach: Van Damme becomes Van Dumb, a lumbering scam artist out for a fast buck. Maybe because *Knock Off* is the first film to play against Van Damme's

**Tsui on the set of *Knock Off*.**

type, it's a better movie than *Double Team* and easily the best film Jean Claude has ever been involved with.

It may also be Tsui's love letter to—and parody of—the Hong Kong of the immediate past. Set during the 72 hours leading up to the 1997 handover of Hong Kong from Britain to China, Tsui presents a Hong Kong ruled by greed and flash. Knock offs—cheap, poorly-made copies of everything from famous toys to designer shoes—are ubiquitous, even if product names are misspelled on the imitations (there's a joke for all Hong Kong film buffs about the need for better translators). Tsui covers the city, from the seedy, seething Kowloon district to Lantau Island's gigantic hilltop Buddha, with a camera that rushes as fast as the pace of Hong Kong life. Even phone calls become spectacular speed events in Tsui's eye, with the high-tech imagery he began experimenting with in *Double Team* used to better effect here, recreating circuits and electrical pathways.

Even the mere act of putting on a shoe becomes a bobsled ride as Tsui ably demonstrates why he may be the best visual stylist in the film world today.

The action is plentiful, albeit unusual for a Van Damme film, with an emphasis less on hand-to-hand and more on Jackie Chan–style outrageousness (it's probably no surprise that regular Jackie Chan collaborator Sammo Hung was *Knock Off*'s second unit director). Instead of a typical car chase, for example, Tsui gives us a rickshaw competition (complete with the unforgettable sight of Rob Schneider slapping driver Van Damme's rear with an eel!). One huge sequence involves a fight and chase in a fruit warehouse (a Chan staple). The principles are constantly leaping onto canopies, sliding down ropes or clambering bare-handed up concrete pillars, with Tsui's dizzying camera spinning around them or capturing it all in slow motion.

Which is not to say *Knock Off* is with-

Marcus Ray (Jean-Claude Van Damme, right) takes on all comers in *Knock Off*.

out the requisite kickboxing scenes. But, since this is a Tsui Hark film, there's gore (one bad guy is accidentally impaled on a bamboo scaffolding), and, in typical Tsui Hark gender-bending fashion, the best fight scenes involve Van Damme battling women: Carman Lee's policewoman at the end of the rickshaw race, and Lela Rochon's CIA agent in a high-tech office. Even in the rickshaw race, one of Van Damme's toughest opponents is a woman.

*Knock Off* keeps the plot surprises coming as fast as the stunts, thanks to a perfectly paced, funky and surprisingly complex script by veteran writer Stephen de Souza (*Die Hard*, *48 Hours*). The title comes to refer as much to the characters— almost none of whom are what they seem — as to the plethora of cheap products flooding out of Hong Kong. It's tempting to place *Knock Off* on Tsui's list of anti-communist films, what with its use of Russian bad guys, but De Souza's script is too smart to case them as the villains for

long — the Russians turn out to be greedy capitalists like everyone else.

*Knock Off*'s cast performs with great zest, if not always great skill. Van Damme manages to actually provoke a few laughs as the buffoonish Marcus Ray, and, fortunately, his speaking lines are at a minimum. Rob Schneider is not entirely convincing as a CIA analyst, but he serves his role of second banana ably. It's probably no surprise that the best performance in the film is given by a Hong Kong actor — Michael Wong, a Hong Kong star reduced here to second lead as the tough local cop, and the only honest character in the film.

Is it just coincidence that the film's only true Chinese character would also be the only truthful one? Probably not. *Knock Off* may be the ode to his hometown Tsui has always wanted to make. It's just curious that he would choose a *gweilo* film to do it.

ABOUT THE MOVIE: *Knock Off*'s budget was $35 million (U.S. dollars). It was the only Western film allowed to film in Hong Kong during the 1997 handover.

Although *Knock Off* was not offered for press screenings prior to its U.S. release (usually a sign that a film's distributor expects the worst from critics), the film opened to some favorable notices, including a rave review from the *L.A. Times.* (According to Kevin Thomas, "It's fast, light and funny and not top-heavy with special effects and epic-scale destruction.")

Russell and Ron Mael, who wrote the score for *Knock Off,* are also known to fans of alternative rock music as the eccentric group Sparks. Their 1995 album "Gratuitous Sax and Senseless Violins" includes the song "Tsui Hark," which features Tsui "rapping" (actually he just talks briefly about himself, and the words are cycled over and over into a fun, rhythmic rap).

After the failure of *Double Team,* Tsui was quoted in the *Hong Kong Standard* as saying that he would go "all out" on the next film, and that he wanted *Knock Off* to showcase his directorial talent.

TSUI ON *KNOCK OFF*: I don't know anything about [Columbia's handling of the film]. I was busy with something else.

[On collaborating with Sparks]: That's a silly song. They didn't say it was a song, they just said to record something. So they play around with it at the studio, and suddenly they find out it is a song! I was lucky I didn't say anything really bad. I was fooling around with my voice. We became very good friends. That's why I was curious to use them on a movie.

# 5

# OTHER FILMS

## Aces Go Places

Actor, 1982. Cantonese: *Jui Gaai Paak Dong*. Mandarin: *Zui Jia Pai Dang*. Literally: *Best Partners*. AKA: *Diamondfinger*; *Mad Mission I*. Director: Eric Tsang. Scriptwriter: Fung Wing. Co-Producer: Nansun Shi. CAST: Sam Hui ("King Kong"), Carl Mak ("Albert)", Sylvia Chang ("Superintendent Ho"). Opening Date: January 16, 1982.

This is the first entry in the immensely successful *Aces Go Places* series, which went on to spawn four sequels and a card deck-full of imitators. It's not hard to see why the film was such a crowd-pleaser — its mix of slapstick comedy, jaw-dropping stuntwork and crime caper is nearly irresistible.

The hilarious Carl Mak stars as Albert (also known in the beginning as "Kodo-jak"), an American cop brought to Hong Kong to help catch White Gloves, a diamond thief. Albert is teamed up with Superintendent Ho, a hot-tempered police-woman whose initial slapping contest with Albert eventually becomes a romance. Their search for White Gloves mistakenly leads them to King Kong, a famed local thief and daredevil. King Kong's partner dies before he can reveal the location of a cache of stolen diamonds, so Albert and Ho work with King Kong to find the missing jewels. Unfortunately, the cops aren't the only ones after King Kong — the diamonds' Mafia-boss owner wants them back, and the Triad leader whose sister slept with King Kong's late partner wants Kong, too. Finally, King Kong and Albert have a show-down with the real White Gloves, hired by the Mafia to retrieve the jewels. King Kong uses specially-made gadgets, including explosive remote-controlled model cars, to finally triumph over White Gloves.

*Aces Go Places* begins as a spoof — first of James Bond films, as King Kong uses intricate planning and machinery to conduct his diamond heist (accompanied by a Bond-like guitar riff), then of American detective series, as Carl Mak riffs on the equally-bald American detective character Kojak. Soon, however, the spoofing gives way to (often amazingly violent) slapstick, such as the slapping contest between Albert and Ho. Before long, the film routinely alternates between slapstick and farce, with car chases, explosions and even a tightrope-walking scene actually performed by Sam Hui. The film also uses the city of Hong Kong to great effect, and local audiences undoubtedly recognized nearly all of the film's many locations.

Where the film occasionally suffers is in its budget. It's far too easy to tell which cars will be demolished in the chase scenes—they're the cheap ones. Shots are sometimes poorly exposed or even out of focus.

But *Aces Go Places* is too smart to suffer from those relatively minor flaws. Director Tsang keeps the pace fast, the action frenetic and the jokes popping throughout. The cast works with great skill and timing — Hui, Mak and Chang are all equally effective and entertaining. The romance between Mak and Chang is especially funny, as it careens between physical fighting, goofy games of peek-a-boo and verbal putdowns. Tsui appears in the film's final third, playing the stage manager of a ballet company who nearly suffers a nervous breakdown as he watches Albert and King Kong destroy a live performance (which, of course, in true comic reversal is finally cheered wildly by the audience). Also notable is Teddy Robin's clever, rock-and-pop musical score, including the obligatory Cantopop ballad (actually not out of place here, used as it is to underscore the burgeoning romances at the right time) and Bond-theme guitar riff.

Director Eric Tsang may be the only man in Hong Kong cinema with even more credits than Tsui: 110 films as actor, director, writer and producer. He started in 1978 with the screenplay for *Dirty Tiger, Crazy Frog*; he also directed *Aces Go Places II*. He's probably most well-known, though, as an actor, and his excellent work has included *Final Victory* (in which he played Tsui Hark's brother) and, most recently, *Gen-X Cops, When I Look Upon the Stars* and *Metade Fumaca*. Tsang is also one of the forces behind UFO (United Filmmakers Organization), along with director Peter Chan; the company has produced such hit films as *Tom, Dick and Hairy* and *He's a Woman, She's a Man* (a gender-bending comedy that owes more than a little to Tsui Hark).

Sam Hui made *Swordsman, Working Class* and the first three *Aces Go Places* with Tsui. Carl Mak made the first three *Aces Go Places, It Takes Two* and *All the Wrong Clues* with Tsui. Sylvia Chang has written, directed and acted, most recently directing/starring in the award-nominated *Tempting Heart* and acting in the international co-production *The Red Violin*; with Tsui she did the first three *Aces Go Places, Shanghai Blues* and *A Chinese Ghost Story: The Tsui Hark Animation*.

*Aces Go Places* was selected as one of the top 10 Hong Kong films of 1982, and finished as the number one money-earner of the year, with a gross of $26,043,773.00. Carl Mak won the award for Best Actor at that year's Hong Kong Film Awards, Sylvia Chang was nominated for Best Actress, and Teddy Robin was nominated for score and Best Song.

Sam Hui was a major star in 1982; he was paid $2 million for *Aces Go Places*, one quarter of the entire budget. Sylvia Chang went on to manage Cinema City's Taiwan branch, beginning in 1983.

## It Takes Two

Actor, 1982. Cantonese: *Naan Hing Naan Dai*. Mandarin: *Nan Xiong Nan Di*. Literally: *Two of a Kind*. Director: Carl Mak. Co-Producer: Nansun Shi. CAST: Dean Shek Tin ("Shek"), Richard Ng Yiu-Hon ("Ai Don Low"), Cherie Chung ("Chu"). Opening Date: April 15, 1982.

*It Takes Two* might have been more appropriately titled *Cinema City Follies of 1982*. It feels less like a real movie than an excuse for the immensely successful Cinema City to celebrate with a parade of its stars at the time. The plot is really nothing more than the tale of two layabouts who set out to con a Triad boss; somehow this is padded out to 90–plus minutes (the script throws in everything from a lengthy pre-credits nightclub act sequence to a bout of amnesia and a trip to Malaysia). What makes it all tolerable is the friendship that binds the two leads; Don Low even takes care of Shek when a head injury turns him into a drooling idiot. And the film has a solid look, thanks in no small part to the art direction of Hee Chung Man and William Cheung; like Tsui's *Shanghai Blues*, it turns poverty and small, cramped apartments into something homey, warm and even lovely.

Richard Ng is dependable, as always, but Dean Shek is broad even by Hong Kong comedy film definitions; what he gives is not so much a performance as an endless stream of facial mugging. Cherie Chung is sweet and pretty in an early role, playing the wheelchair-bound Chu, whose need for a $30,000 operation is what finally forces our boys into action.

That action — which occurs during the film's final twenty minutes—consists of "let's round up our friends." The "friends," of course, are the parade of stars: In a montage sequence they gather together George Lam, Eric Tsang, Carl Mak, Sylvia Chang (the last two reprise their *Aces Go Places* roles), Teddy Robin (doing "Inspector Robin" again, from *All*

*the Wrong Clues*) and Tsui. Tsui plays a priest who ends up posing as a hot-tempered triad leader in the scheme to fleece gangster "Jaws"; needless to say, the scheme is successful, and Chu gets her operation at the end. The film's final shot shows the entire cast of stars singing directly to the camera.

*It Takes Two* was a great success at the box office, finishing number 3 for the year (*Aces Go Places* was number 1). It ran for nearly four astounding months and finished with a gross of $16,724,578. At the second Annual Hong Kong Film Awards, Hee Chung Man and William Cheung received a nomination for Best Art Direction.

Nansun Shi is listed in the opening credits as the film's production supervisor.

## Aces Go Places 2

Actor, 1983. Cantonese: *Jui Gaai Paak Dong Daai Hin San Tung*. Mandarin: *Zui Jia Pai Dang Da Xian Shen Tong*. Literally: *Best Partners Big Show Remarkable Ability*. AKA: *Mad Mission 2*. Director: Eric Tsang Chi-Wai. CAST: Sam Hui Koon-Kit ("King Kong"), Carl Mak ("Albert"), Sylvia Chang ("Ho"). Opening Date: February 5, 1983.

The gang is back in a bigger and better-produced (if not exactly original) sequel. The structure is essentially that of the first film (why tamper with success?): After an exciting action-filled opening sequence (this time King Kong fights off a killer robot and then escapes a gang of motorcycle-riding hitmen), Superintendent Ho shakes down her favorite informant ("Squealie") for information. This time out he tells her about a gang of thieves—led by a brother and sister team, Bull and the beautiful Juju — who con and then frame innocent bystanders into helping them. Unfortunately, Albert and King

Kong (who is hopelessly smitten with Juju) are their latest pawns, as Bull tries to blackmail them into purchasing a collection of diamonds with counterfeit money. As if that weren't enough, the vengeful brother of the last film's villain, White Gloves — a dead ringer for Clint Eastwood called "Black Gloves" — is after them as well. They finally escape the clutches of Bull and Juju, only to confront Black Gloves and his huge killer robot. But King Kong is prepared, and pits an army of superpowered mini-robots against the monster. Our heroes win, escape the killer robot, and finally destroy Black Gloves and his weapon-laden custom Rolls Royce.

*Aces Go Places 2* obviously benefited greatly from the financial rewards reaped by its predecessor; it looks far more polished, with better cars, sharper photography, richer sets and even some decent optical effects. It continues the formula of jaw-dropping stunts (a motorcycle leaping off a freeway bypass onto the roof of a double-decker bus and finally onto the street below — all in one take — is a particular standout) alternated with slapstick comedy (where the Albert-Ho romance is concerned, the emphasis is still on the "slap" part of slapstick) and romance (Sam Hui's googly expressions around Juju are easily as spectacular as any of the stunts). Its only weakness (aside from a meandering plot; but really — who cares?) is that it makes far too little use of Sylvia Chang; she's sadly a background character through most of the film. It isn't until a huge fight breaks out in a nightclub (where Ho gets in more hits than her fiancé Albert) that Chang really gets to shine.

Tsui plays a raving lunatic who passes himself off as an FBI agent — until the men in white coats appear to cart him off again (he appears three times throughout the film and actually saves Albert in the film's climax). Director Tsang has a cameo as Juju's driver, "Fattie."

*Aces Go Places 2* was, strangely, a disappointment at the box office. It placed in the number 80 spot for the year, with a gross of just $2,327,314. It received one nomination at the year's Hong Kong Film Awards, for Best Original Song.

## *All the Wrong Spies*

Producer/Production Designer/Actor, 1983. Cantonese: *Ngoh Oi Ye Loi Heung*. Mandarin: *Wo Ai Ye Lai Xiang*. Literally: *I Love Fragrance of the Night*. Director: Teddy Robin. Script: Raymond Wong. Co-Production Designer: Nansun Shi. CAST: Teddy Robin Kwan ("Chief Inspector Robin"), George Lam Chi-Cheung ("Yoho"), Brigitte Lin ("Bridget"), Tsui Hark ("Hiroshima Tora"), Paul Chun ("The Police Commissioner"). Opening Date: March 31, 1983.

Yoho and Robin from *All the Wrong Clues* are back, this time in a spoof of American '40s spy films. A Jewish scientist has stolen the formula for the atomic bomb from Hitler and is hiding out in Hong Kong until he can deliver it to the Americans. Unfortunately, the Japanese want the formula, too; and before they know it, Yoho and Robin are caught up in a spy war, along with Bridget, a beautiful and deadly female agent.

Two years after the massive success of *All the Wrong Clues* the gang returned with this spy spoof, which, despite a few changes in key personnel, has much of the same anarchic spirit and wit of its predecessor. This time Tsui stepped back and handed directing reins to co-star Teddy Robin (whose later films as director included the epic fantasy *The Legend of*

*Wisely* and the star-laden comedy *Shanghai, Shanghai*), and the film has an obviously different feel (gone are Tsui's abstract images and comic book framing). The superb sets (Nansun Shi and Tsui Hark are listed as the production designers, with Kei Chung Man serving as art director) are striking recreations of old Hollywood, including "Café Casablanca," a wealthy mansion with grand staircase, and forbidding Gothic castle. The cast is just as good here, with Brigitte Lin a welcome addition as Bridget, a glamorous spy clothed in elegant black gowns and lace-top jumpsuits. Also joining the cast are Paul Chun as the Police Commissioner and Tsui as Hiroshima Tora, the godson of the Japanese Emperor, who comes to Hong Kong to retrieve the formula for the atomic bomb.

The pacing is peppy throughout, with plentiful (and actually funny) sight gags and slapstick abounding. The film's best scene is a tango between Robin and Bridget, which Bridget uses to humiliate her former fiancé Yoho. Brigitte Lin and Teddy Robin make the most of their considerable size differential here, and the costuming is to be applauded, as Brigitte uses her long, layered gown to stunning effect (Robin also gets to indulge in a brief *Saturday Night Fever* parody here). Tsui has a standout moment when he tries to lead a Japanese chorus to celebrate the recent Japanese victory at Canton; as he waves his arms to conduct, the Chinese audience breaks into their own anthem, which, of course, Tsui tries more and more frantically to drown out.

The script for *All the Wrong Spies* also betrays some Tsui Hark influence in the code phrase its spy characters rely on: "I am woman." By the end of the film an army of faithful Chinese soldiers is stepping forward, proclaiming, "We all want to be women!" The scene is made that much funnier by Brigitte Lin's quiet, proud smile as she looks on.

Brigitte Lin fans should take note of the weapon she sports in this film: For those who think *The Bride with White Hair* (1993) was the first time she fought with a whip, think again. Tsui also gets to show off with a weapon when he engages in a bit of comic swordplay.

*All the Wrong Spies* was another success for Cinema City. It came in at the number six spot on the year's box office list, with a gross of $13,782,062. It also fared well at the year's Hong Kong Film Awards, garnering nominations for Teddy Robin for both Best Director and Best Original Film Score, for Best Cinematography (Koo Kwok Wah), Art Direction (Kei Chung Man) and Best Original Song.

## Aces Go Places 3

Director, 1984. Cantonese: *Jui Gaai Paak Dong: Nui Wong Mat Ling.* Mandarin: *Zui Jia Pai Dang: Nu Huang Mi Ling.* Literally: *Best Partners: Her Majesty's Secret Order.* AKA: *Aces Go Places III — Our Man from Bond Street; Mad Mission 3: Our Man from Bond Street.* Producers: Carl Mak, Dean Shek Tin, Raymond Wong Bak-Ming. CAST: Sam Hui Koon-Kit ("King Kong"), Carl Mak ("Albert"), Sylvia Chang ("Ho"), Peter Graves ("Tom Collins"), Richard Kiel ("Jaws"), Harold Sakata ("Odd Job"), Neil Connery ("Bond Lookalike"). Opening Date: January 26, 1984.

Tsui Hark takes the directorial reins for the third installment of the immensely successful *Aces Go Places* series, and takes partners King Kong and Albert out of the realm of slapstick and into that of parody. *Aces Go Places 3* seems basically to be one big homage on Tsui's part to other films:

**French lobby card featuring Sam Hui in *Aces Go Places 3* (aka *Mad Mission 3: Our Man from Bond Street*).**

James Bond films, *The Road Warrior*, even *Jaws* get nods here.

The film opens with a shot that sets it firmly apart from the first two films: We pan down from the Eiffel Tower to King Kong, so we know already this one has taken our heroes out of their usual Hong Kong environs for the first time. King Kong is soon being chased by two of the most famous Bond villains: Jaws (Richard Kiel) and Odd Job (Harold Sakata, still hurling that lethal hat). After an exciting fight in the gridwork of the Eiffel Tower, King Kong parachutes to the ground only to be confronted by a beautiful Chinese assassin. He escapes by leaping into the Seine, where he is swallowed up by a shark-shaped submarine (to the accompaniment of the famous *Jaws* music) and meets lookalikes for Sean Connery/Bond (played by Connery's real-life brother) and Queen Elizabeth. They try to convince King Kong

to work for Her Majesty in stealing back some jewels missing from the Royal Crown, but King Kong is reluctant — until they introduce him to the beautiful Jade East. Then he happily agrees.

Back in Hong Kong, Ho and Albert are now married, with a mischievous baby who gets Albert into trouble with an attractive maid. But Albert's troubles are just beginning when King Kong uses him as an alibi during his first daring jewel theft. Meanwhile, an American agent, Tom Collins, is on the trail of a ring of thieves who pose as the Queen and her most famous secret agent; his search brings him to Hong Kong, where he narrowly escapes his own exploding tape recorder.

After King Kong is successful in stealing the first jewel, the duplicitous criminals convince him to try for an even bigger one: the heavily guarded Royal Star.

Ho is in charge of guarding the jewel and has been assured security is foolproof; but King Kong uses a gang of thugs in Santa Claus outfits to beat the system and steal the jewel. The Santa Claus robbers escape via a combination of jetpack, motorcycle and one-man aircraft. However, King Kong has now outlived his usefulness to the gang, who have amassed enough jewels to sell a replicated Royal Crown to a wealthy Saudi collector. The bad guys send a bunch of *Road Warrior*–style barbarians after King Kong, but he escapes. Finally, he and Jade East (who has left the gang in favor of King Kong) are rescued when Tom Collins leads a battle at sea against the villains. But the Bond lookalike escapes and kidnaps Ho and Albert's baby. The climax takes place in a quarry, where little Junior is finally rescued and the villain finished.

*Aces Go Places 3* emphasizes gadgets over the stunts of the two previous entries, and lacks the visceral excitement of the other two films; but it also punches up the satire factor of the first two and becomes almost a visual "Trivial Pursuit," to see how many different films Tsui has riffed on. He accomplished a major coup in casting the actual actors who played the Bond villains, as well as Peter Graves (playing with his *Mission: Impossible* persona). The scene in which Albert's bratty baby literally entangles him with a maid brings to mind the Baby Leroy–W. C. Fields comedies of the early '30s, especially *It's a Gift*, in which the havoc-wreaking child nearly drowns Fields in molasses. Tsui doesn't forget to include certain nods to the other two *Aces Go Places* films as well: Although Ho's stool pigeon "Squealie" is missing, King Kong still throws out his cheery "Bye-bye!" when escaping the clutches of the bad guys.

Tsui also comments wryly on the illusionary nature of film: Twice in *Aces Go Places 3* an image is torn aside to reveal

that it's only an image projected on a sheet. As in *A Chinese Ghost Story*, Tsui is addressing the nature of fantasy, although *Aces Go Places 3* is far too light a movie to hold the warnings contained in the former film. In *Aces Go Places 3* Tsui is merely offering us a playful "don't believe everything you see" funhouse mirror.

The film is technically uneven, with some jarring editing (mainly in stunt sequences—it seems as if they may simply have not had enough coverage of some of the fights) and so-so effects (King Kong and Albert's flight through downtown Hong Kong in the one-man aircraft). But it also contains some genuinely surreal humor (the sight of five Santa Clauses soaring above Hong Kong on jetpacks surely qualifies as surreal!) and the usual excellent work of the leads. Sylvia Chang has possibly the film's most hysterical moment when Albert presents Ho with a necklace in the hospital and she tries desperately not to burst into tears; Tsui holds on her in a lengthy close-up that just gets funnier with each frame.

The cut of the film released under the title *Mad Mission 3* is dubbed and cuts the entire sequence involving Albert, the baby and the maid; it also cuts the scene of Ho in the hospital.

Frequent Tsui collaborator John Sham appears as the heavily-mustachioed policeman.

*Aces Go Places 3* was an immense hit and remains the only film directed by Tsui Hark to reach the number one spot on the year's box office list, with a gross of $29,286,077 (its release during the Chinese Lunar New Year celebration didn't exactly hurt it, either). It was, however, completely shut out of the year's Hong Kong Film Awards, with not a single nomination.

In light of the immense success of the film, it's ironic that at least part of Tsui's decision to direct *Aces Go Places 3* was due to the box-office failure of *Zu: Warriors from the Magic Mountain*.

## *Working Class*

Director/Producer/Actor, 1985. Cantonese: *Da Gung Wong Dai*. Mandarin: *Da Gong Huang Di*. Literally: *Hit Work Emperor* [*Working Class Emperor*]. Scriptwriter: Chan Gam Kuen. CAST: Sam Hui ("Yam"), Tsui Hark ("Sunny"), Teddy Robin ("Hing"), Joey Wang ("Amy"). Opening Date: August 10, 1985.

*Working Class* was the second film made under the Film Workshop banner, and while it's not the film *Shanghai Blues* was, it nevertheless shares much of that film's sweet comic sensibility and empathy with the poor.

It opens with Sunny and Hing rigging a soccer game; right off the bat these characters are set up as scheming and even shiftless. Yam enters and destroys their con job; later he wrecks a car they're supposed to watch, and all three end up losing their respective jobs. In a twist of fate they all land work in a noodle factory. Meanwhile, Yam has fallen for the boss's beautiful daughter, Amy, but is unaware of her real identity (he believes her to be as poor as himself). After a disastrous date Yam realizes who Amy really is and breaks off their relationship. Meanwhile, the factory's villainous supervisors are embezzling, and when they're in danger of being caught they set up Hing as their fall guy, granting him a fake promotion. The promotion nearly destroys Hing and Sunny's friendship, but finally they work past their differences to unite against the supervisors. When the supervisors try to cover their trail by setting fire to the factory while Amy is trapped inside, our three heroes save the day, rescuing Amy and exposing the supervisors. In the end, Amy's father, out of gratitude for saving his noodle factory, grants all the workers shares in the factory, and Amy and Yam are united.

*Working Class* is an atypical film for Tsui Hark, one in which he almost seems to have been taking a deliberate break. Visually it's simple, without the bizarre images of *All the Wrong Clues* or the stylized sets and photography of *Shanghai Blues*; only once does the film venture into surrealism — during a scene wherein the factory's sped-up machinery sends noodles flying over the heads of the workers. The film is like the later comedy *Tri-Star* in using contemporary Hong Kong, but it's a much gentler, tighter movie; like *The Chinese Feast*, it centers around food and a romance between a poor young employee and the boss' daughter, but it lacks that film's panache and reliance on Chinese tradition. In some ways it most closely resembles low-budget American comedies of the early '80s — it uses the same pop music, peppy heroine and working class hero of, say, Martha Coolidge's *Valley Girl* (1983).

Where Tsui Hark's involvement is obvious is in its celebration of the impoverished blue-collar heroes. They may be initially presented as scheming, bumbling fools, but Sunny, Hing and Yam do win sympathy by the film's end for their perseverance and good humor. Like the film itself, they're essentially good-natured and amiable, if not completely lovable.

*Working Class* ends with the victorious factory workers being rewarded for their efforts by being given shares. Although at first this almost seems like a nod to Communism, at closer examination it's clearly a capitalist triumph. The workers, after all, are being given shares to make more money, not to work for the betterment of the state. It seems unlikely that

Tsui — in the second film he made as both director *and* studio mogul — would have made a pro-Communist statement, especially in light of his earlier films *We're Going to Eat You* and *Dangerous Encounter — 1st Kind.*

*Working Class* is buoyed along by the bright performances of its three leads. Teddy Robin and Tsui had already worked together on *All the Wrong Clues* and *All the Wrong Spies,* and they have a kind of Mutt-and-Jeff chemistry together, the gangly tall Tsui playing bewildered foil to the short, conniving Robin's various routines. Balancing these two buffoons nicely is handsome, athletic Sam Hui, who can nonetheless hurl a wet towel or leer as well as they can. *Working Class* also marks the first time Tsui Hark and Joey Wang worked together; unlike her later work with Tsui, in which she typically plays some sort of tragic, doomed heroine, she's appropriately bubbly and cute here.

Though not, perhaps, a major work for Tsui, *Working Class* is a sweet-natured little comic sidetrack, one relatively free of the cruel humor displayed in most modern comedies, and one proudly displaying its *Working Class* sympathies along with its shenanigans.

*Working Class* ended up at the number nine spot on the year's box office list, taking in $16,931,337. The film received one nomination from the Hong Kong Film Awards, for Best Song.

Teddy Robin made *All the Wrong Clues* (actor), *All the Wrong Spies* (actor and director), *Black Mask* (score), *Twin Dragons* (actor), *Working Class* and *It Takes Two* (actor) with Tsui.

## *Run Tiger Run*

Actor, 1985. Cantonese: *Leung Ji Lo Foo.* Mandarin: *Liang Zhi Lao Hu.* Literally: *Two Tigers.* Director: John Woo (Ng Yu-Sam). Cast: Teddy Robin ("Teddy"), Tsui Hark ("Grandfather"). No Opening Date information available.

If the title of this film leads you to expect an *Aces Go Places*–style action comedy, think again — this is a Hong Kong variation on *The Prince and the Pauper* that's so over the top it makes a Chuck Jones Looney Tune look positively subtle by comparison.

The plot (such as it is) concerns two identical little boys: Babe is a spoiled rich brat, cared for by his eccentric old grandfather (Tsui, looking strangely like an Asian Georges Méliès in gray hair, mustache and long beard); his doppelganger, Benny, is a poor kid living with his father, Teddy, in an idyllic shack near a picturesque duck pond. When grandpa dies and leaves his entire estate to Babe, grandpa's estranged other son immediately plots to do away with the boy. Babe's devoted tutor Mary intuits the son's plans, and hides little Babe away. When the son sends his thugs to find the kid, they find instead Teddy and Benny, who are kidnapped and brought back to the mansion. Teddy immediately falls for Mary; meanwhile, the son (also smitten with Mary) plots to secretly do away with little Benny. When all of his attempts fail, he calls in "Mortal Lips," a black-leather-clad female hitwoman, to take out his rival for Mary's affections. The climax turns into a free-for-all as Teddy rounds up the neighborhood kids and they battle to rid the mansion of the son and his thugs (who inexplicably appear in the finale dressed as pirates, witches and cavemen).

This is the kind of film where characters don't just do double-takes, they do *quintuple*-takes; alarm clocks fly into the air as they ring; Teddy's eyes fly from his sockets at first glimpse of Mortal Lips; and an awful lot of pants fall down. The film has the typical low-budget comedy obsession with bodily functions— it's hard to think of another movie that features so many references to urinating. Most of the gags are so broad they elicit more groans than yucks; some (such as one involving Teddy using an enormous unraveling ball of twine to hold up his pants) simply go nowhere. By the end of the film Teddy Robin tries to trade on his "Inspector Robin" image from *All the Wrong Clues* and *All the Wrong Spies* by heroically brandishing pistols, but it's too little, too late. The best scene in the film is one in which Teddy performs a mock Peking Opera routine with a moon goddess (don't ask); here Teddy Robin's own comic talents shine without being hampered by clumsy sight gags or props.

It's difficult to believe that this often-infantile and unfunny collection of gags was directed and produced by John Woo, who just one year later would direct the Tsui-produced *A Better Tomorrow*. Like Tsui's early comedy *Working Class*, this one has the social consciousness of early American comedies, in which the poor are virtuous and the rich lazy and crazy; however, unlike Tsui's film, Woo seems less interested in conveying a point of view than in moving on to the next comic setup. Also unlike Tsui's film (but like some of Woo's later work), the movie is occasionally hampered by sentiment so cloying it could choke the most sympathetic of audience members. It would probably be kindest to simply say that comedy was not Woo's strong point.

The film seems to have virtually disappeared at the box office, leaving no trace on the list of 1985 releases.

*Run Tiger Run* was the last of several films John Woo made in Taiwan before returning to Hong Kong to lens *A Better Tomorrow*.

## Yes, Madam

Actor, 1985. Cantonese: *Wong Ga Si Je*. Mandarin: *Huang Jia Shi Jie*. Literally: *Royal Master Sister*. AKA: *Super Cops*. Producer: Sammo Hung Kam-Bo. Director: Corey Yuen Kwai. Action Directors: Corey Yuen Kwai, Mang Hoi. Screenwriter: Barry Wong Ping-Yiu. CAST: Michelle Yeoh ("Inspector Ng"), Cynthia Rothrock ("Carrie Morris"), Tsui Hark ("Panadol"), John Sham ("Strepsil"), Mang Hoi ("Asprin"). Opening Date: November 30, 1985.

*Yes, Madam* is an entertaining mix of action and comedy, one of the best of the police films to come out of Hong Kong in the mid-'80s. It's chiefly remembered, however, as Michelle Yeoh's breakout film (although she's credited as "Michelle Kheng" here). Yeoh would go on to become Hong Kong's most renowned action actress, displaying her considerable talents in such hits as *The Heroic Trio*, Jackie Chan's *Supercop* (aka *Police Story 3*), and in the James Bond film *Tomorrow Never Dies*.

Here she plays Inspector Ng, and the film is set up to showcase her right from the start, with an opening scene in which she single-handedly foils a gang of armored-car robbers. The scene even ends with her version of Clint Eastwood's famous "feel lucky?" speech, as she faces down the last robber, uncertain of how many bullets are left in her gun.

Cut to: A westerner checks into an exclusive hotel and engages in a deal to sell secret microfilm to a hitman. The deal falls through, and the westerner is murdered. His passport (where the microfilm is hidden) is stolen by Asprin, a con man who is working with his brother Strepsil to fleece the hotel's guests. Inspector Ng arrives on the scene a few moments later and is heartbroken — the murdered man is Richard Nornen, whom she trained with in Scotland and has been romantically involved with.

The authorities soon discover that Nornen was working undercover, and that the microfilm is missing. They call in a Scottish investigator, Carrie Morris, to assist Inspector Ng.

Meanwhile, Asprin and Strepsil have given Nornen's passport to Panadol, a forger. All three men grew up together and are saving to buy their aging mentor a home. Panadol sells the altered passport to a thug, who tries to use it to leave the country. He's caught at the airport, though, by the arriving Inspector Morris. When he refuses to talk, Inspector Ng arranges for his release so they can track him back to the person he bought the passport from. The trail leads straight to Panadol, who is taken into police custody and inadvertently identifies Asprin and Strepsil as his accomplices. Believing them to have the microfilm, Ng and Morris go after them — despite the fact that their work methods clash and they dislike each other.

The man who stands the most to lose if the microfilm becomes police property is Mr. Tin, a dirty-dealing businessmen. Tin has sent his thugs after the three hapless con men; and, under pressure; Strepsil gives in and hands the microfilm over to the police. Unfortunately, none of them are aware that it's another of Panadol's forgeries. The two policewomen try to arrest Mr. Tin, but are told too late their evidence is useless. Their superior, Mr. Wong, tries to remove them from the case; instead they both quit and decide to follow Strepsil and Asprin until the real microfilm can be located. Tin's thugs get to Panadol first, and he is murdered at the very time that Asprin is trying to sell the real microfilm to Tin for $10 million.

When Strepsil finds out Panadol is dead, he panics and heads for Tin, with the policewomen in close pursuit. What follows is an astonishing climax as Ng, Morris and Tin's thugs virtually destroy the businessman's high-tech designer house. The microfilm is destroyed in the fight, however, and at the end the policewomen are arrested as trespassers while Tin is about to walk free. Strepsil, who has just heard the news of Panadol's death, grabs a nearby policeman's gun and shoots Tin; the camera freezes on the grief stricken, gun-wielding Strepsil.

Up until that weirdly-downbeat ending (in which all of the heroes/heroines are either dead or destined for jail), *Yes, Madam* has a bouncy, pleasant feel. Director Yuen keeps the pace fast, the action fairly realistic, and the comedy/action mix just right. In her debut, Michelle Kheng/ Yeoh is determined, athletic and attractive, although both her acting and martial arts skills improved in later films (she and co-star Rothrock both have a tendency to play anger with lots of finger pointing). Rothrock is obviously the real martial artist of the two, and her moves are spectacular, although she lacks Yeoh's natural charisma. John Sham, Mang Hoi and Tsui have a delightful chemistry together as the three brotherly con men, and Tsui's conflicts with some of his disgruntled customers provide the film's best humorous fights. Wu Ma (as a policeman Asprin and Strepsil beat up to try and get police protection), Sammo Hung (as the con men's mentor) and Richard Ng (as Sammo's chicken-loving friend in the nursing home) all have enjoyable cameos.

Aside from the cast and the action (which isn't limited to fights — it also boasts an excellent motorcycle chase, a few car stunts and some spectacular explosions), *Yes, Madam*'s production design is superb. The two best sets — Panadol's labyrinthine forgery lab (which seems to have been copied in 1997's *The Replacement Killers*, Chow Yun-Fat's American film debut) and Tin's multi-level glass-and-wood mansion — give the film a much better look than many others of the period.

This is possibly the best of Tsui's comic performances— he's not as broad here as in *All the Wrong Spies* or even his own *Working Class*, and he creates a genuinely odd, interesting, likable character in the overall-wearing, noodle-cooking Panadol. His death scene is genuinely touching without being maudlin, and he even seems to perform a few of his own stunts in the fight scenes.

*Yes, Madam* performed respectably — if not spectacularly — at the box office, coming in number 21 for the year, with a gross of $10,019,862.00. At the fifth Hong Kong Film Awards, Mang Hoi won for Best Supporting Actor, Michelle Kheng/Yeoh was nominated for Best New Performer, and Corey Yuen Kwai and Mang Hoi were nominated for Best Action Choreography.

## Laser Man

Executive Producer, 1986. Director/Producer/Screenwriter: Peter Wang. Co-Executive Producer: Sophie Lo. Cinematography: Ernest Dickerson. CAST: Marc Hiyashi ("Arthur"), Peter Wang ("Inspector Lu"), Tony Leung Ka-Fai ("Joey"), Sally Yeh ("Susu"). No Opening Date information available.

*Laser Man* is an English-language international production with dialogue so inept it may just make you nostalgic for subtitles. Written, produced, directed by and starring Peter Wang, this high-tech comedy seems to be trying to put a Chinese-American spin on the whitebread

style of Woody Allen (it follows the intertwined lives of various New Yorkers); but Wang makes the mistake of most Allen imitators in thinking "quirkier is better." As a result, he's got a script peopled by characters who are so eccentric they're neither believable nor particularly interesting, especially given the leaden lines they have to utter.

The story begins promisingly with Inspector Lu, who tells us in his voice-over narration (which runs throughout the film) that he takes pride in being a descendent of the legendary Judge Dee. Lu then relates the case of Arthur Weiss, a brilliant young laser scientist who becomes unemployable after accidentally killing his lab assistant. Arthur's family life isn't much better than his professional one: He's got a Jewish mother who is obsessed with all things Chinese, a red-haired sister married to his best friend Joey, an ex-wife who hounds him for child-support payments, a young son and a Caucasian girlfriend who lives in a loft and whose sexual neuroses send him running to masturbate for relief. When Arthur is offered a job by a mysterious research firm, he jumps at the chance; little does he realize that his technology is being turned into weapons. After Joey sells Arthur stolen parts for use in his research, Lu and the police get involved and try unsuccessfully to stop the villainous corporation executives from using Arthur's laser gun to kill Joey. Finally, they try to turn the gun on Arthur himself, and Arthur barely escapes. Arthur finally turns the tables — and the laser — on the bad guys, and discovers that Joey is alive and well; his death was faked as bait for the bad guys. Lu has wrapped up the case, and Joey and Arthur are off on the job hunt again.

While *Laser Man* does have some interesting things on its mind — the identity of Chinese Americans in the United States, personal responsibility in the high-tech age — they're virtually lost in its maze of character relationships and its meandering plot. It works as neither a comedy (none of the performers seem to have the slightest idea of how to play comedy — but, then again, the lines and situations just plain aren't funny) nor an action film (the main plot of Arthur's work within the devious company is reduced to only a few moments of the film's time). Unfortunately, Wang also is not a skilled director; not only do scenes often not cut together, but individual shots within a scene don't connect, giving the film a choppy, uneven pace (the voice-over narration, which runs the length of the film, feels suspiciously like an afterthought added in post-production to try and give the story some coherence). The individual shots are sometimes lovely, but they lack the real elegance and depth of cinematographer Ernest Dickerson's work with Spike Lee.

Even given a good script and talented director, it's debatable whether this cast could deliver. Japanese actor Marc Hayashi lacks either the charisma or the talent to carry a film as the leading man. The various Caucasian actors seem either abrasive or simply at sea with their oddball characters. Wang, as Inspector Lu, looks merely tired (which he probably was, considering he also directed and produced). Tony Leung Ka-Fai is personable enough as the con man Joey, but is plainly struggling with his English lines. Only the perpetually-dependable Sally Yeh gives anything like a good performance (for one thing, she's allowed to speak in her native tongue, with subtitles); she takes the "hooker-with-a-heart-of-gold" role of Susu and dispenses with the clichés, playing the prostitute as warm, attractive and sympathetic.

*Laser Man* apparently sat on the shelf for four years before receiving a U.S. release, at which point it opened to some favorable reviews. (Peter Travers of *Rolling Stone* said, "Maliciously on target. It's that rare comedy with a brain and a heart.")

*Laser Man* has the distinction of being the only English-language film Tsui was involved with prior to his team-ups with Jean-Claude Van Damme in the '90s (and, with *The Master*, is one of the only two Tsui Hark films shot completely within the United States).

## *Happy Ghost III*

Actor, 1986. Cantonese: *Hoi Sam Gwai Jong Gwai*. Mandarin: *Kai Xin Gui Zhuang Gui*. Literally: *Happy Ghost Bumps Ghost*. Directors: Johnnie To Kei-Fung, Raymond Wong Bak-Ming. Producer/Screenwriter: Raymond Wong. Special Effects: Tsui Hark/Cinefex Workshop. CAST: Raymond Wong Bak-Ming ("Hong Sam Kwai"/"Happy Ghost"), Maggie Cheung Man-Yuk ("Tsui Pan-Han"), Fennie Yuen ("Tai Cheuk-yee"), Tsui Hark ("Godfather"). Opening Date: July 3, 1986.

The most supernatural thing about *Happy Ghost III* could be that it's the skeleton in Maggie Cheung's closet. Watching the young Maggie giggle, pout and mug her way shamelessly through this film, it's hard to believe that within two years (after her performance in Wong Kar-Wai's *As Tears Go By*) she would become one of the world's great film actresses. Of course, she's can't be the only one blamed here: Raymond Wong's script is scattered and sophomoric, and Johnnie To (yes, it is the same Johnnie To who would become one of the most successful directors in Hong Kong by the end of the '90s) directs in a flat, barely adequate way. The film is often saved by its colorful and inventive optical effects, which mark Tsui's major contribution to this mess.

This third of five successful *Happy Ghost* films follows the travails of Pan-Han, a dead singer sitting out time in the afterlife while she waits to reincarnate. Tsui (looking uncharacteristically dapper in gleaming white tux) plays the "Godfather" in charge of matching up spirits with potential families, and he finally locates the perfect new musical family for Pan-Han. Unfortunately, high school teacher Sam Kwai blows it for her, taking her new mom to the wrong hospital, and she misses her chance. She's given one month on earth to await her next opportunity for reincarnation, so she spends her thirty days wreaking havoc on poor Sam Kwai. What follows is goofy slapstick of the pants-around-ankles variety, until Sam Kwai summons his ancestor, the Happy Ghost, to help him out.

The film has some mildly amusing moments but sadly mimics one of the worst tendencies of American comedy films by throwing in a mean-spirited subplot involving a Triad boss who prostitutes young girls and tortures the disobedient ones with drug injections. It doesn't matter that this diversion eventually segues into the major plot (Pan-Han's attempt to reincarnate); its tone is so inappropriate that it virtually stops the film dead.

Much of *Happy Ghost III*'s supernatural shenanigans rely on the actors (Pan-Han is fond of possession, especially when it comes to Sam Kwai's young students), but the film gains some visual interest when the opticals take over, which include a spinning, brightly lit tunnel adjoining our world with the next; dancing footsteps; and, in the film's car chase climax, a taxi that careens up and over the walls of Hong Kong skyscrapers. The distorting taxi (it jams itself through a tiny manhole opening at one point) is well done (especially for 1986) and an interesting forerunner of similar effects Tsui would later make

use of for his own *Love in the Time of Twilight*.

*Happy Ghost III* was another hit for Cinema City, coming in number 11 on the year's box office list (only four spots below Tsui's *Peking Opera Blues*), with a total gross of $15,339,277.00.

## *Final Victory*

Actor, 1987. Cantonese: *Jui Hau Sing Lei*. Mandarin: *Zui Hou Sheng Li*. Literally: *Final Victory*. AKA: *Cher, Last Victory*. Director: Patrick Tam Ka-Ming. Screenwriter: Patrick Tam Ka-Ming, Winnie Yu Ching, Wong Kar-Wai. CAST: Eric Tsang Chi-Wai ("Hung"), Tsui Hark ("Bo"), Loletta Lee Lai-Chun ("Mimi"), Margaret Lee Din-Long ("Ping"). Opening Date: March 12, 1987.

Less than a year after John Woo and Tsui Hark released *A Better Tomorrow* — the film that redefined the action movie as an exercise in male bonding — Tsui starred in this intimate character-driven study that dared to question the violence and brutality in that redefinition.

*Final Victory* is certainly one of the most unusual Triad films ever made. Its vision of Triad life is completely lacking in glamour or romance; its bosses live in seedy bars and cheap apartments, play ping pong for fun, and suffer real hurts when they're beaten (which is fairly often). It centers on Bo, a cruel, temperamental Triad boss, and his younger brother Hung, timid and browbeaten from his years with Bo. When Hung fails to stand up to a Filipino who is romancing his girl, Bo steps in, first beating the Filipino to a pulp, then turning on Hung. Finally, Bo tells Hung that he's going to prison for nine months, and he wants Hung to look after his two wives; he leaves Hung some money and instructions that the two women must never know about each other. No sooner is Bo gone than Hung's in trouble; one wife, Mimi, has fled to Japan, while the other, Ping, is in debt to a local loanshark. To escape the loanshark, Hung takes Ping with him to Japan to search for Mimi, who is working as a dancer in a porno club. Hung succeeds in getting her out of the club, but Ping is caught and held for an immense bail. Hung and Mimi consider robbery, but end up winning a fortune in a local pachinko parlor. They ransom Ping, but Hung's troubles are just starting — before long, Ping and Mimi both discover they share a husband. Mimi confesses that she wants to leave her husband, and they return to Hong Kong to face Bo. Bo refuses to let Mimi go and tells Hung to keep an eye on her. Hung tries to hide them from Ping's loanshark, but they find her anyway and threaten her. Hung tries to save her but can't bring himself to use a hatchet; it takes Mimi to put the weapon to use and free Ping. In the ensuing chase Mimi is separated from Hung and Ping, who try to flee in the loanshark's car; Hung orders Ping to go back, and he finally commits an act of true courage by saving Mimi. Mimi and Hung soon realize they've fallen in love, and they make the mistake of thinking that Bo will accept this. Instead, he tells them that he plans on killing them as soon as he's out of prison. Pursued by both loansharks and the vindictive Bo, Hung, Mimi and Ping are desperate enough now to consider robbing a bank, but Hung can't bring himself to do it. It isn't until he's separated from the women that they pull it off; he returns to their hideout and discovers that Mimi has been seriously shot. He also finds Bo waiting for him. Bo walks him to a nearby beach and pulls a knife, but in the end his good memories of their mutual childhood stay his hand. He finally tells

Hung he never wants to see him again, and suggests he and Mimi should flee to Taiwan. Hung runs back to Mimi only to find that he's too late — the cops have tracked the robbers down and taken the two women away. As the ambulance carrying Mimi races by, Hung runs after it, promising to marry Mimi even when she's in prison.

At the opening of *Final Victory* both women are involved with Bo, Mimi because of money and Ping because she likes being the wife of a Triad boss. But by the time the film reaches its two-thirds point, both women have switched their allegiance to Hung, who operates not out of violence and rage but concern and love. At first Hung's refusal to act in a number of situations — whether robbing the old man in Japan or defending himself against Ping's loansharks — seems to stem from cowardice, but we soon realize Hung is capable of extraordinary courage; he simply doesn't want to hurt anyone. In most action films this would doom him from the start, but in *Final Victory* it makes him the hero and survivor.

*Final Victory* is also a poignant meditation on love. All four of its characters go to extraordinary lengths to protect their love: Hung confronts his terrifying brother, Bo fumes in prison and plots revenge, Mimi robs a bank, and Ping threatens to prostitute herself if Bo leaves her. In *Final Victory*, love is such a powerful force that it can force Hung to reveal his bravery, but it can also ruin Mimi. Surely *Final Victory*'s title must be one of the most ironic ever.

Although movie triangles are common, squares (four-sided figures) are almost never seen; it requires not just an adept screenwriter to pull it off, but also fine actors. The film's four leads are astonishing, and director Patrick Tam allows lots of long takes that let them build their performances within individual scenes; take, for example, the shot from the first part of the film when Bo lectures Hung in their small apartment. The shot is a single, long two-shot of the actors, and is incredibly successful in conveying both Bo's fury and Hung's remorse. The film also features numerous individual close-ups, possibly the best being on Mimi as she cries while Hung sings a love song to her in a nightclub. In any other movie that scene would be corny, but in *Final Victory* — and especially in Loletta Lee's subtle, tough performance — it's full of sweet melancholy and release.

*Final Victory* is the only time Tsui Hark played a serious role that was not a cameo, and it's a pity it would be the last; he turns Bo into an unforgettable figure of barely-controlled rage, whose stoic face becomes an image of utter terror. He cuts a striking, surprisingly-large figure (indeed, his nickname throughout the film is "Big" Bo) in his white polyester suit with black shirt, whose creases are almost as sharp as his cheekbones. At the film's end he remains a frightful figure, even though he releases Hung and Mimi. It's to Tsui's credit as an actor that his last scene with Hung never becomes maudlin but instead seems pathetic; we sense that for just a second Bo has some realization of the monster he's become, but doesn't know how to escape.

Tsui is, of course, perfectly complemented by Eric Tsang, one of Hong Kong's best character actors giving possibly his finest performance here. And Loletta Lee also brings a wonderfully tough, almost tomboyish appeal to Mimi; Lee started in Hong Kong's Category III films (their equivalent to our X-rating), and so she's one more example of the differences between the Hong Kong and Hollywood film industries — name one American porn actress who went on to be nominated for several major awards (Hong Kong's actu-

ally had several, Shu Qi — of *City of Glass* and *Viva Erotica* — being the most recent).

*Final Victory* also has an unusual look, even for a Hong Kong film; its shoddy interiors are drenched in vivid, high-contrast colors. A Mah-Jong parlor is lit in bright greens; the nightclubs are rendered in crimsons and dark blues. Faces are sometimes allowed to fall off into shadow, as in one memorable close-up of Tsui near the beginning, as he sits bathed in blue light while contemplating his situation. The lighting gives the film a vital, vivid texture that makes it seem alive and immediate without becoming comic-bookish or overly romanticized.

Director Patrick Tam is often listed as one of the prime directors in Hong Kong's "New Wave" movement of the '80s, along with Tsui, Ann Hui and a handful of others. Tam's 1982 film *Nomad* is considered a seminal film and is also notable for giving Leslie Cheung one of his earliest roles. Tam also designed the film's sets.

*Final Victory* is probably the best-known (and best) film penned by Wong Kar-Wai prior to his career as a director/writer/auteur. Wong is recognizable to Western film viewers for his 1994 arthouse hit *Chungking Express,* but it's his other 1994 film — the martial arts epic *Ashes of Time* — that owes at least a partial debt to the work of Tsui Hark, using, as it does, Brigitte Lin in the dual role of a brother and sister warrior pair.

*Final Victory* was only a moderate financial success, coming in at number 56 for the year, with a gross of $5,795,427.00. But it fared far better at the Hong Kong Film Awards that year, where it was nominated (up against Tsui's *A Chinese Ghost Story* in most categories) for Best Picture, Best Director (Patrick Tam Ka-Ming), Best Actor (Eric Tsang Chi-Wai), Best Supporting Actress (Loletta Lee and Margaret Lee Din-Long), Best Supporting Actor

Kit (Leslie Cheung) confronts Lung (Dean Shek) as Ho (Ti Lung) looks on in *A Better Tomorrow II.*

(Tsui Hark), Best Screenplay (Patrick Tam Ka-Ming, Winnie Yu Ching and Wong Kar-Wai), Best Cinematography (Lam Kwok Wah), Best Art Direction (Patrick Tam Ka-Ming) and Best Original Film Score (Chung Ting Yat); it won for Best Film Editing (Cheung Kwok Kuen).

In the program book for the *21st Hong Kong International Film Festival*, *Final Victory* (which appeared as part of the "Hong Kong Cinema Retrospective") is listed as "one of the great quirky movies produced in the 1980's."

## A Better Tomorrow II

Producer/Writer, 1987. Cantonese: *Ying Hung Boon Sik II*. Mandarin: *Ying Xiong Ben Se II*. Literally: *Heroic Character II*. Director: John Woo [Ng Yu-Sam]. Action Director: Ching Siu-Tung. Co-Writer: John Woo (Ng Yu-Sam). Editor: David Wu. Music: Joseph Koo, with lyrics by James Wong. CAST: Chow Yun-Fat ("Ken"), Ti Lung ("Ho"), Leslie Cheung Kwok-Wing ("Kit"), Dean Shek Tin ("Lung"), Emily Chu Bo-Yee ("Jackie"). Opening Date: December 17, 1987.

*A Better Tomorrow* returns with a sequel that's bigger and bloodier, but is it a better *Better Tomorrow*? Well, the answer is yes and no…

The film opens very promisingly, with a recap of episode one in the form of Ho's nightmare. Ho is now in prison, still grieving over the lost Mark. One day he's taken from his cell and made an offer: The cops want him to spy on his former mentor Lung (suspected of heading a counterfeiting ring). He initially refuses, but accepts when he finds out his brother Kit is already on the case.

Kit has infiltrated the ring by helping Lung's beloved daughter Peggy at a ballroom dancing contest. It's at another event when Ho and Kit meet again; not long after, Lung is framed for two murders and Ho helps him flee Hong Kong for New York. Kit tries to protect Peggy, but when she finds out he's married she leaves him and is murdered.

Ho visits an old friend who is an artist who has immortalized the events from *A Better Tomorrow* in comic-style drawings, and his friend tells him that Mark had a twin brother, Ken, who now lives in New York. Cut to: Ken's restaurant, which is being extorted for protection money by Mafia men. Ken refuses and orders the mob thug at gunpoint to eat the rice he's thrown at Ken.

Lung arrives in New York and hooks up with an ex-Triad member who is now a priest. A shooting leaves the priest dead and Lung shattered; he lands in a mental hospital, where he is rescued by Ken. But Ken's got his own problems—the Mafia has blown up his restaurant and is now after him. Lung doesn't regain his senses until he sees Ken injured in a gun battle; then he finds his courage again and assists Ken in wiping out the thugs. He and Ken then leave New York to return to Hong Kong where Lung discovers that he was betrayed by his assistant Ko. Our four heroes—Kit, Ho, Lung and Ken—finally unite to take on Ko and his thugs. Kit is the first to die, just as his wife Jackie is giving birth to their daughter. Finally, Ho, Lung and Ken head out on a suicide mission to destroy Ko. In a massively violent climax they destroy most of Ko's mansion and dozens of men, finally finishing up Ko

at the last moment. When the police arrive they find the mansion full of corpses—and three dying heroes.

*A Better Tomorrow II* is a more assured film than the first one; director Woo seems to be more consistent and confident with his style, resulting in some spectacular firefights. But those same fights are almost the film's undoing: They've become so impossible here that they flirt with self-parody. When our three heroes effortlessly mow down dozens of heavily-armed men in the finale, we realize Woo has dispensed with the last vestiges of logic; we can either guffaw at the sheer outlandishness of it or give in to the adrenaline-pumping excitement. Woo must have figured it was entertainment either way.

Unfortunately, some aspects of the script are even harder to buy than the massive-body-count action scenes. The biggest contrivance, of course, is the appearance of Chow Yun-Fat, playing Mark's identical twin brother (conveniently never mentioned in the first film); it's another credit to the incredibly gifted Chow that he makes Ken into a different character without resorting to phony mustaches or glasses (he does give Ken the peculiar habit of sucking on a lighter flame, but then Chow *always* endows his characters with some oral fixation, whether it's a matchstick, toothpick or fire). Lung's transformation from tough-if-beleaguered mob boss to drooling idiot and then back again beggars belief, as do numerous occasions when someone shows up just in the nick of time to rescue one or more of our protagonists.

And then, of course, there's the typical Woo treatment of female characters, most of whom serve as nothing more than catalysts to unite the men. Much has been made of Woo's homoeroticism, and while the very idea seems ludicrous, given his love of destroying the male form, there are some scenes in *A Better Tomorrow II* that lend credence to this theory. In the most obvious, Ken cradles a dying Ho so Ho can talk one last time to his wife, who has just given birth to their daughter; Ho is so intent on celebrating the news with Ken that his wife seems to be practically an uninvolved bystander in the conversation. If Woo is not deliberately homoerotic, he is certainly uninterested in allowing women into his tightly-enclosed world of masculine bonding.

As with the first film, *A Better Tomorrow II* is saved from Woo's occasional lapses into machismo and sentimentality by its superb cast. New addition Dean Shek is so good as Lung that it's hard to believe this was the same actor who, five years before, mugged uncontrollably in the comedic *It Takes Two*. Ti Lung gets to revert to his days as a martial arts star when, at the climax, he picks up a sword and carves a path through the bad guys with astonishing grace.

In regards to *A Better Tomorrow II*'s often-discussed climax, it's worthwhile to point out that the action choreography was provided by the always-imaginative Ching Siu-Tung. Most astonishing is a shot in which Chow Yun-Fat throws a hand grenade behind him, then is nearly blown out of the shot (this shot actually set Chow's hair on fire). The sets and actors are often drenched in blood; even the pop ballad (sung by Leslie Cheung) playing near the end contains such tender lines as, "My blood pours out, but I don't want you to know." *A Better Tomorrow II* wasn't quite the runaway hit that its predecessor was, but it nevertheless performed extremely well at the box office, becoming the year's number 6 hit, with a total gross of $22,727,369.00. It received two nominations at the year's Hong Kong Film Awards: one for Best Actor (Leslie Cheung Kwok-Wing) and one for Best Action Choreography (Ching Siu-Tung).

## *I Love Maria*

Producer/Actor, 1988. Cantonese: *Tit Gaap Mo Dik Ma Lei A*. Mandarin: *Tie Jia Wu Di Ma Li Ya*. Literally: *Iron Armor Invincible Maria*. AKA: *Roboforce*. Co-Producer: John Sham Kin-Fun. Director: David Chung Chi-Man. Action Director: Ching Siu-Tung. CAST: Sally Yeh [Yip Sin-Man] ("Maria"/ "Pioneer 2"), John Sham Kin-Fun ("Curly"), Tsui Hark ("Whisky"), Tony Leung Chiu-Wai ("T. Q. Zhuang"), Lam Ching-Ying ("Master"), Paul Chun ("Police Captain"). Opening Date: March 10, 1988.

*I Love Maria* may be the perfect film to illustrate the differences between American filmmaking and Hong Kong filmmaking. Based on the American science fiction hit *Robocop*, *I Love Maria* takes off from the same idea of a near future when killer robots rampage through our cities, but it engages in some serious gender-bending and adds generous dollops of comedy to create an irresistible little gem. Where *Robocop* went for a satirical view of an entire near-future culture, *I Love Maria* chooses to concentrate on a few characters and their interactions with technology; in other words, *I Love Maria* (in typical Hong Kong fashion) is both more down-to-earth and possibly slightly more entertaining than its big American sibling.

The film opens as Hong Kong police are desperately trying to stop a giant robot from committing a bank robbery. Caught in the fray is T. Q. Zhuang, a bumbling reporter who is nearly smashed by the robot when he gets too close to the action. Finally, the robot tells police that it is Pioneer 1 of the Hero Gang, and it issues an ominous warning before rocketing up into the night sky. Upon its return to the industrial plant that houses the Hero Gang, the robot reports to Maria and Big Brother, the gang's leaders. Maria is upset that the robot only accomplished the robbery and did not kill the police. When one of the nearby scientists tries to flee, he is shot down by the cruel Maria. The next day T. Q. Zhuang is covering a news conference at police headquarters when he once again drops his camera. This time it's picked up by Curly, who tells T. Q. he's designing special weapons for the police. Curly has invented an electrosonic cannon that he believes would stop the Hero Gang's robot, but the invention is quashed by Curly's boss, who doesn't want to be shown up by his employee. Dismayed, Curly gets drunk in a bar and takes pity on Whisky, a drunk who is a favorite target of the bar bullies. Curly uses a special gun to defend himself, and gets Whisky out of the bar. T. Q. witnesses the display and follows Curly when he takes Whisky to his laboratory-home to sober up. Unfortunately, Curly doesn't know that someone else is after Whisky: He's left the Hero Gang, and his Master, one-time boss of the gang until Big Brother took over, has come after him. Master is a noble man and tells Whisky he's free — but Maria and Big Brother have other ideas. Big Brother creates a robot duplicate of Maria — dubbed Pioneer 2 — and sends it to kill Whisky. Whisky at first mistakes the robot for Maria, who he grew up with and is still fond of, but Curly finally makes him realize this is a killer 'bot. Curly and Whisky barely escape the machine, which is destroyed when a water tank explodes. When Curly returns to his home he finds the police waiting for him — they believe he's working with the Hero Gang. He's rescued by Whisky, and they escape in Curly's special car; little does Whisky know that Curly has brought the

remains of Pioneer 2 with him. They hide out in an abandoned building near the ocean, and Curly reprograms Pioneer 2 to respond to the phrase "I love Curly." But the Hero Gang has tracked them to the house and unleashes Pioneer 1 on them. A vicious fight ensues, as Whisky runs through the forest, pursued by Maria and the Hero Gang, while Curly and Pioneer 2 fight the bigger, badder Pioneer 1. Whisky escapes only when his Master saves him (aboard a rocket-powered motorcycle), and Curly is saved only when Maria calls on Pioneer 1 to save her from falling off a cliff. Curly and Whisky take their new robot friend and head for a boat repair shed, where they hole up while Curly repairs the robotic Maria. T. Q. stumbles upon them and calls the police; Curly and Whisky are arrested, but the Hero Gang recovers Pioneer 2 and tries to reprogram her. T. Q. breaks into their facility and saves Pioneer 2; she manages to break Curly and Whisky out of jail, and they retrieve Curly's electrosonic cannon, ready to take on Hero Gang. They bust into the industrial plant, and a huge fight ensues. Big Brother — who is now half robot himself — heads for the gang's latest creation: Pioneer 3, a robot that is several stories tall. Master follows Big Brother into Pioneer 3, and they fight for control. Meanwhile, Whisky finally shoots Maria to protect Curly, just as Big Brother loses in his fight with Master; Big Brother and Maria die next to each other. With Pioneer 2's help, Curly's cannon finally succeeds in destroying Pioneer 1, and Pioneer 3 jets off into the stratosphere, disappearing forever(?). Master dies and the greedy Police Captain takes all the credit for destroying the Hero Gang, but our heroes are content to take the robot Maria back to the bar and let her handle the bullies.

*I Love Maria* may be a fast-paced, high-tech action film, but it leaves plenty of time for humor. All three of its main characters are clutzy but sweet-natured — Whisky and Curly may play painful gags on each other, but they befriend a stray dog they find in the seaside building. T. Q., likewise, treats the robot almost like a girlfriend, despite his initial fear of it. When Curly and Whisky first repair the Maria robot, they use it first to power electric appliances, then to beat each other. If *Robocop*'s message was finally about the dehumanizing effects of technology, then *I Love Maria* says that technology — no matter how amazing — will never change human nature.

*I Love Maria* also plays with the traditional hero/heroine roles of science fiction films — there is no conventional, handsome leading man, and the killer robot is female (as is one of the two main antagonists). In opting for a feminine machine, Tsui and director David Chung seem to be paying homage to Fritz Lang's classic *Metropolis* (which also featured a beautiful female robot created in the image of its heroine, Maria) while flipping the typical Western convention of the macho killer robot on its ear. It's hard to believe they didn't create the role with Sally Yeh in mind — she's simply astonishing in both parts. As the robot, she creates both a believable mechanical body language and a poignant look into the soul of the new machine; as Maria, she's vicious and tough as nails. She even spoofs her own image as a pop singer when the robot, while under repair by Curly, picks up a wrench and begins to sing into it.

Tsui and John Sham are an ideal pair to carry this lively, goofy film. Friends in real life, the chemistry carries over onto the screen; and they're a pair we actually care about — even while we laugh at their antics as they scramble to hit each other with the robot. And Tony Leung, normally one of Hong Kong's best serious actors

(John Woo's *A Bullet in the Head*, Wong Kar-Wai's *Happy Together*) has never been funnier than he is here as the butter-fingered, bespectacled T. Q. Zheung. Add to the mix a brief appearance by Paul Chun as the greedy, boastful Police Captain, and you have one of the best comedy ensembles to grace a Tsui Hark-produced film.

The film is technically superlative as well. The robot designs (especially the gigantic "Transformer"-like Pioneer 1) are clever and realistic, as are all of Curly's gadgets. And — as one would expect from a Tsui Hark/Ching Siu-Tung collaboration — there's an emphasis on flying, as the robots propel themselves up over buildings and right through walls. If Tsui and Ching find joy in freeing humans from the bonds of gravity in their other films, here they liberate both humans (in a spectacular airborne chase through a forest, on vines and wires) and machines.

*I Love Maria* was number 80 for the year, with a total gross of $5,259,522. Listen to John Sham in his kitchen near the beginning of the film, and you'll hear him whistling something that sounds suspiciously like the theme to *A Chinese Ghost Story*.

## Diary of a Big Man

Producer, 1988. Cantonese: *Daai Jeung Foo Yat Gei*. Mandarin: *Da Zhang Fu Ri Ji*. Literally: *Big Husband's Diary*. Director: Chor Yuen. CAST: Chow Yun-Fat ("Chow Ting Fat"), Joey Wang Cho-Yin ("Joey"), Sally Yeh [Yip Sin-Man] ("Sally"), Waise Lee Chi-Hung ("Chi-Hung"), Kent Cheng Juk-Si ("Inspector Cheng"). Opening Date: July 21, 1988.

In this sporadically amusing film, Chow Yun-Fat stars as Chow Ting Fat, a

大丈夫♡記

**Chow (Chow Yun-Fat) and Sally (Sally Yeh) live it up in *Diary of a Big Man*.**

stockbroker who has always dreamed of finding a lover who's a cross between Joey Wang and Sally Yeh. Wouldn't you know it, he meets both women during the same rainstorm, and within a short time he's accidentally engaged to both. With the help of his stressed-out, pill-popping business partner Chi-Hung, he connives to marry both women and keep the relationships separate. When he's involved in a minor car accident and winds up in the hospital, police Inspector Cheng begins to suspect, and so Chow must embark on a series of increasingly ludicrous explanations, finally convincing Cheng that he and his male business partner are the real lovers. But in the meantime, Joey and Sally have become friends, and when they run into each other at a wedding photography studio, they finally realize the truth. They promptly scheme to turn the tables on their deceitful husband, but he has the last

laugh: In the end he becomes a Muslim so he can have both wives legally.

This isn't the first film Tsui's been involved with that involved the dilemma of a bigamist; in *Final Victory*, made one year earlier, Tsui himself played the bigamist in a story that added a younger brother assigned to care for the wives in Tsui's absence. Unfortunately, *Diary of a Big Man* isn't nearly so successful in the telling as the earlier film; it often feels like a comedy skit padded out to 90 minutes. Even its self-referential in-jokes (Chow hears on the car radio that Chow Yun-Fat has just been named Actor of the Year and mutters, "Not him again. It's fixed") don't keep it from wearing thin fast. The cast performs with gusto, and the three leads are particularly funny in a fantasy musical montage set to a strange little ditty entitled "Very Nice"; yet, surprisingly, the film is often stolen by Waise Lee as Chow's nervous partner Chi-

Hung. Probably best known for his serious roles in such films as *A Better Tomorrow* and *A Chinese Ghost Story II*, Waise Lee is very funny here, whether pretending to convulse or sleeping at work with fake eyes painted on his eyelids.

The only real evidence of Tsui in this film comes when Chow performs fake Chinese opera to amuse Joey, and again at the end when the two wives abruptly reverse a hostage situation and send the criminals running. Otherwise, the picture is surprisingly flat in its direction (by Chor Yuen) and cinematography, although it does make some clever use of minor opticals to frame Chow when he delivers his to-the-camera "diary" entries.

The film was successful enough to come in at the number 12 spot for the year's box office take, earning $19,419,539.00. *Diary of a Big Man* was also the only Tsui Hark film to receive a nomination at the eighth Hong Kong Film Awards, for Best Original Film Song.

## *The Big Heat*

Producer, 1988. Cantonese: *Sing Si Dak Ging.* Mandarin: *Cheng Shi Te Jing.* Literally: *Big City Special Police.* Director: Andrew Kam Yeung-Wah, Johnnie To Kei-Fung. Screenwriter: Gordon Chan Ka-Seung. Editor/Music Score: David Wu. Theme Song: Lowell Lo. CAST: Waise Lee Chi-Hung ("Wong"), Philip Kwok Chun-Fung [Kuo Chui] ("Kam"), Joey Wang Cho-Yin ("Ada"), Paul Chu Kong ("Han").

Don't be fooled by the poster art for *The Big Heat*, which shows four apparently carefree men happily running towards the camera as if they're trying out for the next *Aces Go Places* entry — *The Big Heat* is a serious dose of ultra-violence Hong Kong-style, an intense mix of action, intrigue and politics.

With a script by Gordon Chan (co-director of Hong Kong's 1998 Best Film winner, *Beast Cops*) and direction by Johnnie To (nominated in 1999 for Best Director on both *Running Out of Time* and *The Mission*), *The Big Heat* is an early entry from two of the brightest future stars in Hong Kong cinema. It tells the story of dedicated cop Wong, who has a degenerative nerve disease slowly crippling his gun hand. Wong is about to retire when he's told that his former partner and close friend Tse has been brutally murdered while undercover in Malaysia. He tears up his letter of resignation and takes the case. He also tells his fiancé that he expects the case to be dangerous, and he wants to postpone their wedding until after he's completed it. He assembles a team which includes naïve rookie Lun, Inspector Ong from Malaysia and his current partner Kam, and they begin by examining photos which were found with Tse's horribly burned corpse. The photos show shipping magnate Ho in a homosexual affair with a young hustler; when Kam goes after the hustler, he finds the boy dead and narrowly escapes from a shootout. The case heats up further when Wong and Lun realize they're being tailed, and a fierce foot chase through Hong Kong's crowded streets ensues. Wong finally chases down the last of the pursuers, only to see the man run over and killed by passing cars. They return to Ho for clues, and, discovering that he plans to leave town on the following day, they attempt to fool Ho into thinking they're blackmailers who will release the photos unless they're paid off. Hoping to get Ho to confess to Tse's murder, the plan backfires when Ho tries to commit suicide instead. They rescue him and send him to a hospital, where he tells them a man called Ching Han is blackmailing him so he can use Ho's shipping company to move illegal cargo. Ong and Wong, following the lead, break into Ho's shipping warehouse and find crates full of cans of powdered milk — which also contain baggies of some black substance. Meanwhile, Kam and Lun are watching Ho at the hospital when he's attacked and finally murdered by a hitman. A furious chase through the hospital finally leads to nothing but a higher body count, and with Ho dead their only hope is the contents of the powdered milk can. They take the can to Ho's girlfriend, Maggie in forensics, and she identifies the substance as refined cocaine. But her news arrives too late — Wong has been set up by Ching Han with a faked $300,000 bribe, and Maggie is murdered by Ching Han's men. The case seems to be over until Lun — now happily involved with pretty hospital nurse Ada — spots one of Ching Han's men at a grocery store. He follows the man to a boat, where Ching Han is meeting with Russians and discussing his drug smuggling operations. Lun manages to tape the conversation and returns to his apartment, but Ching Han and his men follow him there. Lun is tortured, and Ada barely makes it out; Wong arrives only to walk into a trap, which blows up Lun. Ada, Ong, Kam and Wong all take part in the final firefight with Ching Han and his men; they're all injured, but Ching Han is finally killed when Ada and Kam smash his car with a garbage truck. Wong is left only to confront Ng, a cop who was secretly working for Ching Han, but he stops the traitor by forcing his stiff gun hand into action. Ng is killed, and Wong retrieves the tape.

*The Big Heat*'s reputation for violence and gore is well-deserved; during its running time heads and hands are graphically severed, men are struck over and over by speeding cars, and every main character is hit at least five times by bullets. One of the

initial images in the film is Wong's nightmare of a drill going into his hand. The first major sequence involves Wong shooting a hostage in the leg to save his life. If *The Big Heat* seems excessively bloody, its violence also feels more realistic than usual for Hong Kong fare, and the characters react to it in an appropriate way (the rookie Lun is nauseated; even the hardened Wong is occasionally stricken by it). Its violence seems equally authentic; there are no graceful "gun ballets" here, just desperate men trying to reload fast enough to save their lives. In some respects *The Big Heat* foreshadows director To's other 1999 hit, *The Mission*, in which the gun battles are slow and precise, with combatants waiting out long seconds in attitudes of frozen dread.

But what *The Big Heat* might be most remembered for (and what probably most marks it as recognizably a Tsui Hark film) is its political commentary. Villain Ching Han is obsessed with the idea of making money before the 1997 handover; he tells Wong there are only "ten years left." He talks of all those who plan on emigrating, how they'll need money. He and the Russian aboard the boat offer a toast to "drugs and capitalism," and talk again of 1997. In some respects *The Big Heat* is similar to end-of-the-world science fiction films, projecting a real sense of paranoia about a near future event. It's a credit to the film that, in these quiet post–1997 times, *The Big Heat* can still generate a sense of unease.

*The Big Heat* also has a paranoia about *gweilos*. Even though Ching Han's drug partners are Russians, they're nevertheless Caucasian and therefore Westerners. The nurse who tries to kill Ho with an intravenous injection in the hospital is blonde; Wong's cold, always-angry boss is British. In some respects the film's two paranoid themes — the 1997 handover and white intervention — seem to be at odds; after all, '97 is/was the year when the British depart(ed) and return(ed) Hong Kong to the Chinese. But if *The Big Heat* is compared to some of the other films in Tsui Hark's oeuvre — most notably *Dangerous Encounter — 1st Kind* and the *Once Upon a Time in China* series — what emerges is an image of Hong Kong as a place that should belong to neither Western culture nor Communism, but rather to traditional, nationalist Chinese values. In this respect, all that's missing from *The Big Heat* is a lion dance.

*The Big Heat* contains excellent, fresh performances from all of its cast, especially Philip Kwok, cast against type as a mom-loving good guy, and Chu Kong, playing against his sympathetic character from *The Killer* as the grinning, greedy Ching Han. *The Big Heat* is also notable for David Wu's throbbing, martial score, which keeps the pace pumping.

*The Big Heat* was a minor box office disappointment, coming in at only number 94 for the year, with a gross of $4,076,927.00.

Looking back on *The Big Heat*, Johnnie To had this to say: "Tsui had lots of ideas, changing the script all the time, but three days later he would come up with something totally different... Looking at *The Big Heat* now, it's good at places, but it was chaotic" (interviewed by Athena Tsui and Cochran Fung for *Hong Kong Panorama '98–'99*).

## Gunmen

Producer, 1988. Cantonese: *Tin Loh Dei Mong.* Mandarin: *Tian Luo Di Wang.* Literally: *Dragnet.* Director: Che-Kirk Wong Chi-Keung. CAST: Tony Leung Ka-Fai ("Ding"), Waise Lee Chi-Hung ("The Captain"), Carrie Ng Ka-Lai ("Chu-Chiao"), Adam Cheng Siu-Chow ("Mr. Haye"), Mark Cheng Ho-Nam ("Fan"), David Ng Dai-Wai ("Kwong"), Elizabeth Lee Mei-Fung ("Mona Fong"), Elvis Tsui Kam-Kong ("Ting"). Opening Date: October 22, 1988.

Tsui and director Kirk Wong try for a Hong Kong version of Brian De Palma's 1987 *The Untouchables* with this period cop drama. They come close in some respects — the film has solid pacing and performances, with some exciting action throughout — but they miss in its episodic script and uneven production design.

*Gunmen* begins during the Chinese Civil War of 1926. Four soldiers — Ding, Kwong, Fan and their captain — have been captured by the enemy and are awaiting execution when word arrives to the enemy commander that his side has surrendered. He refuses to obey orders and is about to proceed with the execution when a grenade goes off, almost literally blasting our four heroes to freedom. Ding arrives home to embrace his wife, Chu-Chiao, and Sze-Sze, the daughter he's never met.

*Gunmen* now moves to poverty-ridden, French-ruled Shanghai, where Ding takes a job with the police force. He also begins to develop a relationship with Mona Fong, a prostitute who becomes his informant and tips him off about an opium deal going down at a brothel. During a literal firefight (the antagonists are surrounded by fire) in the brothel, Ding's police captain is killed and Ding recognizes the murderer as the enemy commander who wouldn't give up during the war. Ding dedicates himself to catching his late captain's killer, who is now an opium kingpin called Mr. Haye. Ding's task isn't made any easier by the arrival of Ting, a tough, by-the-book cop assigned to take over the police department and clean out the corruption. When Mr. Haye's boss dies as

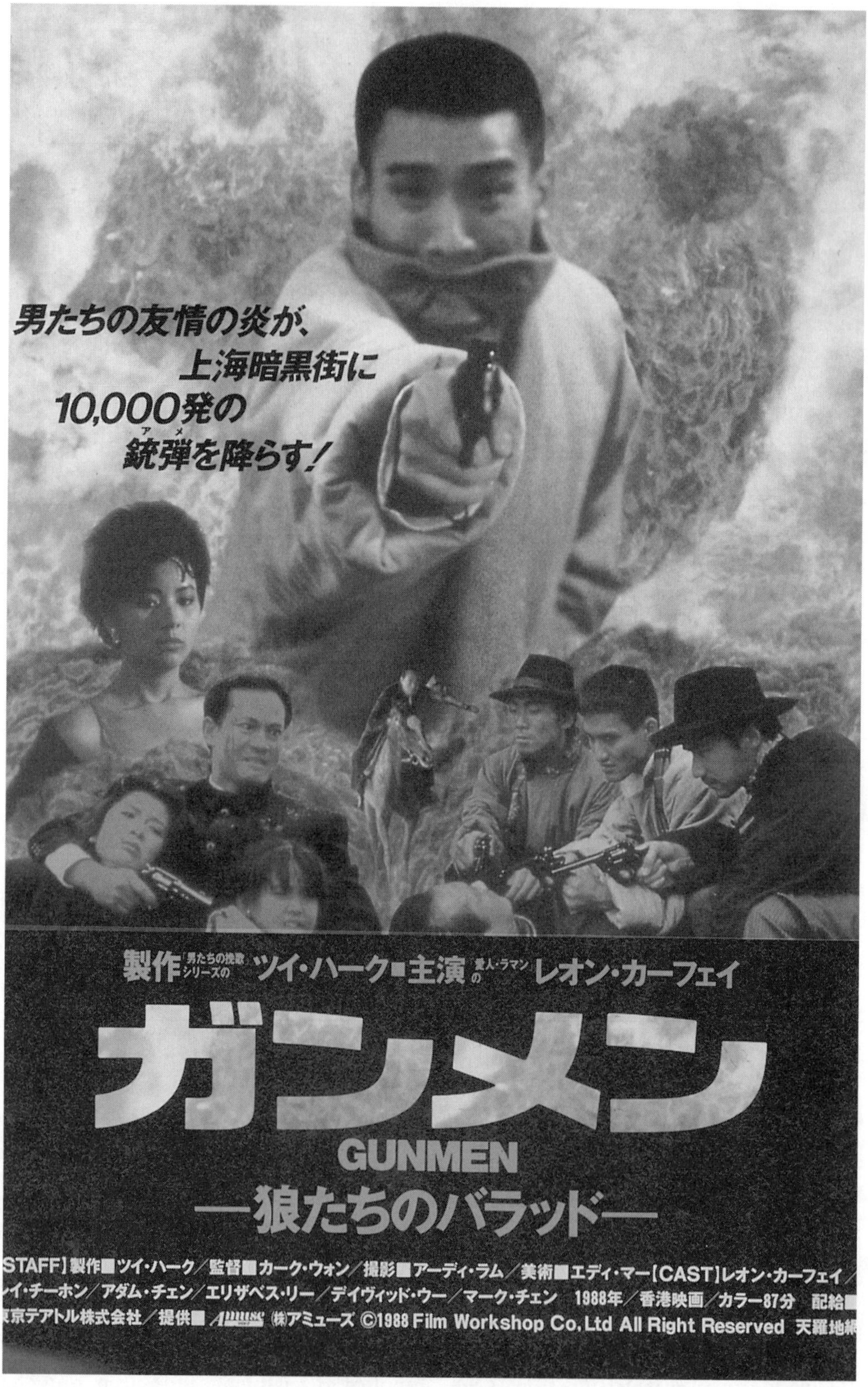


Japanese poster for *Gunmen*.

a result of a gunshot wound inflicted by Ding, Mr. Haye vows vengeance against the cop. Ding stumbles across his three old war buddies— Kwong, Fan and the Captain — one day, and begs them for help. They become cops to protect each other but run afoul of Ting, who fires them. They try to leave Shanghai, but they stumble across an ambush of Ding and decide to remain behind and help their friend. During a shootout at a restaurant, Ting appears, leading the police against Mr. Haye's men, and heavy losses are inflicted on both sides. When Ding tries to get his wife and child to leave Shanghai, they're nearly caught by Mr. Haye's men; but Mona Fong sacrifices herself to save them, and Ding is badly injured. Kwong, Fan, the Captain and Ting show up at the last moment to stop Mr. Haye's thugs, but it's up to Chu-Chiao and Sze-Sze to save Ding when they finally kill Mr. Haye. The film's final image is a photo of Ting with the four heroes and Ding's wife and child, all of whom survived their injuries.

*Gunmen* tries for the appropriate sprawling-epic tone but is hampered by wildly uneven period recreations (too many background extras sport contemporary haircuts and suits, and certain locations look far more like they belong in the '80s than the '20s). The script is also somewhat uneven and occasionally downright weird, as in a chase sequence that abruptly segues into black humor when a funeral is interrupted and the corpse flies out into a racing rickshaw. Kwang, Fan and the Captain are virtually indistinguishable (despite good performances by the actors); a minor subplot involving French ties to the Triad is never really explored.

Where *Gunmen* excels is in the action sequences. Director Kirk Wong would go on to become a major Hong Kong action player with such films as *Rock and Roll Cop* and *Organized Crime and Triad Bureau*,

and the fight scenes display his talents to their fullest. Best of all is the shootout in the blazing brothel, as fire spreads from man to man like plague and a flaming table becomes a weapon. The attempt to ambush Ding at the docks is also a showcase for Wong, with Ding running under the slats overhead and taking out opponents by shooting them in the feet or pulling them down into the muck.

Wong also works his cast well, especially Adam Cheng (from *Zu: Warriors from the Magic Mountain*) as the driven, unstoppable Mr. Haye, and Carrie Ng as Chu-Chiao, Ding's anguished wife. Elvis Tsui — who would later become a minor sensation in Category III films— is also fine in an early role as tough-cop Ting.

If *Gunmen* lacks the expensive, tailored look of De Palma's gangster film, it is at least free from pretension, content to be nothing more than a good, old-fashioned action film.

*Gunmen* placed at number 84 in the year's box office tally, with a gross of $4,825,777.

## The Killer

Producer, 1989. Cantonese: *Dip Huet Seung Hung*. Mandarin: *Die Xue Shuang Xiong*. Literally: *Bloodshed Brothers*. Director: John Woo (Ng Yu-Sam). Action Director: Ching Siu-Tung. Screenwriter: John Woo (Ng Yu-Sam). CAST: Chow Yun-Fat ("Jeff"), Danny Lee Sau-Yin ("Li"), Paul Chu Kong ("Sidney"), Kenneth Tsang Kong ("Sgt. Tsang"), Sally Yeh [Yip Sin-Man] ("Jennie"), Shing Fui-On ("Johnny Weng"), Parkman Wong Pak-Man ("Wong Chan"). Opening Date: July 6, 1989.

*The Killer* is a film so insanely melodramatic that it shouldn't work; that it

喋血雙雄

導演 吳宇森
監製 徐克
領銜主演 周潤發
李修賢
葉蒨文
主演 朱江
曾江
成奎安

電影工作室製

**Li (Danny Lee) and Jeff (Chow Yun-Fat) take on the bad guys at the end of *The Killer*.**

does is as much a credit to the performance of Chow Yun-Fat as to any element of the screenplay or direction. As in the previous John Woo-Tsui Hark-Chow Yun-Fat collaboration *A Better Tomorrow*, Chow's considerable talents carry a film that would otherwise lapse into masculine posturing and maudlin sentiment.

This time out Chow plays Jeff, a professional hitman. When his latest assignment goes awry and causes Jennie, a young singer, to be blinded, Jeff takes it upon himself to pay for the expensive cornea surgery Jennie needs. He takes one last job to get the money: He will knock off mob boss Tony Weng when he makes a public appearance at a Dragon Boat Festival. In charge of Weng's protection is Inspector Li, a tough, dedicated cop who takes off after Jeff when the hit is successful. After a long boat chase, Li tails Jeff to an island

where Jeff is to pick up his payment; instead, he's ambushed. During the shootout a small child is injured and Jeff risks his life to get the child to a hospital. Li follows, but Jeff escapes. Now Jeff is being hunted by both the cops and the Triad; Tony Weng's nephew, Johnny Weng, the new boss, orders Jeff's friend and mentor Sidney to kill Jeff. Sidney refuses and literally begs for Jeff's money; instead, Weng sends a new hitman after Jeff. Meanwhile, Li tracks Jeff to Jennie's apartment, and the two men confront each other in front of the blind woman; Jeff again escapes, eluding both Li and his boss, Sgt. Tsang. Li tells Jennie that Jeff is the man who blinded her, and she agrees to help the police by trying to lure Jeff to the airport; once there, however, she regrets her action and tries to warn Jeff away. With Sidney's help, Jeff again succeeds in evading the police. Li is accused of siding with his quarry, and the case is transferred to new inspector Wong Chan. Li refuses, however, to give up, especially after Sgt. Tsang is killed by Paul Yau, the new hitman; before dying, Tsang tells Li the location of Jeff's new hideout. Li goes there just as Jeff is about to leave with Jennie. Before he and Jeff have time to do much more than level guns on each other, Paul Yau's thugs attack, and Li and Jeff are forced to fight together to protect themselves and the helpless Jennie. They escape, but Jeff is injured. Li fixes him up, and the two men discover a mutual admiration for each other. Sidney makes a last desperate attempt to get Jeff his money, and tells him to meet at their usual place, a semi-abandoned church. Sidney battles Weng and gets the money, but is badly injured; he barely makes it to the church, unaware that Weng and his men are close behind. The final battle takes place around the church, as Weng's men try in vain to stop the determined — and united — Li and Jeff. Jennie is injured again, and finally Jeff is killed. At the end only Li and the malicious Weng are still left alive; as police arrive on the scene, Weng tries to surrender himself to police custody, but Li takes vengeance for Jeff and shoots Weng in front of the witnesses.

*The Killer* reworks many of *A Better Tomorrow*'s themes and situations — both feature men who place honor above all else, and both feature scenes in which two men reminisce about the past and mourn the loss of the old ways — but *The Killer* dispenses with *A Better Tomorrow*'s three leads to concentrate on just one, thus emphasizing Woo's ideal of the solitary hero isolated by his ethics. Even though the film features two male leads (and a mentor/supporting character for each of those), it's really about its eponymous character. Jeff is an ultimate male figure for

Woo: He's strong, quiet, knowledgeable and skilled. Implacable when killing those whom he believes deserve to die, he's compassionate enough to save a child; he takes money for murder but will protect the honor of a friend at the risk of his own life; once he accepts a task he is duty-bound to complete it, at all costs; he stands alone — and above — the baser mass of humanity.

In contrast to Jeff is Inspector Li. Even though they believe themselves to be brothers, Li — ironically the one who believes he's serving "justice" — is Jeff's darker twin. In his first scene Li thinks nothing of a hostage who dies from a heart attack during a shootout; when questioned afterward, he only complains ("how could I know... ?!"), demonstrating no remorse or compassion. Later, when Jeff takes the child to the hospital, Li guesses Jeff's move not so much from empathy but from cold calculation; if their situations were reversed, it's hard to believe that Li would stop to save the little girl. Woo's script is never clear as to whether we're meant to believe that his friendship with Jeff turns Li into a more compassionate man; it doesn't seem likely, considering that by the end of the film Li is still more concerned with justice (i.e., delivering it to Weng) than compassion (seeing to Jennie).

*The Killer* also involves a romantic triangle — in his shadowing of Jeff, Li is also attracted to blinded singer Jennie — but Jennie's character is treated even more badly than Li's. No one goes to a John Woo film expecting strong women (in fact, Woo seems incapable of creating a female character who is even remotely interesting or believable), but his callous treatment of Jennie in *The Killer* marks a low even for him. It's bad enough that the character Jennie obviously exists only to give the two men a pivoting point to circle around, but it's unforgivable that Woo simply never bothers to resolve her character; at the end of the film we are left to just assume that she's crawled off into the brush around the church, perhaps to die there. In *The Killer* Woo's lack of interest in women causes him to violate the basic tenets of good storytelling.

Given their limited characters, Danny Lee and Sally Yeh give the best performances possible, but *The Killer* really belongs to Chow Yun-Fat and the supporting characters that circle him. Chow's brooding, sensitive-but-strong performance virtually redefines the word "charismatic"; that his work wasn't recognized in the year's award nominations is probably only due to the fact that voters felt it was too similar to his Mark in *A Better Tomorrow* (it is, but this is an even more elegant, more emotional Mark — and thus even more compelling). It's hard to imagine any other actor who could make lines such as "I wish I could start all over again" actually work; poor Danny Lee struggles with "I wish I had a friend like you" and comes close to provoking guffaws.

Playing particularly well off Chow's emotional fireworks is Paul Chu Kong as Sidney, Jeff's confused — and so doomed — mentor. Shing Fui-On turns in one of his best performances as the ruthless and rotten Johnny Weng.

Despite the melodramatics and the poor treatment of its female lead, there's no denying that *The Killer* contains some of Hong Kong cinema's most tension-filled and adrenaline-pumping action. Woo's directorial style fully blossomed with this film, and his "bullet ballets" make considerable use of his trademark slow-motion and double-fisted pistol firing. The end shootout in the church is justifiably famous, with Woo intercutting blood, flying doves, grim close-ups and exploding religious icons in furious order.

That *The Killer* is one of the most popular Hong Kong films in America is probably due to its peculiar combination of thrilling lead actor, heart-pumping action, superb craftsmanship and campy melodramatics. Certainly coming as it did at a time when American cinema was cloaked in cool irony, it was a welcome alternative.

*The Killer* was a hit for Tsui and Woo, reaching the ninth position on the year's box office list, with a total of $18,255,083. It was a critical success as well, earning six nominations and two awards at the year's Hong Kong Film Awards: It was nominated for Best Picture, Best Supporting Actor (Paul Chu Kong), Best Screenplay (John Woo) and Best Cinematography (Wong Wing Hang and Peter Pau); it won for Best Director (John Woo) and Best Film Editing (Fan Kung Wing).

Hong Kong film fans often enjoy the "hex errors," or translation mistakes, in subtitles, but *The Killer* includes one of the most amusing signage errors on record: As Jeff rushes the injured little girl to the hospital, he drives by a sign identifying it as "Scared Heart Hospital."

## Just Heroes

Producer, 1989. Cantonese: *Yi Daam Kwan Ying.* Mandarin: *Yi Dan Qun Ying.* Literally: *Righteous Courage Group of Heroes.* AKA: *Tragic Heroes.* Executive Producer: Chang Cheh. Directors: John Woo [Ng Yu-Sam] and Wu Ma. CAST: Danny Lee Sau-Yin ("Tai"), Stephen Chow Sing-Chi ("Jacky"), David Chiang [Keung Dai-Wai] ("Wai"), Wu Ma ("Ma"), James Wong ("Solicitor Wong"), Shing Fui-On ("Wah"), Parkman Wong ("Inspector Lee"). Opening Date: September 14, 1989.

Released just two months after Woo and Tsui's *The Killer,* this one began life as a benefit for the Hong Kong Director's Union (as did the Tsui Hark-Ringo Lam-Jackie Chan effort *Twin Dragons*). The not-half-bad story starts as older Triad boss Tsou is contemplating retirement and a successor. His three possibilities are Tai, a cool enforcer; Wai, bright and devoted but who left the Triads some time back and is now a fish farmer; and Sou, a serious man with a troubled home life. After Tsou is abruptly cut down, his will names Tai, causing strife within the "family." Jacky, a young hothead who is devoted to Sou, overhears a tape one day naming Tai as Tsou's killer, and he goes on a murderous rampage; first he runs down Tai's pregnant girlfriend, then he sets up a meeting with a cop to double-deal Tai. The meeting goes bad, opposing Triad brother Wah and a cop are killed, and Jacky turns himself in to the police, taking the rap for his Triad bosses; Sou is asked by boss Ma and solicitor Wong to leave town. Finally, Tai and Wai realize Sou is the real bad guy, and they come after him — just when he's made his move and is threatening Ma and Wong. A huge gunfight breaks out, Sou is finally destroyed, and the heroes have survived to rebuild the Triad family.

If *Just Heroes* isn't a half-bad story, it also isn't half-good; after the three *Better Tomorrow* films it feels old, and even deliberately recycles elements from those films (a young follower of Wai's plants guns throughout a house, trying to imitate Mark in the first *Better Tomorrow*). It begins promisingly, with Peking Opera under the opening credits, followed by a poignant scene in which Tsou speculates on the similarities between the opera stories and Triad life; but this theme is lost throughout the rest of the film. The opening action sequence — when Tai saves Ma during a dockside battle — is confusing; later fights are better, but they're all of the warehouse or mansion variety done to

death in previous films. Only in one action scene — a flashback shootout in a warehouse — does the Woo macho-brotherhood aesthetic seem prevalent; chances are co-director Wu Ma shot much of the rest of the film, lending it a slightly schizophrenic quality.

The cast is entertaining, with a young Stephen Chow — destined to become Hong Kong's biggest comedic actor in the '90s — good in a serious role as the hotheaded young Jacky. James Wong (yes, that is the same James Wong who co-wrote this score, along with many others for Tsui) plays the mob's attorney, a role he would seemingly repeat in Wong Jing's 1994 *Return to a Better Tomorrow*. David Chiang was an action star of the '70s, just as executive producer Chang Cheh was one of the leading directors of that time. The film's cameo appearances include Ti Lung and Paul Chun as Triad members (near the beginning of the film).

*Just Heroes* actually features two women in leading roles, but the female characters (remember, this is a John Woo film) serve simply as victims to propel the men into action and so are completely forgettable.

If the cast performs adequately, there's also no Chow Yun-Fat here, and perhaps *Just Heroes* serves to demonstrate that without his impossibly-charismatic usual leading man, Woo's films have a hard time standing on their own.

*Just Heroes* came in at number 48 for the year, with a gross of $7,913,229.

## *Web of Deception*

Producer, 1989. Cantonese: *Ging Wan Gei*. Mandarin: *Jing1 Hun2 Ji4*. Literally: *Thrilling Diary*. AKA: *Betrayal*; *Deception*. Director: David Chung Chi-Man. CAST:

**Original poster for *Web of Deception* (featuring, left to right, Pauline Wong, Brigitte Lin, Elizabeth Lee and Joey Wang).**

Brigitte Lin Ching-Hsia ("Jane Lin"), Joey Wang Cho-Yin ("Queenie"/"Cat"), Elizabeth Lee Mei-Fung ("Mimi"), Pauline Wong Siu-Fung ("May"), Waise Lee ("Inspector Li"). Opening Date: October 5, 1989.

*Web of Deception* is a preposterous and intermittently entertaining thriller, often referred to as Tsui Hark's homage to Hitchcock. What makes it most interesting is not its plot or mood, however, but its use of an almost exclusively female cast.

As the story begins, Jane Lin is a barrister with financial problems — she's 1.6 million dollars in debt, she's being blackmailed, and she's losing accounts at work. She's planning on emigrating to Canada soon and would like to take her devoted assistant and close friend May, but she's afraid May won't meet the qualifications for emigration. Little does she know that May is the one blackmailing her; she sus-

pects instead her stockbroker Mimi. After Mimi closes her accounts, Jane ends up with 1.1 million dollars, which she decides to keep in her house. May, delivering files to Jane at the time, sees where Jane hides the money. May tries to convince her roommate Queenie to help her rob the house; Queenie agrees, since she has her own reason for needing money — her identical twin sister Cat, a dangerous ex-con, is being chased by a vicious loan shark who thinks she is Queenie. That night Jane is supposed to attend a party with her boyfriend Li, so Queenie breaks into the house — unaware that Jane has actually fallen asleep and is still at home. Jane discovers Queenie in the house and the two women struggle; finally, Queenie is killed. Jane flees to her upstairs bedroom, and Cat — who had followed Queenie to the house — enters, only to find her dead sister; she vows to avenge her sister's death. Jane gets a gun, but before she can use it

May arrives at the house, sees Cat, and believes it to be Queenie. A long cat-and-mouse game ensues, as May, Cat and Jane stalk each other through the isolated house. Finally, May confesses all to Jane, but the confession is interrupted when Cat — who now has the gun — starts a fire to force them out of the house. Jane knocks May out and flees — with Cat in the back seat of the car. The women duke it out in the speeding vehicle, which finally crashes. As they roll onto the pavement, Cat is nearly run over by a truck but is saved at the last second by Jane. At the end of the film Jane is shown leaving Hong Kong for Canada, while May has a new job and Cat is happy masquerading as Queenie. The only hint of trouble comes when police begin investigating Mimi for a possible murder...

*Web of Deception* is built on one contrivance after another; it occasionally produces unintentional chuckles rather than the chills it's aiming for. In one scene Cat cooks a poisonous dinner for Jane, which she refuses to eat; when Cat suggests that she at least take some "vitamin pills" to boost her strength, Jane's response is "I'm allergic to pills." Logic isn't the film's strong point, either — if Jane and May are such good friends, why hasn't Jane ever met May's roommate? And how could Jane not know her roommate has an identical twin? At one point Cat tells Jane that the tires on her car have been punctured, and yet Jane escapes in the car a few minutes later. Cat actually pushes the loan shark from a tall building at one point — won't she be investigated for that? *Web of Deception* is a house of cards in constant danger of collapse.

The only thing holding it up is the cast. It's startling to see a thriller with four female leads (five if you count Joey Wang's duel role!), and the women all perform well. Joey Wang plainly enjoys the gum-cracking, tough girl Cat, and her gun-and-knife fight with Brigitte Lin in a speeding car is not just the film's climax but also its highpoint dramatically. If the rest of *Web of Deception* had been as tension-filled as those few minutes, it would have been a classic.

*Web of Deception* was not received well at the box office, placing number 115 for the year, with a total of $3,304,768. It should not be confused with the 1998 Hong Kong film *Web of Deception*, which starred Françoise Yip.

## *A Better Tomorrow III: Love and Death in Saigon*

Director/Producer/Editor, 1989. Cantonese: *Ying Hung Boon Sik III*. Mandarin: *Ying Xiong Ben Se III*. Literally: *Heroic Character III*. CAST: Chow Yun-Fat ("Mark"), Anita Mui Yim-Fong ("Kit"), Tony Leung Ka-Fai ("Mun"), Shut Yam Saam Long ("Ho"). Opening Date: October 20, 1989.

The same year that saw the release of John Woo's ultra-macho *The Killer*, this Tsui Hark produced-directed sequel to the two previous Woo-directed *Better Tomorrow* films was released; and the two '89 releases perfectly embody the opposing sensibilities of the filmmakers: Tsui's film is not only led by a woman, but by a woman who essentially teaches her male companions how to be action stars. If Tsui didn't directly intend his film to be a commentary on Woo's sensibilities, he also plainly was not interested in duplicating them. In the process he made one of the most unusual and provocative action films of the decade.

*A Better Tomorrow III: Love and Death in Saigon* begins in 1974, as Mark arrives in Saigon, looking for his cousin Cheung Chi-Mun. He is nearly beaten by corrupt Customs officers before he's saved by Kit, a mysterious and well-connected woman who has also just arrived from Hong Kong. After leaving the airport, Mark heads for the clinic run by his uncle; his cousin Mun is working the Vietnam black market in a desperate attempt to get Uncle out of Saigon before the war worsens. Uncle, however, is determined to stay and has adopted a local boy, Pat, who, despite his inability to talk with Uncle, has become devoted to him. Mun sets up a meeting with a potential new black market buyer, who turns out to be Kit, the woman from the airport; Mun and Mark appeal to her as a fellow Chinese, and she agrees to help them. She's suspicious of Mun's contact, Bong, a wily Army official; however, Mun is sure of Bong, and they set up a night rendezvous to exchange monies. The deal goes bad when Bong shows up with his troops and betrays them, just as Kit had feared. Kit leads Mark and Mun in a firefight against Bong's soldiers, and they're saved at last by the arrival of another cadre whose commander is one of Kit's government friends. The trio celebrates their survival with a shopping spree, when Kit buys Mark his trademark sunglasses; she also talks about her mentor and lover, Ho, who vanished three years ago. With enough money now to leave Saigon, Mark and Mun finally convince Uncle to go, leaving the tearful Pat to look after the shop. After a tense encounter at the airport, Mark, Mun and Uncle finally board the plane — but Kit has to stay. Back in Hong Kong, Mark and Mun help Uncle open a new store, but they worry about Kit as the situation in Saigon worsens. They're relieved when Kit shows up one day, but the triangle situation between Mark, Mun and Kit becomes intolerable, and Mark tries to back out by creating a scene with

some nightclub hostesses; Kit, however, finally admits her love for Mark, and they consummate their relationship. The next day Kit is shocked to find out that Ho has reappeared, and one of his first acts is to bomb the shop of his rivals for Kit; Uncle is killed, and Mun and Mark are forced to flee Hong Kong. When they find out that Kit is returning to Saigon with Ho, they follow her and find the city is now a bombed-out battleground. They locate Pat, now a young soldier and overjoyed to see them. Pat takes Mun to see Kit, but they're ambushed and Mun is shot and lost during the escape attempt. When Mark finds out Mun is missing, he believes Kit shot him, and he angrily disavows their love. After he leaves her (he believes forever), Pat tells him he's found Mun, and he takes Mark to him. Meanwhile, Kit, devastated by Mark's rejection, attends a meeting with Ho and Bong armed with a bomb, intending to destroy them all. Bong launches a surprise attack, and Kit is shot before her bomb explodes and temporarily stops Bong. Mark chooses this time to come after Ho, and Ho is killed in the ensuing firefight — but Kit is also horribly wounded. Mun, Mark, Pat and Kit try to head for the airport, but Bong comes after them in a tank. Mark manages to slide a crate of grenades beneath the tank and Bong is finally destroyed. They rush to the military airport and use Kit's pass to board a copter — all except Pat, who wants to stay and find his family. As the copter lifts off, Mark realizes they're too late — Kit is dead. The film ends on a sobbing Mark.

Tsui establishes his intentions right from the opening of *A Better Tomorrow III* — Mark and Kit step off the same plane, shoulder to shoulder. A few minutes later Kit saves Mark in the airport with her government connections; in the film's first major action scene (after Bong betrays them during the money exchange), Kit is

**Kit (Anita Mui) shows the boys how it's done in *A Better Tomorrow III*.**

the first to fire a gun and the one who carries a pistol in each hand (as her two male companions watch in slow-motion awe). Kit continues to drive the action of the film throughout, and yet Tsui never allows her to become remotely masculine — she's an elegant, completely feminine figure throughout, whose only vulnerability is her love for Mark. Just as Mark's pursuit of honor dooms him in the first of the *Better Tomorrow* films, Kit's love marks her as the central tragic figure in this story. Which also points out another of the major differences between Tsui and Woo: Where Woo is obsessed with honor and brotherhood, Tsui is more interested in the complexities of love and equality. One of the most subversive elements of *A Better Tomorrow III* is the idea that Kit and Mark can stand as equals, and yet also be romantically entwined. It's a tribute to both the script and the performance of Chow Yun-

Fat that, even though Kit is often seen as his teacher, he never seems less than her.

All this, of course, means that Tsui has completely flipped Woo's notion of exclusionary brotherhood on its ear; in fact, it's hard to think of another sequel in all of cinema that so completely reverses the themes of the films it follows. In *The Killer* Woo shows two men firing guns, back to back, a sort of enclosed circle; Tsui has the same shot in *A Better Tomorrow III*, except that it's Ho and Kit. Likewise, Tsui has no interest in copying Woo's "bullet ballet" style of directing action sequences; instead, Tsui emphasizes the characters and the situations. Woo directs action for the sake of the action; Tsui directs it for the sake of the story.

And what a story it is. *A Better Tomorrow III* is simultaneously sprawling and meditative, a politically-minded epic and an examination of gender roles. The recreation of war torn 1974 Saigon is stunning, and Tsui employs a jagged, documentary style to capture the chaos; then, a few moments later, he creates a lovely montage of Mun, Mark and Kit shopping, using gradated filters for a dreamy, romantic feel. He's telling us that life continues even under the worst situations, and can even continue with joy.

As a political epic, *A Better Tomorrow III* reaches its climax when Mark manages to burn Bong's tank. Tsui lingers on the burning, using numerous angles to drive home the importance of this image, which undoubtedly was inspired by the images from the Tian'anmen massacre. The burning of the military tank is Tsui's answer to the massacre; just as he used *Dangerous Encounter — 1st Kind* to convey his anger with a political situation in 1980, so he uses *A Better Tomorrow III* for the same purpose nine years later. (In fact, in his essay "Hong Kong Cinema from June 4 to 1997" in *Fifty Years of Electric Shadows*, Sek Kei singles out *A Better Tomorrow III* as an example of how a few filmmakers used allegory to critique the Tian'anmen incident.)

*A Better Tomorrow III* also reiterates a number of Tsui's favorite themes. There's the celebration of Chinese nationality, when Mark and Mun use their mutual heritage to convince Kit to join them; there's the Chinese notion of fate, as when Ho tells us that "people don't have choices"; and there's the 1997 handover, which Uncle fears more than the Vietnam war.

And, of course, there's the strong woman, here fully realized by Anita Mui. Mui, a pop star often referred to as "the Madonna of Asia," pulls off the nearly impossible task of becoming a female Mark. Not only can she fire an automatic rifle without flinching, she also conveys the pathos of the classic tragic hero(ine). She would return to the action genre with her

role as "Wonder Woman" in the two *Heroic Trio* films, but *A Better Tomorrow III* remains one of her finest performances (along with Stanley Kwan's *Rouge*).

If *A Better Tomorrow III* lacks in any area, it would be Lowell Lo's score, which too often consists of a droning, one-note synthesizer and doesn't propel the action as well as it could; but considering the film's other achievements, it's a small drawback indeed.

*A Better Tomorrow III* was a hit for Tsui, coming in at number 8 for the year (one spot ahead of *The Killer*), earning a total of $18,476,116. It received two nominations at the year's Hong Kong Film Awards— for Best Art Direction (Lok Chi Fung) and Best Original Film Score (Lowell Lo Koon-Ting).

A year later John Woo would release *A Bullet in the Head*, which utilizes many of the same situations and settings of *A Better Tomorrow III* (both films concern young Hong Kong men who find themselves in Saigon during the Vietnam war; both show the protagonists narrowly escaping a street bombing early on; both involve black market trading, and both are about the heroes trying to escape Saigon and return to Hong Kong). *Bullet in the Head* would go on to become John Woo's most critically acclaimed film.

*A Better Tomorrow III* was shot in Thailand, which doubled for Vietnam. During the making of the film, the pyrotechnics expert (who was a local supplied by the state) blew himself and his home up while testing an explosives mix — and smoking a cigarette. His assistant was horribly burned, but lived.

## Swordsman

Director/Producer, 1990. Cantonese: *Siu Ngo Gong Woo*. Mandarin: *Xiao Ao Jiang*

*Hu.* Literally: *Laughing and Proud Warrior.* Co-Directors: King Hu (Wu Kam-Chuen), Ching Siu-Tung, Ann Hui On-Wah, Raymond Lee Wai-Man, Andrew Kam Yeung-Wah. Action Director: Ching Siu-Tung. Scriptwriters: Gwaan Man Leung, Wong Ying, Lam Gei Tiu, Lau Daai Muk, Leung Yiu Ming, Daai Foo Hiu. Cinematography: Lam Gok Wah, Peter Pau. Art Direction: Leung Wah Sang. Editing: David Wu, Mak Chi Sin. Music Score: James Wong, Romeo Diaz. CAST: Sam Hui Koon-Kit ("Ling Wu Chung"), Cecilia Yip Tung ("Kiddo"), Fennie Yuen Kit-Ying ("Blue Phoenix"), Cheung Man ("Ying"), Wu Ma ("Chief of the East Winds Clan"), Jacky Cheung Hok-Yau ("Au Yeung"), Lam Ching-Ying ("Elder Kuk"), Yuen Wah ("Zhor"), Lau Shun ("Eunuch"). Opening Date: April 5, 1990.

*Swordsman* began as Tsui's tribute to one of his favorite directors, King Hu, but ended as a distinctly Tsui Hark film. King Hu, who directed such swordplay classics as *A Touch of Zen* and *Dragon Inn* (remade by Tsui in 1992 as *New Dragon Inn*), left the production after ten days, and Tsui tried to meet the schedule by filling the gap with a number of other directors, including himself. Although Tsui has stated in interviews that he asked the directors to try for King Hu's style, the end result is slightly schizophrenic, a confusing but energetic mishmash of styles and stories.

Based on the epic Louis Cha (aka Jin Yong) novel *The Wandering Swordsman*, the story is set in the Ming Dynasty (King Hu's favorite dynastic period) and centers around a stolen scroll that grants its reader mystical kung fu powers. The investigation, led by an eminent eunuch and his ambitious young assistant Au Yeung, leads to Lam Chun Nam, a recently exiled government minister. Lam's country estate is surrounded, but the circle is broken by

Ling Wu Chung, a skilled swordsman who has come from Wah Mountain with his sidekick, Kiddo, to deliver a letter to Lam. When violence finally breaks out, Ling and Kiddo find themselves fighting on Lam's side; when Lam is slain, he makes Ling swear to deliver a message to his son regarding the location of the stolen scroll. Ling agrees, then he and Kiddo escape, heading home. En route they encounter Elder Kuk, a member of the outlawed Sun Moon Sect; and all are attacked by Zhor, a vicious warrior working for the Ming government. Kuk is slain, and Ling and Kiddo barely survive. They hide out in a ruined house and meet Fung Ching Yueng, an ancient swordsman who once led the Wah Mountain clan, but left over a disagreement about teaching styles; he instructs Ling in some new moves, then disappears. Ling and Kiddo are nearly home when they encounter a wedding procession and discover the bride is a savage highlander princess who may be involved with the dangerous Sun Moon sect. Meanwhile, Au Yeung — posing as the late Lam's son — also finds the procession and tricks Ling into telling him the location of the magic scroll; Ngok, the head of the Wah Mountain clan, eavesdrops and also learns the secret location. Au Yeung and Ngok take off for the Lam estate, leaving behind a poisoned Ling. Ling is saved by the highlander princess, Ying, just in time to fight Zhor. Zhor is finally defeated, with the help of Ying's assistant Blue Phoenix, who has magical control of snakes and bees. The climax takes place back at the Lam estate, as all parties converge on the magical scroll and fight for possession of it. The final battle is between Ngok and his one-time student Ling, who defeats Ngok by using the new techniques he learned at the hands of exiled Elder Fung. Ling spares Ngok's life because Kiddo (who is Ngok's daughter) begs him to. Ling may have Kiddo to ride off with at the end, but the calculating, cruel Au Yeung has made off with the magic scroll.

*Swordsman* must certainly have been shot somewhat in sequence; the first quarter of the film, as the Eunuch and Au Yeung's troops surround Lam's estate, has a stately, elegant style (which most resembles King Hu's, although apparently none of King's footage survived the final cut) that is markedly different from the rest of the film. By the time the plot moves on to Ling and Kiddo's cross-country flight, it begins to bear more visual resemblance to *Swordsman II*, with its layered, smoky forest shots and moody interiors.

*Swordsman*'s stylistic meanderings wouldn't have been such a problem placed in service of a focused script, but the story has the feel of a complicated novel, with numerous details, characters and subplots that would probably have been better left on the printed page. During the film's climax the scroll passes through so many hands it would require an abacus just to keep track of them all; too many questions are left unanswered (what happens when Kiddo gets deathly ill at one point and then is apparently fine the next morning? Just who is Ying marrying, anyways? Who's involved with the Sun Moon Sect and who isn't?).

But despite the film's inconsistencies and erratic flow, it's visually impressive throughout, with stunning costumes (especially the Mongolian-inspired highlanders), sets and photography, all aided by a tremendous James Wong/Romeo Diaz score. At its best, it mixes the pomp-and-circumstance of old-style epics with the manic action of the newer action films (Ching Siu-Tung's hand is plainly visible in the superbly choreographed fight sequences). It also features a large, attractive cast, with three particularly loathsome villains (Tsui favorites Lau Shun and Jacky Cheung, and Jackie Chan "brother" Yuen Wah).

In the Tsui Hark oeuvre, the film may be most memorable for being the first to utilize the character of the woman passing herself off as a man (Kiddo). Although not much is made of it in *Swordsman* (it seems to be more a mild novelty than anything else), Tsui would explore the idea to much greater effect in *New Dragon Inn, The East Is Red (Swordsman III)* and *The Lovers*.

*Swordsman* placed at number 16 on the year's box office list, with a gross of $16,052,552.00. It received nominations at the year's Hong Kong Film Awards for Best Supporting Actor (both Lau Shun and Jacky Cheung — the latter was also nominated in same year for *A Chinese Ghost Story II*), Best Art Direction (Leung Wah Sang), Best Film Editing (David Wu, Mak Chi Sin — Mak was also nominated this year for *A Chinese Ghost Story II* and *A Terracotta Warrior*) and Best Original Film Score (James Wong, Romeo Diaz); it won for Best Action Choreography (Ching Siu-Tung) and Best Original Film Song.

*Swordsman*'s production was lengthy (about two years), with a final budget that was twice the initial amount of $15 million.

The first sequel, *Swordsman II*, strangely features many of the same characters (Ling, Kiddo, Ying), but with new actors; only Fennie Yuen as Blue Phoenix is retained from the original cast.

## A Terracotta Warrior

Producer, 1990. Cantonese: *Goo Gam Daai Jin Chun Yung Ching*. Mandarin: *Gu Jin Da Zhan Qin Yong Qing*. Director: Ching Siu-Tung. Action Director: Ching Siu-Tung. Screenwriter: Lillian Lee. CAST: Zhang Yimou ("Tian Fong"), Gong Li

("Winter"/"Lili"), Yu Rong-Guang ("Bai Yun Fei"), Suk Bung Luk ("Emperor Qin"). Opening Date: April 12, 1990.

An exquisite period fantasy that was two-and-a-half years in the making, *A Terracotta Warrior* is an unusual Tsui Hark-Ching Siu-Tung collaboration in many respects: The film favors romance over action, has a distinctly different look from their other films, utilizes mainland actors (Zhang Yimou and Gong Li) and is virtually free of any gender-identity questions. What it bears in common with other Ching-Tsui films is quality — it is unquestionably one of the lushest and loveliest films to emerge from Hong Kong in the '90s.

The film opens in a cave, with workers excavating as if the story is an ancient artifact being dug out of the earth. When a massive statue that is being moved falls on some of the laborers, warrior Tian Fong proves he's a man of honor and compassion by leaping forward to save the fallen men. Later, Tian Fong foils an assassination attempt on Emperor Qin, and he appoints Tian Fong to be one of his closest protectors. Tian Fong serves the Emperor dutifully, even while he is secretly appalled by the Emperor's cruelty and waste. One day Tian Fong meets one of the Emperor's new concubines, Winter, and he is smitten by her beauty and sensitivity; when she tries to escape her fate, she's captured and brought to Tian Fong. Rather than slay her, he embraces her, dooming himself as well as her. They exchange one last kiss before death, and Winter passes the gift of immortality to Tian Fong; then she is burned to death and Tian Fong is covered in hot clay, becoming one of the Emperor's terracotta warriors.

Cut to: a 1940s plane landing in China. The flamboyantly-dressed Lili — who is Winter's double — steps off a plane, waving hopefully to a cadre of reporters, but they're covering the arrival of Bai Yun Fei, a dashing movie star. Lili is instantly taken by Bai's good looks, style and fame; but he wants nothing to do with her. Lili gets a job as a supporting actress on Bai's new film, and one day she follows him off the set and nearly stumbles into a deal between Bai and some murderous *gweilos*. Bai, who's worried that she's seen too much, lures her into a plane flight that ends when he parachutes out and leaves Lili to go down with the plane. The small plane crashes into a cavern — the very cavern that holds the ancient terracotta warriors. One — Tian Fong — comes to life and, seeing Lili, believes her to be his long-lost love Winter; she, of course, rebuffs him, but begins to appreciate him when he saves her from a gang of ruffians who come after the plane. They make it back to civilization, where Tian Fong discovers he's got a lot to learn — he's never seen glass, electric light, cars or guns. Lili goes to confront Bai, who tries to cover up the murder attempt by romancing her; but the jealous Tian Fong tries to intervene. Lili is reluctantly stuck with looking after Tian Fong, but when he once again saves her from the gang of bad guys, she finds herself caring more for him. When Tian Fong tries to leave her, she stops him, and they embrace. They return to the cavern where she found him, only to find Bai ransacking it with the gang of *gweilos* — he's looking for legendary artifacts to steal. After avoiding the cavern's traps, Bai, Tian Fong and Lili find a vast cavern of terracotta warriors mounted on horses; unbeknownst to them, the cavern's final trap is to bring the warriors and their mounts to life. They crack out of their clay shells and attack Bai's thugs; a fight between spears and guns ensues. Bai tries to escape with Lili in a plane, and Tian Fong finds himself the lone survivor of the battle; then he

Lili (Gong Li) goes for a ride with dashing Bai Yun Fei in *A Terracotta Warrior*.

goes after the plane. He breaks in and fights with Bai, and Lili is shot in the process. As Tian Fong looks after the dying Lili, Bai's greed finally proves his undoing — he triggers the final trap in the cavern's central altar and is blown up with the cavern. Lili dies, and only Tian Fong makes it out alive.

Cut to: modern day. A busload of Japanese tourists arrives to view the contemporary exhibit of restored terracotta warriors. Winter/Lili is one of them, just as Tian Fong is one of the workers; he sees her and knows the wheel has spun again...

If *Terracotta Warrior*'s tale of the noble savage in modern society is universal (try Edgar Rice Burroughs' *Tarzan* for a Western example), the film's design is pure Chinese. Its first third is gloriously rich in pageantry and spectacle: Stiltwalkers dressed as giant herons parade before palace steps, soldiers ride guard on a procession of white-robed women, Tian Fong practices his swordplay in a pavilion amid falling leaves. Even when the film moves to the 20th century it plays the tradi-

tional — rickshaws, village streets, the Great Wall — against the contemporary.

*A Terracotta Warrior* also revels in the re-creation of the 1940s. Western-style clothing and restaurants are in vogue; the roguish Bai, looking the very image of the archetypal old-time movie star, rides a motorcycle with sidecar and a steam-powered train. The film's art direction, costuming and make-up are all stunning; but best of all is Peter Pau and Li Sun Yip's breathtaking cinematography. The film doesn't employ the baroque camera angles and blue-lit night sequences that characterize most of Ching Siu-Tung's other films; it does use lovely sepia tones in its color palette, and inserts that have the feeling of watercolor scroll paintings. In fact, it's safe to say that there's not a single frame in *A Terracotta Warrior* that's not suitable for framing.

The film is as much a feast for the ears as the eyes. Aside from unusually excellent sound effects, *A Terracotta Warrior* also features one of the finest scores by the team of James Wong and Romeo Diaz. Driven by a melancholy piano theme, the score propels the action and comedy perfectly as well — but it works best when running beneath the wistful love scenes.

The unusual casting of mainland Chinese director Zhang Yimou (arthouse favorite in the West for such films as *Raise the Red Lantern*, starring Gong Li) pays off handsomely. Zhang's angular, drawn face (he almost resembles an Asian version of Harry Dean Stanton) already looks like sculptured stone; his performance is alternately kind-hearted, bewildered, comic, strong and tragic. His chemistry with Gong Li — also his real-life leading lady at the time — is palpable; Gong Li, too often cast as a stoic beauty, is lively, funny and physical here. Hers is one more of the pleasant surprises that are found throughout this lovely film.

If *A Terracotta Warrior* can be faulted in any way, it would be for its occasional lifts from Steven Spielberg's *Raiders of the Lost Ark* (the sequence in which Lili encounters a room full of desiccated corpses that fall in on her is copied from *Raiders* almost frame for frame). But at least the stolen bits serve the film, which as a whole is delightfully unique.

*A Terracotta Warrior* was Tsui's most successful film of 1990, coming in at the number 7 slot (ahead of *A Chinese Ghost Story II, Swordsman, Happy Ghost IV* and *Spy Games*); it took home a total of $20,991,782. It also scored with eight nominations in the Hong Kong Film Awards — for Best Picture, Best Actress (Gong Li), Best Cinematography (Peter Pau, Li Sun Yip), Best Art Direction (Yee Chung-Man), Best Action Choreography (Ching Siu Tung, who was also nominated for *A Chinese Ghost Story II* and won for *Swordsman*), Best Film Editing (Mak Chi Sin, also nominated for both *A Chinese Ghost Story II* and *Swordsman*), Best Original Film Score (Joseph Koo, James Wong and Romeo Diaz, who won the award) and Best Original Film Song.

The screenplay for *A Terracotta Warrior* is by Lillian Lee, who also wrote *Green Snake* for Tsui and *Rouge* for Stanley Kwan, among others; all have a similar mix of sensuality, romance and fantasy, undoubtedly a trademark of this talented writer.

Cinematographer Peter Pau would bring a similar look to Ronny Yu's *The Bride with White Hair* (1993), which stars Tsui favorites Brigitte Lin and Leslie Cheung as star-crossed lovers in China's savage past.

*A Terracotta Warrior* is a film often mentioned for remake possibilities; even Jackie Chan (whose 2000 release *Shanghai Noon* similarly featured a lowly guardsman who falls for a princess) has discussed a desire to lens his version.

## Spy Games

Producer, 1990. Cantonese: *Jung Yat Naam Bak Woh*. Mandarin: *Zhong Ri Nan Bei He*. Literally: China Japan North South Cooperation. Director/Editor: David Wu Dai-Wai. Screenwriters: Ng Man-Fai, Philip Cheng, Lam Kee-To, Lau Tai-Mok. CAST: Joey Wang Cho-Yin ("Inspector Joey"), Kenny Bee [Chung Chun-To] ("Ken"), Noriko Izumoto ("Takako"), Waise Lee Chi-Hung ("Lee"), Shut Yam Saam Long ("Kudo"). Opening Date: May 10, 1990.

This amiable, if slightly unfocused, little comedy follows in the footsteps of 1983's *All the Wrong Spies* as a goof on espionage thrillers. *Spy Games* has a contemporary setting and starts when Takako, a Japanese pop star, is late for her birthday party because of her dictatorial manager, Yoshikawa. Takako's bandmate Kudo engineers a scheme to get rid of Yoshikawa: He sends in a troupe of actors who pretend to be secret agents, to convince Yoshikawa that her father is being held hostage "in a castle" in Hong Kong. Unfortunately, the actors have mistaken Takako for Yoshikawa, and the terrified girl immediately jets off to Hong Kong. Aboard the plane she encounters a mysterious man with an eyepatch who she is certain is a real spy. Upon arriving at the airport she tries to escape the one-eyed man by stealing news reporter Ken's van. She wrecks the van and leaves Ken, already in danger of losing his job, with a bill for $387,000 worth of damages. Ken's ex-best friend and rival, Lee, has a field day, and Ken is soon making the news as much as reporting it. When he finds Takako in a department store he takes her home, intending to turn her over to the police; but when he finds out she's looking for her father, he takes pity on her and decides to help. Meanwhile, Kudo and Yoshikawa fly in from Japan to find Takako and are set up by the Hong Kong police with Inspector Joey, whom Kudo instantly falls for. Finally, after Takako accidentally burns down Ken's home, she's kidnapped by CIA thugs who have mistaken her for a KGB informant. Joey, Kudo and Ken find her at the Hong Kong CIA headquarters, where they wage a fierce battle to free her. During the fight Takako discovers that another hostage really is her long lost father, and they're reunited. Finally, the Hong Kong police arrive and Takako is saved. Ken quits his job as a newscaster to become the new saxophonist in Takako's band, a job made available when Kudo quits to become a Hong Kong policeman and Inspector Joey's new partner.

*Spy Games* lacks the wild gags and visual humor of *All the Wrong Spies*; it tries to head more in the direction of screwball comedy but throws in too many characters and a violent ending. When focused on Ken, rival Lee and Takako, it is actually funny, with some pleasant romantic bits mixed in. But its script is (to put it mildly) wildly implausible and sometimes confusing — we're not really told until the end that Takako's father really *was* a CIA intelligence agent, and that she's never met him (he abandoned her mother and her when she was a baby). The movie is full of chance meetings and "love-at-first-sight" gags; the one between Kudo and Joey is visually amusing (they blow smoke rings off their pistols at each other, which form hearts), if completely unlikely.

The film is saved by its cast and its look. Kenny Bee and Waise Lee, both skilled performers and Tsui Hark veterans, propel the film with their on-again-off-again friendship, a subplot more interesting than any of the romantic ones. Joey Wang works hard (and, needless to say, looks great) as the tough Inspector Joey, but doesn't quite pull off the gunplay.

Director Wu has edited a number of Tsui's films, and he plays on this strength in *Spy Games*, which boasts clever editing and good pacing throughout. The film also references some of Tsui's favorite themes: The bad guys are American and Russian spies, Takako is hung up because of her lack of language skills (she only speaks Japanese), and there's even a bowl of goldfish (Tsui has featured goldfish in a number of films, including *Shanghai Blues* and *Working Class*).

*Spy Games* finished at number 107 for the year, with a gross of $3,534,548.

## *Happy Ghost IV*

Special Effects, 1990. Cantonese: *Hoi Sam Gwai Gau Hoi Sam Gwai*. Mandarin: *Kai Xin Gui Jiu Kai Xin Gui*. Literally: *Happy Ghost Rescues Happy Ghost*. Producer/

Director: Clifton Ko Chi-Sum. Action Director: Tony Leung Siu-Hung. Screenwriters: Joe Ma Wai-Ho, Ng Man-Fai, Cheng Chung-Tai. Animation Special Effects: Tsui Hark/Cinefex Workshop. CAST: Raymond Wong Bak-Ming ("Sam Kwai"/"Happy Ghost"), Beyond ("Students"), Lau Shun ("General"). Opening Date: June 30, 1990.

The hapless Sam Kwai and his "Happy Ghost" return in the astonishingly plotless *Happy Ghost IV*.

After a promising beginning, in which General "Crazy" (played with great gusto by Tsui regular Lau Shun) rampages through ancient China, the film moves to the present day, as Sam Kwai still struggles with an arrogant millionaire for the affections of his girlfriend. This time around the wealthy rival turns a bumbling, squeamish hitman lose on Sam Kwai, who is saved (and usually embarrassed) by his ghostly ancestor. Meanwhile, four teenage boys (played by Hong Kong boy band Beyond) find an ancient suit of armor and resurrect General "Crazy." As with the other entries in this series, the film is less interested in telling a coherent story than in showcasing an endless series of sight gags, which include the usual assortment of fart and butt jokes (long before *There's Something About Mary*, Hong Kong comedy cinema was featuring the "peniscaught-in-zipper" bit). The film also heads down some bizarre and pointless sidetracks, including musical numbers and a trip to Egypt. It rallies somewhat for the climactic showdown between the demonic general and Happy Ghost, in which Tsui brings his special effects wizardry to play when a painting of a warrior fighting a tiger comes to life. The animated tiger and warrior fight the live-action general and Happy Ghost á la *Who Framed Roger Rabbit?*; if the match between live action and

animation isn't as good as that American extravaganza's, the quality of the animation is superb and foreshadows the images that would, seven years later, fill the screen in *A Chinese Ghost Story: The Tsui Hark Animation*. Otherwise, this is a completely forgettable film, with actresses Loletta Lee Lai-Chun (*Shanghai Blues*, *Final Victory*) and Fennie Yuen Kit-Ying (*Swordsman* and *Swordsman II*) completely lost in small parts as high school students.

*Happy Ghost IV* was another successful entry in this popular series; it was number 30 for the year, with a take of $11,780,725.

## *A Chinese Ghost Story II*

Producer, 1990. Cantonese: *Sin Nui Yau Wan II: Yan Gaan Do*. Mandarin: *Qian Nu: You Hun II: Ren Jian Dao*. Literally: *Sien Female Ghost II: Human Realm Tao*. Director: Ching Siu-Tung. CAST: Leslie Cheung Kwok-Wing ("Ning"), Joey Wang Cho-Yin ("Windy"), Michelle Reis [Lee Ka-Yan] ("Moon"), Waise Lee Chi-Hung ("Warrior Hu"), Jacky Cheung Hok-Yau ("Autumn"), Wu Ma ("Swordsman Yen"). Opening Date: July 13, 1990.

It took three years (surely a record time in Hong Kong!) for this sequel to reach theaters... was it worth the wait? Certainly it doesn't equal the first film in terms of beauty or romance — it might be more aptly titled *A Chinese Monster Story*, for one thing — but it remains an entertaining and very well-produced follow-up.

As the story begins, Ning is returning to the village near the Orchid Buddhist Monastery, but finds it's now desolate. After narrowly escaping a gang of cannibal bandits, he runs afoul of the local law, who mistake him for the criminal Bing Chow. He's thrown into prison with an old man who was once a writer; when he's told he is to be executed, the old man assists him in escaping, giving him a special talisman. Outside the prison Ning steals a horse, believing the old man left it for him; little does he know the horse actually belongs to a powerful young sorcerer, Autumn. Autumn tracks him down after Ning stops to spend the night in a deserted villa. They try to share the villa but are attacked by ghosts—fake ghosts, it turns out. When the old man's talisman is torn from Ning, the attack ceases instantly—the attackers believe Ning to be Elder Chu, a famous sage and the old man in the prison. The attackers are a family out to rescue their father, Lord Fu, a minister on his way to execution; they expect his party to pass this villa soon. Ning is astonished when he realizes that Windy is the exact double of Hsiao-Ting; although in temperament they couldn't be more different—Windy is a dedicated warrior. Windy's sister Moon is smitten with Ning, setting up an unusual triangle. But there's no time for romance when it turns out the villa really *is* haunted—by a gigantic demonic creature. Autumn tries to teach Ning a spell to freeze the monster, but the spell misfires and the one frozen is Autumn. Ning frantically tries to figure out how to unfreeze Autumn while the monster stalks about them; at one point Ning manages to freeze both himself and the monster. Finally, the spell breaks, and the family of swordsmen attack the monster, carving it into pieces—which run off into the forest. Suddenly the party carrying Lord Fu arrives, and the family successfully frees their father, capturing the noble Warrior Hu in the process. But the forest monster shows up again and is carved into more pieces; its spirit is released and possesses Windy, who becomes

a horrible looking, floating demon. Autumn tells Ning she can only be saved by an infusion of "yang" energy, which must be delivered mouth-to-mouth. Ning gives her a long kiss, and the exorcism is successful, but Ning is drained himself. Before he has time to recover, a procession of monks arrives, led by the Taoist High Priest to the Royal Court. He is actually an evil being and attempts to enslave and destroy all those in the villa with a magic chant; but Autumn fights him, and Windy and Ning escape. Both still drained from the exorcism, they eventually wind up at the Orchid Monastery, where Ning remembers Swordsman Yen and calls on him to help stop the fiendish High Priest. Warrior Hu, meanwhile, tries to stop the creature and trails it to the High Court, which he enters only to discover that all of the officials are dead, and Fu, Moon and Autumn have been captured by the High Priest. Hu tries to fight the Priest but is torn apart by invisible forces. Finally, Swordsman Yen appears, and the demonic Priest transforms into a giant dragon-like insect. Autumn and Yen are swallowed by the horrible monster, but before they're completely digested they destroy it from the inside out. Sadly, Autumn doesn't survive the encounter, and Ning lives only to see Windy married off to another man—but in the end she deserts her own wedding procession to ride off with Ning.

On the surface, *A Chinese Ghost Story II* sounds like little more than an exhilarating monster-coaster, but it's boiling with wit and ideas just beneath that gruesome exterior. Right from the start—when Ning is thrown into prison with Elder Chu—it's full of sly asides on politics (Chu tells Ning that everything he wrote was misread as treason: "If I write a fairy tale, I'm accused of promoting superstition…"; later on, Warrior Hu finds the bodies of all the officials of the High Court but discovers they're just empty shells). But it's not content to stop there, as it also tackles religion, turning an image of a giant, serene golden buddha into a laser-shooting monster.

Where the film is lacking is in its failure to recapture the beauty and sensuality of the first movie. With the exception of the "yang"-infusing kiss during the exorcism (which is a very lovely moment indeed) and some verbal play, the film is nearly devoid of romance. The ending— when Windy leaves her wedding procession to escape with Ning—seems slightly forced; Ning never seems to care for her as anything more than a duplicate of his beloved Hsiao-Ting, so her affection for him is somewhat baffling.

The cast performs well, with Jacky Cheung a welcome new addition as Autumn; he creates the funniest moment in the film (his frozen grimace as he's stalked by the monster) without moving or speaking. Waise Lee brings a solid nobility to the role of Warrior Hu, and Joey Wang, as already mentioned, manages to make Windy a completely different character from the winsome Hsiao-Ting.

The film's look is exquisite (the blue-lit night shots are somewhat reminiscent of *Swordsman II*, which Ching would direct two years later), although the visual effects are slightly uneven. The giant dragon-like creature at the end is good, but the rampaging demon that occupies the middle of the film is not too convincing—it looks strangely like the dinosaur creature from 1961's *Gorgo*. Flying and fighting effects are all, of course, stunning, and the optical effects (especially the giant golden buddha) are quite good.

*A Chinese Ghost Story II* was the number eight earner for the year, bringing in $20,784,824. It received three nominations at the Hong Kong Film Awards—for Best Supporting Actor (Jacky Cheung), Best

Action Choreography (Ching Siu-Tung, Lau Chi-Ho, Wo Chi Loong) and Best Film Editing (Mak Chi Sin, who was also nominated for *A Terracotta Warrior* the same year).

## The Raid

Producer/Writer, 1991. Cantonese: *Choi Suk Ji Wong So Chin Gwan*. Mandarin: *Cai Shu Zhi Huang Sao Qian Jun*. Director: Ching Siu-Tung. Co-Writer: Yuen Kai Chi. Action Design: Ching Siu-Tung, Ma Yuk Shing. Editing: Mak Chi Sin. Music Score: James Wong. CAST: Dean Shek Tin ("Dr. Choy"), Jacky Cheung Hok-Yau ("Bobo Bear"), Tony Leung Ka-Fai ("Masa"), Paul Chu Kong ("Lieutenant"), Fennie Yuen Kit-Ying ("Tina"), Joyce Godenzi [Ko Lai-Hung] ("Miss Kim"), Corey Yuen Kwai ("Big Nose"). Opening Date: March 28, 1991.

Despite an innovative use of comic book–style artwork and storytelling techniques, *The Raid* is the weakest of the Ching Siu-Tung/Tsui Hark collaborations. A good cast and solid production values can't carry a meandering script with nearly a dozen principle characters and too much emphasis on comedy.

The film plays on the real-life historical events of the 1930s, when the Japanese occupied Manchuria and set up the last Chinese emperor, Puyi, as their puppet leader. In a prologue sequence Puyi is delivering a speech to the troops when an assassination attempt occurs. Masa, the cruel Japanese officer assigned to protect Puyi, quickly roots out the assassin and disposes of him. Cut to: The jungle, where Dr. Choy, an elderly healer and ex-soldier, is being taken to see a squadron of dying soldiers who have been poisoned by a new

Japanese gas. Dr. Choy can't help them but decides to follow their Lieutenant when he takes off in search of the poison gas factory. Dr. Choy winds up stuck in Manchuria, caught in the war between two rival gangsters, Big Nose and Bobo Bear. He narrowly escapes their latest axe fight by hiding in a meat truck, which lands him right in the kitchen of the emperor's palace. He disguises himself as a chef and is shocked to discover the Lieutenant and his men are also there, in disguise. The Lieutenant tells him they're looking for a contact, code-named WO-1, who will relay the location of the gas factory. There's just one immediate problem: They must prepare a feast for the emperor, and none of them know how to cook. When the Lieutenant's fake beard appears in Masa's soup, Masa orders an immediate identity search, and a shootout follows. During the shootout they do locate WO-1 (whose real name is Tina), and they escape with her, only to land in the middle of another fight between Bobo Bear and Big Nose. When police intervene, Bobo is forced to flee with Tina and the soldiers, and reluctantly agrees to help them after Tina says she can introduce him to his idol, singing star (and Masa's girlfriend) Miss Kim. Tina takes Bobo to the palace, and a long comedy sequence of mistaken rooms and identities follows; meanwhile, the Lieutenant and his men lead an attack on the main railroad line that supplies the gas factory, and are narrowly saved by Dr. Choy and his two youthful assistants, Nancy and Smartie. As Bobo Bear and Tina make their escape from the palace, Tina is shot, and Bobo gets her back to the camp. He realizes he's in love with her and writes a love letter, which passes through the hands of nearly everyone in the camp before finding Tina. When Tina recovers, she gives the Lieutenant a map of the location of the gas factory, and the raid commences. At first our

heroes are trapped in a gas chamber by Masa and Miss Kim, but Big Nose, who has been working for the Manchurians, relents and frees them. During the ensuing battle Miss Kim is killed and Masa tries to flee in a tank; but he is stopped by Dr. Choy, who blows up the tank and barely escapes with the rest before the factory goes up with the tank.

Where *The Raid* works is in those moments when it stays true to the comic books it's obviously trying to emulate — namely, in the action sequences. Ching brings his usual finesse to a different kind of fighting, utilizing '30s-style biplanes and machine guns over wire-rigged kung fu (although the film also features some stunning swordfights, particularly the final one between Dr. Choy and Masa). The film makes considerable use of comic book-ish artwork, which occasionally even animates, providing probably the film's best moments.

Unfortunately, the film too often lapses into lame, clichéd comedy (possibly due to the involvement of production company Cinema City, looking to recapture the comedy crown they held in the early '80s). The sequence near the film's middle when Bobo Bear and Tina hide out in Masa's bedroom in the palace is nearly interminable, with one mixup after another until Bobo and Tina are discovered and must escape. Likewise, the passing of the love letter — one of the oldest tricks in the comedy book — seriously hampers the pace of the film at the very point when it's building to its climactic raid.

And then there's the cast, featuring six male leads and three female leads. The film's plot sometimes takes strange, sudden turns to try and work in all those roles (for example, in one scene Dr. Choy is in the middle of running from pursuing bad guys when he hears the imprisoned Tina calling to him, and he must halt the chase long enough to save her). The final battle in the gas factory is similarly fractured, as Ching desperately tries to bring all the characters into some kind of resolution.

On the other hand, Ching and Tsui have assembled a fine, entertaining cast. Tony Leung Ka-Fai stands out as the sadistic, proud Masa, and Joyce Godenzi (Sammo Hung's wife) is stunning as Masa's seductive, cool partner, Miss Kim. Dean Shek brings a sweet, aging nobility to Dr. Choy, and Jacky Cheung is fun in yet another of his greedy-guy-who-turns-into-a-hero roles. It's also interesting to see Hong Kong action film director Corey Yuen (*Yes, Madam* and a number of Jet Li films, including *Fong Sai Yuk*) in an acting role as Big Nose.

The film does give some clues as to Tsui's involvement, both in its use of the Japanese as villains (see also *All the Wrong Spies, A Better Tomorrow III, The East Is Red* and several others) and its physically strong female leads (one of the film's solid fight scenes takes place between Miss Kim and Tina). Technical credits for the film are good, with James Wong providing an unusual score — a mixture of martial, military themes and odd, pseudo-jazz action cues (music editing is a problem in the film, though — cues will sometimes cut off abruptly or segue into a completely different cue).

*The Raid* came in at number 86 for the year at the box office, with a total of $3,694,660 earned.

# A Chinese Ghost Story III

Producer/Writer, 1991. Cantonese: *Sin Nui Yau Wan III: Do Do Do*. Mandarin: *Qian Nu: You Hun III: Dao Dao Dao*. Literally: *Sien Female Ghost III: Tao Tao Tao*. Director: Ching Siu-Tung. Co-Writer: Roy Szeto. Action Directors: Ching Siu-Tung, Ma Yuk Shing, Cheung Yiu Sing. CAST:

Joey Wang Cho-Yin ("Lotus"), Jacky Cheung Hok-Yau ("Yin"), Tony Leung Chiu-Wai ("Fong"), Nina Li Chi ("Butterfly"), Lau Shun ("Master"). Opening Date: July 18, 1991.

After the monsterfest of *A Chinese Ghost Story II*, Ching and Tsui returned to the sensuality and romance of the first *Chinese Ghost Story* with this third entry in the popular series; unfortunately, the film swings almost too far away from the horror of the other two movies, and often plays like a romantic comedy with mild supernatural elements.

The film opens with a spectacular display of bloodletting, as two travelling monks (Fong and his Master) witness master swordsman Yin carving up a troupe of opponents. They meet Yin again when they arrive at the village outside Orchid Buddhist Monastery, where we learn that Yin is less interested in spilling blood than he is in making money. Since they're secretly conveying a precious golden buddha back to their monastery, the two monks decide to spend the night in the deserted temple. Little do they know they've been followed by a gang of thieves, who are distracted by a female voice coming from a nearby pavilion; they enter and see two beautiful women smoking opium and languidly tattooing each other. Inflamed by desire, they attack the two women — and soon fall victim themselves when it turns out the two women are ghosts who work for a demonic Priestess. Lotus seizes the men with supernaturally long hair, while Butterfly slays with long curling fingernails. The Priestess sends Lotus out to seduce Fong, while she fights the Master. Although Lotus' seduction fails, the gold buddha is lost during the attempt, and Fong must deceive his Master until he can find it again. He tricks Master into going into town while he stays in the haunted monastery, and the next night Lotus returns to continue the seduction; she helps Fong fight off the snakes that live on the monastery's floor, and then they find the buddha — in pieces. When Master returns, Lotus is still there and hides; Master tries to seal the monastery against ghosts and nearly destroys Lotus until Fong intervenes to save her. The Priestess takes advantage of the confusion to attack Master, and he is captured; his last words to Fong are to return when the buddha — which has powers against demons — has been repaired. Fong takes the buddha into town and falls victim to a deceitful goldsmith, who tries to melt the buddha down. Fortunately, Fong encounters Yin, who agrees to work on credit to help Fong and his Master. They save what's left of the buddha and return to the monastery. That night Lotus and Butterfly both try to seduce Fong (much to the annoyance of Yin), but when the attempts are unsuccessful the Priestess attacks. Yin fights her with a magic suit of armor that grants the wearer super-speed, and Fong promises Lotus that they'll help her by finding her urn of ashes and moving it. When morning comes they find the urn under an enchanted tree — and Master inside the tree. They free Master and try to escape with Lotus' urn, but the Priestess' magic tricks them and they're separated. Yin and Master find Fong at the Monastery — about to be given to the Mountain Devil, along with Lotus. Yin and Master fight the Priestess while Lotus frees Fong; the Priestess sucks Butterfly dry in an attempt to renew her energy, but she's finally destroyed by Yin and Master. With the Mountain Devil approaching, Yin, Master, Fong and Lotus try to flee on Master's magic cloak, but they're too late — suddenly the entire monastery rears up, now part of the head of the Mountain Devil. Yin and Master are unable to stop the gigantic demon until Master turns Fong into a liv-

ing golden buddha; Fong gathers the sun's energy and uses it to dispel the clouds shrouding the Mountain Devil. Caught in the sunlight, the demon evaporates. At first Yin and Fong fear Lotus has vanished as well, but she has survived by hiding in a small cave. Fong finds her and she returns to her ashes; as Yin bids them farewell and departs, Fong sets off with Master to find a new resting place for Lotus.

If *A Chinese Ghost Story III* sounds structurally similar to the first film — it is. In fact, they're almost exactly the same story, with *III* featuring a more extended interior seduction scene rather than *I*'s forest adventures. *Three* also introduces the notion of two beautiful ghosts fighting over the innocent young man — in this case a monk who is desperate to keep his virginity; in fact, *III* occasionally feels more like a play than a film, with lengthy scenes of comic bantering between Fong, Lotus and Butterfly. This also makes *III* considerably less of a horror film; while this isn't necessarily a bad idea (especially not after the demons and creatures of *II*), it is nonetheless disappointing in the wake of the previous entries in the series.

On the plus side, though, *III* features some of the series' most imaginative design. The ghosts are lovelier than ever, the heroes seem costumed more deliberately as colorful fantasy characters, and Ching's flying effects are at their most astonishing, especially when the Priestess soars through the forest with her entourage in tow. Tsui also has a chance to conduct an early experiment with CGI (computer-generated imagery) when Yin creates his magical suit of armor. The effect is so successful that it backfires slightly when the Mountain Devil finally appears as a disappointing puppet; fortunately, the climax is saved by the excellence of the effects around Fong's transformation into the golden buddha and his harnessing of the

**Joey Wang in *A Chinese Ghost Story III*.**

sun's power. Interestingly enough, when Tsui would create his animated version of *A Chinese Ghost Story* in 1997, part *III* of the original series would provide more inspiration than either of the first two installments (the long-earlobed character of the Master would be virtually duplicated for the animated film's White Cloud).

Frequent Tsui character actor Lau Shun (*Once Upon a Time in China, Swordsman II* and many more) is delightfully bizarre as Master, with Jacky Cheung and Joey Wang good as always. Tony Leung Chiu-Wai is fine as the naïve young Fong but lacks Leslie Cheung's natural comedic grace (Leung's comic skills were used to better advantage when he played the bumbling, bespectacled reporter in *I Love Maria*).

*A Chinese Ghost Story III* reached the number 20 spot for the year, with a gross of $15,018,584. At the year's Hong Kong Film Awards it was nominated for Best Art Direction (James Leung and William Cheung), Best Action Choreography (Ching Siu-Tung, Yuen Bun, Ma Yuk Shing and Cheung Yiu Sing), Best Film Editing (Mak Chi Sin, who won for *Once Upon a Time in China* this year) and Best Original Film Score (Romeo Diaz and James Wong — Wong won the award for *Once Upon a Time in China*). It won the Best Special Effects award at the Opporto Film Festival in Portugal.

## The Banquet

Director, 1991. Cantonese: *Ho Moon Ye Yin.* Mandarin: *Hao Men Ye Yan.* Literally: *Powerful Family Midnight Banquet.* Co-Directors: At least four others. CAST: Eric Tsang Chi-Wai ("Boss Tsang"), George Lam Chi-Cheung ("Prince Alibaba"), Stephen Chow Sing-Chi (as himself), Aaron Kwok Fu-Sing (as himself), Leon

Lai Ming (as himself), Jacky Cheung Hok-Yau ("Jacky"), Anita Mui Yim-Fong (as herself), Maggie Cheung Man-Yuk ("Peking Opera Singer"), Carina Lau ("Peking Opera Singer"), Michael Hui Koon-Man (as himself), Andy Lau Tak-Wah (as himself), Richard Ng Yiu-Hon ("Dad"), Rosamund Kwan Chi-Lam ("Sister"), Tony Leung Ka-Fai ("Brother-in-Law"), Joey Wang Cho-Yin ("Jacky's Wife"), Sammo Hung Kam-Bo ("Boss Hung"), Gong Li (as herself), Leslie Cheung Kwok-Wing (as himself), Sally Yeh [Yip Sin-Man] (as herself), James Wong ("Street Food Vendor"), Sandra Ng ("2nd Waitress"), John Sham ("Hung's Assistant"), Tony Leung Chiu-Wai ("Mr. Cheung"), Teddy Robin ("Soccer Player"), Simon Yam ("Gigolo"), Waise Lee (as himself), Lau Kar Leung ("Uncle Nine"), Sylvia Chang (as herself), Carl Mak ("Mr. Mak"), David Chiang (as himself), Kenneth Tsang (as himself), Ti Lung (as himself). Opening Date: November 30, 1991.

*The Banquet*, a benefit film made quickly as an effort on the part of the Hong Kong film community to help the victims of the disastrous flooding of mainland China in 1991, is a well-intentioned, good-natured comedy. It may be plotless, shot almost exclusively in wide shots, and lacking even a hint of depth or sophistication, but the "hey, kids, let's put on a show" enthusiasm with which *The Banquet* is performed is hard to resist.

The plot — what little there is — concerns a greedy businessman, Boss Tsang, his scheming assistant Jacky, and their rival, Boss Hung. Boss Tsang is out to get a multi-billion dollar contract to rebuild Kuwait, but to do so he must impress the Arabian Prince Alibaba with his devotion to his father. Unfortunately, Tsang hasn't spoken to his father (who lives in public housing with Tsang's sister and brother-

in-law) in ten years, so to regain his father's affection quickly Tsang claims to have cancer. Dad agrees to stay with Tsang, but Tsang's public relations man Mr. Cheung reminds him that in one interview Tsang described his father as wealthy. Tsang sets about to remake his father, hiring experts who put the aging man through a regimen of workout programs and diets. But on the night of the big party for the visiting Prince, Dad overhears Tsang confess the fake cancer, and he walks out. To Tsang's surprise, the Prince awards him the contract anyway — because Tsang's father and the Prince have actually known each other since the Prince was a child. Tsang regrets his deception, and to make up for it he throws a huge dinner party for the residents of the public housing project.

*The Banquet* is less a film and more an excuse for an endless parade of stars, many of whom play themselves. Some — like Stephen Chow and Simon Yam — shine by spoofing themselves; others do little more than walk through a scene and deliver a line. A few have genuinely funny bits, perhaps the best being a spoof of Chinese opera, which Eric Tsang, Maggie Cheung and Carina Lau try desperately to sing in English (suffice it to say, some things don't translate well).

*The Banquet* is shot in mostly long takes and wide shots, since its shooting schedule obviously didn't allow for many setups or different angles. Given this context, it's no surprise that it's virtually lacking in directorial style; only a few bits of clever editing (especially a montage sequence in which Tsang bounces all over his bedroom while talking to his wife) save the film from being one master shot after another. The most interesting thing about *The Banquet* technically is that it seems to have been photographed with synch sound (still rare for Hong Kong films); it was probably cheaper and faster to do it this way than to dub it later.

Still, given these limitations, *The Banquet* can be enjoyed simply as a star parade (a familiarity with Hong Kong stars is a must), with some sweet-if-clichéd little messages about family, devotion and greed.

*The Banquet* succeeded in its task, raising $21,921,687 and coming in at the 15th spot in the year's box office take.

## The Twin Dragons

Director/Writer/Cameo, 1992. Cantonese: *Seung Lung Wooi.* Mandarin: *Shuang Long Hui.* AKA: *Double Dragon, Brother vs. Brother.* Producer: Teddy Robin Kwan. Co-Director: Ringo Lam Ling-Tung. Co-Writers: Barry Wong, Tung Cho "Joe" Cheung, Wong Yik. CAST: Jackie Chan ("Ma Yau"/"Die Hard"), Maggie Cheung Man-Yuk ("Barbara"), Teddy Robin Kwan ("Tarzan"), Nina Li Chi ("Tammy"), David Chiang [Keung Dai-Wai] ("Policeman"), James Wong ("Twins' Father"), Sylvia Chang ("Twins' Mother"), Kirk Wong ("Crazy Kung"). Opening Date: January 25, 1992.

This Hong Kong version of the Jean-Claude Van Damme vehicle *Double Impact* was another of Tsui Hark's benefit films (this one, like *Just Heroes*, was to benefit the Hong Kong Directors Union), and if it's missing Tsui's usual style and themes, it does have energy, humor, a cameo by nearly every Hong Kong director, and the always-watchable Jackie Chan.

This time Jackie plays twins separated at birth after a criminal breaks out of the hospital, using one infant as a hostage. This child — Die Hard — ends up being raised by a hooker; the other — Ma Yau — is brought up in America as a concert pianist. Die Hard, a garage mechanic by trade, is perpetually in trouble, thanks in part to his friend Tarzan; things get particularly rough the night Tarzan tries to crash a party to show off his newest crush, a singer named Barbara. The party, given in honor of a notorious racecar driver, turns into a rumble, with Die Hard, Tarzan and Barbara escaping only after Die Hard agrees to a race the following day. When he and Tarzan try to blow town rather than race (they don't have a car), they're caught at the docks and a boat chase follows. Every move of Die Hard's boat is felt by Ma Yau, in town to give a concert and having lunch in an exclusive restaurant; lunch ends abruptly when Ma Yau is so shaken that he dumps his water glass on his date, Tammy. Finally, Tarzan is captured, and Die Hard is told he'll be contacted. Die Hard goes off to lunch with Barbara — and doesn't even know Ma Yau and Tammy are one booth away. When Tammy's jealous boyfriend comes after the delicate Ma Yau, he gets Die Hard instead, who beats him (to the applause of onlookers). Die Hard ends up going off with Tammy, while Barbara gets Ma Yau; needless to say, Barbara is surprised when Ma Yau heads off to a concert rehearsal. Another mixup follows, and this time Ma Yau is taken to free mob boss Crazy Kung, while Die Hard tries to conduct a symphony before a paying audience. Both twins are successful, and Ma Yau even walks off with a mob suitcase. The twins have something to bargain with now, and they join forces to free Tarzan from the bad guys. A meeting is arranged at the docks, and Tarzan is freed, but the thugs chase them into a "Vehicle Testing Centre," where a wild fight breaks out throughout the high-tech plant. Finally, Ma Yau is left alone to face Crazy Kung, but Die Hard (locked in storage cell) takes psychic control of Ma Yau and knocks the villain out. The boys wind up marrying their respective girlfriends—although neither of the girls is really sure who they're getting stuck with...

Among Jackie Chan fans, *The Twin Dragons* is usually rated in the middle of Jackie's work, somewhere between the superb *Project A* and the nearly unwatchable *The Protector*. The emphasis is definitely on comedy, with very few of the spectacular stunts Jackie is most known for; fortunately, Chan is genuinely funny, with comedic skills honed from years of training (in Peking Opera) and experience. The fight scenes in *Twin Dragons* have slightly more of an emphasis on actual martial arts, as compared to Jackie Chan's usual "grab anything and turn it into a weapon" schtick. The use of real martial arts may be attributable to co-director Ringo Lam (Tsui has claimed in at least one interview that Lam directed most of the action), who would helm the martial arts film *Burning Paradise* for Tsui two years later.

As a comedy of identity, *Twin Dragons* works reasonably well, although the script does let some sequences go on too long. Jackie is terrific as both the snorting, earringed Die Hard and the polite, impeccably-groomed Ma Yau; he manages to create such distinct characters for both twins that we always know who's who, even if the other characters don't. Jackie is ably assisted by Maggie Cheung and Nina Li Chi as his bewildered leading ladies, and Teddy Robin as pint-sized troublemaker Tarzan.

*The Twin Dragons* is also a virtual feast for star-spotters, especially those who like directors. Like the benefit film *The Banquet*, *The Twin Dragons* lured dozens of walk-on appearances; unlike *The Banquet*, these cameos are almost all directors,

not actors. Look for Tsui as one of the guards playing poker at the entrance to the Vehicle Testing Centre (he's playing with co-director Ringo Lam and producer Ng See-Yuen). There's also Kirk Wong (*Gunmen*) as "Crazy Kung," the mobster Ma Yau breaks out of the prison bus, John Woo (*The Killer*) as the priest presiding over the end wedding, Wong Jing (*Return to a Better Tomorrow*) as a supernatural healer in the hospital, Lau Kar Leung (*Drunken Master II*) as a kickass doctor, Eric Tsang (*Aces Go Places*) as the hotel guest on the phone in the lobby, and a host of others.

Jackie Chan has said that he was interested in doing *The Twin Dragons* because he wanted to test just how special the effects could be, but he was unimpressed with the final outcome. Indeed, the opticals are uneven; there are shaky mattes around one of the twins in many shots, and often the two Jackies don't seem to be looking at each other at all. When the angle is slightly farther away the opticals are fine; and in shots where body doubles must have been used, the switch is completely unnoticeable.

*The Twin Dragons* received an American theatrical release, premiering on April 9, 1999, in a newly-dubbed and edited version. The American print excised a number of scenes, including the cameos of Wong Jing and Lau Kar Leung in the hospital, a fantasy sequence of Maggie Cheung singing during Ma Yau's concert, and a scene in which Tammy's defeated boyfriend mistakenly begs Ma Yau to take him on as a kung fu student. The American release was received fairly well critically but not financially, taking in only $8,332,431.

In its original Hong Kong theatrical release, *The Twin Dragons* scored as the year's ninth most popular film, with a box office gross of $33,225,134.

## The Master

Director/Producer, 1992. Cantonese: *Lung Hang Tin Ha*. Mandarin: *Long2 Xing2 Tian1 Xia4*. Literally: *Dragon Travels Land Under Heaven*. AKA: *Wong Fei Hong '92*. CAST: Jet Li Lian-Jie ("Chuck"), Yuen Wah ("Uncle Tak"). Opening Date: May 28, 1992.

Although *The Master* didn't receive a release in Hong Kong until 1992, it was shot earlier, on location in Los Angeles. As the first collaboration between Jet Li and Tsui Hark, it should have been a minor classic; instead, it's a poorly made and uninvolving kung fu melodrama.

It starts when Tak, an aging herbalist/kung fu expert living in Los Angeles, is badly beaten and nearly driven out of business by rival kung fu wiz Johnny; he calls on his best student, Chuck, for help. Chuck arrives from Hong Kong determined to find a peaceful conclusion, but within hours of his arrival he's robbed by a Latino gang, conned by an unscrupulous cabdriver, hassled by an attractive female police officer and hounded by Johnny's gang, who are determined to annihilate every other Kung Fu school to prove their dominance. Chuck manages to create his own gang by teaching the Latinos his martial arts; and in the end Tak, Chuck and their students finally take on the evil Johnny.

*The Master* is a film so mind-numbingly bad it's almost impossible to believe this could be the same Tsui Hark who delivered *Once Upon a Time in China* and *Peking Opera Blues*. The plot is the oldest one in the kung fu book — rival school beats up old master, young student comes to his defense — and Tsui and company do virtually nothing to enliven it here. The photography is not merely static, it's often technically inept, with shots under- or overexposed. There's none of Tsui's usual skill with camera movement or color palette on view here; even the film stock looks cheap. The humor (often a strong point in a Tsui Hark film) is weak and lifeless, sometimes depending on clichéd depictions of Latinos; while the romance between Chuck and the policewoman is undeveloped and passionless. The only interesting production design is offered by Uncle Tak's Po Chi Lam herb shop, which glows with burnished wood and backlit shelves; and there's a section of the final showdown that takes place in an industrial complex with spinning fan blades and thick shutters. But that's hardly enough to make up for the inexcusably horrible dubbing or the excruciating synthesized music score.

Only the considerable presence of Jet Li makes *The Master* endurable at all. Li, as usual, is the epitome of dignity and grace, and seems completely out of place in the dingy urban L.A. surroundings. He manages to evoke a few gasps with his stunning martial arts moves, even if the camera seems barely capable of capturing them. Yuen Wah, a dependable character actor (and one of Jackie Chan's Peking Opera "brothers"), is wasted as Uncle Tak, a role which requires him to play far older than he obviously is. The American and Latino actors all could use another few years of acting classes.

*The Master* was obviously Tsui's attempt to break into the American action market, and it's ultimately not much worse than most American B-films from the same time — but it's also not any better.

Tsui had this to say: "Golden Harvest came and talked to me and said, 'What do you think of Jet Li?' I said, 'Jet Li is being wasted. We should use Jet Li, do all sorts of things with him, restart the action kung fu film again after Jackie Chan.' Jackie Chan is really like a stuntperson, and Jet

**Chuck (Jet Li) heals the LAPD in *The Master*.**

Li is like a martial artist. So I left for America for three months to do the movie. I was a bit lost. I think the production team on that movie was not up to my expectation. It was the first time I worked with Jet, and I found out there's a lot of things he doesn't do, doesn't like to do, he likes to do. So the movie was finished in two very short months; I was there for three months, preparation for one month, production on one-and-a-half months, then we came back. It was a bit weird. I was thinking about something and it didn't work out — the casting, the story, everything. And supposedly I was doing this *Swordsman* series, and instead I went to America to do this one. And also Jet got hurt in the middle of production, so I can't show his hands, I can only show his feet. I can't show his whole body. And whenever he'd go walking, I'd have to hide his hands, so that was kind of weird, too. I thought it was supposed to be a comedy, but... Jet doesn't act in the way that I expect him to act. And that's something that I realized in the middle of production. I found that it didn't work."

*The Master* was renamed *Wong Fei-Hung '92* after the success of *Once Upon a Time in China*. It performed adequately at the Hong Kong box office, coming in at number 59 for the year, with a total gross of $8,096,542.

## King of Chess

Director/Producer, 1992. Cantonese: *Kei Wong*. Mandarin: *Qi Wang*. Literally: *Chess King*. Co-Director: Yim Ho. Screenwriters: Yim Ho, Tony Leung Ka-Fai. CAST: Yim Ho ("Chung"), Tony Leung Ka-Fai ("Wong Yat Sun"), John Sham Kin-Fun ("Ching as Adult"). Opening Date: September 25, 1992.

Based on two separate novels (by Chang Shi Kui and Zheng Acheng) and helmed by two directors, *King of Chess* has (as one might suspect) an unbalanced sense of pacing and story. Although both stories deal with our need for heroes, one, set in 1967, is a critique of Communism and the loss of individuality; the other story, set in contemporary Taiwan, is a contrasting commentary on capitalism and greed. Despite some stunning moments throughout (especially in the 1967 sequences), an attempt to meld the two stories in the film's final shot seems forced and ultimately renders the film unsuccessful.

*King of Chess* begins with a superbly edited montage of actual documentary footage from the Cultural Revolution. At the conclusion of this sequence the film cuts to present day Taipei, where a young television hostess, Jade, is being fired because of low ratings for her show, *Whiz Kids' World*. Jade goes to her friend Ching, an advertising expert, for help; when she mentions that her next "whiz kid" is a young chess king, Ching flashes back to his childhood when he was sent to a labor camp as part of the Cultural Revolution. On the train to the camp with his cousin Ngai, he first meets Wong Yat Sun, a famous chess player who has never lost a game. He also meets Chung, an artist who has been denounced because his parents were major literary figures. Ngai and Chung befriend Wong, who is an innocent with a constant hunger and a genius for chess. Likewise, the modern chess king, little Wan Shing Fong, is a psychic superman who can read minds and predict the future, but is terrified of the grandfather who beats him. Ching genuinely cares about the little boy and begins to regret the way they plan on using him as a media figure. Ching thinks back to his past when his cousin Ngai gave away a valuable

antique chess set to rescue Wong from prison, where he'd been placed for committing a breach of Communist etiquette; when Wong discovered what Ngai had sacrificed, he refused to participate in the upcoming chess tournament, since he'd feel too guilty. After the tournament is over, however, Wong challenges the champions to a game; after he wins the first one, he challenges nine players, including the retired, elderly King of Chess, to "blind chess," meaning he'll play all nine at once without even looking at the boards. And in the modern story, Wan is forced to play on *Whiz Kids' World* against Professor Lau, an arrogant, selfish chess champion who agrees to help save Jade's career if she'll become his mistress. At the film's climax the two chess tournaments are intercut, but both end with the same result: The respective chess kings are so exhausted from their ordeals that one (Wong) dies while the other (Wan) collapses. On the way to the hospital, Wan senses a building front collapsing and leaps from the ambulance to save a little girl. The sign falls on him, killing him — but his spirit is alive and is joined by Wong's. The two chess kings walk off hand-in-hand, and the film closes with a montage intercutting the Cultural Revolution with modern-day Taiwan.

*King of Chess* works best in the sections set during the Cultural Revolution. After its rousing, joyous opening montage, it shows the Revolution in a completely different light: Cold, cruel, oppressive and petty. The villain is a young girl with a round peasant face and a permanent frown who constantly looks for actions to denounce. The labor camps are intended to force everyone into the same mold, and yet the need for heroes— those who are willing to use their natural talents regardless of the party's demands— is so overwhelming that one man (Ngai) is willing to part with his most precious possession to glimpse a hero in action.

The contemporary sections of *King of Chess* also deal with the creation of a hero and the toll said creation takes on its reluctant chosen one; yet this part of the film practically wallows in cynicism. The media (Jade's television program) attempts to create a hero that no one really seems to want; the hero they already have (current Chess King Professor Lau) is jaded, arrogant and greedy. If the 1967 sequences come close to becoming maudlin, at least they have genuine emotion; the contemporary sequences echo (perhaps all too well) the shiny, shallow media culture.

The two sequences, aside from their thematic differences, also have distinctly separate directorial styles and performances. Yim Ho has said that he basically directed only the sequences that he acted in, and these happen to be the best in the film; they have a cinéma vérité quality, with extensive use of handheld camera and natural lighting. The cast for the 1967 sequences is exemplary, with Tony Leung Ka-Fai giving one of the finest performances of his career as Wong; hidden behind coke-bottle-bottom glasses, his Wong is a man whose ultimate heroism is simply that he's so in love with life. By contrast, the actors in the modern scenes are sometimes barely adequate, with only John Sham giving anything close to a believable, naturalistic portrayal.

A good score helps to meld the disparate sequences together, but the ending — when Wong and little Wan finally meet — feels like nothing but an attempt to tie the two halves together in the last moment. Unfortunately, it's too little, too late.

*King of Chess* feels very little like a Tsui Hark film. Aside from the critique of communism during the Cultural Revolution, it's curiously lacking in either Tsui's

visuals or thematic obsessions. The female lead — usually one of the strong points in a Tsui film — is weak here, willing to sell herself for financial comfort even as her male companions are deciding that money isn't everything.

Despite Tony Leung Ka-Fai's stunning work and some very fine moments, *King of Chess* was one of Tsui's biggest flops at the box office, coming in at number 179 for the year, with a dismal take of $1,151,165. It did garner a Best Actor nomination for Tony Leung at the year's Hong Kong Film Awards, and also won the Golden Flaiano Award at the Script and Image International Film Festival in Italy.

## The Wicked City

Writer/Producer, 1992. Cantonese: *Yiu Sau Do Si*. Mandarin: *Yao Shou Du Shi*. Literally: *Monster City*. Director: Peter Mak Tai-Kit. CAST: Jacky Cheung Hok-Yau ("Ying"), Leon Lai Ming ("Lung"), Michelle Reis [Lee Ka-Yan] ("Gaye"), Carman Lee Yeuk-Tung ("Loh"), Tatsuya Nakadai ("Yuen"), Roy Cheung Yiu-Yeung ("Gwei"), Yuen Wo-Ping ("Commander").

*The Wicked City* is possibly Tsui's most wickedly witty commentary on the 1997 handover of Hong Kong to China, and is also his homage to *anime* (Japanese animation). Based on the Japanese animated feature *Supernatural Beastie City*, Tsui's live-action version is pure mind-blowing over-the-top eye candy.

The story begins in Tokyo, with a shot of the sun setting — not rising — over Japan. In a scene that closely echoes the beginning of the original animated source film, a man brings a hooker to a hotel room but gets more than he bargained for when the woman turns into a horrible, spidery monster. The man is Lung, an agent with a special anti-monster squad based in Hong Kong; his partner is Ying, a half-man half-monster who is constantly under suspicion in the squad because of his heritage. Upon their return to Hong Kong, Lung meets with the squad commander, who tells him that things are heating up in the war between the humans and the monsters; as the commander puts it, "The handover will be a good time for the monsters." The monsters have unleashed a killer drug, Happiness, into the human world, and a multi-billionaire named Yuen is suspected of being the monster behind the campaign. Lung is assigned to investigate Yuen, but when he asks for Ying as a partner, he's denied. Lung confesses to Ying that he's had a secret affair with a beautiful monster named Gaye, who once saved his life but whom he hasn't seen in some time. Later, when Lung crashes a birthday party for Yuen, he meets Gaye again, and this time he shoots her as a monster — but she saves his life a few moments later when he is attacked by Yuen's malicious son Gwei. Meanwhile, Yuen reveals to a group of highly-placed monsters that he wants to make peace with the humans, but the talks are interrupted when the party is attacked by a rival gang of monsters, led by a female assassin who can take the shape of any machine. Her followers are liquid monsters who have infiltrated all of Yuen's men through the party drinks; now they're all murdered from the inside out, and Gaye is injected with Happiness. Yuen, Lung and Gaye narrowly escape; later, when Lung reports to the Anti-Monster Squad Commander that the monsters are fighting among themselves, the Commander responds, "That's their nature." Gaye and Yuen are tracked to a power plant, where they're stealing

energy to recharge themselves; Yuen allows himself to be captured so Gaye can escape. Yuen is taken to the Squad's laboratory, where he is kept sealed in special magnetic bonds, unaware that his son, Gwei, is the one behind the release of Happiness. Gwei is working with a female Anti-Monster Squad agent, Loh, to get the drugs into Hong Kong; when Ying finds out, he sees a way to prove he's not the traitor within the Squad, and tries to get back to headquarters with the information. He arrives only to find that the Commander doesn't believe him, so he frees Yuen and, along with Lung, they escape to fight Gwei themselves. As they enter the city, they find out that Gwei has managed to stop time and is planning on moving time so far back that humans become easily-controlled primitives. They track Gwei to IM Pei's famous Bank of China Tower, where Gwei has Gaye held captive. Gwei forces Ying to revert to his monster form, while Yuen finally defeats the female monster assassin by forcing her to turn into a motorcycle, then riding her off the top of the building. Yuen and Gwei finally face each other, using a telepathically-controlled jumbo jet as a weapon. Gwei is finally defeated, but Ying is killed and Yuen is dying. At the end Gaye escapes with Yuen, and Lung returns to the Squad.

*The Wicked City* is rich with metaphor for the 1997 handover. Hong Kong is already a city in which humans (read: Chinese) and monsters (indeed, the key monster assassin is a Caucasian woman) are fighting for control; even though the Commander mentions that "the Handover will be a good time for the monsters," the intent is clearly to drive the monster/Caucasians/British from Hong Kong. The battleground becomes Hong Kong's most famous architectural wonder, the Bank of China building; at the film's end the Anti-Monster Squad seem as intent on saving the building as their own men. Half-monster half-human Ying is despised, even though he is a courageous, valuable member of the Squad.

And yet the film also makes a plea for unity — not only is Ying a figure to be felt for and admired, the film's real hero is Yuen, the monster businessman who wants peace between the two worlds. Interestingly enough, even though he's worth 500 billion, Yuen is the film's most compassionate, honest figure; if this seems almost in direct contrast to some of Tsui's earlier work (*Working Class, Shanghai Blues*), it does seem to suggest that the assets left by the monsters/British are to be valued and used, not hated and discarded.

The film also has a wry obsession with time. The female assassin several times takes the form of a giant clock to pursue the heroes (while they engage in a running dialogue of time jokes, along the "time flies" lines); at the end Gwei is turning time back; and Lung wants to go back in time to the romantic moment when he first met Gaye. It should come as no surprise that when *The Wicked City* was made (1992), time was foremost in the minds of many Hong Kongers — the handover was only five years away, after all.

But *The Wicked City* is first and foremost a comic book movie, and it succeeds very well at that. Tsui Hark is a great fan of both *manga* (Japanese comic books) and *anime*, and his live-action film manages to translate much of the look and feel of the animated form. The film makes considerable use of special effects, both physical (the monsters can fly) and optical (at one point Ying and Lung are chased by the monster assassin in the form of a giant clock). It also uses such simple lighting effects as blacklighting to good effect (Gwei turns into a collection of glowing tentacles), and uses effects like double-exposure and step-frame printing to heighten the monster transformations and abilities.

Unfortunately, those same effects are often the downfall of *The Wicked City*. In 1992 computer effects were still in their gestation period (at least in Hong Kong), and *Wicked City* could have benefited greatly from them: It is occasionally forced to cut around the effects, making for some confusing editing and jagged pacing. Camerawork by Andrew Lau (who would go on to direct the Tsui Hark-inspired *Storm Riders*) and Joe Chan is drenched in deep, vivid colors and shadows. Sadly, the film possesses only a lackluster synthesizer score.

But what it does have is a good cast. As Lung, pop sensation Leon Lai is slightly dull but has terrific chemistry with the lovely Michelle Reis (whom he also starred with in Wong Kar-Wai's *Fallen Angels*). Jacky Cheung is marvelous as Ying, the tormented half-breed; Cheung makes him sympathetic without ever being weak. Roy Cheung — who would later go on to make a career out of playing Triad gangsters in such films as *Young and Dangerous 3* and *The Mission* — exudes malevolent sex appeal as Gwei. Carman Lee makes her film debut here (she would go on to work with Tsui several more times, most recently in 1998's *Knock Off*) and is effectively duplicitous. But most interesting are the film's two older stars: Martial arts choreographer and director Yuen Wo-Ping (*Iron Monkey*, *Once Upon a Time in China II*, etc.) is the Squad Commander, and Japanese star Tatsuya Nakadai is absolutely commanding as Yuen. Nakadai was one of the actors in Tsui's favorite film, *Yojimbo* (directed by Akira Kurosawa), so it must have been a particular pleasure for Tsui to cast him.

Although *The Wicked City* performed just adequately in Hong Kong (it came in at number 38 for the year, with a gross of

$10,778,465), it remains one of Tsui's most popular American/European films—it had a major U.S. video release in 1995 from Fox Lorber, and still plays festivals and midnight shows around the country.

## *Once Upon a Time in China III*

Director/Writer/Producer, 1993. Cantonese: *Wong Fei Hung Ji Saam: Si Wong Jaang Ba.* Mandarin: *Huang Fei Hong Zhi San: Shi Wang Zheng Ba.* Literally: *Wong Fei Hong 3: Lion King Struggle for Supremacy.* Cinematography: Andrew Lau. Art Direction: Sip Gam. Action Design: Yuen Tak. Editing: Mak Chi Sin. Music Score: Woo Wai Laap. CAST: Jet Li Lian-Jie ("Wong Fei-Hung"), Max Mok Siu-Chung ("Fu"), Rosamund Kwan Chi-Lam ("Aunt Yee"), Lau Shun ("Wong Kei-Ying"), Xiong Xin-Xin [Hung Yan-Yan] ("Club Foot"). Opening Date: February 11, 1993.

With *Once Upon a Time in China III*, Tsui Hark firmly moves Wong Fei-Hung into the mythological realm, placing him amid the dragons and legendary creatures of the traditional Chinese lion dance. Tsui set Wong Fei-Hung up as an icon right from the beginning of the first film in the series, so the setting in *III* is appropriate, although Wong moves dangerously close to becoming a supernaturally-endowed superhero here. Nevertheless, *Once Upon a Time in China III* is a colorful, exciting film which moves the characters and themes of the first two movies along in some fascinating new directions.

The film opens with a lion dance, performed for the benefit of the aging Empress Dowager, while top-hatted foreigners also observe (and film, with an early hand-cranked camera). During the festivities, President Li suggests that a Lion King Competition would demonstrate Chinese strength to the foreigners, and the Empress Dowager agrees. Cut to: Wong Fei-Hung, aboard a train (just as in the beginning of *Once Upon a Time in China II*), coming into Peking. Wong now wears a Western hat and sunglasses, and tells Aunt Yee he wants to learn English. Aunt Yee meets a friend, the handsome Russian Tomansky, whom she knew when she traveled abroad; he claims that he's come to China just for her, and Wong is instantly jealous. Tensions are running high throughout Peking—Fu nearly gets in a fight at the train station, and, at the Cantonese Association, local thug Chiu Tin Bai harasses Wong's father, Wong Kei-Ying, threatening him if he tries to enter the Lion King Competition. Chiu Tin Bai introduces his secret weapon, a whirling dervish of destruction named Club Foot who nearly demolishes the building. By the time Wong Fei-Hung arrives, the fight is over, but the building is in a shambles and Kei-Ying has been injured. That night Fei-Hung attends to his injured father and tries to ask his permission to marry Aunt Yee, but his father talks about the new steam engine he's bought to increase production at his medical plant, and Fei-Hung loses his nerve. The next day Fei-Hung discovers men from many different associations are fighting over the Lion King Competition, and he tries to establish peace by asking President Li for help; but the President turns him down. On the way back from the President, Chiu Tin Bai tries to coerce Fei-Hung into joining his Lion Dance team, but Wong turns him down, saying he doesn't plan on entering the Competition. Unfortunately, he soon realizes he has no choice, when a parade of Lion King entrants leads to major violence; Aunt Yee attempts to film the parade with her own movie camera, but the camera is knocked down and she's rescued by Fei-Hung in the nick of time. During the melee, Club Foot (in a knife-studded Lion head) is trampled by horses set free by Fu, and is badly injured; when he tries to return to Tin Bai, he's laughed at and beaten. Fei-Hung finds him in a pouring storm, takes him in and tries to cure him; Club Foot's pride nearly sends him away, but he's finally won over during a celebration when Aunt Yee shows off her movies. When Tin Bai tries to lure Wong Fei-Hung into a trap, it's Club Foot who helps save him, his loyalty now completely given over to his savior. Meanwhile, Aunt Yee discovers a piece of film in her camera that shows the Russians murdering a man; she follows the clue and finds out that the Russians are planning on using the (literally) explosive climax of the Lion King Competition to cover their assassination of President Li. Wong finally agrees to join the Competition in order to stop the assassination, and he enters the arena with Fu and Club Foot. Fu is soon injured, leaving just Wong and Club Foot to face Chiu Tin Bai's immense dragon and his army of murderous followers. Aunt Yee confronts Tomansky, who nearly kills her, but he's shot by his own comrades, who fear he's a spy. Wong and Club Foot finally defeat Tin Bai to win the Lion King Competition, but Wong refuses the medal and strides defiantly from the arena.

*Once Upon a Time in China III* contains a number of brilliant sequences, but it suffers from an overuse of wire work in the fight scenes. Wong and his fellow martial artists are no longer grounded — they can now seemingly fly, jump over tall buildings and essentially ignore the law of gravity. This has the net effect of depriving Wong of the status of "blue-collar" hero he earned in the first two films, and setting him in a world that seems more firmly placed in fantasy than reality. While

this idea works given the context of the Lion King Competition, it moves the series from epic historical drama to action fantasy. Wong Fei-Hung is still fighting for China, but he's no longer fighting for a realistic China.

Still, as action fantasy, *Once Upon a Time in China III* is astonishingly good. The actual Lion King Competition itself occupies nearly the entire last fifth of the film, and it's a masterwork of controlled chaos. As Wong, Fu and Club Foot work their way through dozens of fighting lions towards the tower (and the medal) at the arena's center, Tsui packs his frames with movements and bodies, but never loses screen direction or sense. He also manages to seamlessly intercut the very physical confrontations of the Lion King Competition with the more intimate struggle between Aunt Yee and her one-time friend and mentor Tomansky (he thus also makes his female lead a vital ingredient in the Lion King Competition).

The editing is also spectacularly good in the earlier Lion King parade, when the daylight procession breaks out into a riot and Wong must rescue Aunt Yee at one point. In the midst of the tense, exciting action Tsui inserts one of the most romantic images in the entire *Once Upon a Time in China* series, as Wong swings over the heads of the combatants while Yee hangs on, forgetting the battle as she blissfully clutches Wong. It's an image of pure beauty and one that lingers long after the film.

The Fei-Hung/Yee romance is advanced well in *III*. After the shadow play of the first two films, the couple finally considers marriage and stun the onlookers at one point with a gleeful embrace. The shadow play theme is cleverly advanced as well — it's now become the shadows cast by a movie projector. As Aunt Yee cranks the projector, showing images of Fei-Hung practicing his martial arts, he and Yee gaze at each other adoringly. This is the same moment when Club Foot gives in to Wong Fei-Hung's compassion, when he and Fu share food during the movie. In *Once Upon a Time in China III* movies are a powerful force, shedding literal light on both mysteries (the Russian murder) and relationships.

*Once Upon a Time in China III* continues the series' fine acting and production credits. Lau Shun is a welcome addition as Wong's father (compare his affectionate, slightly befuddled portrayal to Donnie Yen's stern, upright version in *Iron Monkey*), and Rosamund Kwan is given more opportunity here to show Yee as a strong, progressive woman. Yet the film is nearly stolen by Xiong Xin-Xin's dynamic, fierce performance as Club Foot. In his first scene, when he takes on the Cantonese Association, he's positively demonic, with his strange body language, cocked head and grimace; after he's injured and cast out by Chiu Tin Bai, his fury and pride are extraordinary. If the image of Wong and Yee sailing gracefully over the heads of the rioters is memorable, so is the one of Club Foot trying desperately to drag himself through the rain and mud while Wong tries to help him. Xiong earned a nomination as Best New Performer for his portrayal of the head of the White Lotus Sect in *Once Upon a Time in China II*, but it's in *III* that this unique performer finally shows that he's considerably more than just another martial arts actor.

*Once Upon a Time in China III* was very successful, coming in at number 7 on 1993's box office list, with a gross of $27,461,435. It received one nomination in the Hong Kong Film Awards—for Best Film Editing (Mak Chi Sin and Lam On-Yee).

*Once Upon a Time in China III* was photographed by Andrew Lau, who would later become one of Hong Kong's premier action directors (*Young and Dangerous*, *The Storm Riders*).

## *Once Upon a Time in China IV*

Producer/Writer, 1993. Cantonese: *Wong Fei Hung Ji Sei: Wong Je Ji Fung*. Mandarin: *Huang Fei Hong Zhi Si: Wang Zhe Zhi Feng*. Director: Yuen Bun. CAST: Zhao Wen-Zhou [Chiu Man-Cheuk] ("Wong Fei-Hung"), Jean Wong Ching-Ying ("Aunt May"), Max Mok Siu-Chung ("Fu"), Xiong Xin-Xin [Hung Yan-Yan] ("Club Foot"), Lau Shun ("Wong Kei-ying"). Opening Date: June 10, 1993.

*Once Upon a Time in China IV* is like the exploitation version of the Wong Fei-Hung story—the subtler shadings have been completely erased in favor of action and melodrama. With a plot that borrows heavily from the first three entries in the series, *Once Upon a Time in China IV* will probably spark more déjà vu than excitement.

The film begins immediately after the events in *III*—Wong Fei-Hung has won the Lion King Competition, and the governor arrives to attempt to persuade him to accept the gold medal he refused at the end of the earlier film. The governor, anxious to see Wong's skills, has brought his own dragon, and they engage in a playful dragon competition. Then the governor reveals his real reason for coming: Another Lion King competition is about to be held, this one to be international, with China's global standing partially riding on the outcome. Wong, of course, accepts. Shortly thereafter, Wong pays a visit to Aunt Yee's sister, Aunt May, who runs a newspaper no one will read; Wong tells her the

Chinese people, many of whom are illiterate, must receive better education. As they talk, a procession of the Ladies of the Red Lantern Sect strides by; they're an organization of women dedicated to ridding China of foreigners. They launch an attack on a German clinic, and Wong tries to fight them off. In the process he and Lady Miu San, one of the cult members, are captured by the Germans and threatened with execution, until kindly Father Thomas rescues them. Wong escapes home only to find that the Red Lantern Sect have invaded his house and captured Fu, Club Foot, young protégé Yan and Wong's father, since they believe Wong is actually working with the foreigners. Wong trails them to their headquarters, where he must undergo a series of tests before the sect members release him. His last trial involves facing the Holy Mother, the sect's leader, whose kung fu is nearly Wong's equal; but he defeats her, and his men are released. They return home only to find that the Lion King Competition has begun; they attempt to enter the arena but are barred. By the time they gain entrance, the contest is nearly over — the foreigners have hidden swords, flamethrowers and guns in their dragons, and slain the Chinese participants, including the governor. Wong invites the foreigners to face him in a new Lion King competition two days later, and they accept. That night Wong receives a propitious gift: an immense, heavy, copper lion head. He takes the head into the Competition and, wielding it as a great weapon, finally defeats the foreigners. He leaves the field triumphant, only to discover that while the contest raged, the Forbidden City was invaded by foreign troops.

*Once Upon a Time in China IV* went into production without most of the principals from the first three films — gone were Tsui as director, and stars Jet Li and Rosamund Kwan; virtually the only holdovers from the previous films are Lau Shun as Wong Kei-Ying and Max Mok as Fu. Assigned to direct in Tsui's place was action choreographer Yuen Bun; sadly, he is neither a Tsui Hark nor a Ching Siu-Tung in the director's chair. He overuses wide angles, slow-motion and gradated filters, giving the entire movie a strange, unnatural look and choppy rhythm. His direction of his actors is also unimpressive — poor Zhao Wen-Zhou as the new Wong has the looks and physical agility, but he seems completely at sea when it comes to the right Wong mix of stoicism and emotion. This Wong Fei-Hung (in sharp contrast to Jet Li's) laughs, cries and plainly eyes Aunt May. Likewise, Xiong Xin-Xin's Club Foot has been denuded of his savagery and consigned to the role of eccentric second banana. Max Mok is the standout performer here, finding new, fresh humor for Fu; he obviously is at home in Fu's skin, playing him for the third time here.

The plot is almost a "Wong Fei-Hung's Greatest Hits" (no pun intended), taking the element of the sympathetic white priest from *Once Upon a Time in China*, the dangerous anti-foreign-intervention cult from *II*, and the Lion King Competition from *III*. It does give some new spins to these recyclables, making the sect a sisterhood and creating almost Godzilla-like monsters for the new Lion King Competition; but when it tries to set up new ideas, they vanish almost instantly in the sea of plot elements. Near the beginning of the film Wong promises Aunt May that he'll work to provide education for illiterate Chinese, but he never mentions it again; Club Foot, Fu and Yan are all badly wounded by machine gun fire at the film's climax, but are shown unharmed in the end shots; and the ending, intriguing as it is, is introduced virtually out of nowhere and left to dangle there, as if it knows it's out of the film's reach.

The film is a minor disappointment on the technical front as well. Aside from the aforementioned overuse of wide angles and slow-motion (some fights are virtually nothing but slow-motion shots), much of the music is recycled from the other films and sometimes is badly edited. Most of the budget seems to have gone to the Lion King Competition monsters, which are colorful and unique, including a giant centipede whose sections crush each other, a bird that dive-bombs its opponents and an insect studded with swinging swords.

Coming in the wake of the first three entries, *Once Upon a Time in China IV* is a pale imitation and easily the weakest entry in the series.

Opening only four months after *III*, *Once Upon a Time in China IV* placed considerably lower on the year's box office list (at number 39), with a gross of $11,189,826.

## *The Magic Crane*

Producer/Writer, 1993. Cantonese: *Sin Hok San Jam*. Mandarin: *Xian He Shen Zhen*. Literally: *Immortal Crane Magical Treasure*. Director: Benny Chan Muk-Sing. Co-Writer: Tsui Daat Choh. Cinematography: Lau Moon Tong, Ko Chiu Lam, Mau Gin Fai. Art Direction: Cheung Sek Wah. Editing: Mak Chi Sin. Music Score: Wong Bong. CAST: Anita Mui Yim-Fong ("Pak Wan Fai"), Tony Leung Chiu-Wai ("Kwun Mo"), Rosamund Kwan Chi-Lam ("Butterfly Lam"), Damian Lau Chung-Yun ("Yat Yeung Sze"), Lawrence Ng Kai-Wah ("Pang Hoi"), Norman Chu Siu-Keung ("Lam Hoi Ping"). Opening Date: August 19, 1993.

Although *The Magic Crane* is often placed alongside *Green Snake* as Tsui Hark's two period fantasies, it actually resembles *Dragon Inn* and *The East Is Red* far more closely. Its first half, featuring warring kung fu schools battling in an inn, has *Dragon Inn's* claustrophobic action; the second half is like *The East Is Red* in both setting (it even seems to use the same set — a large ship at sea) and situation (two women involved in a long mortal combat). And therein lies the problem with *The Magic Crane*: Although it's often exciting and exquisitely shot, it also feels like two different films that never fully mesh together.

It begins as the story of Kwun Mo and Yat Yeung Sze, two martial arts students who travel from their native Tein Chong mountain to distant Kah Chou Fu for a meeting of martial arts schools. En route, Kwun Mo has an encounter with Pak Wan Fai, a beautiful woman who rides a giant crane and has never seen a man before. Upon their arrival at Kah Chou Fu they meet Pang Hoi, venomous head of the Tien Lung school, and his seductive but deadly sister. Pang Hoi is plainly out to eliminate the other schools, even though local law officer General Tsao warns him of the consequences. After Pang Hoi tries to use killer bats to knock off his rivals, Kwun Mo seeks out Pak Wan Fai for help; she has a Sacred Text full of healing secrets. Together they go to find a 1000-year-old tortoise, but after Pak Wan Fai slays the tortoise, the organ they need to cure the bats' victims is stolen by Butterfly Lam, who fights Pak Wan Fai's magic flute with her own enchanted lute. Butterfly Lam was abandoned as a child by her father, who is Pak Wan Fai's sifu; now she's out to wreak vengeance on both the teacher and the student. She escapes with the tortoise gall to her ship; Pak Wan Fai pursues, and they fight. Both are badly injured in the battle, and Pak Wan Fai escapes to confront her sifu, Lam Hoi Ping; he tells her that she is a princess of a vanished kingdom, and that he once chose to save her over his own daughter. Pak Wan Fai is devastated by this revelation. Kwun Mo finally returns to Kah Chou Fu with the tortoise gall and discovers that the real villain is General Tsao, who plans on taking over all of the kung fu schools himself. When Tsao sees that Kwun Mo also has the Sacred Text, he chases Kwun Mo and Yat Yeung Tze; they tear the Text in half and split up. Tsao eventually chases half of the Text literally over a cliff, where he is captured by a hideous aged cannibal who lives in a cave there. Abused by the cannibal, Tsao is forced to eat the Text — and becomes a supernaturally-endowed kung fu artist as a result. He escapes to challenge both Pak Wan Fai and Butterfly Lam, who has killed both her father and the magic crane; now the two opposing women must unite to battle Tsao. Fortunately, Lam Hoi Ping has been rejuvenated by the other half of the Sacred Text, and with his help the women defeat Tsao; however, Pak Wan Fai has apparently been killed in the attempt. At the end, the repentant Butterfly goes to search for Pak Wan Fai, while Kwun Mo and Yat Yeung Tze decide to give up martial arts and become businessmen instead.

In its first half — as the different schools gather and battle in Kah Chou Fu — *The Magic Crane* seems like standard (albeit very well-made) kung fu fare. Tony Leung Chiu-Wai is playing virtually the same virtuous, virginal young man he essayed in *A Chinese Ghost Story III*, lending the story a light, comic tone; his romance with Pak Wan Fai has a sweet-natured, simple innocence about it (not unlike the romance between Mo-Yin and Chow in *New Dragon Inn*). At this point Pak Wan Fai and Butterfly Lam both seem

destined to support Kwun Mo's story, but the situation is reversed in the film's second half when the film focuses on the relationship between the two women, and Kwun Mo becomes a love interest for both of them. The second half of the film is far more unusual and intriguing, even though it bears more than a slight resemblance to *The East Is Red* (especially the dynamics between Asia and Snow). The story of General Tsao's conversion to kung fu superman is intrusive; had the film chosen to concentrate on Pak Wan Fai and Butterfly Lam, it could have been a minor classic; as it is, it's an unfocused, scattered work of entertainment.

The cast is uniformly good, with Anita Mui (usually cast as world-weary heroines in the likes of *A Better Tomorrow III* and *Rouge*) bringing a wonderful naïvete to Pak Wan Fai, a naïvete later transformed to bewilderment and finally rage. Rosamund Kwan is playing a similar character to Ying, her role in *Swordsman II*, but she does it extraordinarily well. Also look for *We're Going to Eat You* star Norman Chu, buried under hair pieces as Lam Hoi Ping.

Like *Green Snake*, *The Magic Crane* relies on extensive use of special effects, and, also like *Green Snake*, the effects are uneven. Optical effects are generally good, with an especially noteworthy shimmer whenever the two women use their magical instruments; the title character, however, is somewhat unconvincing in close shots. Flying effects are, as always, beautifully done, especially in one sequence where Pak Wan Fai saves Kwun Mo by using long streamers of brightly-colored cloth.

*The Magic Crane* also has a solid music score, making good use of the instruments carried by its female leads.

*The Magic Crane* clocked in at number 59 on the year's box office list, with total earnings of $8,173,544.

## *Iron Monkey*

Producer/Writer, 1993. Cantonese: *Siu Nin Wong Fei Hung Ji Tit Ma Lau*. Mandarin: *Shao Nian Huang Fei Hong Zhi Tie Ma Liu*. Literally: *The Young Wong Fey Hung: Iron Monkey*. AKA: *Iron Monkey: The Young Wong Fei Hong*. Director: Yuen Wo-Ping. Action Directors: Yuen Wo-Ping, Yuen Cheung-Yan, Yuen Shun-Yee, Kuk Hin-Chiu. Co-Writers: Tang Pik-Yin, Lau Tai-Mok. CAST: Yu Rong-Guang ("Dr. Yang"), Donnie Yen Ji-Dan ("Wong Kei-Ying"), Jean Wong Ching-Ying ("Orchid"), Yan Yee Kwan [Yam Sai-Koon] ("Legate Officer"), James Wong Jim ("Governor Cheng"). Opening Date: September 3, 1993.

*Iron Monkey* is a diverting — if not exactly entrancing — spinoff from the *Once Upon a Time in China* series. Released two years after the first film in Tsui Hark's landmark series, *Iron Monkey* deals with a pre-adolescent Wong Fei-Hung and his father, Wong Kei-Ying. The two Wongs are passing through a province ruled by the corrupt Governor Cheng when they are attacked by thieves. Kei-Ying defends himself expertly and is mistaken by some guards for Iron Monkey, a masked Robin Hood-ish superhero who has been using his amazing martial arts skills to attack Cheng. The real Iron Monkey is a local healer, Dr. Yang; he is assisted by the lovely Orchid, a former prostitute whose contract he bought out and who is now his devoted disciple. When Wong Kei-Ying is forced by the vile Governor to find Iron Monkey (Cheng holds little Fei-Hung hostage), he soon discovers that he and Iron Monkey are really on the same side. Dr. Yang uses his cunning first to free Fei-Hung and then to disguise himself as the Legate Officer, Cheng's superior (with Orchid by his side in drag!). When the real Legate Officer arrives, Cheng

is sent packing, and Wong Kei-Ying and Dr. Yang find they have a vicious new common foe. They unite to defeat first the Legate Officer's thugs (who include a facially-deformed, high-kicking woman), then the Officer himself, in a climax that takes place atop twenty-foot-tall bamboo poles while a fire rages beneath them.

*Iron Monkey* is both far more comic book in style than *Once Upon a Time in China* and less interested in eliciting emotional responses. Under Yuen Wo-Ping's direction, it goes for the gut rather than the head or heart; characters are either pure evil (the Legate Officer), stoic, upright heroes (Yang, Kei-Ying), or hissable buffoons (Governor Cheng). The film has some amusing references to *Once Upon a Time in China* — the score riffs on it throughout, and Fei-Hung learns to fight with his father's umbrella — but the main reason to see this film, of course, is the fight choreography. Yuen Wo-Ping (who shot to Western stardom after his work on the 1999 American sci-fi film *The Matrix*) is in his element here, and several of the film's fights are justifiably famous in martial arts film circles. A rooftop combat between Iron Monkey and Wong Kei-ying is perhaps the high point; it uses relatively little wire work and lets the performers shine through with some truly astonishing footwork. Donnie Yen, in particular, is spectacular; he's probably second only to Jet Li among contemporary cinematic martial artists. Unfortunately, Yuen's wire-rigging actually hampers a few scenes more than it helps them — by removing all semblance of reality. For the most part, *Iron Monkey* wants to be a Robin Hood or Batman-type comic, not a *Swordsman* supernatural fantasia, so impossible leaps and flights seem jarring rather than startling.

That said, the film works well as a simple action flick and is ably served by good production values and a very capable cast. Donnie Yen (*Dragon Inn*, *Once Upon a Time in China II*), Yu Rong-Guang (*The East Is Red*), Jean Wong (*Once Upon a Time in China IV*) and Yan Yee Kwan (*Swordsman II*, *Once Upon a Time in China*) all seemed to be working regularly with Tsui around this time, and it shows—the cast has a fine chemistry together. And James Wong is delightful as the sleazy, greedy Cheng; after providing the scores and singing voices for any number of Tsui films (including *A Chinese Ghost Story* and *Once Upon a Time in China*), it's a pleasure to see him onscreen in a Tsui Hark-produced film.

*Iron Monkey* fared somewhat poorly at the box office, placing at number 73 for the year, earning $6,810,899. It received one nomination from the Hong Kong Film Awards—for Best Action Choreography (Yuen Wo-Ping, Yuen Cheung-Yan, Yuen Shun-Yee and Kuk Hin-Chiu).

## Red Lotus Temple

Producer, 1994. Cantonese: *Foh Siu Hung Lin Ji*. Mandarin: *Huo3 Shao1 Hong2 Lian2 Si4*. Literally: *Burning Red Lotus Temple*. AKA: *Burning Paradise*; *Burning Paradise in Hell*; *Rape of the Red Temple*. Director: Ringo Lam Ling-Tung. Action Director: Chris Lee Kin-Sang. Screenwriter: Nam Yin. CAST: Willie Chi Tian-Sheng ("Fong Sai Yuk"), Carman Lee Yeuk-Tung ("Tou Tou"). Opening Date: March 31, 1994.

*Red Lotus Temple* is the second collaboration between Tsui Hark and Ringo Lam (the first was the benefit film *The Twin Dragons*); despite the auspicious pedigree, the resulting film is a bleak, hollow exercise, with some so-so fight scenes and a considerable amount of pointless cruelty.

The film is set during a time when the evil Manchus are persecuting and imprisoning Shaolin monks. Young Shaolin student Fong Sai Yuk is being pursued through the desert with his master; when they pause to hide out in an abandoned shack, they encounter Tou Tou, a former prostitute. The Manchu forces attack; after a valiant struggle the master is slain; and Fong Sai Yuk and Tou Tou are captured and sent to Red Lotus Temple, a Manchu prison. The prison warden is ex-general Kung, who has set himself up as a cruel god in this isolated place; he takes Tou Tou as a concubine and proudly displays his foreman Hong, a former Shaolin hero. Fong is horrified by Hong's betrayal and engages him in fights until Hong reveals that he's actually working to create a map of Red Lotus Temple's many traps, so the prisoners can escape. Finally, Hong and Fong lead the prisoners (including Shaolin Master Chi Sin) through the Temple's maze of trap doors, collapsing bridges and spiked pits to freedom. In the end, Fong and Tou Tou ride off together into the desert.

*Red Lotus Temple* is curiously lacking in subtext or even context. Although the premise is one rich with possibilities, director Lam never lets us into the rage or anguish of his characters; there are few films so lacking in close-ups as this one. Possibly Lam realized he was stuck with actors of limited range; although agile and athletic, young Willie Chi as Fong Sai Yuk possesses none of Jet Li's dramatic intensity or innate charisma. This leaves the film with a hole at its center and, unfortunately *Red Lotus Temple* can offer nothing to fill that void. The entire cast is dull (only Carman Lee would go on to regularly appear in other films, including Tsui's *Knock Off*), and the script offers neither philosophy nor subplot. It does offer numerous scenes of gratuitous sadism, especially one in which Kung kills one of his concubines and then rapes Tou Tou; in another, Kung cuts the hands of his concubines and paints on the walls with their blood. While this would work if the concubines were part of the final rebellion, they aren't (with the exception of Tou Tou).

Lam chooses to shoot his action scenes in long takes and wide shots, and while this eliminates the possibility of any wire work, it also makes for fights that seem stagy, slow and slightly awkward. The film's emphasis is clearly on its sets, and they are impressive, particularly an eerie cavern where Kung keeps the preserved corpses of his concubines; but *Red Lotus Temple* proves all too well that sets alone can't carry an entire film.

*Red Lotus Temple* was poorly received at the box office, placing only at number 145 for the year, with a gross of $1,819,697.

The film is commonly known in America (where it is inexplicably well-regarded) under the title *Burning Paradise.* It is also the second Tsui Hark film to feature legendary Chinese folk hero Fong Sai Yuk — the first was Tsui's debut, *The Butterfly Murders.* Jet Li also played the role twice for director Corey Yuen (*Fong Sai Yuk* and *Fong Sai Yuk 2*, both 1993).

# Once Upon a Time in China V

Director/Producer/Writer/Music, 1994. Cantonese: *Wong Fei Hung Ji Ng Lung Sing Chin Ba.* Mandarin: *Huang Fei Hong Zhi Wu Long Cheng Jian Ba.* Literally: *Wong Fei Hong 5: Dragon City's Exterminator Tyrant.* Co-Producer: Ng See-Yuen. Action Director: Yuen Bun. Co-Writers: Lau Tai-Mok, Lam Kee-To. Cinematography: Ko Chiu Lam, Lau Moon Tong, Peter Pau, Wan Man Git. Art Direction: Bill Lui. Editing: Mak Chi Sin. CAST: Zhao Wen-Zhou [Chiu Man-Cheuk] ("Wong Fei-Hung"), Rosamund Kwan Chi-Lam ("Aunt Yee"), Max Mok Siu-Chung ("Fu"), Kent Cheng Juk-Si ("Porky Lang"), Xiong Xin-Xin [Hung Yan-Yan] ("Club Foot"), Jean Wong Ching-Ying ("Aunt May"), Lau Shun ("Wong Kei-Ying"). Opening Date: November 17, 1994.

It's "Yo-ho-ho and a bottle of Wong!" as Tsui Hark returns to the director's chair and takes his *Once Upon a Time in China* series for a wild pirate ride in the fifth installment.

For *Once Upon a Time in China V* Tsui has jettisoned most of the political overtones and serious approach in favor of a film that's a pure treasure chest of entertainment. The first half is mainly a romantic/situational comedy, as Wong Fei-Hung and the crew from the last film meet up with Aunt Yee, Porky Lang and Bucktooth Sol from the first film. They all come together in a lawless town; it seems the governing magistrate fled with the downfall of the Empress Dowager, and the local constables don't have enough money to feed themselves, let alone fight off the bloodthirsty pirates ravaging the coastline. Wong tries to intervene but finds the pirates aren't the town's only problem — the rice merchants are making a fortune inflating the price of their goods. Wong's got his own problems, too — Aunt May is plainly attracted to him, but he wants to stay loyal to Aunt Yee. Yee mistakes a scene between Wong's father and Aunt May for a romantic rendezvous, and she and Wong quarrel; when Wong finally decides to take off after the pirates, the relationship is still uneasy. Wong Fei-Hung, Fu, Club Foot, Porky and Sol take the constables' stash of guns and sail off disguised as merchants. They're attacked at sea by Flying Monkey, a pirate leader; once they've subdued the

Thai lobby card for *Once Upon a Time in China V* (featuring, in inset, Xiong Xin-Xin).

cutthroat, they force him to reveal the hidden location of the pirates' base. They find the base, located in island caverns, and Wong goes after Sister Ying, the pirate leader's wife. As if two women already weren't enough, Sister Ying tries to seduce Wong, but the seduction turns deadly when Ying tries to pull Wong down onto her knife-studded bed. A fight breaks out, but Wong and his men have a surprise weapon in the form of Bucktooth Sol, who is unexpectedly expert with pistols. Finally, Wong and the others find the pirates' hidden stash of treasure, but it's guarded over by Cheung, the 100-year-old leader of the pirate clan. Wong and Cheung fight while balancing atop wobbling vases; Cheung is defeated when his own crates of loot fall on him. Wong takes the treasure, the captured pirates and Sister Ying back to town, knowing full well that Cheung's son will come after them. Wong stages a trap for the new pirate king, a trap that's nearly

sprung too early when Ying and the other pirates break out of jail on their own. Wong chases them to a rice storage barn and finally shoots Ying; then, in the final confrontation, he faces Cheung the younger in a town street packed with barrels of gunpowder. The fight ends when Cheung is blown to smithereens. Aunt May goes sailing off to Hong Kong, but Wong, Yee and the rest decide to stay until order is restored to the town.

If the first half of *Once Upon a Time in China V* is light on action, the second half more than compensates—its frames are so packed with movement and color that it's almost intoxicating. This is a perfect example of Tsui Hark's mastery of controlled chaos: Each shot is like a comic-book panel threatening to explode out of its linear confines, but the action is never confusing, only breathtaking. The production design is a veritable catalogue of pirate-movie tropes—chests of jewels, caverns studded with stalactites, scarves and bandoleros... all that's missing is a skull-and-crossbones. The addition of kung fu into the pirate world works perfectly, a melding so seamless it's hard to believe they haven't been part of each other all along.

There's more genre mixing going on here as well—kung fu and gunplay. In the previous *Once Upon a Time in China* films there's always been a notion that martial arts and firearms were completely separate, in opposition to each other; but here they blend into a new style of—call it gun fu. Wong and his men trade shots with the pirates while flipping, spinning and swinging upside-down; Tsui manages to avoid making it look like John Woo's "bullet ballets," creating instead something uniquely Tsui Hark.

And, lest we forget this is a Tsui Hark movie, Tsui gives the pirates a female leader. Sister Ying, with her Veronica Lake haircut, spectacles and boyish garb, is a true Tsui Hark woman: Tough, strong, but successful because of her femininity, not in spite of it. She almost destroys Wong by seducing him; later she frees herself from jail by using one of her hair pins as a lock pick. Unlike the Red Lantern sect women from *IV*, she's not interested in foreign intervention, politics or religion, just her own desires; she may just be the single most interesting villain in the entire *Once Upon a Time in China* series.

*V*'s cast recovers beautifully from the stumbles in *IV*. As Wong, Zhao Wen-Zhou comes into his own here, capturing the right combination of righteousness and comic befuddlement (to say nothing of his astonishing physical agility). Xiong Xin-Xin likewise triumphs here, endowing Club Foot with some of the ferocity he showed in *III*, even though he's a second banana now. Rosamund Kwan's return is welcome, and the scene where Aunt Yee

casually stabs pirates while fuming at Wong's possible infidelity is one of the film's blackest and funniest.

The tech credits are superb, with a small army of cinematographers granting the film a vibrant, almost manic look. Tsui is credited with the film's excellent score, which seems to be a mix of cues culled from existing sources superbly grafted to the film.

*Once Upon a Time in China V* was a bit of a box office disappointment, coming in at only number 80 for the year, with a gross of $4,902,426.

## *Love in the Time of Twilight*

Producer/Director/Writer, 1995. Cantonese: *Fa Yuet Gaai Kei*. Mandarin: *Hua Yue Jia Qi*. Literally: *Flower Moon Wedding Day*. Action Director: Yuen Bun. Co-Writers: Hui Sa-Long, Roy Szeto. CAST: Nicky Wu [Ng Kei-Lung] ("Kong"), Charlie Yeung Choi-Nei ("Yan Yan"), Eric Kot Man-Fai ("Little Shrimp"), Lau Shun ("Yan Yan's Father"). Opening Date: April 13, 1995.

*Love in the Time of Twilight* is often thought of as Tsui Hark's follow-up to his hit *The Lovers*, but the similarities essentially end at the use of the two lead actors. What *Love in the Time of Twilight* really feels more like is Tsui Hark flexing his special effects muscle within the framework of a strange, supernatural love story. Despite some fine humor, engaging performances and several sequences that equal anything in the cinema of the surreal, *Love in the Time of Twilight* more often than not trips over its own outlandish conceits and is ultimately unsuccessful.

The overly-complicated story concerns a 1930s travelling opera troupe. Yan

**Charlie Yeung in *Love in the Time of Twilight*.**

Yan is the actress daughter of the company's leader, but she's living in the shadow of the beautiful So So. Both women are pursued by Little Shrimp, a hulking but genial young actor who has an imaginary friend called "Tsui Hark." On Affinity Day, Yan Yan goes to an oracle in hopes of finding out about her future husband, but she has a series of misadventures with a young man named Kong, and both leave angry and disheveled. Yan Yan returns to the opera theater just in time to see the installation of the first light bulb; there's talk of turning the theater into a cinema. And Kong meets his dream girl, Cheung Siu Yung, who takes him home, seduces him and asks him to deposit her expensive jewelry in the bank he works at. The next day Yan Yan sees a newspaper article that says Kong robbed the bank and escaped; later she sees Kong appear in a variety of odd places throughout the theater. Finally,

he talks to her and tells her that he was used by Cheung Siu Yung, who actually gave him a case of guns, not jewels, which Devil King and his gang used to rob the bank. Devil King then strangled Kong with a wire, and his departing soul entered the electrical stream that led to the theater's light bulb. Kong begs Yan Yan's help in going back in time to stop his murder; he explains that they can travel through the lightbulb as long as it's turned on. She agrees, and they journey back to the past, where there are now two Yan Yans and two Kongs. They are initially unable to change the events, and Kong is killed again. They go back again, and this time they're sucked through an electrical wire into a horrific limbo, where any fast movement causes them to literally fall apart. They manage to escape this place and once again relive Kong's murder; but this time they find out Cheung Siu Yung murdered Devil King to take all the robbery money. In their last attempt to change the past, they fight the ghostly Devil King, who has been partly burned by exposure to sunlight and has become a monster. They defeat Devil King at last, and Yan Yan and Kong realize their original antagonism has now turned to love.

*Love in the Time of Twilight* may have been partly inspired by the success of the romantic fantasy *Ghost*, but its story is so scattered it's difficult to say exactly what it is supposed to be about. Is it a love story about two people who hate each other and end up as lovers; is it a supernatural time travel adventure; is it a comedy laden with special optical effects á la *The Mask*; or is it a poignant comment on the time when film replaced stage? As if all that weren't enough, it also tries to be a gross-out comedy (vomiting is a major theme), a surrealistic art film and a horror film. By trying to cram so many different themes and genres into one film, it ends up being unable to concentrate on any of them.

Certainly individual scenes have plenty of charm. Charlie Yeung and Nicky Wu recreate the chemistry that served them so well in *The Lovers*; and Eric Kot brings a bumbling, likable silliness to Little Shrimp (when he isn't vomiting, that is). Tsui's playful use of optical effects is often delightful, especially a scene in which Yan Yan and Kong get stuck together back-to-back after a return from the ghost limbo; in another scene, animated exclamation points and question marks float in space over Yan Yan's head in imitation of a thousand cartoons.

And there's the notion of the end of theater and the beginning of cinema. This seems like an exceptionally rich idea, and one that Tsui could explore well, but this is probably the smallest of the film's many subplots. The title *Love in the Time of Twilight* is actually the name of a film within

the film, but this important detail is mentioned in only one line, a virtual throwaway.

The climax of *Love in the Time of Twilight* is Tsui's special effects showstopper, with supernaturally-elongated limbs and flying, but the scene is nearly destroyed by the obvious rubber mask worn by Devil King. Hong Kong has never reached the Hollywood level of make-up effects, but this is a new low; it's so bad it seems deliberate, as if Devil King will reach up any moment to snatch the mask away and reveal the real horror beneath. Sadly, that never happens.

The real effects highlights—and the all-round best scenes in the film—are found in the strange electrical limbo where time is sped up and quick motion causes disintegration. In this world night becomes day in an eyeblink, the sun and moon whirl through the sky overhead, and the landscape is littered with other stranded souls. The limbo scenes are stunningly surreal, easily the equal of anything in the work of Luis Buñuel or David Lynch. Although it would be virtually impossible to spread this kind of weirdness out over the length of a commercial feature film, it's nevertheless unfortunate that it couldn't have been better integrated into a film that matched it in tone; as it is, these scenes stand out, and not just because of their visual brilliance.

*Love in the Time of Twilight* is worth watching for its individual moments, but overall it must stand as perhaps the most ambitious Tsui Hark failure.

The film was not the equal of *The Lovers* at the box office, where it placed at number 71 and earned $5,126,023.

It received two nominations at the Hong Kong Film Awards—for Best Supporting Actor (Eric Kot Man-Fai) and Best Original Film Score (Woo Wai Laap and Raymond Wong).

*Love in the Time of Twilight* was a major film for Tsui's effects company, Cinefex Workshop, and the first for which they made extensive use of "FLINT," a revolutionary real-time digital compositing system.

When asked if *Love in the Time of Twilight* might have been partially inspired by the effects-laden comedies of Robert Zemeckis (especially *Back to the Future*), Tsui had this to say: "Not *Back to the Future*. *Back to the Future* is something I cannot do because it's a sci-fi film. The concept has been around in things like *Groundhog Day*. The idea is you go back in time and you change the matter, but it's like you change yourself in a way and you mix with yourself. It's a bit like *Back to the Future*, come to think of it!"

## Tri-Star

Director/Producer/Writer, 1996. Cantonese: *Daai Saam Yuen*. Mandarin: *Da San Yuen*. Literally: *Big Three Round*. Co-Producer: Raymond Wong. Co-Writers: Che Chung Taai, Tiu Wan. Cinematography: Arthur Wong. Art Direction: Bill Lui. Action Design: Xiong Xin-Xin. Editing: David Wu, Chan Kei Gap, Chow Gok Chung. Music: Lowell Lo. CAST: Anita Yuen Wing-Yee ("Baiban"), Leslie Cheung Kwok-Wing ("Zhong"), Lau Ching Wan ("Fa"), Xiong Xin-Xin ("Tai"). Opening Date: February 15, 1996.

After the success of *The Chinese Feast*, Tsui cast stars Leslie Cheung and Anita Yuen in this follow-up comedy about a cop, a priest and a hooker. *Tri-Star* opens as tough cop Fa first meets prim, proper Father Zhong when he mistakes the priest for a bank robber during a high-speed chase; but the two men intersect again when both pursue the same woman for

different reasons. Fa thinks Baiban, a debt-laden young prostitute, may be involved in blackmailing wealthy married businessmen, but Father Zhong is more interested in saving Baiban from her profession. As Fa is pulled deeper into a dangerous gang situation involving Baiban's debts, Zhong finds himself in a different sort of danger: falling in love.

If *We're Going to Eat You* was Tsui Hark's parody of communism, than *Tri-Star* is his parody of Catholicism; unfortunately, where the former film worked because of a lightning-fast pace and a simple plot, *Tri-Star* is weighed down by a lack of focus and a strange uncertainty. The film's overall tone veers wildly from sophisticated relationship comedy to an *All the Wrong Clues*–type chaotic comedy of errors to toilet-humor gross-out. The film even opens with an action scene, a car chase that humorously juxtaposes classical music with squealing tires and crashes; and yet Tsui sets up *Tri-Star*'s low comedy early on when slop cop Fa interrupts the chase to vomit on himself after sniffing his own feet. After the chase the film settles into its story, which centers on a young prostitute, Baiban, who is sought by both Fa and righteous young priest Father Zhong; yet the plot lacks even the focus of a romantic triangle, since the priest and the cop have virtually no interaction and are interested in Baiban for entirely different reasons. While Zhong tries to convert her to his faith, Fa pursues her as part of a case involving prostitutes and an extortion ring, but not even Fa's mission is clear; somewhere near the film's third act Fa becomes more interested in Zhong's psychoanalyst cousin than in Baiban.

And through all of this confusion there's a constant thread of jokes relating Catholicism to sex or gangs. Some are amusing — when a potential landlady asks

**Priest Zhong (Leslie Cheung) tries to withstand the charms of Baiban (Anita Yuen) in *Tri-Star*.**

Zhong what he does, he tells her, "A sacred profession," to which she blithely responds, "Oh, sex"—but more fall flat, often embarrassingly so. If Tsui was out to make a scathing satire, he missed the boat—the film closes with Baiban and her prostitute friends happily belting out a disco "Ave Maria" in the church, while Zhong has avoided temptation and kept his vows of chastity.

Which is not to say that *Tri-Star* is completely without its charms: The cast in particular is sensational, with each of the three leads playing against type, all successfully. Leslie Cheung (the "bad boy" of such recent films as Wong Kar-Wai's *Happy Together*, Ronny Yu's *The Bride with White Hair* and Tsui's own *The Chinese Feast*) is sweetly convincing as the compassionate Father Zhong; Lau Ching Wan, usually suave and cool, is having the time of his life playing the bearded, rumpled Fa;

and Anita Yuen moves past her impish ingenue image to play a hardened whore who is blasé about her profession, even if she's emotionally confused (she laughs when she's sad and cries when she's happy). Yuen and Cheung again demonstrate the chemistry that served them so well in *He's a Woman, She's a Man*; and despite Lau Ching Wan's considerable presence, it's almost too bad *Tri-Star* didn't focus solely on the star-(and God-)crossed couple.

*Tri-Star* also has a characteristically (for Tsui, that is) lovely look to it, one uncommon for comedies: Streets are a riot of neon colors, prostitutes strut in purple hair and mirrored shoes, and the camera's movements give the story whatever momentum it has. However, Tsui often seems intent on overpacking his frames here: Instead of centering on just Baiban, he includes her in a troupe of four prostitutes, giving poor Yuen all-too-few close-ups.

Compared to the earlier *The Chinese Feast*, *Tri-Star* feels heavy-handed, although it's still light years beyond the typical current Hollywood comedy.

*Tri-Star* was one of 1996's biggest Hong Kong hits, coming in at number 8, with a gross of $25,218,13.

The title's literal translation, *Big Three Round*, refers to a winning hand in mahjong.

If the musical rooftop scene in *Tri-Star* looks stylistically very different from the rest of the film, there's a reason: It was shot by renowned cinematographer (and frequent Wong Kar-Wai collaborator) Christopher Doyle.

Lau Ching Wan wears a fake beard throughout *Tri-Star*; Tsui said, "I just wanted to change his look. I think he looks kind of serious. I wanted to change his image."

On the subject of religion in *Tri-Star*, Tsui had this to say: "That was something I always wanted to touch on, but I didn't handle it that well. I didn't even handle Anita Yuen's character that well, so it's kind of like a very strange piece. It didn't come out as what I wanted."

## *Shanghai Grand*

Producer, 1996. Cantonese: *San Seung Hoi Taan*. Mandarin: *Xin Shang Hai Tan*. Literally: *New Shanghai Beach*. Director: Poon Man-Kit. Action Director: Stephen Tung Wai. Cinematography: Poon Hang-Sang. Art Direction/Costume and Make-Up: Yu Ka On. Screenwriters: Sandy Shaw [Siu Lai-King], Matthew Chow Hoi-Kwong, Poon Man-Kit. Music Score: Woo Wai-Laap. Songs: Joseph Koo, James Wong. CAST: Leslie Cheung Kwok-Wing ("Hui

Man-Keung"), Andy Lau Tak-Wah ("Deng Lik"), Lau Shun ("Uncle Lau"). Opening Date: July 13, 1996.

It's almost surprising that *Shanghai Grand* wasn't titled *Once Upon a Time in Shanghai*; its tremendous scope, gorgeous period recreation, superb acting and heart-pounding action scenes all have the feel of Sergio Leone's 1984 gangster epic *Once Upon a Time in America*. If the film seems slightly atypical for Tsui Hark (despite its anti-Japanese sentiment, the usual Tsui themes aren't present), it nevertheless displays Tsui's talents as a producer to the fullest and finest effect.

*Shanghai Grand* is essentially the classic gangster tale of the small-time hood's rise and fall. In this case the hood is Deng Lik, an ambitious young man who works in sewage disposal (meaning he collects the contents of commodes around the city); Deng lives under the thumb of Shorty Chiu, a cruel, medium-level gangster. One day Deng finds a man and a gun washed up on the shore; the castaway is Hui Man-Keung, a member of the Taiwan Peoples League who escaped from a boat after his comrades were all slain by a vicious woman. Deng is secretly in love with Fung Ching Ching, the daughter of mob boss Fung King-Yiu; one day he rescues Ching Ching from Shorty Chiu, and Chiu retaliates by burning down Deng's house. Deng's mother is rescued by Hui, and a bond is formed between the two men. Deng arranges a meeting with Chiu's boss, Wing, and although Wing manages to chop off one of Deng's fingers, Deng and Hui kill Wing and escape. Boss Fung is grateful to Deng for saving his daughter, and so he awards all of Wing's territories to Deng, who shares them with Hui. Deng rises quickly in the organization and soon proposes to Ching Ching; however, the next day he finds her with Hui. Hui, whom

Deng Lik (Andy Lau) and Hui Man-Keung (Leslie Cheung) in better days in *Shanghai Grand*.

Ching Ching has been in love with since they first met a year ago, didn't know his lover was Deng's intended, but Deng won't listen and ends his friendship with Hui. Hui tells him he'll leave Shanghai once his mission is finished: to find the woman who shot his comrades. What he doesn't know is that the woman is working for Fung, who was the real power behind the shooting on the boat. When Fung finds out that Deng wants to marry Ching Ching, he secretly arranges to have Deng killed by the same woman, but the plan backfires and she is killed by a giant constrictor snake she'd tried to unleash on Deng. Meanwhile, an accidental meeting between Fung and Hui ends in tragedy when Hui kills Fung and the enraged daughter retaliates, wounding Hui and ending their romance. Ching Ching is devastated, and finally Fung's right-hand man, Uncle

Lau, comes to Deng and begs him to help Ching Ching. Deng takes over as mob boss but warns his men that Hui is off-limits—he wants Hui for himself. The two men meet for a last time at a plush New Year's party where Deng shoots Hui; then, regretting his action, Deng tries to get Hui out of Shanghai. Deng tries to cover Hui's escape by claiming to have killed him, but he is overheard by a follower of Hui's who avenges Hui by killing Deng. Hui is left alone, dying, on a car out of Shanghai to think back to his friendship with Deng.

*Shanghai Grand* is rich in both story and design. It tells its saga in a non-traditional style, with printed chapter headings (á la silent film title cards) and intricate flashbacks spaced throughout. The plot is constantly involving and well-paced, wisely focusing on Deng and Hui (although a large cast of supporting characters is solid as well). Visually, *Shanghai Grand* makes lovely use of a sepia-toned palette, some unusual gradated filters, black-and-white for some of the flashbacks, and superb production design.

*Shanghai Grand* does seem slightly anachronistic at times— Ching Ching is obsessed with *Gone with the Wind*, a 1939 American film, which probably played in Shanghai while it was under occupation by the Japanese, but there's virtually no mention made of this (the Japanese are involved, however, in one flashback sequence, when Hui was an escaped Chinese soldier making his perilous way through Japanese-occupied regions). It also seems strange that Hui is involved with a Taiwan organization and not a resistance movement in Shanghai (or even Hong Kong); perhaps the answer is as simple as a small homage to the ties between the Hong Kong and Taiwanese film industries.

But these are questions that are unlikely to arise while watching the film, especially in light of the two stellar lead performances. Andy Lau imbues Deng with a quiet, stoic rage, but still finds time to flash a million-dollar smile. The film really belongs to Leslie Cheung as Hui, though; Cheung, so good as the delicate lead in films like Tsui's *A Chinese Ghost Story* and Stanley Kwan's *Rouge*, is equally superb here as the tough, passionate Hui. His death scene, as a soft smile lights his face and one tear edges down his cheek, is one of the best in all of Hong Kong cinema; even the hardest-bitten cynics can't fail to be moved by it.

*Shanghai Grand* is also considerably more than an epic gangster tale — it contains one of the most memorable action sequence to grace any non-martial arts extravaganza when Deng and Hui take on Wing in the upper floor of a ritzy club. The choreography works perfectly for the two protagonists: Deng has just had his hand nailed to a table top, while Hui knows a gun is dangling near the window just out of reach. All hell breaks loose when Hui grabs the gun, which only has three bullets; after that it becomes Hui's club, while Deng shatters the table and uses the nail-studded board still stuck to his hand as a deadly glove.

Add to the splendid visuals some lovely Joseph Koo-James Wong songs and a lush musical score by Woo Wai Laap, and you've got one of the best period gangster films to come out of Hong Kong.

*Shanghai Grand* was a financial success, placing at number 13 for the year, earning a total of $20,837,056. It also received four nominations from the Hong Kong Film Awards— for Best Cinematography (Poon Hang-Sang), Best Art Direction (Yu Ka On), Best Make-Up and Costume Design (Yu Ka On), and Best Action Choreography (Stephen Tung Wai).

## Black Mask

Producer/Writer, 1996. Cantonese: *Hak Hap*. Mandarin: *Hei Xia*. Literally: *Black Hero*. Director: Daniel Lee Yan-Kong. Action Director: Yuen Wo-Ping. Co-Writers: Koan Hui On, Teddy Chan Tak-Sum, Joe Ma Wai-Ho. Art Direction: Eddie Ma Poon-Chiu, Bill Lui. Make-Up/Costume Design: Fung Kwan Man, Kwan Mei Bo. Music Score (Hong Kong version): Teddy Robin. CAST: Jet Li Lian-Jie ("Tsui Chik/Black Mask"), Lau Ching Wan ("Inspector Shek"), Karen Mok [Mok Man-Wai] ("Tracy"), Françoise Yip Fong-Wah ("Yeuk-Lan"), Xiong Xin-Xin [Hung Yan-Yan] ("Kau's Lieutenant"), Moses Chan Ho ("701 Man"), Anthony Wong Chau-Sang ("King Kau"). Opening Date (Hong

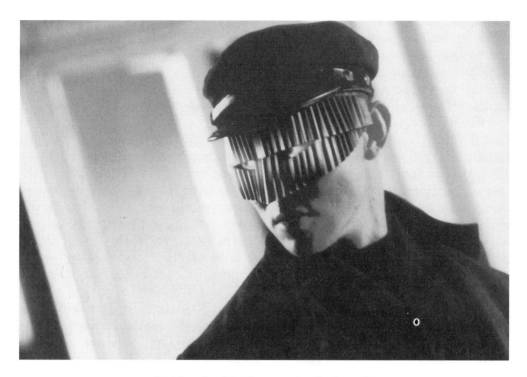

**Jet Li as the title character in *Black Mask*.**

Kong): November 9, 1996. Opening Date (U.S.): May 14, 1999.

*Black Mask* is probably the comic book-superhero film that Tsui Hark the comic book fan has been itching to make for years. It's got a powerful lead, secret identities, supervillains, hidden lairs, gadgetry galore, funny girlfriends and gallons of high-octane action; because it's in the contemporary style of comic books (i.e., *Batman: The Dark Knight Returns*), it also has a hero with a tortured psyche, a dark visual look, drugs, twisted sex and gore. About the only thing it's missing is a cape.

It's the story of Tsui Chik, who was once part of the elite 701 Squad, a corp of soldiers who had their nerves surgically destroyed so they would feel no pain. When their creators realized the 701s were dangerous, they tried to destroy them; Tsui Chik got himself and Yuek-Lan out, then went into hiding. Tsui now works in a library, trying to forget his past; he's a man of mystery to co-worker Tracy, who has a slight crush on him. Tsui's best friend is a cop, Inspector Shek, whose brooding aura and violent tendencies have earned him the nickname "The Rock"; Shek worries that Tsui's pacifist philosophy is at odds with the real world and will get him hurt. He mentions a case he's involved with, in which someone is gruesomely knocking off all the drug lords in Hong Kong. Shek sets up a meeting with the last of these mob bosses, King Kau; during the meeting the 701s attack but are stopped by the sudden appearance of Black Mask (Tsui Chik), who throws razor-edged CDs at his foes. King Kau is injured and taken to the hospital, and Shek is reprimanded by his boss, who thinks Shek is the Black Mask. Tsui Chik, worried that he may be endangering the lives of his co-workers, quits the library but is pursued by Tracy, who is with him when the 701s attack. They manage to escape, and he takes her to his home, an old factory in an industrial area. Tsui now realizes what the 701s are up to: Led by the fiendish, long-haired Commander Hung, they're trying to take over drug operations in Asia. Their goal: to make enough money to repair the surgical damage inflicted on them as 701s. When the 701s issue an ultimatum about the hospitalized King Kau, Black Mask and Shek both fight them as they rampage through the hospital. Black Mask finally saves Yeuk-Lan but is badly injured himself. Yeuk-Lan chases him to his home, and they fight as they climb one of the tall scaffoldings atop his building. When Yeuk-Lan has a clear shot at him, she hesitates— and is killed in that moment by Commander Hung. Black Mask and Tracy escape, and Tracy nurses him back to health. Meanwhile, Shek has tracked down the location of the 701s— right beneath the police station. He goes after them and is captured, but Black Mask appears to save the day. Black Mask fights his way through the 701s, frees Shek, and finally faces Commander Hung, who fights him with laser guns, poisonous gas and kung fu. Black Mask finally kills Hung with one of his CD weapons, and the 701s are terminated. Tsui Chik — no longer Black Mask — bids farewell to Tracy and Shek; he's leaving Hong Kong in hopes of finding a cure to repair his mutilated nerves.

As undeniably fun as *Black Mask* is, it suffers from some of the same problems that plagued *Love in the Time of Twilight*— chiefly, a meandering, unfocused script. The film opens with a slam-bang action sequence of Black Mask taking on a small army, but we have no real idea of who he's fighting or why. Ideas and characters are established only to be dropped abruptly; for example, by the film's climax Tracy has adopted the role of sidekick to Black Mask, but she doesn't appear in the finale after that. Likewise, King Kau — the film's main

villain, aside from the 701s— is taken to the hospital and becomes the center of a conflagration, but is never shown after his initial scene.

But the script's biggest and most unforgivable problems revolve around its eponymous hero. *Black Mask* wants to both revel in the superhero mythos and deconstruct it (the film has scenes of television commentators editorializing on the psychology of superheroes), but the script doesn't pursue either idea far enough. We know nothing about Tsui Chik or the 701s; questions far outweigh answers. What country were the 701s working for (they're a mix of ethnic types; at one point Tsui Chik mentions that he's going to Asia, so the 701s are apparently not based there)? Why did destroying their nerves turn them into superheroes? If they were thought to be so dangerous, why aren't they being hunted now?

The film also hints at a radical idea that it never explores: That tough Inspector Shek and/or Tsui Chik himself might be gay. Although Jet Li has tremendous chemistry with Françoise Yip, neither Tsui nor Shek has a girlfriend; Shek at one point invites Tsui to live with him; after Black Mask saves Yeuk-Lan in the hospital, Shek is furious with him; Shek dislikes Tracy and nearly beats her up at one point in the library; and Tsui tells Tracy that he doesn't like women because "they're snobbish." The film ends with Tracy, Tsui and Shek posing together for a photo, implying a triangle, but the closest thing to flirtation that's existed between any of them has been with Tsui and Shek. It would certainly have put *Black Mask* into a whole different arena had it seriously explored the psychology of a cop in love with a masked vigilante, but it would also have removed *Black Mask* forever from the mainstream, a financial risk that even Tsui's not willing to take.

*Black Mask* may be reminiscent of *Love in the Time of Twilight* in terms of failures, but *Black Mask* is ultimately a far more successful film. Despite the muddled script and plot holes, it's held together by its design, action and the sheer star presence of its leads. Jet Li has always been underappreciated as an actor, and he gives Tsui Chik both great inner strength and desperation; but it is as Black Mask that he really shines, of course, moving with panther-like grace and agility (plus he looks extraordinarily good in a mask!). He's matched by Lau Ching Wan, who has perfected the driven cop character in a number of terrific films, including *Expect the Unexpected* and Johnnie To's astonishing *Running Out of Time*. Karen Mok, one of the most vivacious performers around, is great fun as Tracy, with Françoise Yip providing the ideal balance as the intense Yeuk-Lan. Of course, the film is stolen at one point by Anthony Wong as King Kau. Wong is arguably the best character actor in the world today (check out his award-winning work in *The Untold Story*, *Beast Cops* or *Ordinary Heroes*), and it's a pity that he and Tsui haven't worked together more. The always-inventive Wong plays scumlord King Kau as a long-haired, gold-toothed freak in leather print underwear and very little else. Watch Wong in the scene where he opens a box to display his daughter's severed leg to Shek; any other actor would play the scene for pathos or rage, but Wong plays it as if he understands the cruel joke being played on him and is determined to laugh along. Wong — like Tsui — never takes the easy way out.

*Black Mask*'s superb cast is matched by the talent on the other side of the camera. The film has a smoky, lived-in industrial look; even the Black Mask itself looks like used, corrugated metal. The optical effects (by Tsui's Cinefex Workshop) are excellent, with Black Mask being required

periodically to dodge red and blue laser beams and the strange circular ray fired by Hung's special gun in the film's finale. Teddy Robin provides a pounding score fueled by a catchy surf guitar–style riff. And, of course, Yuen Wo-Ping's action choreography is topnotch; his over-the-top wire-rigging fits *Black Mask*'s superhero theme to a tee.

*Black Mask* even comes with its share of in-jokes, nods and winks. Black Mask's weapon of choice is a razor-edged CD, which he hurls out with such accuracy and force that his victims die instantly; is it pure coincidence that pirated video CDs were killing off part of the Hong Kong film industry at the same time (and still are)? Airplanes are featured throughout the film, either in the background of shots or on the soundtrack; *Black Mask* was released six months before the handover and a year-and-a-half before the relocation of the airport, so the planes serve as a reminder of a changing Hong Kong. Considering that *Black Mask* is the last Tsui film shot in Hong Kong before the handover, it's surprising that it's not more politically oriented.

*Black Mask* performed adequately upon its initial Hong Kong release, showing up in the number 29 spot for the year, with $13,286,788.00. On its American release it took in $12,491,455 (U.S. dollars). It received three nominations at the 16th Hong Kong Film Awards: for Best Art Direction (Eddie Ma Poon-Chiu, Bill Lui), Best Make-Up and Costume Design (Fung Kwan Man, Kwan Mei Bo), and Best Action Choreography (Yuen Wo-Ping).

Director Daniel Lee Yan-Kong should not be confused with Danny Lee the actor, who appeared in the Tsui-produced *The Killer*. Daniel Lee Yan-Kong also directed the wrenching drama *Till Death Do Us Part*, with Anita Yuen taking a serious role as a housewife abandoned by her husband.

Poster for *Once Upon a Time in China and America.*

For its American release, *Black Mask* received a number of changes, the most significant being the loss of Teddy Robin's score (it was replaced by a collection of rap songs). Tsui Chik's voice-over was expanded in the beginning, and certain character scenes (notably of Tracy and of King Kau) were cut. Although a good voice actor was provided for Jet Li, the quality of the English dubbing was poor overall and didn't seem to have really been mixed with the rest of the film's sound.

## Once Upon a Time in China and America

Producer/Writer, 1997. Cantonese: *Wong Fei Hung Ji Sai Wik Hung Si*. Mandarin: *Huang2 Fei1 Hong2 Zhi1 Xi1 Yu4 Xiong2 Shi1*. Literally: *Wong Fei Hung: West Territory Mighty Lion*. AKA: *Once Upon a*

*Time in China 6.* Director: Sammo Hung Kam-Bo. Action Director: Sammo Hung Kam-Bo. Co-Writers: Sharon Hui Sa-Long, Roy Szeto, Philip Kwok Wai-Chung, Sze Mei-Yee, So Man-Sing. CAST: Jet Li ("Wong Fei-Hung"), Rosamund Kwan ("Aunt Yee"), Xiong Xin-Xin ("Seven"), Jeff Wolfe ("Billy"), Kwok Pong Chan ("Sol"). Opening Date: February 1, 1997.

Tsui Hark continues Wong Fei-Hung's genre-hopping in the sixth *Once Upon a Time in China* feature film. After tackling pirates in *V*, now Wong Fei-Hung, Aunt Yee and Club Foot (called "Seven" here) head to the American West to help Bucktooth Sol, who is opening a Po Chi Lam herb shop in a Texan town. En route they encounter hostile Indians, and when Wong is injured in the aftermath of an attack he loses his memory and winds up in the Indian camp, where he's reluctantly accepted as a new member of the tribe. Yee and Seven, meanwhile, encounter the white man's hostility in the Texan town, unaware that the town is rife with corruption. Only Billy, a likable young gunslinger, stands with the Chinese when the town's whites finally turn against them, and it's up to Wong Fei-Hung to recover his identity and save the day in a final showdown with the corrupt officials' hired guns.

It's so easy to think of Sammo Hung as "that Hong Kong movie star who proves you don't have to be thin to kick ass" that Sammo's career as one of Hong Kong cinema's best and most influential directors is sometimes overlooked. Sammo made the first great new wave kung fu horror film with *Encounters of the Spooky Kind* (1981), the excellent character piece *Pedicab Driver*, and one of the best recent Jackie Chan films, *Mr. Nice Guy*. Somehow the hardworking Sammo found enough time in between directing Jackie and starring in the American television series *Martial Law* to direct *Once Upon a Time in China and America*, the film which reunited Jet Li and the role of legendary hero Wong Fei-Hung. Tsui stepped back to produce, and while this marriage of titans could have ended in disaster, instead it produced a film sparkling with wit, excitement and unexpected pathos.

Sammo and Tsui's vision of the American Old West is the one that movies had half-a-century ago, before political correctness and post-modernism forever destroyed the childhood game of cowboys and indians. After our heroes arrive in the Old West via train and stagecoach, the film really picks up speed with an old-fashioned Indian attack, complete with whooping braves, rifle-slinging cowpokes and flying tomahawks. Of course, they simultaneously subvert tradition by inserting Wong and his entourage into the mix, writing a whole new set of rules for a favorite youthful pastime. Sammo's cam-

era work is as smooth as his famous fight choreography, moving effortlessly from capturing breathtaking widescreen landscapes to whirling with Wong's lightning-fast blows.

This is, though, a Wong Fei-Hung movie (which has its own set of established rules), and so most of the white cowboys must fall into the role of evil, Chinese-hating bigots; fortunately, there's also a genuinely likable American good guy, young Billy (delightfully played by Jeff Wolfe). And there are Chinese villains, too—aside from the required character of the betrayer who has sold out his own people to the Westerners, there's a half-breed, mustachioed man-in-black who kills wolves for fun and proves to be Wong's ultimate nemesis.

Where *Once Upon a Time in China and America* delves into the Western's post-modernist possibilities is in its depiction of Chinese emigrants struggling to establish their own identity in a Western town. They must deal with more than merely the prejudice of the townspeople; even their architecture doesn't mesh. It's telling that the film's final triumph is not Wong's defeat of the antagonists but the erection of a Chinese arch leading into Chinatown.

The film's take on Native Americans tries (with only partial success) to straddle a line between old and new representations. While the Indians are scalping, howling killers in the initial fight sequence, they become noble savages once Wong enters their world. Wong's amnesia provides for both humor and sentimentality—he becomes an Indian brave basically because of his astonishing kung fu skills (which he employs to defeat a rival tribe), but also because he shares a love of homeland with his new benefactors, even while realizing their homeland is not the one he loves.

The other great love of Wong's life — Aunt Yee — becomes paradoxically more and less interesting in this installment. She demonstrates more of her own fighting abilities here than previously seen, but she's definitely out of place in the macho world of cowboys, Indians and kung fu fighters (in fact, she's even told throughout the film that there are "no women allowed!"). Sammo has also dropped Tsui's "shadow play" approach to Yee and Wong's romance, although he's kept in the nearly-obligatory scene in which Yee puts on male clothing (it is genuinely outrageous fun to see her walk into a bar decked out in her cowboy duds). Sammo has also added one of the loveliest shots of Yee's yearning in the entire series: When Wong goes missing after the Indian attack, Yee stands alone in the nighttime rain under an umbrella, crying silently.

Jet Li slides back into his trademark role elegantly, once again bringing grace and humor to the ultimate kung fu fighter. He still proudly utters English syllables, which are utter nonsense; he lectures his friends, completely ignorant of the fact that they're nodding off around him. His bewilderment over his amnesia-induced loss of identity is heartfelt and poignant, and his rage toward his opponent in the climactic fight is palpable. Rosamund Kwan is as lovable as ever, despite her reduced role, but the film is nearly stolen (as Once Upon a Time in China III was) by Xiong Xin-Xin as Club Foot/Seven. Xiong is a hurricane of intensity, and his combat with Jet (when he attempts to bring back Wong's memory by forcing him to use his kung fu) may be the best scene in the film.

Once Upon a Time in China and America keeps the series fresh by inserting Wong into a whole new situation while maintaining the values and ideals of the previous films. It's also a fascinating "out-sider's" look at the Western genre; and, as pure entertainment, it's a hoot from first frame to last.

Once Upon a Time in China and America was a smash at the Hong Kong box office, placing at number 5 for 1997 and grossing $30,268,415.

Sammo Hung was nominated for a 1998 Hong Kong Film Award for Best Action Choreography.

The budget for Once Upon a Time in China and America was $12 million (U.S. dollars), an almost-unheard-of amount for a Hong Kong film.

In Hong Kong Panorama '97–'98 critic Li Cheuk-To notes that 1997's three main martial arts films—Once Upon a Time in China and America, Jackie Chan's Who Am I? and Donnie Yen's Legend of the Wolf—all dealt with amnesia, suggesting a desire on the part of a handover-obsessed Hong Kong to simply forget the past.

In 2000 Jackie Chan released his similarly-themed Shanghai Noon, in which he played an Imperial Guard who must head to the turn-of-the-century American West, where he becomes first an Indian brave, then a desperado, all to rescue the Princess. Chan claimed in some interviews that Once Upon a Time in China and America was based on his original idea.

## Double Team

Director, 1997. AKA: The Colony. Producer: Moshe Diamant. Co-Producers: Rick Nathanson, Nansun Shi. Screenwriters: Don Jakoby and Paul Mones. Music: Gary Chang. Production Designer: Marek Dobrowolski. Cinematography: Peter Pau. CAST: Jean-Claude Van Damme ("Jack Quinn"), Dennis Rodman ("Yaz"), Paul Freeman ("Goldsmythe"), Mickey Rourke

("Stavros"). Opening Date (U.S.): April 4, 1997. Opening Date (Hong Kong): May 8, 1997.

*Double Team* was Tsui Hark's debut as an English-language director, and as such it should have been a cause for celebration; unfortunately, the only celebration it's likely to spawn is a wake. Although it is undeniably a gorgeous-looking film with some witty production design and solid action, a cliché-ridden script and abominable acting by the leads dooms it from the get-go.

You know you're in trouble when a film opens with a hero named Jack Quinn, a villain named Stavros (inexplicably, considering he's played as an American) and a second banana named Yaz. After an exciting pre-credits sequence of Quinn in action as a spy (plainly influenced by the James Bond films), the film settles into its plot: Quinn wants to retire to spend time with his pregnant wife, but he's called back into "the game" when his old foe Stavros, a terrorist, reappears. Quinn jets to Antwerp, where he hooks up with Yaz, a rainbow-haired and pierced black market arms salesman. Then it's on to Belgium, where a tip places Stavros at an amusement park. Quinn sets his trap, but the trap closes instead on Stavros' young son, who is killed by a tiger on display at the park. Quinn pursues Stavros through the amusement park and into a nearby hospital, but the terrorist finally escapes after badly wounding Quinn. Quinn awakens to find that he's in "The Colony," a mysterious island where failed spies who are still useful are kept captive. The Colony is a high-tech anti-terrorist institute/prison; Quinn immediately begins planning an escape. When Stavros sends him a message that he's got Quinn's pregnant wife, Quinn steps up his plans and succeeds in getting away. He heads to Yaz, who equips him and finally agrees to help him. They fly to Rome, where Stavros is masquerading as an art dealer and holding Quinn's wife. Quinn — also sought now by The Colony's Goldsmythe — tries to lure Stavros out into the open, but Stavros has a sniper waiting for him. Quinn ends up chasing the sniper, hoping to obtain information on Stavros, but all he gets is an empty pill vial with his wife's name on it. Yaz takes the vial to his contacts in Rome, a brotherhood of high-tech monks who track the prescription to a particular hospital where Quinn's wife is about to give birth. Quinn and Yaz fight through Stavros' men at the hospital but find that Stavros has taken Quinn's new son to the Coliseum. Quinn and Yaz follow and find that Stavros has set up a particularly vicious game: The floor of the ancient monument is studded with landmines, and Quinn must fight his way past both explosives and Stavros to reach his infant son before a tiger is released into the arena. Yaz bursts forth on a motorcycle and retrieves the baby, but Quinn must elude the hungry tiger. He finally leads the tiger to Stavros, who steps on one of his own mines; Stavros and the tiger are annihilated together. Just when Quinn thinks he's won, Goldsmythe appears, but Yaz pulls a smoke bomb and Quinn and his son escape.

The first distressing thing about *Double Team* is how completely lacking it is in the elements that make Tsui Hark's work so identifiable. It is extremely well shot by Hong Kong cinematographer Peter Pau, but otherwise it feels like a standard, hero-driven American action vehicle. In the second English-language outing *Knock Off*, Tsui was recognizably at the wheel, with references to the handover, strong women and technology. Here only the latter is visible; the film's middle act, when Quinn is held prisoner at The Colony, is easily the best part of *Double Team*, with some

**Tsui directs on the set of *Double Team*.**

spectacular CGI optical effects, excellent production design and a good sense of building tension as Quinn plots his escape.

But the film's first and third acts (even the three-act structure is atypically formulaic for Tsui Hark) are standard action fare, with Van Damme playing the stoic good guy (who wants to retire, another overused cliché of this genre). Stavros has the potential to be the film's most interesting character — he's driven by a desire to avenge the death of his son and even seems to feel an attraction to Quinn's wife — but the script sadly consigns him to the role of villain, plain and simple. *Double Team*'s script is obviously more interested in getting to the next display of Van Damme's brawn than in exploring its characters.

Even so, it could have been a fine little action film... were Tsui not saddled with two of the most embarrassingly-inept performers to grace the screen in some time. At least with Van Damme no one expects Oscar-winning work, and his physical attributes can carry him most of the time; but Dennis Rodman lacks even that. And Van Damme can honestly claim that English is not his native language.

Mickey Rourke turns in a completely forgettable performance as Stavros. The only two performers of merit are Paul Freeman (who was so good in *Raiders of the Lost Ark*) and — no surprise here — Xiong Xin-Xin, the film's only Hong Kong actor, as a Chinese hitman who takes on Quinn. Xiong's presence in the film is utterly inexplicable, but when a knife pops out from between his toes as he whirls around Quinn, who cares?

*Double Team* flopped in both the U.S.

and Hong Kong: It grossed $11,328,565 (U.S. dollars) in America and only $3,785,520 in Hong Kong, where it placed at number 98 in the year's box office list.

*Double Team* won three coveted "Razzies," given to honor the worst film achievements of the year: Worst New Star (Dennis Rodman), Worst Screen Couple (Dennis Rodman and Jean-Claude Van Damme) and Worst Supporting Actor (Rodman again). Despite such awards, *Double Team* also opened to some decent reviews, especially from Kevin Thomas in the *L.A. Times* ("A slam-banger… one of Van Damme's best!") and the *Chicago Tribune's* Michael Wilmington ("A stylish action show, it's fast, sassy and beautifully shot, shaped and edited by a master director").

Van Damme (who has done more to promote the Hong Kong film industry in America than nearly anyone else by hiring directors John Woo, Ringo Lam and Tsui) said he chased Tsui for nearly five years; Tsui said he was intrigued by *Double Team's* script, which reminded him of the Bond films he adores. The film was shot on location throughout Europe, with the Arles Coliseum in France doubling for the Roman Coliseum.

## Time and Tide

Writer/Director/Producer, 2000. Cantonese: *Shun Lau Yik Lau*. Co-Screenwriter: Koan Hui. Cinematography: Ko Chiu Lam, Herman Yau. CAST: Nicholas Tse, Wu Bai, Anthony Wong, Joventino Couto Remotigue, Cathy Chui, Candy Lo Hau Yam. Opening Date: October 2000.

Produced by the new Columbia Pictures Film Production Asia, *Time and Tide* marks the first Hong Kong–based film directed by Tsui in four years (since *Tri-Star*). Although Columbia Pictures Film

Production Asia also financed Ang Lee's *Crouching Tiger, Hidden Dragon* and bought world rights to Zhang Yimou's films *The Road Home* and *Not One Less*, *Time and Tide* is the first film shot completely in Hong Kong to be financed by an American major. In the article "Hollywood Jumps In" (from *Far Eastern Economic Review*, April 20, 2000, article by Karen Mazurkewich), Tsui noted that, although he was originally somewhat apprehensive, he agreed to the deal when it was clear that he would have artistic freedom. Columbia Pictures Film Production Asia's managing director noted: "What makes Hong Kong cinema successful is its energy and spirit, and I was mindful to harness that." With a budget of HK$25 million (about $3 million in U.S. terms), the only compromises were legal ones: Brand names couldn't be shown and original music had to be purchased, not simply licensed.

In an interview with Stephen Short for Time@CNN.com (May 3, 2000), Tsui mentioned that the idea for *Time and Tide* first came to him about four years ago, and that it was inspired by a line in a famous song: "It's a song I listen to when I feel depressed or very moody. I decided I wanted to translate that feeling into something thematic. It's a film about capturing moments." It tells the story of Tyler, a young man who is forced to take a job as a Triad bodyguard when his girlfriend unexpectedly becomes pregnant; Tyler's path crosses with a legendary hitman returning to Hong Kong after many years in exile, and together they unite to defeat a South American drug cartel.

In the film's first major review, Richard Corliss wrote of *Time and Tide*: "If it doesn't win a Best Film prize, this spectacle of perpetual motion is surely the movie-est movie of the year. Like graffiti written in blood, it spells out Tsui's message to the industry he left in 1996: I'm back, lean and mean, guns blazing." (From *Time Asia*, October 30, 2000).

new actors and utilizing state-of-the-art special computer effects.

## The Legend of Zu

Director, 2001. Cantonese: *Sook San Jing Juen*. AKA: *Zu Mountain Official Legend*. CAST: Ekin Cheng Yi-Kin, Louis Koo Tin Lok, Cecilia Cheung Pak-Chi, Patrick Tam Yiu-Man, Zhang Ziyi. Opening Date: 2001.

Tsui remakes/follows up his 1983 classic *Zu: Warriors from the Magic Mountain* with this new edition, filmed in Beijing with some of Hong Kong's hottest

## Black Mask II: City of Masks

Director, 2001. In production as of this writing, *Black Mask II* lacks the considerable presence of Jet Li in the title role, but what it gains is Tsui as director. With a cast that includes several well-known American wrestlers (Tsui seems to have an interest in American wrestlers—his office decoration includes several action figures), the film is being shot in Thailand.

# 6

# NON-FILM PROJECTS

## I. Television

*A Coup in the Family*; *Aries, Scorpio, Aquarius*; etc. (1978, TVB): Two of the series Tsui worked on as a director at TVB, one of the main Hong Kong television stations. When executive Selina Chow hired Tsui for TVB, he requested a job in journalism, but she placed him in the drama section (Chow also hired other New Wave directors for TVB, making her an important behind-the-scenes figure in Hong Kong film). In Hong Kong, television production works at the same frantic pace that feature film production does; many shows appeared every week night.

*Golden Dagger Romance* (Director, 1978, CTV): Tsui left TVB for rival CTV (apparently following Selina Chow), where he directed this nine-episode series, which propelled him to fame and led to his career as a film director. He created a sensation by shooting this costume drama (which was based on the Gu Long novel) as if it were a feature film. The series starred Eddy

Ko Hung, who would also star in Tsui's first two feature films. Tsui later recalled that someone might have suggested him for this series because they'd heard him pitching the idea for *A Chinese Ghost Story* and thought he had an interest in period pieces. His work on *Golden Dagger Romance* led directly to his first feature, *The Butterfly Murders*.

*Wong Fei-Hung: The Series* (Producer, 1996): Tsui Hark's most successful film series continues on in forty episodes of this made-on-video television series. Zhao Wen-Zhou (who played Wong in the fourth and fifth feature films), Max Mok and Kent Cheng all recreate their film roles in this beautifully shot and produced series.

## II. Filmed Interviews

*Portrait of Lin Ching Hsia* (ca. 1988): A Taiwanese feature-length documentary on Lin Ching-Hsia (Brigitte Lin). Tsui is

221

one of a series of host/interviewers. The documentary (which is unsubtitled) features extensive interviews and traces Lin to her childhood home. Even unsubtitled it's interesting, especially for the look at how Tsui and one of his leading ladies interact.

*The Incredibly Strange Film Show* (1989): Jonathan Ross hosted this highly entertaining British television series that focused on two directors in each hour. The segment on Tsui features interviews with Tsui, Nansun Shi, film critic and historian Tony Rayns, and frequent Tsui collaborator John Sham. It also includes clips from *A Chinese Ghost Story, Dangerous Encounter — 1st Kind, Zu: Warriors from the Magic Mountain, We're Going to Eat You* and *A Better Tomorrow*. There's also a brief glimpse of Tsui directing on the set of *A Better Tomorrow III*.

*The Making of "A Chinese Ghost Story II"* (1990): Issued with the Japanese edition of the film, this features many behind-the-scenes shots, including the creation of the special effects.

*Film Without Bounds — The New Hong Kong Cinema* (1992): Produced and directed by Ralph Umard, this short (43 minute) film includes interviews with Tsui and Sylvia Chang, Jackie Chan (Sing Lung), Ringo Lam Ling-Tung, Chow Yun-Fat, John Woo (Ng Yu-Sam), Stephen Chow Sing-Chi and Ching Siu-Tung.

*The Making of "The Wicked City"* (1992): Issued with the Japanese edition of the film.

*Yang + Yin: Gender in Chinese Cinema* (1996): This documentary was made by Hong Kong director Stanley Kwan (*Rouge, Centre Stage*) as part of the British Film Institute's "100 Years of Movies" celebration. Overall, it's a fascinating look at gender and sexuality in Chinese cinema, although the emphasis is on male homosexuality (Kwan "came out" in this film himself). The segment with Tsui is disap-

pointing; although the film's title would lead the viewer to expect an extensive and favorable review of Tsui's work, Kwan uses the segment on Tsui to first focus on Brigitte Lin, then to interrogate Tsui regarding homosexuality in *The Lovers* (Kwan questions Tsui's choice of words in describing homosexual love as being "not real").

## III. Commercials

"China Motion" (1998): Tsui's commercial for this mainland telecommunications company may have had him following in the footsteps of John Woo and Wong Kar-Wai (both of whom had already directed major commercials), but Tsui's is a virtual masterpiece of short-form film, similar in scope and style to Ridley Scott's breakthrough 1984 spot for Apple Computers. This 90-second mini-epic is broken down into three sections: The first, set in the past, shows villagers frantically drumming and sending out birds to warn of an impending flood; the second, in the present, shows engineers working out the logistics of a dam; and in the final segment, futuristic technicians man computerized consoles from which they create their own weather.

According to an interview Tsui gave to the *South China Morning Post*, he only shot for eight days, but post production work took more than two months because almost all of the shots required special effects. The 90-second format was also a challenge: "In films you can spend more time on detail and the atmosphere and mood of the scene. In this, each scene must give your message, clearly and quickly, so you have to be very clear about the message. Everything has to be up front."

Tsui encountered great difficulties shooting on location, including a flooding

Tsui's Photoshop art from *Red Snow*.

Yellow River and arduous treks. In the end, the lengthy ad was usually cut and shown as three 30-second commercials.

"Singapore National Day" (1998): Tsui was given the assignment here of essentially creating a patriotic music video. The spot was created in honor of Singapore National Day, and Tsui was given a song to build his short film around. Unfortunately, he was hampered by both the astonishingly vapid song and a low budget. To emphasize the idea of Singapore moving into the future, he utilized a small, simple story of a boy who grows up to be an astronaut. Later on the spot received some criticism — on the basis of the fact that Singapore has no space program!

## IV. Comic Books

*Red Snow* (1999): Created with Ma Wing Shong, who also created the original comic book that inspired *The Storm Riders*. Tsui provided about 20 percent of the artwork used throughout the comic; his material is easily distinguishable from the rest, since his panels are created in a photorealistic style (they were created on Photoshop — he told me it takes him approximately four hours to create one of the gorgeous, richly-detailed renderings seen in the book!). Tsui also provided several stunning pencil sketches used in the book.

Nansun Shi told me that comic books are Tsui's one big vice, and that his intention in creating *Red Snow* was to prove that Hong Kong comic books — which are normally 90% action, and much of that very bloody — could be beautiful as well.

*Old Master Q*: On October 21, 1999, Tsui gave an interview to *Oriental Daily* in which he announced that he would team up with Wong Jat, creator of the classic comic strip "Old Master Q" ("Lo Fu Ji"), to produce the first web comic theater. Tsui, who is an avowed fan of the "Old Master Q" comics, has also talked about making a live-action feature film based on the comic, which features the bumbling (if very traditional) Master Q.

# FILMOGRAPHIES OF SELECTED COLLABORATORS

Below are listed a few of the actors and/or technical personnel who have worked with Tsui. I have chosen either those who have worked repeatedly with him, or those who may have only done one project with him but have a standing in the industry that makes the collaboration notable. These are by no means complete filmographies, but are rather films made with Tsui Hark (in some cases I have briefly listed other notable films). Abbreviations are as follows: A=Actor, AC=Action Designer, AD=Art Director, CIN=Cinematographer, CMU=Costume and Make-Up, COM=Composer, D=Director, E=Editor, P=Producer, W=Writer, *=Nominated for a Hong Kong Film Award, **=Won a Hong Kong Film Award.

**Kenny Bee** (A)— Amiable leading man.
  *The Chinese Feast*
  *Shanghai Blues*
  *Spy Games*

**Yuen Biao** (A, AC)— One of Jackie Chan's Peking Opera "brothers," a top action actor.
  *Once Upon a Time in China* (A)
  *Zu: Warriors From the Magic Mountain*
    (A, AD)

**Jackie Chan** (A)— Hong Kong's "Big Brother," and one of the world's top action stars.
  *The Twin Dragons*

**Moses Chan** (A)— Lanky young actor.
  *Black Mask*
  *The Blade*

**Sylvia Chang** (A)— One of Hong Kong's finest comedic actresses; recently won the

225

HK Film Award for Best Screenplay for *Tempting Heart* (which she also directed); appeared in international arthouse hit *The Red Violin*.

*Aces Go Places**
*Aces Go Places 2*
*Aces Go Places 3*
*The Banquet*
*A Chinese Ghost Story: The Tsui Hark Animation*
*It Takes Two*
*Shanghai Blues**
*The Twin Dragons*

**Che Chung Taai** (W)

*The Chinese Feast*
*Tri-Star*

**Adam Cheng** (A)—Exotic-looking actor and singer.

*Gunmen*
*Zu: Warriors from the Magic Mountain*

**Kent Cheng Juk-Si** (A)—Amiable, rotund actor.

*Diary of a Big Man*
*Once Upon a Time in China*
*Once Upon a Time in China V*

**Mark Cheng Ho-Nam** (A)—Handsome, serious actor, most recently seen as a Japanese ninja in *A Man Called Hero*.

*Gunmen*
*Peking Opera Blues*

**Jacky Cheung Hok-Yau** (A)—Popular singer/actor; is also featured in Wong Kar-Wai's films *Days of Being Wild*, *As Tears Go By* and *Ashes of Time*.

*A Chinese Ghost Story II**
*A Chinese Ghost Story III*
*The Banquet*
*Once Upon a Time in China**
*The Raid*

*Swordsman**
*The Wicked City*

**Leslie Cheung Kwok-Wing** (A)—Boyishly good-looking (and ageless) pop superstar who is also one of Hong Kong's finest actors. Known to Western audiences for such art films as *Farewell My Concubine*, *The Bride with White Hair* and *Happy Together*.

*The Banquet*
*A Better Tomorrow*
*A Better Tomorrow II**
*The Chinese Feast*
*A Chinese Ghost Story*
*A Chinese Ghost Story II*
*Shanghai Grand*
*Tri-Star*

**Maggie Cheung Man-Yuk** (A) Former Miss Hong Kong and ingenue who is now considered one of Hong Kong's finest actresses. Her work also includes Stanley Kwan's *Centre Stage***, *The Heroic Trio*, and the Western films *Irma Vep* and *The Chinese Box*.

*The Banquet*
*Green Snake*
*Happy Ghost III*
*New Dragon Inn**
*The Twin Dragons*

**William Cheung Suk Ping** (AD, CMU)—Talented art director and designer who has also worked for Wong Kar-Wai (*Happy Together, Ashes of Time,** etc.).

*The Blade** (AD)
*The Chinese Feast* (AD, CMU)
*A Chinese Ghost Story III* (AD)
*The East Is Red** (CMU)
*Green Snake** (CMU)
*It Takes Two** (AD)
*The Lovers** (AD/CMU)
*New Dragon Inn* (AD)
*Swordsman II*** (CMU)
*Zu: Warriors from the Magic Mountain** (AD)

**Cheung Taan** (W)

*The East Is Red*
*New Dragon Inn*

**David Chiang (Keung Dai-Wai)** (A)—
'70s-era martial arts star who, like Ti
Lung, also found success as an older leading man.

*The Banquet*
*Just Heroes*
*Once Upon a Time in China II*
*The Twin Dragons*

**Ching Siu-Tung** (D, AC)—Probably Tsui's
most important (and frequent) collaborator. Ching also showed his directorial flair
in *The Heroic Trio*.

*A Better Tomorrow II\** (AC)
*A Chinese Ghost Story\** (nominated for
  both D and AC)
*A Chinese Ghost Story II\** (D, AC—
  nominated for AC)
*A Chinese Ghost Story III* (D, AC—
  nominated for AC)
*Dangerous Encounter—1st Kind* (AC)
*The East Is Red* (D, AC)
*Happy Ghost III* (AC)
*I Love Maria* (AC)
*The Killer* (AC)
*New Dragon Inn\** (AC)
*Peking Opera Blues\** (AC)
*The Raid* (D, AC)
*Swordsman\*\** (AC)
*Swordsman II\** (D, AC—nominated for
  AC)
*A Terracotta Warrior\** (D, AC—nomi-
  nated for AC)

**Chow Yun-Fat** (A)—Probably the second
most popular Hong Kong actor in the world,
with appearances in the Western films *Anna
and the King* and *The Corruptor*.

*A Better Tomorrow\*\**
*A Better Tomorrow II*
*A Better Tomorrow III*

*Diary of a Big Man*
*The Killer*

**Norman Chu Siu-Keung** (A)—Suave star
who can also be seen in *Wing Chun* with
Michelle Yeoh.

*The Magic Crane*
*We're Going to Eat You*
*Zu: Warriors from the Magic Mountain*

**Paul Chu Kong** (A)—Fine character actor,
best known as the doomed Sidney in *The
Killer*.

*The Big Heat*
*The Killer\**
*The Raid*

**Paul Chun Pui** (A)—Wonderful comic
actor, recently seen in *Viva Erotica*.

*All the Wrong Spies*
*I Love Maria*
*Peking Opera Blues\**

**Cherie Chung Cho-Hung** (A)—Sweet-
faced actress, also seen in John Woo's *Once
a Thief*.

*It Takes Two*
*Peking Opera Blues*

**David Chung Chi-Man** (CIN, D)

*Dangerous Encounter—1st Kind* (CIN)
*Deception* (D, CIN)
*I Love Maria* (D, CIN)
*The Lovers* (CIN)
*Once Upon a Time in China\** (CIN)

**Dang Bik Yin** (W)

*Once Upon a Time in China*
*Swordsman II*

**Romeo Diaz** (COM)—Usually works with
James Wong.

*A Chinese Ghost Story\*\**
*A Chinese Ghost Story III\**

*Swordsman**
*A Terracotta Warrior***

**Ho Kim-Sing [Hiu Gim Seng] (AD)**
*The Banquet*
*A Chinese Ghost Story II*
*Peking Opera Blues**

**Sam Hui Koon-Kit** (A) — Hugely popular singer/comic actor.
*Aces Go Places*
*Aces Go Places 2*
*Aces Go Places 3*
*Working Class*

**Sammo Hung** (A, AC, D, P) — Multi-talented, stoutly-built martial artist, and another of Jackie Chan's "brothers." Currently an American television star thanks to *Martial Law*.
*The Banquet* (A)
*A Chinese Ghost Story: The Tsui Hark Animation* (A)
*Knock Off* (D, 2nd unit)
*Once Upon a Time in China and America* (D, AC)
*Yes Madam* (P, A)
*Zu: Warriors from the Magic Mountain* (A, AC)

**Eddy Ko Hung** (A) — Long-time character actor, most recently seen in Johnnie To's *The Mission*.
*The Butterfly Murders*
*The East Is Red*
*We're Going to Eat You*

**Joseph Koo [aka Joseph Goo, aka Goo Fung Fai] (COM)** — Frequently collaborates with James Wong.
*A Better Tomorrow**
*A Better Tomorrow II*
*The Butterfly Murders*
*Happy Ghost III*
*Shanghai Grand*
*A Terracotta Warrior***

**Eric Kot** (A) — Large comic actor.
*A Chinese Ghost Story: The Tsui Hark Animation*
*Love in the Time of Twilight**

**Rosamund Kwan Chi-Lam** (A) — Strikingly pretty actress, also paired with Jet Li in *Dr. Wai and the Scripture with No Words*.
*The Banquet*
*The Magic Crane*
*Once Upon a Time in China*
*Once Upon a Time in China II*
*Once Upon a Time in China III*
*Once Upon a Time in China V*
*Once Upon a Time in China and America*
*Swordsman II*

**Leon Lai Ming** (A) — Immensely popular singer/actor, more recently seen in *Comrades: Almost a Love Story* and *City of Glass*.
*The Banquet*
*The Wicked City*

**George Lam Chi-Cheung** (A) — Popular singer and very capable comic leading man.
*All the Wrong Clues*
*All the Wrong Spies*
*The Banquet*

**Lam Ching-Ying** (A) — Eccentric character actor made famous after playing the ghostbuster in *Mr. Vampire*.
*I Love Maria*
*Swordsman*

**Ringo Lam Ling-Tung** (D) — Action film director whose *Full Contact* made him an international sensation.
*Red Lotus Temple*
*The Twin Dragons*

**Andrew Lau** (CIN) — Cinematographer who later became one of Hong Kong's hottest directors with the *Young and Dangerous* series and *The Storm Riders*.

*Once Upon a Time in China III*
*The Wicked City*

**Andy Lau Tak-Wah** (A)—Handsome singer/actor who is nearly ubiquitous in Hong Kong; recently won the Best Actor award for *Running Out of Time*.

*The Banquet*
*Shanghai Grand*

**Lau Ching Wan** (A)—Often called the "Spencer Tracy of Hong Kong," he made his mark in *C'est La Vie, Mon Cheri*; recently seen in *Running Out of Time* and *Where a Good Man Goes*.

*Black Mask*
*Tri-Star*

**Damian Lau** (A)

*The Magic Crane*
*Zu: Warriors from the Magic Mountain*

**Lau Moon Tong** (CIN)

*A Chinese Ghost Story*
*The Magic Crane*
*New Dragon Inn**
*Once Upon a Time in China V*
*Swordsman II*

**Lau Shun** (A)—Possibly Tsui's favorite character actor, he is one of Hong Kong's best chameleons.

*The Chinese Feast*
*A Chinese Ghost Story III*
*The East Is Red*
*Happy Ghost IV*
*Love in the Time of Twilight*
*The Lovers*
*New Dragon Inn*
*Once Upon a Time in China III*
*Once Upon a Time in China IV*
*Once Upon a Time in China V*
*Shanghai Grand*
*Swordsman**
*Swordsman II*

**Lau Siu-Ming** (A)

*The Butterfly Murders*
*A Chinese Ghost Story*
*A Chinese Ghost Story II*
*A Chinese Ghost Story III*
*Swordsman*

**Carman Lee** (A)

*Knock Off*
*Red Lotus Temple*
*The Wicked City*

**Danny Lee Sau-Yin** (A)—Lee is also well known for his appearances in such horrific thrillers as *The Untold Story*.

*Just Heroes*
*The Killer*

**Elizabeth Lee Mei-Fung** (A)

*Gunmen*
*Web of Deception*

**Lillian Lee Bik Dut** (W)—Maybe Hong Kong's best supernatural love story screenwriters, she also penned Stanley Kwan's *Rouge*.

*Green Snake*
*A Terracotta Warrior*

**Loletta Lee Lai-Chun** (A)—Baby-faced former Category III actress.

*Final Victory**
*Happy Ghost IV*
*Shanghai Blues**

**Raymond Lee** (D)

*The East is Red*
*New Dragon Inn*
*Swordsman*

**Waise Lee** (A)—Fine young character actor also known for John Woo's *Bullet in the Head*.

*The Banquet*
*A Better Tomorrow** (for both Supporting Actor and Best New Performer)

*The Big Heat*
*A Chinese Ghost Story II*
*Diary of a Big Man*
*Gunmen*
*Spy Games*
*Swordsman II*
*Web of Deception*

**James Leung** (AD)

*A Chinese Ghost Story III**
*Swordsman II**

**Tony Leung Chiu-Wai** (A)—Sometimes referred to as "Little Tony," he's also appeared in Wong Kar-Wai's *Happy Together* and *Chungking Express.*

*The Banquet*
*A Chinese Ghost Story III*
*I Love Maria*
*The Magic Crane*

**Tony Leung Ka-Fai** (A, W)—The "Big Tony" of the two Leungs; also appeared in Wong Kar-Wai's *Ashes of Time.*

*The Banquet* (A)
*A Better Tomorrow III* (A)
*Gunmen* (A)
*King of Chess** (A, W, nominated for A)
*Laser Man*
*New Dragon Inn*
*The Raid*

**Jet Li Lian-Je** (A)—Mainland kung fu champion who is also a gifted actor and one of Tsui's major star creations.

*Black Mask*
*The Master*
*Once Upon a Time in China*
*Once Upon a Time in China II*
*Once Upon a Time in China III*
*Once Upon a Time in China and America*
*Swordsman II*

**Brigitte Lin Ching-Hsia** (A)—Gorgeous Taiwanese actress turned Hong Kong

superstar, thanks to Tsui's casting of her as the cross-gendered Asia the Invincible. Last seen under a blonde wig in *Chungking Express.*

*All the Wrong Spies*
*The East Is Red*
*New Dragon Inn*
*Peking Opera Blues*
*Swordsman II**
*Web of Deception*
*Zu: Warriors from the Magic Mountain**

**Lo Lieh** (A)—Actor who made it big in the '70s and '80s appearing in such bizarre horror films as *Black Magic 2.*

*Dangerous Encounter—1st Kind*

**Lowell Lo** (COM)

*A Better Tomorrow III**
*The Big Heat*
*The Chinese Feast*
*Tri-Star*

**Bill Lui** (AD)

*Black Mask**
*The Blade*
*Green Snake**
*Once Upon a Time in China V*
*Tri-Star*

**Mark Lui Chung Dak** (COM)

*Green Snake**
*The Lovers**

**Ma Poon-Chiu** (AD)

*Black Mask**
*New Dragon Inn*
*Once Upon a Time in China II**

**Ma Yuk Shing** (AC)

*A Chinese Ghost Story III**
*The East Is Red*
*The Raid*
*Swordsman II**

**Mak Chi Sin** (E)—One of Tsui's most frequent—and frequently honored—collaborators.

*The Chinese Feast*
*A Chinese Ghost Story II**
*A Chinese Ghost Story III**
*The Lovers*
*The Magic Crane*
*Once Upon a Time in China***
*Once Upon a Time in China II**
*Once Upon a Time in China III**
*Once Upon a Time in China V*
*The Raid*
*Swordsman**
*Swordsman II**
*A Terracotta Warrior**

**Carl Mak** (A, P, D)—Rubber-faced comic actor who was also one of the founders of Cinema City.

*Aces Go Places*** (A)
*Aces Go Places 2* (A)
*Aces Go Places 3* (A)
*All the Wrong Clues* (A, P)
*The Banquet* (A)
*It Takes Two* (D, A)

**Mang Hoi** (A, AC)

*The Blade** (AC)
*Yes Madam*** (for A, also nominated for AC)
*Zu: Warriors from the Magic Mountain* (A, AC)

**Max Mok Siu-Chung** (A)—Bug-eyed comic actor.

*Once Upon a Time in China II*
*Once Upon a Time in China III*
*Once Upon a Time in China IV*
*Once Upon a Time in China V*

**Anita Mui Yim-Fong** (A)—Talented actress/singer also called "The Madonna of Asia." Also appeared in Stanley Kwan's *Rouge* and *The Heroic Trio*.

*The Banquet*

*A Better Tomorrow III*
*The Magic Crane*

**Carrie Ng Ka-Lai** (A)—Solid, serious actress who is also a cult favorite due to *Naked Killer* and *Remains of a Woman*.

*Gunmen*
*The Lovers**

**Lawrence Ng** (A)—Long-faced young character actor, excels at arrogant bad guys.

*The Magic Crane*
*New Dragon Inn*

**Ng Man-Fai** (W)

*The Chinese Feast*
*Happy Ghost IV*
*Spy Games*

**Richard Ng Yiu-Hon** (A)—Very sympathetic older character actor.

*The Banquet*
*It Takes Two*

**Peter Pau** (CIN)—One of Hong Kong's finest cinematographers; his recent work includes *Crouching Tiger, Hidden Dragon***.

*The Chinese Feast*
*Double Team*
*The Killer**
*Once Upon a Time in China V*
*Swordsman*
*A Terracotta Warrior**

**Poon Hang-Sang** (CIN)—Another great cinematographer, he also photographed *Centre Stage* and *The Heroic Trio*.

*A Chinese Ghost Story**
*King of Chess*
*Peking Opera Blues**
*Shanghai Grand**

**Michelle Reis** (A)—Lovely actress more recently seen in Wong Kar-Wai's *Fallen Angels*.

*A Chinese Ghost Story II*
*Swordsman II*
*The Wicked City*

**Teddy Robin Kwan** (A, COM, D, P) — Diminutive former pop star (of Teddy Robin and the Playboys), one of Hong Kong's busiest talents over the last twenty years.

*Aces Go Places** (COM)
*Aces Go Places 2* (COM)
*All the Wrong Clues* (A)
*All the Wrong Spies** (D, COM — nominated for both)
*The Banquet* (A)
*Black Mask* (COM)
*Run Tiger Run* (A)
*The Twin Dragons* (A, P)
*Working Class* (A)

**John Sham Kin-Fun** (A, P) — Fuzzy-haired actor and producer.

*The Banquet* (A)
*I Love Maria* (A, P)
*King of Chess* (A)
*Yes, Madam* (A)

**Dean Shek Tin** (A, P) — One of Cinema City's heads turned actor.

*Aces Go Places 3* (P)
*All the Wrong Clues* (P)
*A Better Tomorrow II* (A)
*It Takes Two* (A)
*The Raid* (A)

**Nansun Shi** (P) — Co-founder of Film Workshop, former Production Designer (*All the Wrong Spies*), she was also a principal at Cinema City. Oh, and she's married to Tsui.

*Aces Go Places*
*A Chinese Ghost Story: The Tsui Hark Animation*
*Double Team*
*It Takes Two*
*Knock Off*

**Shing Fui-On** (A) — Large, scary-looking actor who has appeared in over 100 films, almost always as villains.

*A Better Tomorrow II*
*Just Heroes*
*The Killer*
*Tri-Star*

**Shut Tiu Cheuk Hon** [aka Roy Szeto, aka Si To Cheuk Hon] (W) — Probably the writer who has worked with Tsui more than any other.

*A Chinese Ghost Story III*
*Dangerous Encounter — 1st Kind*
*Love in the Time of Twilight*
*Once Upon a Time in China and America*
*Shanghai Blues*
*Zu: Warriors from the Magic Mountain*

**Shut Yam Saam Long** (A) — Lanky actor usually cast as Japanese.

*A Better Tomorrow III*
*Spy Games*

**Ti Lung** (A) — Distinguished actor, former alumni of '70s martial arts epics. Recently won Best Supporting Actor for *The Kid*.

*The Banquet*
*A Better Tomorrow**
*A Better Tomorrow II*

**Johnnie To Kei-Fung** (D) — Probably the most popular Hong Kong director at the end of the '90s, he won 1999's Best Director award for *The Mission*.

*The Big Heat*
*Happy Ghost III*

**Raymond To Kwok-Wai** (W)

*Peking Opera Blues*
*Shanghai Blues*

**Eric Tsang Chi-Wai** (A, D) — Chubby actor who is also a Hong Kong mogul (as one of the forces behind United Filmmakers Organization). Tsang was most recently seen in *Gen X Cops* and *Metade Fumaca*.

> *Aces Go Places* (D)
> *Aces Go Places 2* (D)
> *All the Wrong Clues* (A)
> *The Banquet* (A)
> *Final Victory** (A)
> *The Twin Dragons* (A)

**Kenneth Tsang** (A) — One of HK's busiest character actors.

> *The Banquet*
> *A Better Tomorrow*
> *A Better Tomorrow II*
> *The Killer*
> *Peking Opera Blues*

**Elvis Tsui Kam-Kong** (A) — Huge, intense-looking actor whose best work might be in Derek Yee's *Viva Erotica*.

> *Gunmen*
> *The Lovers*
> *New Dragon Inn*

**Stephen Tung** (AC)

> *A Better Tomorrow*
> *The Blade**
> *Shanghai Grand**

**Jean-Claude Van Damme** (A) — Belgian kick-boxer.

> *Double Team*
> *Knock Off*

**Joey Wang Cho-Yin** (A) — Lovely actress/ singer who has contributed to the soundtracks of *Green Snake* and *The East Is Red*, among others.

> *The Banquet*
> *The Big Heat*
> *A Chinese Ghost Story**
> *A Chinese Ghost Story II*
> *A Chinese Ghost Story III*
> *Diary of a Big Man*
> *The East Is Red*

> *Green Snake*
> *Spy Games*
> *Web of Deception*
> *Working Class*

**Jeff Wolfe** (A) — Young blonde American actor.

> *Knock Off*
> *Once Upon a Time in China and America*

**Anthony Wong Chau-Sang** (A) — The bad boy of HK cinema and one of the world's great character actors (see *Untold Story***, *Beast Cops*** or *Ordinary Heroes**).

> *Black Mask*
> *Time and Tide*

**Arthur Wong Ngok Taai** (CIN)

> *New Dragon Inn**
> *Once Upon a Time in China**
> *Once Upon a Time in China II**
> *Tri-Star*

**James Wong** (A, COM) — Second only to Ching Siu-Tung as Tsui's most frequent — and highly regarded — collaborator.

> *The Banquet* (A)
> *A Better Tomorrow 2* (COM)
> *A Chinese Ghost Story*** (COM)
> *A Chinese Ghost Story III** (COM)
> *A Chinese Ghost Story: The Tsui Hark Animation* (COM, A)
> *Green Snake** (COM)
> *Iron Monkey* (A)
> *Just Heroes* (A)
> *The Lovers** (COM)
> *Once Upon a Time in China*** (COM)
> *The Raid* (COM)
> *Shanghai Blues* (COM)
> *Shanghai Grand* (COM)
> *Swordsman** (COM)
> *Swordsman II** (COM)
> *A Terracotta Warrior*** (COM)
> *The Twin Dragons* (A)

**Jean Wong Ching-Ying** (A)

*The East is Red*
*Iron Monkey*
*Once Upon a Time in China IV*
*Once Upon a Time in China V*

**Wong Kar-Wai** (W)—Screenwriter who later became an arthouse fave as director of such films as *Chungking Express*.

*Final Victory**

**Raymond Wong Bak-Ming** (P, A, W, D)

*Aces Go Places 3* (P)
*All the Wrong Spies* (W)
*The Chinese Feast* (P)
*A Chinese Ghost Story: The Tsui Hark Animation* (A)
*Happy Ghost III* (D, A)
*Happy Ghost IV* (A)
*Tri-Star* (P)

**Wong Wing Hang** (CIN)

*A Better Tomorrow**
*A Chinese Ghost Story**
*The Killer**

**John Woo** (D, W, A)—Famed action director who's hit it big in America with such fare as *Face/Off* and *Mission Impossible 2*.

*A Better Tomorrow** (D, W, A, nominated for D, W)
*A Better Tomorrow II* (D, W)
*Just Heroes* (D)
*The Killer*** (D, W, nominated for both, won for D)
*Run Tiger Run* (D)
*The Twin Dragons* (A)

**Woo Wai Laap** (COM)

*The Blade*
*The East Is Red*
*Love in the Time of Twilight**
*The Lovers**
*Once Upon a Time in China III*
*Shanghai Grand*

**David Wu Dai-Wai** (E, COM, D)

*The Banquet* (E)
*A Better Tomorrow II* (E)
*A Better Tomorrow III* (E)
*The Big Heat* (E, COM)
*A Chinese Ghost Story* (E)
*Diary of a Big Man* (E)
*Gunmen* (E)
*Happy Ghost III* (D)
*Peking Opera Blues** (E)
*Spy Games* (D, E)
*Swordsman** (E)
*Tri-Star* (E)

**Wu Ma** (A, D)—Moon-faced character actor who's been around forever.

*A Chinese Ghost Story**
*A Chinese Ghost Story II*
*Just Heroes*
*Once Upon a Time in China*
*Peking Opera Blues*
*Swordsman*
*Yes, Madam*

**Nicky Wu [Ng Kei-Lung]** (A)—Pop star-turned-actor.

*A Chinese Ghost Story: The Tsui Hark Animation*
*Love in the Time of Twilight*
*The Lovers*

**Xiong Xin-Xin [Hung Yan-Yan]** (A)—Fearsome-looking, muscular martial arts actor. Possibly Tsui's favorite bad guy.

*Black Mask*
*The Blade*
*The Chinese Feast*
*Double Team*
*New Dragon Inn*
*Once Upon a Time in China II**
*Once Upon a Time in China III*
*Once Upon a Time in China IV*
*Once Upon a Time in China V*
*Once Upon a Time in China and America*
*Tri-Star*

**Yan Yee Kwan** (A)—Large actor with rough face and martial arts skills.

*Iron Monkey*
*New Dragon Inn*
*Once Upon a Time in China*
*Once Upon a Time in China II*
*Swordsman II*

**Yee Chung-Man** (AD)—Also known for his work on the stylish cult fave *Saviour of the Soul*\*\*.

*A Chinese Ghost Story*\*\*
*Once Upon a Time in China*\*
*A Terracotta Warrior*\*

**Sally Yeh [aka Sally Yip]** (A)—She may have been the biggest female singer of the '80s in Hong Kong, and one of Tsui's favorite actresses.

*The Banquet*
*Diary of a Big Man*
*I Love Maria*
*The Killer*
*Laser Man*
*Peking Opera Blues*\*
*Shanghai Blues*

**Donnie Yen Ji-Dan** (A)—Like Jet Li (and not Jackie Chan), Yen is a real-life skilled martial artist; he has also directed *Legend of the Wolf*.

*Iron Monkey*
*New Dragon Inn*
*Once Upon a Time in China II*

**Charlie Yeung Choi-Nei** (A)—Has also appeared in *Downtown Torpedoes* and Wong Kar-Wai's *Fallen Angels*.

*A Chinese Ghost Story: The Tsui Hark Animation*
*Love in the Time of Twilight*
*The Lovers*

**Yu Ka On** (AD, CMU)

*Shanghai Grand*\* (AD, CMU, nominated for both)
*Swordsman II*\* (CMU)

**Yu Rong-Guang** (A)—Dashing actor, recently seen in *The Storm Riders*.

*The East Is Red*
*Iron Monkey*
*A Terracotta Warrior*

**Anita Yuen Wing-Yee** (A)—Elfin actress who rose to fame with *C'Est La Vie, Mon Cheri* and was recently seen in *Till Death Do Us Part*\*.

*The Chinese Feast*
*A Chinese Ghost Story: The Tsui Hark Animation*
*Tri-Star*

**Yuen Bun** (AC, D)

*The Blade*\* (AC)
*The Chinese Feast* (AC)
*A Chinese Ghost Story III*\* (AC)
*Love in the Time of Twilight* (AC)
*New Dragon Inn*\* (AC)
*Once Upon a Time in China IV* (D, AC)
*Once Upon a Time in China V* (AC)
*Swordsman II*\*

**Yuen Cheung-Yan** (AC)

*Iron Monkey*\*
*Once Upon a Time in China*\*\*

**Corey Yuen Kwai** (D, AC, A)—Another of Jackie Chan's Peking Opera school "brothers."

*The Raid* (A)
*Yes, Madam*\* (AC, D—nominated for AC)
*Zu: Warriors from the Magic Mountain*\*

**Fennie Yuen** (A)

*Happy Ghost IV*
*The Raid*
*Swordsman*
*Swordsman II*

**Yuen Kai Chi** (W)

*A Chinese Ghost Story*
*Once Upon a Time in China*

**Yuen Wah** (A)—The Jackie Chan "brother" with the somewhat wizened face.

*The Master*
*Swordsman*

**Yuen Wo-Ping** (AC, D, A)—Martial arts director who achieved Western fame with *The Matrix*.

*Black Mask\** (AC)
*Iron Monkey\** (AC, D—nominated for AC)

*Once Upon a Time in China II\*\** (AC)
*The Wicked City* (A)

**Zhao Wen-Zhou** (A)—Handsome young martial arts actor.

*The Blade*
*The Chinese Feast*
*Green Snake*
*Once Upon a Time in China IV*
*Once Upon a Time in China V*

# ANNOTATED BIBLIOGRAPHY

Accomando, Beth. "Army of Harkness: Hong Kong Director Tsui Hark Takes on the West." *Giant Robot.* No. 8, 1997. Possibly the single best magazine interview with Tsui. Highly recommended.

"Asian Diary: Hong Kong/Film Workshop — Cinefex." *Logik: For the Digitally Correct.* Issue No. 3, 1995.

Baker, Rick, and Toby Russell. *The Essential Guide to Hong Kong Movies.* London: Eastern Heroes, 1994.

Berry, Chris. *Perspectives on Chinese Cinema.* London: British Film Institute Publishing, 1991.

Bordwell, David. *Planet Hong Kong: Popular Cinema and the Art of Entertainment.* Cambridge: Harvard University Press, 2000. The best examination yet of the aesthetics of Hong Kong cinema, with an excellent chapter on Tsui.

Browne, Nick, Paul G. Pickowicz, Vivian Sobchack and Esther Yau. *New Chinese Cinemas: Forms, Identities, Politics.* New York: Cambridge University Press, 1994.

Chan, Jackie, with Jeff Yang. *I Am Jackie Chan: My Life in Action.* New York: 1998. Includes good information on the Hong Kong film industry in the '70s, and how the death of the Peking Opera schools impacted it.

Charles, John. *The Hong Kong Filmography, 1977–1997.* Jefferson, NC: McFarland, 2000.

Dannen, Fredric, and Barry Long. *Hong Kong Babylon: An Insider's Guide to the Hollywood of the East.* New York: Miramax/Hyperion Books, 1997. One of the earliest and most entertaining looks at the Hong Kong film business. Includes interviews, filmographies, reviews, critics lists and more.

Gentry, Clyde III. *Jackie Chan: Inside the Dragon.* Dallas: Taylor Publishing Co., 1997. Probably the best book on Jackie Chan written by someone else. Packed with interesting data.

Hammond, Stefan. *Hollywood East: Hong Kong Movies and the People Who Make Them.* Chicago: Contemporary Books, 2000. Entertaining, chatty, somewhat sketchy.

_____, and Mike Wilkins. *Sex and Zen & a Bullet in the Head: The Essential Guide to Hong Kong's Mind-Bending Films.* New York: Fireside/Simon and Schuster, 1996. Includes a good section on Tsui — hardly comprehensive, but still worthwhile.

Hampton, Howard. "Once Upon a Time in Hong Kong: Tsui Hark and Ching Siu-Tung."

*Film Comment.* Vol. 33, No. 4, July/August 1997. Over-written, academic look at Tsui and Ching's work.

Hearn, Lafcadio. *Some Chinese Ghosts.* New York: Modern Library, 1927.

Hong Kong International Film Festival. *Fifty Years of Electric Shadows.* Hong Kong: Urban Council, 1997. Another excellent collection of articles on Hong Kong cinema, this volume includes "A Magical Witch's Brew: *A Chinese Ghost Story.*" by Sam Ho; and Sek Kei's "Hong Kong Cinema from June 4 to 1997." Highly recommended.

Hong Kong International Film Festival. *Hong Kong Cinema '79–'89.* Hong Kong: Urban Council, 2000. An invaluable collection of articles from ten years of Hong Kong cinema, and a rare opportunity to see how the New Wave directors were viewed at the beginning of their careers.

_____. *Hong Kong New Wave: Twenty Years After.* Hong Kong: Urban Council, 1999. A superb analysis of Hong Kong's New Wave, by some of the territory's finest writers. Includes Lee Yi-Chong's article "Artist Provocateur — On Tsui Hark's Artistic Character."

_____. *Hong Kong Panorama 97–98.* Hong Kong: Urban Council, 1998. Includes an interview with Tsui about *A Chinese Ghost Story: The Tsui Hark Animation*; also several excellent overviews of the Hong Kong film industry during the '97-'98 period.

_____. *Transcending the Times: King Hu and Eileen Chang.* Hong Kong: 1998. A lovely tribute to King Hu, which includes some material relating to his work on *Swordsman.*

*Hong Kong Movie Database,* http://www. hkmdb.com — New home of the most well-known Hong Kong movie resource (formerly located at Stanford University). Includes not only extensive information and reviews, but also the Chinese characters for titles and names.

Hu, Jason C. *An Overview of the Chinese Film Industry.* Taipei: 1993. A government brochure with some interesting facts.

Hwang, Ange. "The Irresistible: Hong Kong Movie *Once Upon a Time in China* Series— An Extensive Interview with Director/Producer Tsui Hark." *Asian Cinema.* Vol. 10, No. 1, Fall 1998. Interview with Tsui almost exclusively centered on Wong Fei-Hung and the *Once Upon a Time in China* films.

"Interview with Tsui Hark." *South China Morning Post,* 1997.

*The John Woo and Tsui Hark Action Web.* http://www.geocities.com/Hollywood/6648/index. html — Good place to find current information and news, as well as a poster gallery.

Lent, John A. *The Asian Film Industry.* Austin: 1990.

Lo Che-Ying. *A Selective Collection of Hong Kong Movie Posters.* Hong Kong: 1992. A gorgeous book, with surprisingly-good text to match the art.

Logan, Bey. *Hong Kong Action Cinema.* New York: 1996. One of the first major books on Hong Kong cinema, and still very useful.

Lu Hsun. *A Brief History of Chinese Fiction.* Peking: 1964.

Macias, Patrick. "Animerica Interview: Tsui Hark." *Animerica,* Vol. 7, No. 10. Very good interview with Tsui, mainly covering *A Chinese Ghost Story: The Tsui Hark Animation* and his interest in manga.

*The Making of a Chinese Ghost Story: The Tsui Hark Animation.* Hong Kong: 1997. This gorgeous book includes artwork, cue sheets, etc. Sadly, there is no English text.

Mazurkewich, Karen. "Hollywood Jumps In." *Far Eastern Economic Review.* April 20, 2000. Interesting article on how Hollywood majors are taking an interest in Hong Kong film production, specifically Tsui's *Time and Tide.*

*Movieworld Hong Kong,* http://www.movie world.com.hk — An invaluable resource that includes award and box-office information.

Price, E. Hoffmann. *The Devil Wives of Li Fong.* New York: 1979. A Western retelling of the *Green Snake* story.

Pu Sung-Ling, translated by Herbert A. Giles. *Strange Stories from a Chinese Studio.* London: 1916. The quintessential collection of traditional Chinese tales, it has provided the basis for such films as *A Chinese Ghost Story*, *Painted Skin* and more.

Rayns, Tony. "An Introduction to the Aesthetics and Politics of Chinese Cinema." *On Film.* Issue No. 14, Spring 1985. A very good article on mainland cinema.

Reynaud, Berenice. "High Noon in Hong Kong." *Film Comment.* Vol. 33, No. 4, July/

August 1997. Solid article on the state of Hong Kong cinema at the time of the handover.

Ross, Jonathan. *The Incredibly Strange Film Book: An Alternative History of Cinema.* London: 1995. The fabulously entertaining book accompaniment to the fabulously entertaining television series. Includes a section on Hong Kong in general and Tsui in particular.

Server, Lee. *Asian Pop Cinema: Bombay to Tokyo.* San Francisco: 1999. Well-designed but somewhat vacuous book.

Short, Stephen. "Tsui Hark: 'You Have to Touch People With Film': The Hong Kong Film Director on Sex, Violence and Leading Ladies." Time@CNN.com, May 3, 2000. Very good interview with Tsui, emphasizing the future of Hong Kong cinema.

Stokes, Lisa Odham, and Michael Hoover. *City on Fire: Hong Kong Cinema.* London/New York: 1999. A massive book which, despite the authors' attempt to force Hong Kong cinema into a leftist slot, is extremely well-researched.

Taylor, Chris, et al. *China: A Lonely Planet Travel Survival Kit.* Oakland: 1996. Includes a good, brief overview of Chinese history, customs and language.

Teo, Stephen. *Hong Kong Cinema: The Extra Dimensions.* London: British Fi lm Institute Publishing, 1997. Probably the best book written in English on Hong Kong cinema. Includes a complete history, critical overviews and a very good section on Tsui.

Ting Wai Ho. "From *A Better Tomorrow* to *Zu: Warriors*: Tsui Hark, Hong Kong Movie Maker." *Eastern Heroes.* Special Issue No. 5 — A film-by-film interview with Tsui.

Tombs, Pete. *Mondo Macabro: Weird & Wonderful Cinema Around the World.* New York: St. Martin's, 1997. Includes a section on Hong Kong movies and some coverage of Tsui.

"Tsui Hark Brings a Classic Comic to the Web." *Oriental Daily.* October 21, 1999.

Weisser, Thomas. *Asian Cult Cinema.* New York: Boulevard Books, 1997. Handy reference guide, with capsule reviews, filmographies, credit listings, etc.

Williams, Tony. "Kwan Tak-Hing and the New Generation." *Asian Cinema.* Vol. 10, No. 1, Fall 1998. A fine article on the history of Wong Fei-Hung in Hong Kong cinema and how the character has changed.

Women of China. *Women in Chinese Folklore.* Beijing: Women of China, 1983. This lovely little book includes the original stories that provided the basis for *Green Snake* and *The Lovers*, as well as a good afterword by Wu Chao.

Wood, Miles. *Cine East: Hong Kong Cinema Through the Looking Glass.* Surrey: FAB Press, 1998. Interviews with a number of different Hong Kong film VIPs. Tsui isn't here directly, but he comes up in well over half of the interviews.

## Other Resources

Five Star Laser — The best place in the U.S. to get Hong Kong VCDs, DVDs and soundtracks. Online at http://www.fivestarlaser.com

Taiseng Video — They still sell videotapes and laserdiscs of Hong Kong movies. They have a good online listing at http://www.taiseng.com

HKMovie — Located in Hong Kong, this shop carries VCDs, DVDs, movie posters, lobby cards and more. Check them out at http://www.hkmovie.com.hk

eBay — One of the best places to get good deals on Hong Kong movies and movie memorabilia. HKMovie often deals there, as do other reputable direct-from-Hong Kong dealers. http://www.ebay.com

# INDEX

241